ISLAMIC RADICALISM

AND

GLOBAL JIHAD

ISLAMIC RADICALISM

AND

GLOBAL JIHAD

Devin R. Springer

James L. Regens

David N. Edger

GEORGETOWN UNIVERSITY PRESS
Washington, D.C.

All statements of fact, opinion, or analysis expressed are those of the authors and do not reflect the official positions or views of the CIA or any other U.S. Government agency. Nothing in the contents should be construed as asserting or implying U.S. Government authentication of information or Agency endorsement of the authors' views. This material has been reviewed by the CIA to prevent the disclosure of classified information.

Georgetown University Press, Washington, D.C. www.press.georgetown.edu
© 2009 by Georgetown University Press. All rights reserved. No part of this book may be reproduced or utilized in any form or by any means, electronic or mechanical, including photocopying and recording, or by any information storage and retrieval system, without permission in writing from the publisher.

Library of Congress Cataloging-in-Publication Data

Springer, Devin R.
   Islamic radicalism and global jihad / Devin R. Springer, James L. Regens, David N. Edger.
        p.   cm.
   Includes bibliographical references and index.
   ISBN 978-1-58901-252-3 (cloth : alk. paper)—ISBN 978-1-58901-253-0 (pbk. : alk. paper)   1. Jihad.   2. Islamic fundamentalism.   3. Terrorism—Religious aspects—Islam.   4. Qaida (Organization)   I. Regens, James L.   II. Edger, David N.   III. Title.
   BP182.S67   2008
   363.325—dc22

                                                                              2008029497

⊗ This book is printed on acid-free paper meeting the requirements of the American National Standard for Permanence in Paper for Printed Library Materials.
15   14   13   12   11   10   09   9   8   7   6   5   4   3   2
First printing

Printed in the United States of America

CONTENTS

FIGURES

TABLES

PREFACE

The dreamers of the day are dangerous men, for they may act their
dreams with open eyes, to make it possible.

T. E. Lawrence, *The Seven Pillars of Wisdom*

Our motivation for writing this book grew out of our desire
to understand the inherent complexity of Islamic radicalism and the
global jihad. In the years after the catastrophic September 11 attacks,
what was once an obscure movement on the other side of the world has
become the subject of unprecedented attention: the average bookstore is
filled with studies of terrorism, television shows—both fictional ones like
24, and nonfiction documentaries—have attracted large audiences, and
words such as *jihad* have quickly entered into common usage. Unfortunately, far too often emotion rather than careful analysis has led to an
oversimplification of the capabilities, motivations, and intentions of our
adversaries. In the case of al-Qa'ida and its jihadist contemporaries, emotional reactions to them often result in mistakenly viewing what is in fact
a diverse movement with a persistent ideology as a single, monolithic
entity. To see our adversaries in this way is a disservice and a hindrance
in combating their vision of intolerance, extremism, and terror.

Instead, in this volume, we seek to analyze systematically the actions
and statements of the jihadists in order to understand their doctrines,
strategies, and tactics. In essence, we have attempted to engage in rigorous
and dispassionate analysis of the jihadist movement. We recognize that
far too many experts on terrorism draw sweeping generalizations based on
selectively assembling isolated facts to advocate a priori positions. We also
recognize that possessing Arabic language skills is not synonymous with
being a terrorism expert. In the chapters that follow, we have made a
conscious effort to avoid falling prey to either pitfall in order to link
together understanding of the language and knowledge about terrorism.
Our analysis of terrorism and the global jihad is evidence-based and
grounded in the application of the scientific method. That is, we systematically examine the doctrine, strategy, and tactics of the jihadists, especially al-Qa'ida, in order to draw conclusions. We draw heavily on our
own experiences with terrorism, counterinsurgency, and intelligence. In

doing the research for this book, we made the deliberate choice to rely exclusively on public sources so that our readers can have ready access to the information that we have examined in writing this book.

With this in mind, we began to piece together the ideology, strategy, and tactics of jihadists, with special attention to their primary driver, al-Qa'ida. We want to present a panorama of the differing ideas, goals, and vulnerabilities of the movement. Our book, therefore, is the result of an ongoing intellectual journey that has included spirited discussions among the authors as well as with colleagues who have contributed to crystallizing our perspectives and interpretations. We hope that this study will contribute to the understanding of Islamic terrorism and prospects for counterterrorism. Our goal is to provide the reader with a basic understanding of the jihadist movement's common philosophical foundations and underlying beliefs, its diverse strategies and tactics, and the dynamics of recruitment to the jihad. The book also offers insights into trends in the ongoing evolution of the jihadist movement and ways to exploit its potential vulnerabilities.

The transliteration of Arabic into Romanized script is always a difficult undertaking. Because there is no universally accepted standard in the West for transliterating Arabic words and names into English, we have tried to use a phonetic system that accurately approximates the original sound of the Arabic word, yet is simple enough for nonspeakers to recognize and repeat. We also have used several of the "accepted" spellings of names and terms where it made sense. Hence, our use of Arabic terms and names may not mirror what others have used, accounting for the various spellings of al-Qa'ida, Usama, and other names or terms quoted from the works of other authors. Naturally, we are responsible for any inconsistencies or inaccuracies in our Romanization and translation of Arabic.

Our work on this book benefited greatly from the collegial and supportive environment of the Center for Biosecurity Research at the University of Oklahoma Health Sciences Center. Portions of this material build on prior research we conducted that was sponsored by the Defense Threat Reduction Agency and the Air Force Research Laboratory under Cooperative Agreement FA8650−05−2−6523. We submitted the manuscript to the CIA's Publication Review Board (PRB) for review to ensure that active intelligence sources and methods are not compromised. The PRB completed its review to ensure that we do not reveal sensitive material previously unavailable in open sources. For the sake of readability, we have chosen not to black out any excised portions of the text or endnotes to indicate material redacted by the PRB. In no instance does redacting material compromise our analysis or limit readers' ability to weigh the intellectual merits of our arguments. As authors, we accept full responsibility for the views and conclusions contained in this book. They should not be interpreted as necessarily representing the official policies or endorsements, either expressed or implied, of the CIA, DTRA, AFRL/HE, or the U.S. government.

Don Jacobs, our editor at Georgetown University Press, deserves special thanks. He has been an enthusiastic partner whose helpful comments have guided us well in completing this book. We also appreciate the assistance provided by other press staff to ensure that our book moved smoothly through the publishing process. The anonymous reviewers for Georgetown deserve mention for their critical feedback and useful advice. Naturally, any remaining errors or faults are ours alone.

Special thanks are due to those individuals who provided encouragement throughout the process of researching and writing this book. They graciously endured our preoccupation with this project since its inception. Their patience and support has been invaluable! Devin would like to express profound gratitude to his family. Larry and Dave express special thanks to their wives, Leslie and Ruth, and to their children.

Devin R. Springer
James L. Regens
David N. Edger

LIST OF ABBREVIATIONS

AQAP: Al-Qa'ida in the Arabian Peninsula is the al-Qa'ida branch that waged a terrorist campaign in Saudi Arabia starting in 2003 and ending in 2005. The group continued to maintain a presence on the Internet, occasionally redistributing previously released literature from its *al-Battar Camp* and *Sawt al-Jihad* magazines in addition to some new material. In February 2007, the group released the first issue of *Sawt al-Jihad* magazine in nearly two years.

AQI: Al-Qa'ida in Iraq, also referred to as the al-Qa'ida of Jihad Organization in the Land of the Two Rivers, and formerly known as Tawhid wa al-Jihad: the jihadist network built and led by Abu-Mus'ab al-Zarqawi until his death in June 2006.

EIJ: Egyptian Islamic Jihad was an Egyptian Near Enemy jihadist group run by Ayman al-Zawahiri, until he merged it with al-Qa'ida in June 2001.

GIA: Armed Islamic Group: Algerian jihadist group created during the Algerian insurgency in response to the government's 1991 cancellation of elections in which Islamists were poised to win. The GIA later carried out widespread massacres of Algerian civilians, leading to serious losses in public support and the creation of the GSPC.

GSPC: Salafist Group for Preaching and Combat: Algerian jihadist group created in the wake of the GIA's civilian massacres. The group became formally allied with al-Qa'ida in 2006 and, in January 2007, changed its name to al-Qa'ida in the Lands of the Islamic Maghreb.

IAI: Islamic Army in Iraq: local jihadist insurgent group in Iraq. Major competitor of al-Qa'ida in Iraq and its umbrella groups.

ISI: Islamic State of Iraq: jihadist umbrella organization created by the al-Qa'ida-led Mujahidin Shura Council and other less-influential insurgent groups in October 2006. Upon the creation of the Islamic State, the MSC moniker was dropped from insurgent statements completely.

JRF: Jihad and Reform Front was created in May 2007 during a period of open hostilities between al-Qa'ida in Iraq supporters and other Sunni jihadist insurgents; the Jihad and Reform Front aimed to counter AQI influence in Iraq. The group initially was created by the Islamic Army in Iraq, the Ansar al-Sunnah Group Shari'ah Council splinter group, and the Mujahidin Army. The al-Fatihin Army joined the JRF in June 2007, but withdrew from the JRF in January 2008.

MSC: Mujahidin Shura Council: jihadist umbrella organization including al-Qa'ida in Iraq. Created in January 2006.

INTRODUCTION:
THE CALL TO JIHAD

Abandoning Jihad is the cause of the humiliation and division in which Muslims live today.

Muhammad Abd-al-Salam al-Farag, *The Neglected Duty*

Violent confrontation between Islamic radicalism and the West has been one of the defining features of the first decade of the twenty-first century.[1] The tragic events of September 11, 2001, in the United States and subsequent attacks in Madrid and London, combined with the wars in Afghanistan and Iraq, have shown how the resurgence of Islamic fundamentalism has fostered among some Muslims the belief that a religious war (*jihad*) is required to fight against infidels, who are thought to be invading holy places or working against the Islamic faith as a result of Christian beliefs.[2] *Jihad* means "to strive" or "to struggle" in Arabic. The term has a dual religious connotation, involving an outwardly directed struggle against oppression and tyranny and an inwardly directed personal struggle for holiness. The terrorism that has resulted from the fusion of Islamic radicalism and violent jihad has led to intense debate over whether the West and the Islamic world are engaged in a clash between civilizations; it has also led to regime change in Afghanistan and Iraq, electoral defeats of conservative governments allied with the United States in Spain and Italy, conflict over the balance between civil liberties and security, abuses of human rights, and the deaths of thousands of people.[3] Originally, the conflict was perceived to be a battle against a specific group, al-Qa'ida. However, with the passage of time it has become increasingly apparent that the battle has evolved into an ongoing struggle against an amorphous and seldom understood network of religious extremists who believe they are engaged in a holy war against enemies of Islam. Although this book focuses on violence committed and justified in the name of Islam, it is important for readers to recognize the lack of convincing evidence that the religion itself makes its adherents violent.

The nexus between the global jihad and Islamic radicalism, including the use of terrorism as the basis for restoring the caliphate, is the subject of this book. The term *caliphate—al-Khilafah* in Arabic—refers to a unified system of temporal authority exercised by a successor to the Prophet Muhammad over the community of believers.[4] During his lifetime, Muhammad was not only the Muslim political and military leader, but also the source of religious revelation as the Muslim prophet. All law and spiritual practice proceeded from Muhammad. Most academic scholars agree that Muhammad had not explicitly established how the Muslim community was to be governed after his death in 632.

The caliphate was created in response to the two critical questions his followers faced: (1) who was to succeed Muhammad? and (2) what political, military, legal, and/or religious authority could he exercise? The answer was to follow standard Arab practice at the time and use a *shura* (Arabic for consultation), in which his leading followers selected one of Muhammad's relatives to be *caliph* with full temporal authority but no authority over religious doctrine. Historically, the caliph—frequently called the *Amīr al-Mu'minīn*, which in Arabic means "Commander of the Faithful"—ruled over the territory called *Dar al-Islam* (Land of Islam), which was controlled by the caliphate and subject to Islamic law. The caliphate was created after Muhammad's death when Abu Bakr, his close companion and kinsman, became the first of the *Rashidun* (righteously guided) caliphs. Sunnis recognize all four of the patriarchal caliphs who were Muhammad's kinsmen—Abu Bakr, Umar ibn al-Khattab, Uthman ibn Affan, and Ali ibn Abi Talib—as the Rashidun, but Shi'ites consider Ali to be the first caliph. After Ali's death, a series of dynasties—sometimes competing as rivals for primacy—assumed control over the caliphate. The title was claimed by the Umayyads, the Abbasids, and the Ottomans, as well as by other competing lineages in Spain, North Africa, and Egypt, primarily as a result of their successful use of military power. At its zenith under the Ottomans, the caliphate encompassed the Middle East, North Africa, and the Balkans, and extended into portions of Central Europe. The historical caliphate was abolished in 1924 as a part of Mustafa Kemal Atatürk's reforms.[5]

The current jihadist view of the caliphate differs significantly from historical experience and traditional understanding. The concept of the caliphate, as used by al-Qa'ida and others, is not based on leadership or territory. Instead, it symbolizes the ultimate goal to be achieved by a successful global jihad. It represents the final point of victory in which Muslims live under God's authority without interference by corrupt elements. The lack of well-delineated geographical limits for the caliphate helps foster the underlying universalism of jihadist ideology, since it supports assertions that the caliphate should be restored wherever Muslims live so that they can flourish under Islamic law.[6]

Prior to September 11, the threat posed by Islamic terrorism was most often viewed as a local or regional phenomenon, even when media coverage brought vivid images such as the carnage at the 1972 Munich Olympics or the 1998 bombings of the American embassies in Kenya and Tanzania onto the global stage. Mirroring the Israeli-Palestinian conflict, however, the actual risks of terrorism remained primarily confined to the Middle East. Starting in the 1980s, three key factors linked to the emergence of Islamic radicalism contributed to the transformation of modern terrorism. Mass movements such as Hizballah and Hamas explicitly grounded their political objectives in Islamist rhetoric with calls to jihad while remaining focused on local or regional goals. The defeat of the Red Army by the mujahidin and the former Soviet Union's withdrawal from Afghanistan in 1989 after ten years of brutal war was heralded widely as proof that Islam had triumphed over a superpower. At the same time, al-Qa'ida emerged as an explicitly jihadist-oriented organization espousing even more expansive political objectives: removal of existing Muslim governments and borders along with restoration of the caliphate throughout the Islamic world. In fiery public statements, Usama bin Laden placed the Western world squarely in the crosshairs, both for its support to Israel and for what was considered to be an intolerable Western presence and influence in Muslim lands, as well as for its perceived opposition to the goals of jihad. In the aftermath of September 11, the transformation of the underlying dynamics of terrorism became a reality once the jihadist movement targeted the United States and friendly nations' interests on a worldwide basis. Terrorism is a deliberate tactic adopted by the jihadist movement. It is also an extremely efficient way to impact the political and social climate of the West because of its sensitivity to casualties. The jihadists have quite clearly identified their enemies as legitimate targets of violence, and we make no apology for characterizing their actions as terrorist in this work.

We recognize that far too many experts on terrorism draw sweeping generalizations, based on selectively assembling isolated facts, in order to advocate an a prioi position. We also recognize that possessing Arabic language skills is not synonymous with being a terrorism expert. In the chapters that follow, we have avoided falling prey to either pitfall by linking understanding of the language and knowledge about terrorism. Our analysis of terrorism and the global jihad is evidence-based and grounded in the application of scientific method. We systematically examine the doctrine, strategy, and tactics of the jihadists, especially al-Qa'ida, in order to draw conclusions. We draw heavily on our own experience with counterterrorism, counterinsurgency, and intelligence combined with analysis that incorporates Arabic language statements made by the jihadists themselves in their writings, chat rooms, websites, and blogs. Blogs as we know them in the United States have not proliferated widely in the Arabic-speaking jihadist community. The vast majority, if not all, of the jihadist sources we rely on were posted originally to website forums. Chat rooms generally do not have the volume or quality of literature and discussion that website forums do. Being able to understand the language is an essential tool in order to rely on original sources rather than secondary analysis of translations. As a result, we are able to make heavy use of published material that is not commonly available to non-Arabic speakers. We also draw on statistical analysis of open-source data and the scholarly insights of other observers of terrorism and counterinsurgency. Our hope is that our analysis and conclusions will stimulate ongoing dialogue among both specialists in terrorism and the broader public about the implications for international security of this nexus between terrorism and the global jihad.

ELEMENTS OF JIHADIST IDEOLOGY

The jihadist movement evokes imagery of a holy war promising, after victory, that everything will be vastly improved and that engagement in the noble cause gives meaning to life. For the jihadists, a mythic struggle is raging and through their actions they are able to affect its outcome.[7] Those who point out the inconsistencies between jihadist ideology and Islamic law are automatically considered apostates for their sympathy for the infidel or the killer of Muslims and are therefore also targeted. The need to be accepted as a full-fledged member of the group and not to be considered an outsider can heighten the drive to please one's comrades-in-arms in this religious struggle. Moreover, by stressing the mythic aspects of the undertaking and limiting combat roles to terrorism and sporadic insurgency, the jihadist organizations have essentially lengthened the fighting lifespan of their mujahidin.[8]

The jihadist movement grows out of and is sustained by a pervasive ideology that is constantly evolving. For purposes of this book, *ideology* is defined as a set of structured cognitive and affective attitudes that form a belief system for an individual or group. The elements of that belief system provide a philosophical foundation or mental framework for interpreting and explaining both observable and nonobservable phenomena. In addition to ethical or moral guidance, goals and means to attain those goals also are subsumed under a belief system. As such, a belief system provides a basis for determining the "good," long-term end points, and proper actions to attain those end points. Perhaps ironically, its ongoing evolution has been a key factor in making the jihadist ideology's appeal so pervasive, creating recruits and sympathizers while simultaneously fostering doctrinal strife within the movement, especially over tactics. Analysts of al-Qa'ida and its associated groups must take into account their differences and how those differences affect relations with other groups and the movement as a whole.

This book examines major elements in the ideology of the jihadist movement led by al-Qa'ida in order to identify and explain instances of disagreement and dissent, and to understand how the movement's ideology has evolved over time. Significant attention is devoted to jihadist strategic and tactical ideology, in which much variation in approach and emphasis is evident. We readily concede that most jihadists are not philosophers or strategic thinkers, but strategy and tactics are often presented in connection with the movement's underlying philosophical foundations, both political and religious. In some cases, such as Abu-Mus'ab al-Suri's theories on decentralization, strategy and tactics actually rely completely on ideology. We also assess how the movement has been transformed into a symbolic guide for a new generation of jihadists who may operate independently, following and adapting the al-Qa'ida ideal into the basis for self-directed local action. This new trend towards idea-based, autonomous action may actually prove to be the biggest security threat yet. The jihadist movement's evolution may hold the key to decreasing its lethality and effectiveness. The easiest way to identify and understand these changes is to pay attention to what they say and what they do. Unless we understand their doctrine, strategy, and tactics, we are inevitably doomed to failure in our attempts to understand and thwart the logic driving their rhetoric and behavior.[9]

It is worth noting that religion per se is not the exclusive focal point for all of jihadist ideology. Some parts of the ideology are quite political.

And, in some senses, elements of the jihadist ideology are even secular in orientation. Taken as a whole, however, even its less overtly theological elements typically are presented in the context of religious goals.

Jihadist ideology can be evaluated on three distinct levels. First, it is grounded in a set of broad philosophical foundations that provide the underlying rationale for the movement. Those philosophical foundations comprise the ideology's core religious, moral, and ethical justifications for action, including terrorism. They are essentially universal in scope with a few common themes articulated across the broad spectrum of jihadist groups. Those shared values play a central role in holding together the global jihad as a nonhierarchical social movement, and one subscribes to these values when declaring: "I am a jihadist." As such, the macro-level philosophical component changes very little from group to group and is the most prevalent component in propaganda. Because it has mass appeal, a shared philosophy allows jihadist cooperation across borders and oceans, playing as well in London or Madrid as it does in Karachi. The philosophical foundations bind the jihadist movement together and foster cooperation between jihadist groups with strategic and tactical differences.

The second level offers insights into the movement's long-term strategic goals and vision for the future. Many strategic aspects of jihadist action, such as shifting between targeting the Near Enemy and focusing on the Far Enemy, are increasingly important in defining the overall worldview of the movement. For the jihadists, the Near Enemy consists of secular "apostate" regimes in Muslim countries, such as Egypt or Syria, that the jihadists oppose, while the Far Enemy is the Western governments such as the United States and the United Kingdom that support those local regimes. However, because strategic doctrine inescapably reflects changing circumstances and provides insights into an individual's or group's short-term and long-term goals, it typically is more fluid than the underlying philosophical foundations of jihadist ideology. Inevitably, in order to be successful, strategy must reflect situational reality and change as the jihadists adapt to new challenges, threats, or opportunities. Consequently, jihadist strategic ideology is more likely to be specific to certain elements of the movement. It is likely to have more local coloration as the larger philosophy gets interpreted regionally or nationally into on-the-ground actions. Although globalizing the jihad has taken the spotlight off of the core al-Qa'ida leadership somewhat, its two most visible leaders—Usama bin Laden and his deputy, Ayman al-Zawahiri—still hold great importance in the movement, especially in articulating a strategic vision for guiding, inspiring, and justifying the jihad.

The third level consists of tactical guidance for organizing and executing actions to advance the jihadist cause. The word *tactics* refers to specific organizational and operational forms of guidance that are elements of the ideology. For example, discussions of suicide or martyrdom tactics or assassination in a particular manner such as beheading have ideological significance and meaning. The choice of tactics for jihadist operations is greatly impacted by the philosophy of the movement and changes in strategy. Tactical ideology frequently is presented in a precise, phase-oriented way and is often the most logical and pragmatic part of jihadist ideology. Moreover, tactical thought is even more variable and specific to individual jihadist leaders, usually revolving around targeting doctrine. Not surprisingly, the fluctuations in tactics over time that are evident when one examines the operations of jihadist groups reflect ongoing changes in the resources of the various groups and the security environments in which they operate.[10] As a result, the tactical program that has been adopted by the jihadist movement is generally leader-specific and changes over time. Hence, when these programs change, the changes are quite significant and often involve a shift or refocusing in targeting doctrine. For example, although the public has been horrified and repulsed by images of extreme violence and destruction carried out by religious-based terrorists, ideology plays a large part in many targeting practices by legitimizing them theologically. It has functioned as an essential element in the emergence and evolution of al-Qa'ida, which currently is the preeminent terrorist organization seeking to advance a global jihad.

Because ideas bind individuals to the movement, a coherent ideology is important, something that jihadist organizations such as al-Qa'ida consciously strive to maintain.[11] Although a common ideology does not create common interests, it makes such interests much easier to be discovered and exploited to mutual benefit.[12] The fact that the al-Qa'ida ideology is so broad-based, malleable, and able to be applied to a number of countries and regions is a major reason that it is able to resonate with militants across boundaries of class and education. This reflects the fact that the global jihadist movement is based on a shared ideology that imparts to its adherents a philosophical certainty that violent actions must be carried out to further divinely inspired edicts. Al-Qa'ida and bin Laden's embrace of terrorism, coupled with their effective use of history, religious thought, and philosophical tenets, have allowed them to successfully carry out a series of terrorist attacks against the United States. Those attacks have elevated them to near mythological status in the jihadist movement; this in turn has resulted in al-Qa'ida being an ideal that Islamic militants around the world now wish to emulate. This underscores the importance of examining its political dimensions in order to illuminate what is frequently referred to as the root causes of Islamic terrorism.

THE ASCENDANCY OF RADICAL ISLAM

Islam, since its earliest days in the seventh century, has had a political valence. The teachings of Islam, especially the Qur'an, provide much of the vocabulary for expressing political ideas, since politics and religion are seen as part of the same sphere, unlike the secular and religious dichotomy that dominates contemporary Western political theory. Islamist groups—both violent and nonviolent—are able to use this vocabulary to their advantage in order to make the case for reform, justice, and social change.[13] Political Islamist groups, primarily led by individuals who are not ulemas, advocate structuring Muslim society according to their interpretations of an integrated cultural-political framework that embodies their perceptions of the core tenets of Islam.[14] This is not surprising because Islam functions as a social force to very powerfully reinforce the self-identity of Muslims, especially in states with intense religious and ethnic conflicts over Muslim community rights and aspirations for autonomy.[15] As a result, Islamist thought shapes much of the political landscape throughout the contemporary Muslim world by default, since no other ideology is generally seen as offering solutions to everyday problems while maintaining Muslim values.

The shortcomings, including rampant corruption and official venality, of secular regimes in the Middle East have contributed to support for Islamist opposition groups. These groups routinely have the largest number of supporters in political movements and seek to challenge the authority of existing rule in hopes of influencing political and social change.[16] Unrest in Algeria, Egypt, and Syria and the fall of the Shah's regime in Iran are examples. Each of those countries has severely limited popular participation in governance. Moreover, each has been characterized as being plagued with institutional corruption. Moreover, each has limited or excluded Islamist groups from wielding political power. As a result, the Islamists have been able to avoid sharing any of the blame for the shortcomings of those regimes. Instead, they offer themselves as opposition forces that would benefit the masses while grounding their appeals in the rhetoric of a presumably pristine Islam. The lack of confidence in secular institutions and their ability to meet the needs of impoverished people can cause individuals in search of support to turn to a religious or quasi-religious institution. In the domestic sphere, Islamist organizations frequently act as nongovernmental organizations (NGOs) and provide social services, often exceeding the state's own services, which give Islamist organizations still another avenue of support. For example, social services are regularly provided by groups like Hizballah and Hamas. Al-Qa'ida, interestingly, has opted not to provide social services and specifically states in its bylaws that its ideology is to "fight a holy war and not be distracted by relief and aid operations or anything similar."[17] Thus, it has chosen to focus solely on the sword to advance the agenda of Islamic radicals.

With the collapse of the Soviet Union and the end of the cold war, several trends coalesced to link political Islam and the global jihad. The arms market was saturated, and many arms found their way from the Soviet Union to the Middle East, Central Asia, and Southeast Asia.[18] The porousness of borders made it easier for people and ideas to cross boundaries. Perhaps most significantly, the great collapse of faith in communist and socialist ideologies was paralleled by the resurgence of ethnically and religiously based organizations and ideologies throughout the 1990s. Moreover, the Soviet defeat in Afghanistan gave widespread credence to the belief within both radical Islamist circles and the wider Muslim world that the mujahidin's faith brought down a superpower. The widespread availability of weapons, mass-produced during the cold war, further provided the means for armed activity. Finally, the globalization of information technology—especially the widespread availability of the Internet, e-mail, satellite phones, and text messaging—and ubiquitous media coverage provided a previously unknown capacity for Islamist groups to publicize their messages and garner new recruits to their cause.

Although each of those factors has contributed to the emergence of global jihad, religious fundamentalism forms its cornerstone.[19] As one of the five pillars of Islam, meeting the obligation to pray brings a great number of Muslims to mosques on a daily basis.[20] It is reasonable to assume that those individuals for whom religion is a defining feature of their identity will be more likely to expend the time and effort necessary to participate in prayers at a mosque. Similarly, believers who embrace a literal interpretation of the Qur'an as a guide to both attitudes and behavior (such as following Islam's ban on alcohol and prescriptions on modesty and premarital sex) are most likely to find that fundamentalism at the mosque helps spur networking with those who embrace the same values and ideas—the first step in creating a coherent ideology capable of making an impact. Thus, the mosque becomes a convenient place to meet others who share a common Muslim religious bond, whether one is a native of the country or an immigrant.[21] The tendency to gravitate towards the familiar is recognizable to all expatriates. So, it should come as no surprise that, particularly for devout Muslims, religious centers are places where many immigrants and their children or grandchildren find a comforting connection to their original culture or community.

This phenomenon is not threatening per se. The problem is that some mosques are centers of radical fundamentalist teaching. They attract like-minded people and persuade still others. For example, during the 1990s, the North Central London Mosque in Finsbury Park became infamous as the "Finsbury Park Mosque" due to the fact that a variety of militants, including individuals associated with al-Qa'ida such as Richard Reid, attended services there led by its radical imam, Abu-Hamza al-Mazri. However, after a 2003 British antiterrorism police raid found weapons and passports, the mosque was taken over by a new board of more moderate Muslims who replaced al-Mazri as imam and who sought to have a positive relationship with the non-Muslim community. This example provides a cautionary note: the fact that mosques attract devout Muslims and homesick immigrants is not necessarily nefarious. It only becomes dangerous if a specific mosque actively engages in attracting extremists and promoting violence.

This is the true danger when radicalization and religious faith become intertwined. Violence legitimated by religion becomes self-sustaining because the actions themselves are seen as the true path that has been divinely sanctioned. When framed this way, the jihad represents an apocalyptic battle between the forces of good and evil. Not surprisingly, victory in such a struggle is worth any cost, thereby removing the normal ethical restraints on savagery.[22] This is a central theme of the jihadist organizations. In their propaganda, they increasingly refer to *Jahiliyah*, a term used most often to reference the pagan time before the rise of Islam—literally "ignorance"—to signify the modern era. This application of the term *Jahiliyah* to modern government and situations was made popular by Sayyid Qutb, a key ideologue of the Muslim Brotherhood in Egypt, who was executed by the Egyptian government in 1967. This concept has been his legacy to the world of political Islam. Qutb asserted that the entire world, even "Muslims" holding power, is living in a state of Jahiliyah. Only through practicing Islam uncorrupted by modernity can Jahiliyah be escaped and the *umma* be set on the right course. This reflects the Salafi conviction that it is imperative to return to the path of righteousness by following the practices of the Prophet Muhammad and his companions.

In the ideology of many of the most visible violent jihadist elements active today—especially al-Qa'ida and al-Qa'ida-like groups—reenergizing religious fervor to bring an end to the state of jahiliyya can be done only through terrorism, guerrilla insurgency, and aggressive preaching.[23] The anti-Western, extremely violent rhetoric of al-Qa'ida—and of the increasing number of groups modeled after bin Laden's strategy and approach—assigns blame to the West, either because of Western values or because of an alleged sinister conspiracy between Western Christianity and Judaism, for the current state of jahiliyya. Three themes are emphasized by these organizations and individuals: (1) the West is implacably hostile to Islam; (2) the only way to address this threat (and the only language that the West understands) is through the rhetoric of violence; and (3) jihad is the only option.

Although the jihadists are interested in forming an Islamic state in place of these *jahili* regimes, it is not a state conceived as a government administering Islamic policy. According to their doctrine, any government organized by humans is viewed as heretical because it asserts its rules upon the population. From an ideological perspective, this makes those regimes inherently illegitimate, since the jihadists claim that rule-making is solely the province of God, not man. As a result, they maintain that the state will be comprised of the *umma*, the community of believers, and will simply live according to Islamic principles because it is the right thing to do. They envision a sort of utopian Islamic nation without borders or government and with God as the head of state. Violent jihad is viewed as essential to restore "authentic" Islam.

Sayyid Qutb's call for action against *jahili* targets was pushed to the extreme by Muhammad Abd-Al-Salam al-Farag, an Egyptian electrician who wrote what is arguably the most important and influential book for groups like al-Qa'ida. In *The Neglected Duty*, Farag stated that jihad is a duty for Muslims worldwide and that it should be considered the "6th Pillar of Islam," thereby making it a requirement of the faithful. He argues that jihad has been neglected, and that this neglect is entirely unjustified.

The long-standing tradition of undertaking jihad (as a military action) only when there is an *Amir*, leader, to rally behind is meaningless to Farag, who states that the appropriate leadership would spring from the faithful in times of need.

For adherents of the jihad, the struggle against alleged Western-perpetrated Jahiliyah is monolithic and apocalyptic, and it gives rise to terrorist action and guerrilla insurgency when pursued through violent means to convey a clear message to the target audience. Because the ultimate objective is changing the minds and policies of the enemy's political leadership, the intermediate objectives are essentially milestones in shifting the opinion and actions of the various target audiences. Operations, therefore, are all about the message being sent. In terms of psychological impact, an operation's message is made more dramatic by enhancing the terrorist event's size, scope, and audacity. Whether it be by crashing a plane into a building, car-bombing an embassy, hijacking, or kidnapping and beheading, every operation, legitimized by the ideology, aims to send a message to the enemy in hopes of influencing a policy change or simply destroying morale; such operations also aim to send a message to the supporters, ranging from those who sympathize with the group to those who actively participate in operations, whether by contributing monetarily or by being involved in the planning and execution of an operation. Characteristically, the audience of operations is not a single, unified entity, but rather a fragmented field of "interest groups that shift sides depending on how a campaign affects their issues."[24] If the message is ignored, the support base for action dwindles, making it harder to legitimize terrorist action in the eyes of the public—in this case, the Islamic community—and thus making it harder for insurgencies to operate in such areas as Chechnya, Afghanistan, and now, Iraq. For example, because such a large number of al-Qa'ida fighters have been caught or killed since September 11, the group has increasingly needed to rely on nonhierarchical structures to remain relevant and, to some extent, to remain operationally capable. Al-Qa'ida has turned to using previously established networks for attacks and logistical support where possible, in addition to relying on existing infrastructure to promote the jihad as a social movement, thereby involving thousands of anonymous jihadist supporters through propaganda on the Internet and recruitment via personal contacts.

The unifying effect of religion is very useful to groups such as al-Qa'ida, who attempt to establish a worldwide network, capable of reaching anywhere. Sunni Muslims, especially Wahhabis, have traditionally been hostile toward Shi'ite Muslims, as seen historically in Saudi Arabia or by the current internecine struggle between Sunnis and Shi'ites in Iraq. But, when united under the banner of God, terrorist groups from these two opposing sects can cooperate in opposing what they view as the Greater Evil, provided hard-line Wahhabis can get over their long-standing prejudice against Shi'ite Muslims. There is, however, no evidence of ideological shifts on either side that could signal long-term, full cooperation between these organizations and others like them. Given the deep-seated enmity between Sunni jihadists and the Shi'ites, any accommodation is likely to be short-term rather than enduring.[25]

THE RISE OF THE AL-QA'IDA ORGANIZATION

The origins of al-Qa'ida are grounded firmly in the anti-Soviet jihad in Afghanistan. In 1979, when the Soviet Union launched its invasion of Afghanistan to support that country's new communist government, many Afghans took up arms to resist Soviet forces, initiating a conflict that would rage for the next decade. Although the majority of the Afghan resistance movement was composed of Afghan nationals, Muslims from around the world rallied to the call for an anti-Soviet jihad.

Palestinian cleric Abdullah Azzam and Usama bin Laden, the son of a wealthy businessman with close ties to the Saudi royal family, were among those who came from the Middle East to participate in the jihad. Azzam and bin Laden quickly established a wide facilitation network for providing foreign fighters for the jihad. Their organization became known as the Services Bureau, or Maktab al-Khidmat (MAK). The MAK created a global network of financiers and recruiters to bring fighters from around the world, especially Arabs from the Middle East, to Pakistan and Afghanistan. Once there, the foreign fighters were often hosted in MAK guesthouses before traveling to the front. Azzam's fatwa characterizing jihad in Afghanistan as an individual duty—*fard ayn*—aided the MAK's efforts. The MAK brought fighters from around the world, especially Arabs from the Middle East. For example, a contingent of Egyptians—including Ayman al-Zawahiri, who at the time was the leader of the Egyptian Islamic Jihad group—joined Azzam and bin Laden. However, unlike Azzam, the Egyptians saw the jihad in Afghanistan as temporary and hoped to use the campaign to promote bringing the jihad back to Egypt.

After Moscow's April 1988 announcement that Soviet forces would withdraw from Afghanistan over the next nine months, Azzam and bin Laden started planning the MAK's future. It was during this time period that al-Qa'ida—*the base*—was formally created by Azzam and bin Laden. Although both of them wanted to preserve the MAK's facilitation network and bring its resources to bear in future jihadist campaigns, they had two very different visions for the future. Azzam, who was firmly committed to solidifying Islamist control of Afghanistan, preferred to continue the MAK's support to the Afghan resistance. He also wanted potentially to move on to organizing a similar resistance movement against Israel on behalf of the Palestinians. Bin Laden, on the other hand, seems to have shared the viewpoint of the Egyptian contingent, which wanted to use al-Qa'ida to prepare fighters for conflicts elsewhere—in bin Laden's view, worldwide. This dispute over the strategic direction of al-Qa'ida, in addition to disagreements over which Afghan fighters to support and bin Laden's wishes to become the unchallenged leader of al-Qa'ida, drove bin Laden and Azzam apart. Bin Laden was, at this time, already the amir of al-Qa'ida. However, Azzam remained an influential figure among foreign fighters.

This schism within al-Qa'ida and the struggle over its leadership and future direction were resolved while bin Laden was back in his native Saudi Arabia. Azzam and his son were killed by a car bomb in Peshawar, Pakistan, on November 24, 1989. Azzam's assassination remains unsolved, but many suspect that the Egyptian mujahidin were involved, given their desire to see al-Qa'ida pursue a global strategy.

Back in Saudi Arabia, bin Laden received considerable attention as a result of his exploits in Afghanistan. However, he quickly began to lose favor with the Saudi royals after Iraq's 1990 invasion. Following the Iraqi invasion of Kuwait, bin Laden approached the Saudi royal family with a proposal to defend Saudi Arabia and use his organization to repel Iraq. Instead, the Saudi government rejected bin Laden's proposal in favor of American assistance and opted to bring thousands of American and other Western troops into the Kingdom. Furious with this turn of events, bin Laden and a number of other Saudi radicals denounced the Saudi royal family's decision to welcome non-Muslim military forces into the Kingdom. As a result, bin Laden was placed under surveillance and subjected to increased pressure by the Saudi government.

In response to the Saudi government's actions, bin Laden accepted the offer of Sudanese political leader Hassan al-Turabi, who urged him to move his organization to Sudan. Bin Laden was assured that he could freely prepare for future jihads and manage the group's various business interests. So, instead of returning to Saudi Arabia after a 1991 trip to Pakistan, bin Laden moved to Sudan. Once in Sudan, bin Laden invested heavily in construction projects in the country and also continued—along with al-Zawahiri and his inner circle—to prepare for jihadist operations. Al-Qa'ida expanded contacts with and support of jihadists worldwide, especially by providing training and other assistance to a number of new jihadist groups in South East Asia. During his stay in Sudan, bin Laden built up his vast network of militant contacts, which formed the foundation for the al-Qa'ida global network.[26] From its base in Sudan, al-Qa'ida continued to denounce the Saudi government and urged the eviction of Western forces from Saudi Arabia. It also became involved in the conflict in Somalia in 1992, began to prepare for attacks inside Saudi Arabia, and established cells in East Africa. The group and its Sudanese hosts, however, began to suffer from financial difficulties. Its financial problems made Sudan vulnerable to significant pressure from Saudi Arabia and other countries to cease acting as a host country and expel bin Laden and his al-Qa'ida followers.

In May 1996, bin Laden and around 150 supporters and their families fled Sudan for Afghanistan. They took refuge with the Taliban and recognized Mullah Omar as the *amir al-mu'minin*—the Commander of the Believers. Although promising the Taliban that he would keep a low profile while in Afghanistan, bin Laden issued a 1996 fatwa declaring war against Westerners in Saudi Arabia. Recovering from the financial difficulties and other restrictions from which al-Qa'ida suffered in Sudan, bin Laden and his followers were given extraordinary protection and autonomy by Mullah Omar and the Taliban. The Taliban allowed thousands of foreigners to enter Afghanistan to train at bin Laden–sponsored training camps. Most of these trainees did not become al-Qa'ida members and returned to their countries of origin. Others who passed through those camps, however, were recruited and joined al-Qa'ida. While in Afghanistan, bin Laden was able to assert more control over al-Zawahiri's Egyptian Islamic Jihad group. As a number of sources, including the *9/11 Commission Report*, have noted, it was during this period that al-Qa'ida organized itself around individuals with varying levels of commitment.[27]

In February 1998, bin Laden issued another statement in which he declared that "to kill the Americans and their allies—civilians and military—is an individual duty for every Muslim who can do it in any country in which it is possible to do it."[28] Less than six months later, two car bombs were detonated outside of the American embassies in Nairobi, Kenya, and Dar es Salaam, Tanzania. Both bombings were the work of al-Qai'da East African cells. Al-Qa'ida attack planning continued. In January 2000, al-Qa'ida operatives attempted an unsuccessful attack against the *USS Sullivans* while it was anchored in Yemen. A subsequent al-Qa'ida attack planned and supervised by bin Laden, utilizing an explosives-laden boat detonated by a suicide bomber, succeeded in heavily damaging the *USS Cole* and killing seventeen of its crew during a port call in Yemen ten months later, on October 12, 2000.

At the same time, planning for the September 11 attacks was well under way, and al-Zawahiri formally merged the Egyptian Islamic Jihad organization with al-Qa'ida after internal EIJ turmoil and financial problems in June 2001. After the September 11 attacks and the subsequent U.S.–led campaign against al-Qa'ida and the Taliban, al-Qa'ida's central leadership dispersed and continued to operate from Afghanistan and Pakistan. The launch of the Iraq war in March 2003 breathed new life into al-Qa'ida's global movement. In October 2004 the group merged with the Tawhid wa al-Jihad group, a largely foreign fighter group run by Jordanian al-Qa'ida associate Abu-Mus'ab al-Zarqawi. Al-Zarqawi's group had already established itself in Iraq, enabling bin Laden and al-Qa'ida Central to become part of a major insurgency against Western forces. In essence, and consistent with its underlying doctrine, al-Qa'ida has moved aggressively to institutionalize the strategic and tactical use of terrorism to advance its cause.

Unlike early analyses that attributed terrorism to psychiatric pathologies, more recent studies underscore the rationality of political violence.[29] The actions of the jihadists are not grounded in individual psychopathology or mass antisocial behavior. Instead, they are rooted in purposeful albeit savage actions in pursuit of rather clearly defined goals. Moreover, the movement is growing as a result of the power of its ideas. Its power, therefore, can only be neutralized by making those ideas unappealing to potential adherents, while persuading or preventing the current generation of jihadists from acting violently to advance its beliefs.

1

PHILOSOPHICAL FOUNDATIONS

The reasons for Jihad . . . are these: to establish God's authority in the earth; to arrange human affairs according to the true guidance provided by God; to abolish all the Satanic forces and Satanic systems of life; to end the lordship of one man over others since all men are creatures of God and no one has the authority to make them his servants or to make arbitrary laws for them. These reasons are sufficient for proclaiming Jihad.

Sayyid Qutb, *Milestones*

WIDESPREAD MEDIA COVERAGE of the martyrdom videos and terrorist operations of the jihadists has sparked growing interest in trying to understand the ideological roots of Islamic terrorism. The advent of twenty-four-hour news networks with correspondents and, more important, camera crews around the world has made people more aware of the devastation and pain caused by terrorist attacks and, in turn, more sensitive to real or perceived vulnerabilities to terrorism. It is not surprising that, in the age of globalized information, the agenda of the radical Islamists appears to be driven by an information strategy of maximizing attention to their cause. Moreover, their strategy seeks to convey images that weaken the resolve of their adversaries while signaling the inevitability of victory in a long war. This has forced leaders, the public, and scholars in the West to ask: Who are these extremists whose agenda previously was absent from Western concerns? Why are they steadfast in the pursuit of jihad and change in the name of God?

As the West struggles to come to grips with its newest enemy, efforts to understand the emergence of the global jihad have fostered awareness of an ideological battle that started over fifty years ago. Originally limited

17

to the urban and rural centers of the Middle East and Central Asia, the underlying philosophy and acts of violence associated with the jihadist movement have spread beyond the core of the Muslim world. Hence, to understand the rise of and trends in Islamic radicalism, we turn our attention to the historical origins and philosophical foundations of the global jihad. In the context of this study, Islamic radicalism is defined as a sometimes violent movement seeking to radically change local, national, and global social and political landscapes. Radical Islamists believe such actions are justified by the tenets of Islam, thereby making it God's will.

Origins of the Islamic Resurgence

While the charred rubble of the Twin Towers was still smoldering, the United States began to realize more fully the danger posed by radical Islamic groups. Although the term *jihad* has become linked to terrorism, it is important to note that it frequently has a nonviolent connotation as a religious obligation. This spiritual jihad, or *jihad bil-nafs*, is seen by most Muslims as the "greater jihad." On the other hand, there also is the concept of *jihad bil-sayf*, literally "jihad by the sword," or violent jihad, traditionally viewed as the "lesser jihad."

Violent jihad, whether by war, insurgency, or terrorism, has become an increasingly popular tool for extremist organizations that maintain that violent jihad is the greater or only jihad. The Qur'an, the holy text of Islam, provides a number of verses pertaining to jihad that are seen as particularly significant in the eyes of the Islamic extremists. John Esposito notes that these verses, "sometimes referred to as the 'sword verses' are quoted selectively to legitimate unconditional warfare against unbelievers and were used by jurists to justify great expansion."[1] The jihadists use those interpretations of violent jihad in the name of Islam.[2] Although relatively small in numbers in comparison to the overall population of the Muslim community, radical Islamists who endorse violence frequently cite the same ideologues and reasons for action, using the rhetoric of *jihad*, meaning "to strive" or "to struggle" in Arabic.

It is critical to recognize that the adherents of violent jihad are absolutely convinced that their cause is right, both politically and morally, since they believe it is divinely sanctioned. It should come as no surprise, therefore, to learn that Usama bin Laden believes that he has received divine sanction to use weapons of mass destruction in his jihad. Moreover, they are extremely dedicated and, regardless of their savagery, are actually quite rational in the pursuit of their strategic goals. Examining the series of tasks listed in an al-Qa'ida jihad manual illustrates this point. Islamic militant organizations are instructed to remove those personalities who block the group's path to success. They are admonished to properly utilize an individual's unused capability while striving for precision in performing tasks and working collectively. The jihadists similarly are instructed to control work to prevent fragmentation or deviation. The manual differentiates between tasks tied to achieving long-term goals, such as establishing Islamic law, and tasks for achieving short-term goals, such as performing operations against individuals and the enemy sector. It also offers guidance on how to go about establishing conditions for possible confrontation with repressive regimes. Not surprisingly, since Islamic militant organizations often operate clandestinely, the manual addresses achieving discipline in secrecy and through performing tasks.

The participants in jihadist activities, like any other social movement, are also products of their own environments and have been influenced strongly by the "Islamic Resurgence," which emerged in the Middle East in the second half of the twentieth century. The origins of this Arab-led resurgence can be seen in part as a reaction to the decline of the Ottoman Empire and to colonial rule by the British and French, starting in the nineteenth century and, subsequently, under League of Nations mandates following World War I.[3] In addition, the establishment of Israel in 1948, encompassing part of the former Ottoman province of Palestine, and the support that Israel has enjoyed from Western nations, particularly the United States, is also a key ingredient. Thus, extremist Islam has become more prevalent in reaction to a series of external and internal events.

Secular regimes in Egypt, Syria, and Iraq—and governmental corruption in many countries—led a number of hard-line Muslim extremists to feel frustrated by their inability to impact the social and political dynamics of their own countries in the immediate aftermath of World War II. Moreover, it has not been unusual for them to view their traditional norms and customs as being under assault by the ongoing modernization and secularization occurring in the urban areas of their countries. Some have attempted to lobby for change and traditional mores in a nonviolent manner, while others have opted to take the other path to change. In their eyes, Islam has been seen as losing the battle against the decadence of the West. Failed economies, repressive regimes, the catastrophic Arab loss of the 1967 war against Israel, overcrowding, high unemployment, the breakdown of traditional religious and social values in the face of global-ization,[4] and revolution have all led to the Islamic resurgence. In the fol-lowing sections, we examine in more detail the ongoing Israeli-Palestinian problem along with a number of the key developments in Egypt, Iran, Algeria, and Saudi Arabia that were crucial to the emergence and evolution of modern-day violent political Islam as embodied by groups like Hamas, Hizballah, and al-Qaeda.

Israel and Palestine

It would be naïve not to recognize the Israeli-Palestinian question, which is embedded in the wider Israeli-Arab conflict, as one of the key elements of the ongoing confrontation between the West and Islamic radicalism. On a symbolic as well as substantive level, when the Arab states rejected the 1947 UN General Assembly plan to partition Palestine into separate Jewish and Arab states, the conflict became a struggle between two peoples seeking to define their national identities within the same territory. The 1948 creation of the state of Israel within the heart of the Muslim world and the accompanying flight of almost one million Palestinians, who were expelled from or left their homes in the last six months of the British Mandate or during the first Arab-Israeli war, clearly demonstrated the Arabs' military and political weaknesses.[5] That refugee exodus (*al-Hijra al-Filasteeniya*), referred to by the Palestinians and other Arabs as the *Nakba* (Arabic meaning disaster, catastrophe, or cataclysm), has had the enduring legacy of shaping the collective narrative of the Palestinians as being an occupied people forced by colonizing Zionists to flee their ancestral homes. As such, it provides a highly emotionally charged rally-ing cry for both Fatah and Hamas to appeal for support within the Pales-tinian community. Israel's subsequent victories in the 1956, 1973, and 1982 wars, combined with massive U.S. aid, reinforced a sense that the Arabs have been thwarted by foreign forces and created a rationale for terrorism targeting the Israelis. Combined with the burgeoning Palestin-ian refugee problem, which resulted in entire generations living in camps, this series of Arab defeats provided fertile ground for radicalization, trig-gering an ongoing cycle of Palestinian terrorism and Israeli repression. The imagery of the refugee exodus is extremely powerful, and it resonates strongly with Muslims in general. As a result, the presence of permanent refugee camps has been used by Arab regimes to deflect discontent away from their own shortcomings, while the rhetoric of jihadist groups points to the very existence of Israel—and of American support for Israel—as justification for their own actions.

Egyptian Brotherhood

Egypt is the largest traditional breeding ground for Muslim extremism. When Gamal Abd-al-Nasser assumed power after the 1952 coup that ousted King Farouk, his government imprisoned members of the Muslim Brotherhood, an organization founded by Hassan al-Banna in 1928 to promote Islam in the political arena during the monarchy, specifically against British colonialism and the monarchy. Although the Muslim Brotherhood previously backed Nasser and the Free Officers in their rise to power, its members quickly began to protest when they realized that the Brotherhood was being used to legitimize the new secular regime. Mass punishment of the Brotherhood followed their vocal attempts to mobilize Egyptian society against the Nasser regime's pursuit of a secular agenda. Under Nasser's Arab-nationalist agenda, Islam was pushed out of the public sphere. Instead, the state and its leaders were to be revered; Nasser hoped that Egypt would become a modern and secular nation.

On January 16, 1953, all political parties in Egypt were abolished by the government. However, the Muslim Brotherhood was exempted, since it officially was an association and not a political party. Despite the Brotherhood's exemption from the ban, it was the largest organized popular movement in Egypt, and thus the government began to suppress its agenda and slowly drain its capability for instigating reform. After a Brotherhood member tried to assassinate Nasser on October 26, 1954, the government stepped up its campaign against the Brotherhood by destroying its headquarters, arresting and torturing its leaders and members, and, through the use of propaganda, disgracing the Brotherhood in the eyes of the population. However, these actions taken by the government failed to end its problems with Islamist groups.[6] Throughout the remainder of the century, Egypt's leaders would resort to mass arrests, torture, and execution in the battle against political Islam. Many of the men who were arrested and subjected to harsh treatment in prison camps would be released eventually in negotiations between the Egyptian government and the Islamists. Once released, many of them became the new voices of Islamic extremism, affecting successor generations both inside and outside Egypt.

Iranian Revolution

Unlike their Sunni counterparts in the Egyptian Brotherhood who failed to gain control in Egypt, the Shi'ite clerics and their followers who participated in the Iranian revolution of 1979 were successful. The secular, pro-Western regime of the Shah was overthrown and replaced with a radical Islamist regime led by senior Shi'ite clerics. Especially after the 444-day seizure of the U.S. Embassy in Tehran by supporters of the new regime, coupled with the Carter Administration's failed rescue attempt, the first successful Islamic revolution in modern times became an inspiration for radicals and invoked fear among Sunni rulers throughout the Muslim world. Suddenly, a group of believers were able to take the reins of their country, oust the secularized government, and build an Islamic state with the clerical class as the leadership. Although the new Iranian regime was Shi'ite, this demonstrated to the Sunni jihadists that a religiously based political leadership could gain power. The events in Iran simultaneously made the establishment of a Sunni-based Islamic power that would counter Shi'ite influence all the more urgent.

Algeria's Downward Spiral

Since 1991, Algeria has been plagued with jihadist-related violence of varying intensity. The experiences of the Armed Islamic Group (GIA) have been studied by jihadist strategists worldwide as a case study that offers valuable lessons about what not to do.

After the secular Algerian government lost a majority of seats in the National Assembly to the Islamic Salvation Front (FIS), the Algerian military canceled the second round of elections in 1991, which the FIS was certain to win, and banned religious political parties. The Islamist FIS responded with violence in an effort to force a return to elections, taking care to limit attacks to the Algerian government in order to avoid losing its broad popular support.[7] The GIA began its campaign by advocating all-out war with the Algerian government, but eventually it began to attack French civilians in Algeria. The French government responded by cracking down on the large Algerian population inside France. This prompted the GIA to begin directly attacking France. The group hijacked an Air France airplane in 1994 and initiated a series of bombings in France in 1995.

As a coalition of various jihadist factions, the GIA suffered from serious infighting stemming from differences in ideology and personal rivalries.[8] Additionally, the group had a number of leaders in the 1990s, each with different agendas and often with different methods. The inner-GIA tensions resulted in a number of changes in who they chose as targets, (such as government officials, civilians, and foreigners), and in group purges as the definition of loyalty shifted over time. The first amir of the GIA, Abd-al-Haq Layada, declared nonviolent elements of the FIS to be apostates. He also threatened journalists and the families of Algerian soldiers.[9] The GIA then expanded its range of targets to include not only the Algerian government but anyone linked with it. A series of assassination attempts began in March 1993, resulting in the deaths of a number of people, many of whom had no connection to the Algerian government. In the same year, the GIA began targeting foreigners in Algeria, killing twenty-six in all. After Layada's death, Djafar al-Afghani became the new amir and intensified violence in the country. Upon his death, the third amir of the GIA, the 26-year old Sherif Gusmi, took over. Gusmi firmly established that the GIA's goal was not to force a return to elections or open a dialogue with the Algerian government. Instead, the goal was to rid the land of apostates and establish an Islamic state through jihad.[10]

Gusmi's successor, Djamel Zitouni, in addition to expanding the GIA's operations to France, also condemned all Islamist factions that did not support the GIA, although he did stop short of condemning society as a whole. Zitouni also oversaw the kidnapping of seven French monks, who were later beheaded. Upon Zitouni's death, Antar Zouabri took over, killing anyone who dared to question his authority. In 1997, Zouabri's chief theorist, Abu-Hamzah, published an article in the group's *al-Ansar* magazine, which set the course for events to come in Algeria.[11] Abu-Hamzah noted that Algerian society was not fertile ground for the jihad—that it was not ready to join the GIA in opposing Algeria's secular regime, which he characterized as being ruled by apostates. Abu-Hamzah portrayed Algerians as resisting the obligation of jihad, and that thereby they had "forsaken religion and renounced the battle against [their] enemies."[12] After the article's publication, Zouabri and Abu-Hamzah declared the whole of Algerian society to be apostate. Declarations of apostasy are commonly referred to as *takfir* (declaring an individual or group previously thought to be Muslim unbelievers). The GIA then proceeded to carry out a series of massacres of Algerian civilians, often murdering entire communities with knives and axes. The acceptability of indiscriminate violence as part of its doctrine is illustrated by a GIA communiqué that stated: "There is no neutrality in the war we are waging. With the exception of those who are with us, all others are apostates and deserve to die."[13] Not surprising, by adopting such an exclusionary, violent ideology and targeting agenda, the GIA rapidly lost its public support. This led to the rise of the Salafist Group for Preaching and Combat (GSPC), which eclipsed the GIA in terms of public support, in great part due to its pledge to avoid civilian casualties.

Numerous statements by senior al-Qa'ida leaders point to lessons to be learned from the Algerian experience, which engendered caution among jihadists worldwide. For example, in a 2005 letter to Abu-Mus'ab al-Zarqawi, Ayman al-Zawahiri reproached the al-Qa'ida in Iraq leader for his tactics and targeting agenda, which decreased popular support for both the mujahidin in Iraq and the overall jihad. In the conclusion of his letter, al-Zawahiri made a reference to the Algerian jihad, indicating his wariness of repeating the GIA's experience: "The subject of the Algerian brothers at our end, there are fears from the previous experiences, so if you're able to get in touch with them and notify us of the detail from them, we would be very grateful to you."[14] This short excerpt is the only Algeria-related line in the letter and appears to be in response to a conversation between al-Zawahiri and al-Zarqawi. It is likely that the "Algerian brothers" are the GSPC or another Algerian jihadist faction. When considered along with a September 2006 video statement from al-Zawahiri, in which he announced that the GSPC has joined al-Qa'ida, it is possible that al-Zawahiri was speaking about a potential merger between the two groups and, therefore, of al-Qa'ida's caution in bringing in Algerian jihadists who may have been involved in the GIA's campaign.

In December 2005, a letter to al-Zarqawi from "Atiyah"—who counterterrorism officials believe to be Atiyah Abd-al-Rahman, a Libyan jihadist with connections to both bin Laden and al-Zarqawi—was made public.[15] In the letter, Atiyah reproaches al-Zarqawi for taking unnecessary action in the name of al-Qa'ida, asserting that all operations should support al-Qa'ida's ultimate goals. Judging from his letter, Atiyah spent time in Algeria during the 1990s, and he uses the Algerian case as an example of excessive violence that does harm to the overall movement:

> I had previously talked with you and with many of the brothers about what happened in Algeria, so do remember that. My brother, what use is it for us to delight in some operations and successful strikes when the

immediate repercussion is a defeat for us of our call, and a loss of the justice of our cause and its logic in the minds of the masses who make up the people of the Muslim nation, who are ignorant and simple, and upon whom the afflictions of stultification, misguidance, and corruption pile, and increased domination by the enemies, more oppression, more humiliation visited upon us, and more ills, troubles, loss in capabilities, and wasted opportunities?[16]

Atiyah also mentions Algeria later in the letter, this time pointing out how quickly a positive situation can be undermined through the alienation of the public:

Ask me whatever you like about Algeria between 1994 and 1995, when [the movement] was at the height of its power and capabilities, and was on the verge of taking over the government. The government was on the verge of a downfall at any moment. I lived through that myself, and I saw first hand; no one told me about it. However, they destroyed themselves with their own hands, with their lack of reason, delusions, their ignoring of people, their alienation of them through oppression, deviance, and severity, coupled with a lack of kindness, sympathy, and friendliness. Their enemy did not defeat them, but rather they defeated themselves, were consumed and fell.[17]

Atiyah and al-Zawahiri are not alone in their awareness of the experiences of the GIA in Algeria. In his 1,600-page book, *The Call to Global Islamic Resistance*, senior al-Qa'ida strategist Abu-Mus'ab al-Suri evaluated the collapse of the Algerian jihad.[18] Al-Suri is the nom de guerre of Mustafa Setmariam Nasar, a Syrian who was a key figure involved with the London-based *al-Ansar* magazine, which functioned as the GIA's media cell. He attributed the Algerian jihad's failure to the escalation of violence by a deviant leadership that played into the hands of the Algerian intelligence service:

The issue of jihad in Algeria took many turns, which, after the martyrdom of its sincere, conscious leadership, led in the end to the devolution of the leadership of the GIA to a few deviant ignoramuses, who embraced ideas somewhere between *takfir* and delinquency that were in turn mixed with certain basic jihadist concepts. This went according to the intelligence service's exact plan, and led to the group's failure and dissolution at the beginning of 1996.[19]

As a result, insights garnered from the failure of the Algerian jihad are likely to have influenced substantially many of al-Suri's "recommendations and warnings" at the end of his book:

> Beware not to wrongly accuse Muslims of faithlessness, and beware not to follow those who aid in the faithlessness of Muslims.
>
> Beware and exercise vigorous caution not to shed the blood of Muslims in the course of the battle against the infidels and apostates.
>
> Beware not to cause the resistance and the Mujahidin to lose the public opinion of Muslims.
>
> Beware not to target neutral parties in this confrontation, even if they are infidels.[20]

Saudi Arabia

During the 1970s and 1980s, the conservative Sunni monarchy in Saudi Arabia experienced the effects of a burgeoning influx of oil wealth and rapid population growth. The Saudi regime funded expanded social programs and spent lavishly on fundamentalist educational programs that stressed a strict Wahhabist interpretation of Islam. Saudis relied on foreigners to perform numerous jobs, while high birth and low infant mortality rates produced a large and growing population. This in turn created a generation of Saudi males, grounded in fundamentalism, who entered adulthood during the 1980s; many of these young men participated as mujahidin in the Soviet-Afghan war, inspired by an intensely puritanical view of how society should be structured. It also created a widespread sense of entitlement to generous social programs. Both factors led to discontent that could be mobilized by Islamists. For example, declining oil revenues in the late 1980s and early 1990s, coupled with a stagnant domestic economy, forced the Saudi monarchy to institute cuts in entitlements. When combined with awareness of how much of the oil revenue had actually gone into the pockets of the rulers to support lavish lifestyles, feelings of resentment deepened, with their heavily religious educations, these young men became easy targets for radicalization.[21]

The resentments of the most radical elements within the Saudi public grew when King Fahd asked the United States to station troops in the Kingdom to protect it against Iraq and Iran during the 1980s. Those resentments were exacerbated and spread more widely across Saudi society after the 1990 Iraqi invasion of Kuwait. Many segments of the public were furious that the Saudi government had approved a massive influx of U.S. and other Western troops in the face of threats to its oil fields in the north. There was open dissent among the people of the Kingdom in response to this move by their rulers. King Fahd needed religious sanctions for his initiative to put to rest the anger over letting infidel troops roam the land of the two Holy Cities (Mecca and Medina); thus, he persuaded Wahhabi clerics to give him the theological cover the king needed in exchange for allowing the establishment clerics to exercise even greater social control over the Kingdom.[22]

In reaction to the establishment clerics' move, many young Wahhabis and Salafis who were influenced by Egyptian writer Sayyid Qutb, including Usama bin Laden, began to split ideologically and socially from the traditional Wahhabi establishment. This split continues to cause a great sense of unrest in the Kingdom among the Wahhabi Ulama. The younger clerics, who are more numerous because of the Saudi baby-boom in the 1970s and 1980s, tend to oppose the Royal Family, which is supported by the older generation of clerics. The older generation of Wahhabi clerics, many of whom were essentially bought off by the Royal Family, supported the jihad in Afghanistan by supplying ideology and money to the religious schools that provided the ideological base for the anti-Soviet war. However, as soon as the USSR collapsed, the United States withdrew its active involvement in Afghanistan. The Saudis' influence also waned as Pakistani influence increased. Arguing that this was a mistake, the young Wahhabi clerics and their followers were vocal in expressing disapproval of the actions of the United States and Saudi Arabia.

INTELLECTUAL FATHERS

Having placed the origins of the modern global jihad in historical perspective, we now turn to the writings that inspired the Islamists. Examining the ideas underlying the rhetoric of the jihad is important in order to understand how this disheartened community has organized itself and adopted a radical interpretation of its religious beliefs to legitimize the systematic use of violence against a variety of targets.

A number of well-known earlier religious scholars and contemporary Muslim writers, some of whom are relatively obscure ideologues, have influenced modern Islamic extremism.[23] The earlier figures are religious scholars whose works were written prior to 1900. The writings of those scholars, especially Ibn-Taymiyyah and Ibn-Abd-al-Wahhab, allow the modern jihadist movement to assert that their beliefs are firmly grounded in the traditions of Islam and its Salafi interpretation. The contemporary authors come overwhelmingly from the ranks of the jihadists themselves. The majority of these have been laymen instead of clerics, and like Sayyid Qutb they have lacked formal training in Islamic scholarship. Others, such as Abdullah Azzam, have trained as Islamic scholars. It is worth noting that not all of these influential figures have been militants or terrorists; several have sought to emphasize Islamic values in society or to bring Islam into the political arena.

In this section we turn to an examination of a number of the more prominent and influential authors whose works provide the philosophical foundations for the global jihad.[24] In selecting key contributors to the jihadist canon, we have chosen authors whose arguments are generally accepted throughout the jihadist community as authoritative. Each of them is also commonly acknowledged to rank among the most influential thinkers. As a consequence, their writings are broadly representative of the established tenets underlying jihadist doctrine. Although no single individual is the intellectual father of the modern jihadist movement, its philosophical foundations are grounded in the writings of a number of key individuals: Ibn-Taymiyyah, Ibn-Abd-al-Wahhab, Rashid Rida, Hasan al-Banna, Abu-A'la Mawdudi, Sayyid Qutb, Shukri Mustafa, Abd-al-Salam al-Farag, and Abdullah Azzam. The importance of their concepts to establishing the philosophical foundations of the modern jihadist movement cannot be overstated. Reliance on the Qur'an is a common thread that runs through the writings of all of the advocates of violent jihad. *Fatwas,* or Islamic rulings by a member of the religiously learned class called the *Ulema,* frequently cite different Qur'anic verses involving jihad to legitimate violence. Such citation, however, is extremely selective and often focuses on a few excerpts commonly referred to as "sword verses." We readily concede that other writers, not included here, also have influenced the movement, but their works are less prominent.

Ibn-Taymiyyah

Because al-Qa'ida has become the new face of Islamic extremism, it is important to recognize the great influence of Ibn-Taymiyyah over al-Qa'ida's ideology. Ibn-Taymiyyah was born in 1269 in Syria and became a professor of Islamic law like his father. The majority of Ibn-Taymiyyah's writings focused on statecraft and good governance. He sought to redefine politics and believed that any further interpretation of the Qur'an would be heretical. Refusing to accept the subjugation of religion under the state, he declared all rulers who did not enforce *Shari'ah* (Islamic law) to be apostates and, consequently, legitimate targets of rebellion and attack. Ibn-Taymiyyah was the first to issue a fatwa against Muslims when he declared that the Mongols, who were locked in a bitter struggle with the Muslim Mamluk rulers of Egypt, were apostates due to their failure to implement Shari'ah law.[25] Ibn-Taymiyyah's labeling of the Mongols as apostates is still used by jihadist groups to draw an analogy to governments run by Muslims who similarly fail to implement Shari'ah law.

Ibn-Taymiyyah argued that the requirements for jihad were clearly indicated through the stories of the Prophet, and that they should be put on "the same level as the 'five pillars' of Islam: prayer, pilgrimage, alms, the declaration of faith ('There is no deity but God, and Muhammad is his Prophet'), and the fast of Ramadan."[26] Ibn-Taymiyyah also established a new basis for legitimizing jihad: "When the enemy has entered an Islamic land, there is no doubt that it is obligatory on those closest to the land to defend it, and then on those around them . . . for the entire Islamic land is like a single country."[27] Similarly, in pursuing the jihad, violence against fellow Muslims was acceptable: "If with the Kuffar [unbelievers] there are pious people from the best of mankind and it is not possible to fight these Kuffar except by killing them, then they are to be killed as well."[28]

This argument has been adopted by groups like al-Qa'ida for a number of reasons: it sanctions taking their fight to the enemy, unites the Islamic world by Islam alone (and rejects worldly borders), and provides the theological groundwork for allowing the killing of Muslims as "collateral damage." Ibn-Taymiyyah also prescribed that in jihad, one should deal with the greatest of the kuffar first; this has been one of the primary influences on al-Qa'ida's campaign against the United States, especially in regard to the Middle East. The works of Ibn-Taymiyyah are often overlooked by Western analysts, but his comments on jihad have influenced generations and given sanction to those groups that seek to use violence to achieve their goals.

Muhammad Ibn-Abd-al-Wahhab

As the father of arguably the most puritanical sect of Islam, Muhammad Ibn-Abd-al-Wahhab (1703–91) was greatly influenced by Ibn-Taymiyyah. Commonly referred to as Wahhabis, and also as Salafis (from the

Arabic word *Salaf*, meaning ancestors and referring to Muhammad's companions), followers of al-Wahhab's teachings perceive themselves as practicing the purest form of Islam. He called for an Islam "that returned to its revealed sources,"[29] declared jihad against "bad" Muslims, named all non-Wahhabi Muslims to be infidels,[30] and called for an absolute monotheism that rejected idolatry completely. In his teachings, Ibn-Abd-al-Wahhab rejected all Islamic practices after the third century of the Muslim Era (approximately 950 C.E.), rejecting them as *bid'a*, or heretical innovations, and set his followers on a path to conquer all heretical sects of Islam. Like Ibn-Taymiyyah, Ibn-Abd-al-Wahhab called for a literal interpretation of the Qur'an free of analogies and metaphors.

Ibn-Abd-al-Wahhab was the first to reintroduce the Kharaji concept of *takfir*. Derived from the Arabic word for declaring someone to be a disbeliever, takfir is the process of declaring another Muslim to be an apostate and, in turn, saying that their murders are legitimate. The growing use of takfir to justify terrorist activities is a controversial idea.[31] In large measure, this reflects the fact that scholars traditionally have been extremely reluctant to use takfir for fear that widespread application could be detrimental to the Islamic community.[32]

To determine whether someone was takfir, al-Wahhab promulgated a system of "voiders" of Islam. If only one of the voiders is met, then that person is found to be an apostate and therefore eligible for execution. The voiders are (1) polytheism; (2) using mediators for God; (3) doubting that non-Muslims are disbelievers; (4) judging by non-Islamic laws and believing that these are superior to divine law; (5) hating anything the Prophet practiced; (6) mocking Islam or the Prophet; (7) using or supporting magic; (8) supporting or helping nonbelievers against Muslims; (9) believing that someone has the right to stop practicing Islam; (10) turning away from Islam by not studying or practicing it.[33] Abd-al-Wahhab also established a second principle that is often quoted in jihadist justifications: whoever does not declare takfir against the disbeliever is a disbeliever himself.

Al-Wahhab's forces set out to destroy shrines and other sacred objects. They even destroyed the sacred Shi'ite pilgrimage site in Karbala, Iraq, which housed the tomb of Hussein, one of the two grandsons of Muhammad and a central figure in Shi'ism. In helping the al-Sa'ud family take control of the Arabian Peninsula, al-Wahhab was able to shape the country's religious beliefs and provide key philosophical rationales for future generations to pursue the global jihad.

Rashid Rida

In Egypt, a Cairo intellectual named Rashid Rida (1866–1935) argued that "only a salafiyah Islam, an Islam purged of impurities and Western influences, could save Muslims from subordination to the colonial powers."[34] Although his argument is similar to that of Wahhabism, Rida's writings take the novel step of employing the Qu'ranic term *Jahiliyah* to characterize Muslim lands of his own time. *Jahiliyah* previously had referred to the pre-Islamic time on the Arabian Peninsula and literally means "godlessness" or "barbarity." Rida employed the term against his own time because of the widespread failure to implement Shari'ah law in Muslim lands. He also condemned secular government. His writings "cleared the way for future radicalism."[35]

Hassan al-Banna

Egyptian schoolteacher Hassan al-Banna (1906–49), the founder of the Muslim Brotherhood in Egypt, launched his organization as a way to respond to, not retreat from, modern society. Al-Banna's views need to be examined in terms of their historical context, including the colonial experience in Palestine during the British Mandate from 1918 to 1948, the creation of Israel, and the social and economic deficiencies he attributed to Arab nationalism. He felt that Arab weakness could only be reversed by returning to the path of true Islam. Moreover, because Muslim lands were occupied at the time, al-Banna argued that violent jihad was necessary, making it an obligation of all Muslims to repel the invaders and reject governments that were not Islamic.

Realizing that change would come slowly, al-Banna was more an anti-colonial Islamic revivalist than he was a revolutionary, focusing on training future generations according to the precepts of his Islamic system. Many social services, including schools, infirmaries, and classes and lectures on Islam, were established. Several widely read newspapers and magazines were published by the Brotherhood, which eventually began to establish factories and take control of trade unions. While denouncing colonialism and imperialism, al-Banna emphasized that to rebuild a community of the faithful, the primary goal must be to call Muslims to "return and reappropriate their faith in its fullness or totality of vision."[36] Along with advocating reforms, al-Banna and the Brothers began looking toward a military option. They sought members within the ranks of the military and also organized their own paramilitary groups, commonly referred to as phalanges, as a step towards seizing power in the future.

After the execution of al-Banna at the hands of the Egyptian government, the Muslim Brotherhood continued to grow. Even as an underground group after the banning of their organization, the Brotherhood strengthened its resolve and hatred of the Egyptian leaders. Membership increased from approximately seventy thousand at the time of al-Banna's execution to hundreds of thousands only a decade later. In the intervening years, the Brotherhood has inspired groups all over the world to take up the same cause, under the aegis (to varying degrees) of the Muslim Brotherhood. The Brotherhood has been particularly successful in appealing to students and is a presence on nearly every university campus in the Islamic world.

Abu-al-A'la Mawdudi

At the same time of al-Banna's mobilization of the Muslim Brotherhood, Abu-al-A'la Mawdudi, a journalist, began to write about the need to cleanse Muslim society of Western influence and corrupt, heretical traditions. Like al-Banna, Mawdudi was an Islamic revivalist very much concerned with reform. Mawdudi drew upon Wahhabism, the writings of Rashid Rida, and the Indian anti-imperialist Deobandi school of Islam in an attempt to organize a group to respond to society, much like al-Banna's Muslim Brotherhood. The Deobandi label is derived from a school (Daral Uloom Deoband) in India and refers to a Sunni religious revivalist movement.

Mawdudi argued that it was important to develop science and technology within an Islamic context in order to avoid Westernization and the secularization of society. He also called for the implementation of Shari'ah. This is consistent with the viewpoints articulated by al-Banna, and their shared perspective has helped to shape jihadist ideology and to inspire future generations of jihadists. For example, Mawdudi established the Jamaa a-Islami group, which later became a central group in Pakistani politics following the creation of Pakistan in 1947. Like the Brotherhood, Mawdudi's Jamaa a-Islami organization focused on the indoctrination of future generations through the use of schools, mosques, publications, and social programs.[37]

In his writings, Mawdudi portrayed jihad as a transcendental battle of absolutes between good and evil forces. He maintained that it is the duty of believers to "wipe out oppression, wrongdoing, strife, immorality, arrogance and unlawful exploitation from the world by force of arms. It is their objective to shatter the myth of the divinity of 'demi-gods' and false deities and to reinstate good in the place of evil."[38] Writing on the subject of jihad, Mawdudi argued: "Jihad is as much of a primary duty of the Muslims concerned as are the daily prayers or fasting. One who shirks it is a sinner. His very claim to being a Muslim is doubtful. He is a hypocrite whose 'Ibadah and prayers are a sham, a worthless, hollow show of devotion."[39]

Although he addressed the question of jihad, Mawdudi's primary concern was working towards an Islamic state and the importance of Shari'ah. His writings on that topic still resonate powerfully with jihadist groups today. Like Ibn-Taymiyyah, he asserted that the moral high ground belongs to the jihadist. As such, his writings offer the jihadist movement another respected source to call out those Muslims who do not fight and to perhaps even bring violence against them as kuffar, or unbelievers.

Sayyid Qutb

Born in 1906 in Musha, Egypt, Sayyid Qutb became the leading Islamic thinker for the Muslim Brotherhood group, and his texts are still studied by current followers of jihadist movements around the world. Although Qutb was an author and not a *faqih* (doctor of Islamic law), virtually every jihadist group in the last forty years has used his philosophy—or at least parts of it—to propagate and protect Islam by violent means, whether by attacking Western interests or by fueling insurgency in the Muslim world. For example, given their objective to apply Islamic law, Egyptian jihadists used Qutb's arguments to legitimize attacks against the government. Islamists who accepted Qutb's views succeeded in assassinating Egyptian president Anwar Sadat on October 6, 1981.

As a child, Qutb became very politically aware thanks to his father's interests in anti-British nationalism. He also memorized the Qur'an by the age of ten. Following three years at Dar al-Ulem, a teacher-training institute, Qutb graduated and went on to work at the Ministry of Public Instruction, where he drafted many proposals for school reform in Egypt. Qutb began writing journals, essays, and novels, some of which were politically based primarily in support of the Wafd party. Qutb abandoned his party affiliation in 1945 out of frustration with Wafd due to its corruption and the softening of its anti-British-colonialism position. Politics in Egypt during this time was pretty chaotic, and the people—not only Qutb—were losing faith in Wafd, which increasingly was seen as corrupt and unable to respond to the needs of the people. Until the end of World War II, Qutb wrote mostly literary criticism.

The seminal event for Qutb occurred in 1948, when he was sent for a three-year stay in the United States to study the American education system under the sponsorship of the Egyptian Ministry of Public Instruction. His American experience had exactly the opposite effect from the outcome his superiors desired. Qutb returned to Egypt in the summer of 1951 extremely disenchanted with American ideals and culture. While in the United States, Qutb rediscovered Islam, and he began praying five times a day and preaching to other Muslims. Qutb claimed his religious reawakening was in reaction to the rampant sexual promiscuity, drunken behavior, and capitalism he encountered in the United States.

Upon his return to Egypt, he was forced to resign from the Ministry of Public Instruction because of his bitter denunciations of American society. Jobless, Qutb began frequenting Brotherhood establishments and was recruited into the organization in 1951 by Salih 'Ashmawi. The next year, he was elected to the Brotherhood's leadership council and headed up the department for the propagation of Islam.

After a brief period of cooperation between the Free Officers and the Brotherhood, Nasser and his colleagues began to see the Islamists as threats to their government. Qutb was imprisoned in 1954 for three months and released. After a crackdown on the Brotherhood following a failed attempt to assassinate Nasser, Qutb again was arrested and tortured along with the majority of the Brotherhood's militants. After a sham trial in July 1955, he was sentenced to twenty-five years of hard labor.[40]

Imprisonment gave Qutb the time to write a series of Qur'anic commentaries, especially his most influential work, *Milestones,* a work that went beyond the Brotherhood's traditional focus on revivalism, taking a revolutionary perspective and providing the theological underpinnings for jihadist policies. The book was, in fact, so controversial at the time that the Brotherhood immediately denounced it. Qutb's ideas in the book were shaped by the writings of Ibn-Taymiyyah, Rida, and Mawdudi. According to Qutb, the West and other secularized societies were demonized and portrayed as legitimate targets for believers to attack since these societies were viewed as enemies of Islam:

> The *jahili* society is any society other than the Muslim society; and if we want a more specific definition, we may say that any society is a *jahili*

society which does not dedicate itself to submission to God alone, in its beliefs and ideas, in its observances of worship, and in its legal regulations. . . . Lastly, all the existing so-called 'Muslim' societies are also *jahili* societies.[41]

Qutb emphasizes the importance of true belief in Islam, and thus he argues for bringing the Muslim world to believe sincerely that there is only one God and Muhammad is his messenger. Qutb also asserts that the basis for building the community must be grounded in religious beliefs instead of laws. Thus he argues:

> Islam provides a legal basis for the relationship of the Muslim community with other groups. . . . This legal formulation is based on the principle that Islam—that is, submission to God—is a universal Message which the whole of mankind should accept or make peace with. No political system or material power should put hindrances in the way of preaching Islam. It should leave every individual free to accept or reject it, and if someone wants to accept it, it should not prevent him or fight against him. If someone does this, then it is the duty of Islam to fight him until either he is killed or until he declares his submission.[42]

Like Ibn-Taymiyyah, Qutb felt disdain for the non-Muslim People of the Book (Christians and Jews), who, like Muslims, recognize the God of Abraham as the one and only god and practice faiths based on divine ordinances. He espoused the idea that Jews have conspired against Muslims at all times and that anyone who leads the community of Muslim believers away from its religion is quite obviously a "Jewish agent."[43] Seeking to reorganize the community of believers and to erase the competition, Qutb essentially deepened the Good vs. Evil divide portrayed by Ibn-Taymiyyah, al-Banna, and Mawdudi.

Qutb also clearly states the rationale for jihad: "to establish God's authority in the earth; to arrange human affairs according to the true guidance provided by God; to abolish all the Satanic forces and Satanic systems of life; to end the lordship of one man over others since all men are creatures of God and no one has the authority to make them his servants or to make arbitrary laws for them. These reasons are sufficient for proclaiming Jihad."[44] However, while Qutb very clearly articulates the reasons for jihad, he leaves questions about the means of jihad—and whether or not the jihad is spiritual or "by the sword"—to the reader's interpretation: "one should always keep in mind that there is no compulsion in religion; that is, once the people are free from the lordship of men, the law governing civil affairs will be purely that of God, while no one will be forced to change his beliefs and accept Islam."[45] In his works, he continually stresses the need for total, unwavering belief in the *shahadah*, or declaration of faith, and he asserts that this is the core of Islamic theory. For Qutb, without total belief in the fact that "there is no god but God and Muhammad is his Prophet," there can be no homogeneity in the community, since everyone would be bound by different levels of faith. Qutb echoes the Qur'an by asserting that people must come to this belief of their own accord, and that people can only accept it if they want to— that forcing conversion is not the same as belief, and that therefore it is unnecessary. Still, the "assault" by the West and forces of impurity through globalization are very often seen as hostile actions towards Muslims, and therefore the groups that follow Qutb's ideology very much believe that they are fighting a defensive jihad and will continue to believe so until the enemy has been subjugated, or at least until the community of believers has risen to a position of authority above the enemy.

According to Qutb, the real reason for jihad is not to defend Muslim lands but to uphold Qur'anic law, so there should be no reason for Muslims to refrain from violent force to preserve and advance Islam in the world. In his works, Qutb asserted that Western societies and the Islamic world, especially Egypt, are in a state of Jahiliyah. As David Zeidan explains, "There is only one law, *Shari'ah*. All other law is mere human caprice. There is only one true system, Islam. All other systems are *jahiliyya*."[46]

Throughout *Milestones* and other works, Qutb emphasizes the need for the return of a true community of believers to fight oppression, but the method of that return is left open to interpretation. That method could very easily be interpreted as violence due to his assertion that there is no reason not to use violence against the apostate regime. His legacies to future generations of extremists include the use of takfir, the theory that modern society is jahili, and the belief of a Christian-Jewish conspiracy against Islam. Since his philosophy is based on his interpretation of Islam, Qutb was, and still is, one of the best sources for understanding Islamic extremist thinking and how Muslim extremists legitimize attacks on foreign populations—and also on their own.

Shortly before publishing *Milestones*, Qutb was released from prison and became the central figure in the deeply shattered Muslim Brotherhood. Less than a year after Qutb's release, Nasser had him arrested again, stating that Qutb was the ringleader in a new Brotherhood conspiracy. On August 29, 1966, Qutb was hanged along with two of his companions.

He died before being able to clarify his concept of worldwide Jahiliyah and its various implications. Because he never declared if his pronouncement was to be taken literally or allegorically, the concept has often been taken in the most literal form by today's jihadists. In this form, the most logical next step after declaring the world to be ignorant and un-Islamic would be to pronounce takfir against someone: Qutb stated in *Milestones* that Muslim societies are jahili "not because they believe in other deities beside God or because they worship anyone other than God, but because their way of life is not based on submission alone."[47] Therefore, such people are not to be seen as apostate, only ignorant. Many Egyptian militants, looking to assign guilt for worldwide Jahiliyah to an apostate entity, turned to the Egyptian leadership. Militants blamed Jahiliyah on secular governments, in this case the Egyptian government. They believed the government's policies, specifically the lack of Shari'ah, were keeping people in a state of Jahiliyah. They thought that, if the secular government were replaced by genuine Islamic leadership, the people would awaken and pull themselves out of Jahiliyah.

Shukri Mustafa

Shukri Mustafa, another of the Egyptian extremists released after he was tortured in prison camps for Islamic activists, believed modern society to be jahili and urged a withdrawal from it. However, unlike the spiritual withdrawal that many followers of Qutb, al-Banna, and Mawdudi pursued, Shukri advocated a physical separation from Jahiliyah. His group, known in the West as Takfir wa al-Hijra, withdrew from the "unbelieving" society and set up a new, more Islamic society. The reasoning was that, in a period of temporary weakness, the Prophet fled from Mecca to Medina, where he would gather strength and later return to conquer Mecca in the name of Islam.

Shukri spent six years in the Tura prison camp, where he became an adherent of Qutbist/Mawdudist ideology. The time that he and many of his contemporaries spent in these camps points to how the camps served as incubators for increased radicalization; essentially the camps served as tools for networking with other militants, indoctrination, and even training in clandestine activity. The torture of militants may have added to

Shukri's withdrawal from society. John Conroy explains that a defense mechanism of some torture survivors is to retreat from the world around them.[48]

Shukri believed that the four traditional schools of Islamic law and interpretation were unnecessary, and he stated that all that was needed to understand the Qur'an and its meaning was a good dictionary. Essentially, he was against any interpretation and believed that the words of the Qur'an should be taken at face value. Shukri's interpretation was much like the viewpoint articulated by Ibn-Abd-al-Wahhab.

Shukri and his group rejected state education and state-run mosques, believing that education through Islam is the only real education and that piety and prayer are individual obligations that should not be run by the government, especially by an apostate government such as that in Egypt. His new community welcomed women into its membership, something that most Islamist groups did not do, provided housing for members, and arranged marriages between them. Diplomas from universities were meaningless in Shukri's society, and the community was supported financially through farming, peddling, and money sent to the community from Shukri's supporters in the Gulf.[49]

The ultimate objectives of Shukri's group were to reconstitute the caliphate as it was during the four "Rightly-Guided" caliphs (he believed that every ruler after the last of the four caliphs to be jahili); to restore the Golden Age of Islam; and to establish Islamic rule worldwide. Shukri's leadership was absolute: he was seen as the Mahdi, or a Muslim who is destined to fulfill God's original mandate of spreading Islam and to bring about God's final reign on earth. Certain of his apocalyptic role, and quite possibly believing himself to be infallible, Shukri declared the action of breaking with his group equivalent to apostasy and punishable by death. This led to disillusioned members, many of whom cooperated with the Egyptian secret police.

In 1976, Shukri reacted violently to the splintering of his group and to other groups recruiting Takfir wa al-Hijra members by attempting to kill two rivals. Egyptian authorities, in a crackdown on Islamist groups throughout the country—and partially in reaction to violence by Shukri's group—pursued Shukri and arrested a number of Takfir members. After Takfir wa al-Hijra kidnapped and executed a high-ranking state cleric, Shukri was brought to trial, where he mocked the ulema for insisting that jihad is an internal battle to overcome the impurities of a person. His attacks upon the ulema led to a broad takfir of those who followed the clerics. Daniel Benjamin and Steven Simon explain: "As far as Shukri was concerned, the clerics were simply protecting their prerogatives and concealing their intellectual cowardice. Even worse, he argued, this practice set the great commentators up as idols, competing with God and the Prophet. Those who relied upon these jurists were denying the oneness of Allah and deserved death."[50]

Shukri's trial (1977) badly discredited the ulema in the eyes of the Egyptian people and further fueled radicalization within the region. Shukri was executed along with four other members of Takfir wa al-Hijra the following year.

Abd-al-Salam al-Farag

Contrary to the expectations of the Egyptian government, the prisons that housed members of the Egyptian Muslim Brotherhood served as schools for the indoctrination and even clandestine training of many future leaders of the global jihad. Similarly, the repressive tendencies of the Egyptian government also fostered increased radicalization, particularly within Egypt's student population. For instance, Abd-al-Salam al-Farag (1952–1982) was the leader of the al-Jihad group that came out of the radicalization of Egyptian universities in the 1970s. The group had two specific grievances: the peace treaty with Israel, and the enactment of a new secular law that governed family affairs.

Al-Jihad was unlike previous Islamist organizations in Egypt because it was first and foremost a committed revolutionary group. Farag was the intellectual leader of the group; he in turn had been inspired by Shaykh Umar Abd-al-Rahman, commonly referred to as the "Blind Shaykh." Abd-al-Rahman was involved in the assassination of Egyptian president Sadat and in the 1993 bombing of the World Trade Center in New York. Armed robberies, especially against businesses owned by Coptic Christians, helped fund the activities of the organization.

In his book *The Neglected Duty*, Farag followed Ibn-Taymiyyah's assertion that jihad should be the sixth pillar of Islam, insisting that "abandoning Jihad is the cause of the humiliation and division in which the Muslims live today."[51] Farag described jihad as "the forgotten" or "neglected" duty, and he insisted that all Muslims are obligated to spread the word of Islam to the entire world before the end of time and the coming of the *Mahdi*, a messianic figure in Islam who will establish a perfect Islamic society on earth.[52] He also insisted that the traditional belief that jihad could not be issued without an *amir*, or leader, of the community was false—jihad was obligatory even when leaderless and fragmented. This idea is clearly applicable to jihadists of the present day who conduct jihad in furtherance of an idea as much as in support of a leader.

While Shukri Mustafa argued that much of the Egyptian public was apostate, Farag argued that only the regime was apostate, saying that "what they carry of Islam is nothing but names, even if they pray, fast and claim to be Muslims."[53] Farag, by shifting the focus back to the regime, also argued that "it is obligatory upon the Muslims to raise their swords against the rulers who are hiding the truth and manifesting falsehood, otherwise the truth will never reach the hearts of the people."[54] As a result, Farag's major contribution to religious-nationalists in Egypt and elsewhere in articulating a strategic vision may have been his ability to provide a coherent rationale for the belief that fighting the Near Enemy takes precedence. He paraphrases this concept by stating that "fighting the enemy that is near to us comes before fighting that which is far."[55] Farag explains his vision:

> Verily the main reason behind the existence of Imperialism in the Muslim lands is these rulers. Therefore to begin with destroying the Imperialists is not a useful action and is a waste of time. We have to concentrate on our Islamic issue, which is to establish the laws of Allah in our land first and make the word of Allah the highest. This is because there is no doubt that the prime field of Jihad is to remove these leaderships and replace them with the complete Islamic system, and from here we start.[56]

Farag believed that the people could only be judged by God. Because Farag did not condemn Egyptian society, al-Jihad was able to increase its "technical competence as a clandestine group" by recruiting government workers, soldiers, journalists, and intelligence operatives.[57] The group posed a large threat to the Egyptian government because most of the recruiting took place at private mosques after observation of recruits, and because of the nearly tribal structure of al-Jihad, in which family and friends were entrusted with the most sensitive positions.

In the jihadist movement, takfiri ideology plays a central role in defining a legitimate set of targets (especially when the target is Muslim) and in justifying violent jihad. For example, in *The Neglected Duty* Farag argued that both the Qur'an and the Hadith (compilations of sayings by the Prophet) were fundamentally about war. Faraj called upon Muslims to take up jihad—Al-Faridah al-Gha'ibah (the "absent obligation" or "neglected duty" depending on translation)—against apostate regimes in the Middle East, particularly Egypt. Farag's call for the deaths of apostate Muslims is greatly influenced by Ibn-Taymiyyah, the medieval Islamic scholar, whom he quotes extensively in his own book.[58] Saudi jihadist scholar Shaykh Ali bin Khudayr al-Khudayr further expanded the concept of takfir by declaring that all Muslims who know the principles of takfir have the right to do takfir, regardless of whether or not they are scholars or religious leaders.[59]

Hoping that the Egyptian population would rise up against the regime after a catalytic event, Farag's group carried out the assassination of Sadat in 1981, along with a failed attempt to create an armed revolt in Cairo. Farag argued, "It is obligatory upon the Muslims to raise their swords against the rulers who are hiding the truth and manifesting falsehood, otherwise the truth will never reach the hearts of the people." [60] The population, however, did not launch a popular revolution following Sadat's murder. After the aborted uprising was quelled by the security services, Farag and many others involved in the assassination were tried and executed. Abd-al-Rahman, on the other hand, was acquitted in a show of leniency by the Egyptian government.

Abdullah Azzam

The preceding writers, intellectuals, and theologians are among the most important influences on modern groups like al-Qa'ida; but the most direct influence on such groups has been Abdullah Azzam, a former Brotherhood member. Azzam, unlike many of the other ideologues discussed thus far, studied theology and held a doctorate in Islamic jurisprudence (*fiqh*).[61] Azzam was born in 1941 in Palestine. He became the major Arab advocate of the jihad against the Soviets in Afghanistan when he founded the Office of Services (MAK), which "disseminated propaganda, raised funds and recruited new members through a network of offices in thirty-five countries."[62] Many of these jihadist recruits were from Arab countries. His partner and protégé in this endeavor was Usama bin Laden.

The MAK enacted Azzam's four phases of the organization: (1) *hijra*—emigration or withdrawal from other influences; (2) *tarbiyyah*—

recruitment and training of believers for the cause; (3) *qital*—fighting the enemies of Allah; and (4) *shari'ah*—implementing Islamic law and creating an Islamic state. Once completed, according to Azzam, the organization would move on to the next jihad and repeat the cycle. In fact, the transnational foundation for funding and training mujahidin was adapted by al-Qa'ida, itself a transnational organization that funded and trained insurgencies and, later, terrorist operations as part of the global jihad.

Because he provided the initial intellectual and spiritual inspiration for al-Qa'ida, Azzam's importance must not be understated, and his works should not be ignored. Azzam's *Defense of the Muslim Lands: The First Obligation after Faith* frequently quotes and borrows extensively from Ibn-Taymiyyah. Azzam asserts that neglecting jihad is as bad as neglecting prayer or fasting, and that jihad is obligatory if the mujahidin are in need. Like Farag, Azzam asserts that jihad must be pursued even without an amir. In his writings, Azzam lays out the conditions for defensive jihad and also reiterates Ibn-Taymiyyah's call for the continuation of violence against the infidel even when Muslims are being used as shields. He also says that the obligation to jihad outranks obedience to parents and spouses, and that young men and women should work to expel the enemy without parental permission. The wealthy are also required to give money to the mujahidin if they are in need of it.[63]

Azzam, in his influential tract *Join the Caravan*, wrote that one of the reasons for jihad was to establish control through combat over some territory (or "piece of land") that could serve as a homeland:

> Establishment of the Muslim community on an area of land is a necessity, as vital as water and air. This homeland will not come about without an organized Islamic movement which perseveres consciously and realistically upon Jihad, and which regards fighting as a decisive factor and as a protective cover.
>
> The Islamic movement will not be able to establish the Islamic community except through a common, people's Jihad which has the Islamic movement as its beating heart and deliberating mind.[64]

Perhaps the most relevant of Azzam's assertions concerns the legality of receiving help from one group of infidels while fighting against another. Azzam states that for this to be permissible, the following conditions must be met:

> (1) The rule of Islam must have the upper hand, that is to say, the Muslims must be stronger than the combined group of the *Mushrikun*

[unbelievers, infidels, idolaters, etc.] from whom they are seeking help as well as the *Mushrikun* they are fighting. In case of the collaboration of the *Kuffar* against the Muslims.

(2) The *Kuffar* must have a good opinion of the Muslims, and the Muslims must feel safe from their treachery and this is estimated from their behavior.

(3) The Muslims must be in need of the *Kaffir* or the *Kuffar* they ask help from.[65]

The above criteria were allegedly met when the mujahidin were receiving aid from the United States and its allies to fight against the Soviet Union.

Azzam's legacy, however, lies especially in his having redefined jihad, departing from the traditional view that jihad was to be a collective duty—*fard kifayah*—carried out by the community, and not mandatory for individuals as long as the community sends a sufficient number of mujahidin. After Azzam, jihad was held by jihadists to be *fard ayn*—an individual duty—to be carried out by every Muslim as a requirement of Islam, along with daily prayer and pilgrimage to Mecca. The idea of jihad as an individual duty is a major item of belief shared by most modern jihadists.

Azzam was assassinated by a car bomb in Peshawar, Pakistan, in 1989. After his death, nobody came forward to claim credit for having killed him. However, because of the rivalry between Azzam and al-Zawahiri for influence within the jihadist movement, many suggest that al-Zawahiri and his Egyptian jihadists were behind the attack. There are also questions about whether bin Laden was personally involved, including whether he ordered the assassination due to his disagreements with Azzam over a set of training camps that would be converted for terrorist use against noncombatants, a practice that Azzam repudiated. Miriam Abou Zahab and Olivier Roy maintain that "the militants who went to Afghanistan were far from being entirely hotheads. Indeed, the assassination of Abdullah Azzam took place when he was preparing to transfer his allegiance to the most moderate of the mujahidin," guerrilla leader Ahmad Shah Massoud.[66] Even if he was not involved, Usama clearly failed to condemn the action or show outrage over it. After Azzam's death, the MAK and al-Qa'ida were firmly aligned with the militant elements and under bin Laden's control.

Ayman al-Zawahiri

Regarded by many as al-Qa'ida's leading ideologue and strategist, Ayman al-Zawahiri instigated one of the most important changes in jihadist ideology by arguing that the primary targeting emphasis should shift from regimes in the Middle East (Near Enemy) to Western governments, especially the United States (Far Enemy). Al-Zawahiri believes, along with most of the jihadist movement, that the basic problem is the domination of corrupt regimes in the Arab and Islamic world. These regimes do not govern by Islamic law, and they open up the land to foreign enemies; opposition to the latter policy is most often displayed through continued jihadist outcries against the stationing of American troops in Saudi Arabia during the Gulf War. These corrupt regimes, and the foreigners who support them, make up what al-Zawahiri terms the "Alliance of Evil," perhaps a subtle dig at President George W. Bush's "Axis of Evil" terminology.[67] According to his theory, focusing attacks on the West will result in the removal of Western support and cause the local regimes to fall.

In a July 2007 video, al-Zawahiri offered viewers near- and long-term plans for resisting what he called the "Zionist Crusade" against Islam:

> The near-term plan consists of targeting Crusader-Jewish interests, as everyone who attacks the Muslim Ummah must pay the price, in our country and theirs, in Iraq, Afghanistan, Palestine and Somalia, and everywhere we are able to strike their interests. . . . And the long-term plan is divided into two halves: The first half consists of earnest, diligent work, to change these corrupt and corruptive regimes.

Al-Zawahiri conceded that, because the circumstances in every country are different, he was unable to "offer a single prescription for change to every country." He did, however, offer five general characteristics that he thought are applicable to all countries: (1) the mujahidin must be patient; (2) the mujahidin must strive to garner popular support; (3) change must be forced, whether by military coup, mass popular uprising and disobedience, guerrilla warfare, or armed political resistance, noting that "whatever its form, method and means, force remains a necessary element for bringing about change . . . after all paths to peaceful change have been blocked"; (4) the Ummah must "get used to challenging falsehood, and declaring the truth in its face, even if that leads to sacrifice of wealth and self"; and (5) an organization and leadership cadre must be "leading the change, guiding progress, and taking advantage of the opportunities which present themselves."

The second half of al-Zawahiri's long-term plan for resisting the "Zionist Crusade" focused on exhorting Muslims to take personal action. He argued in the same video that they needed to meet his call to arms "by hurrying to the fields of jihad like Afghanistan, Iraq and Somalia, for jihad preparation and training. Thus, it is a must to hurry to the fields of jihad for two reasons: The first is to defeat the enemies of the Ummah and repel the Zionist Crusade, and the second is for jihadi preparation and training to prepare for the next stage of the jihad."[68]

Because al-Zawahiri constantly argues that violence is the only language Americans understand, his strategic thinking places a premium on martyrdom and mass-casualty operations. He argues that those types of attacks are easy to carry out, that they are psychologically distressing to the enemy, and that they erode public support in the West for continued engagement in the Middle East.

Throughout his statements and correspondence, al-Zawahiri declares that the mujahidin need to march under a clear, identifiable banner and conduct a successful public relations campaign in an effort to unite not only the mujahidin but all Muslims in general.[69] Al-Zawahiri argues that al-Qa'ida must assert its leadership of the Islamic nation in order to bring about a direct confrontation that is clear-cut jihad, or to force the West to make policy changes in the Islamic world:

> The masters in Washington and Tel Aviv are using the regimes to pro-
> tect their interests and to fight the battle against the Muslims on their
> behalf. If the shrapnel from the battle reach their homes and bodies,
> they will trade accusations with their agents about who is responsible
> for this. In that case, they will face one of two bitter choices: Either
> personally wage the battle against the Muslims, which means that the
> battle will turn into clear-cut jihad against infidels, or they reconsider
> their plans after acknowledging the failure of the brute and violent con-
> frontation against Muslims.[70]

Like all jihadists, al-Zawahiri has emphasized the need to control territory from which the mujahidin can wage war as essential to restoring the caliphate. Al-Zawahiri explains:

> The jihad movement must adopt its plan on the basis of controlling a
> piece of land in the heart of the Islamic world on which it could establish

and protect the state of Islam and launch its battle to restore the rational caliphate based on the traditions of the prophet. . . . Armies achieve victory only when the infantry takes hold of land. Likewise, the Mujahid Islamic movement will not triumph against the world coalition unless it possesses a fundamentalist base in the heart of the Islamic world.[71]

There is some disagreement, however, among jihadists over where the "center" of the caliphate should be located. From this letter, it is apparent that al-Zawahiri believes that the Islamic state would be centered in the Levant and Egypt.[72] Iraq and Afghanistan, from his perspective, will be established as Islamic Emirates and serve as bases from which jihad can be launched in an effort to expand the caliphate. Not surprisingly, however, al-Qa'ida in Iraq (AQI) advocates the position that Baghdad should be the capital. AQI bases its claim on the historical fact that Baghdad was the capital of the Abbassid caliphate before it was sacked by the Mongols, allegedly with the help of the Shi'ite minister Ibn-al-Alqami, who is a major figure in AQI's examples of a Shi'ite conspiracy against Sunnis.[73] Bin Laden's idea about where to locate the capital of the Islamic state was unclear until July 2006, when he addressed the mujahidin in "Baghdad, the seat of the Caliphate."[74] This is the first public statement by the leader addressing the issue of the caliphate's center, although in earlier statements bin Laden alluded to the caliphate being based in Saudi Arabia and Afghanistan.

Al-Zawahiri's 2005 letter to al-Zarqawi, released by the Office of the Director of National Intelligence,[75] offers insights into al-Zawahiri's strategic thinking. Listing goals for the mujahidin in Iraq, al-Zawahiri offers a multiphased approach to establishing and maintaining an Islamic state until the "Hour of Resurrection." Although it is clear that the short-term goal has to be expelling the Americans, he expresses concern that some of the mujahidin in Iraq will lay down their weapons and stop engaging in jihad when U.S. forces leave that country. Al-Zawahiri thinks that, if this happens, the jihadists will lose the initiative and Iraq will be ruled by secularists and traitors. As a result, he outlines a series of stages. The first stage in al-Zawahiri's plan involves expelling the Americans from Iraq. Second, he hopes to establish and maintain an Islamic Emirate. Third, operating out of this base, he anticipates extending the "wave of jihad" to secular countries neighboring Iraq. Fourth, al-Zawahiri wants a direct confrontation with Israel. Iraq, in particular, is important to al-Zawahiri because of its proximity to Jordan, which shares a long common border

with Israel. Al-Zawahiri hopes that the mujahidin will be able to penetrate Jordan and launch attacks on Israel.[76] As noted in a U.S. Military
Academy study, the strategy al-Zawahiri advocates in this letter mirrors
past al-Qa'ida strategic programs dating back to a mid-1990s al-Qa'ida
statement. In that document, the anonymous author proposes a five-point
plan to unite Somali forces and create an Islamic national front:

1. expulsion of the foreign international presence;
2. rebuilding of state institutions;
3. establishment of domestic security;
4. comprehensive national reconciliation; and
5. economic reform and combating famine.[77]

In his 2005 letter to al-Zarqawi, al-Zawahiri asserts that the "strongest
weapon" that could be possessed by the mujahidin is the support of the
Muslim masses in Iraq and in surrounding Muslim countries. He warns
that the mujahidin should avoid any action that the masses do not understand or approve. Without the active support of the masses, al-Zawahiri
says, the Islamic mujahidin movement would be crushed. To avoid this
outcome, he argues that the mujahidin must work to involve the masses
in the battle. Al-Zawahiri then, very subtly, begins to address al-Zarqawi's war on Shi'ites and his beheading of hostages. Al-Zawahiri states
that the reason for the popular support of the mujahidin in Iraq is more
because of the occupation by a foreign enemy, especially one that is seen
as Jewish and American, than because of religious sectarianism.

In a future Islamic state in Iraq, al-Zawahiri says, Muslims will elect
individuals with expertise in Islamic law to represent them. Because of
this plan, al-Zawahiri urges al-Zarqawi and his colleagues to begin the
necessary "fieldwork" to gather the support not only of the masses, but
also of its tribes, elders, scientists, merchants, and otherwise distinguished
persons. The mujahidin will be "a nucleus around which" these people
will gather.

The overriding theme of al-Zawahiri's strategic thought is the necessity
of popular support.[78] Without it, al-Zawahiri recognizes, the jihad against
the West is doomed to failure, just as the jihad against Egypt failed. In
his 2001 autobiography, al-Zawahiri details an attack on the Prime Minister of Egypt in the 1990s; in this particular attack, a twelve-year-old girl
named Shayma was killed. The Egyptian government responded through

a media campaign portraying the death as anything but an accident, saying that Shayma was the target. This devastated the Egyptian jihadist groups' popular support and caused some of the Egyptian jihadist leadership to leave the jihad. The event obviously affected al-Zawahiri greatly and is likely the cause of his emphasis on popular support in jihadist strategy. A 1997 attack on tourists in Luxor, Egypt, by the Islamic Group similarly inflicted severe damage to the popular support for militant Islamists in Egypt, throwing the movement into disarray.

As a result of their own bitter personal experiences, jihadist veterans are well aware of the power of popular support; this is especially true of those who were active in Egypt from the 1970s through the 1990s. In the eyes of many former Egyptian militants, they were "naïve, arrogant, and immature, fired up by the spirit of youth." With a combination of all of these factors, many of the Egyptian groups tested, and indeed exceeded, the limits of violence that the public was willing to accept.[79]

Drawing lessons from this experience, al-Zawahiri warns that participation in governance must not be limited to the mujahidin. He points out that the Taliban similarly failed to mobilize widespread support when it limited participation in Afghanistan to their students. Al-Zawahiri concludes by repeating that the mujahidin must "direct political action equally with the military action, by the alliance, cooperation and gathering of all leaders of opinion and influence in the Iraqi arena." He adds that al-Zarqawi's disparagement of the Ulema, or Islamic scholars—an attitude that had long been characteristic of the now-deceased al-Zarqawi—is counterproductive, since these people are "a symbol of Islam and its emblem. Their disparagement may lead to the general public deeming religion and its adherents as being unimportant."[80]

Abu-Muhammad al-Maqdisi

The writing of al-Zarqawi's former mentor, Abu-Muhammad al-Maqdisi, is also important to takfiri ideology, especially in the case of the insurgents in Iraq. He asserts that democracy is equivalent to a religion because it puts power in the hands of the people rather than in those of God. Following this line of reasoning, anyone who takes part in the democratic process could be considered a polytheist. This concept, which was laid out in al-Maqdisi's book, *Democracy Is a Religion*, was further expanded upon by al-Zarqawi's Legal Committee in January 2005 in a short statement outlining seven grievances against democracy, all firmly rooted in al-Maqdisi's writings.[81] Al-Zarqawi's Legal Committee's grievances with democracy are as follows:

1. the people are the source of authority, not God;
2. because of freedom of religion, people are able to renounce religion;
3. people are the sole arbiters in disputes, not God;
4. freedom of expression allows people to criticize and curse God and Islam;
5. the separation of religion from the state;
6. political parties are protected, regardless of their beliefs, ideas, and morals;
7. democracy upholds the stand of the majority, even if the majority approves evil.[82]

Although al-Maqdisi's concepts greatly influenced al-Zarqawi and his targeting in Iraq, the two disagreed about al-Zarqawi's application of takfiri targeting. In July 2004 al-Maqdisi published an open letter to al-Zarqawi entitled "Advice and Support" that criticized al-Zarqawi's tactics in Iraq. This schism received more publicity upon al-Maqdisi's 2005 release from Jordanian prison. He granted a series of interviews to a number of media outlets in which he appeared to make significant revisions and clarifications to his previously espoused tenets concerning takfir, and even criticized al-Zarqawi and his jihadist brethren for an overreliance on suicide bombing, attacks on the Shi'ites, and the killing of both civilian and allegedly "apostate" Muslims. For al-Maqdisi, the battle is with the occupiers of Iraq, not the Shi'ites, and the continued targeting of Shi'ites should be stopped, "regardless of their history and animosity."[83] Al-Maqdisi went even further by asserting that al-Zarqawi should not excommunicate people in general, perhaps suggesting that takfir should only be decided on the personal level, not en masse.[84]

The disagreement between al-Maqdisi and al-Zarqawi underscores the fact that jihadists vary in the intensity of their beliefs about takfir. Although bin Laden and al-Zawahiri are takfiris, they are much less intense than was al-Zarqawi, who frequently targeted Muslims—many of whom were Shi'ites—who he claimed had cooperated with the Coalition in Iraq or the new Iraqi government in attacking Sunnis. Such cooperation, for al-Zarqawi, was a mortal sin. Bin Laden and al-Zawahiri's use of takfiri ideology is much less broad and specifically targets "apostate" regimes, such as those in Iraq, Jordan, Saudi Arabia, and Pakistan, by encouraging the masses to topple these governments.

Al-Maqdisi's writings also furthered the important though often overlooked jihadist concept of *al-Wala' wa al-Bara'*—allegiance and disavowal. According to this concept, good Muslims should not only separate themselves from jahili societies. They should live and associate only with other devout Muslims, to whom they must remain loyal, while also showing open hatred toward infidels. In an influential text on the concept, Muhammad Sa'id al-Qahtani quotes jihadist-favorite Ibn-Taymiyyah as urging Muslims to love what God loves and hate what God hates. Al-Qahtani goes so far as to say that Muslims are required to oppose disbelievers "even if they are your closest kin."[85]

A number of Qur'anic verses viewed through the standard Salafi lens—literal interpretation—provide the foundation for the concept. Frequently cited verses include 3:28: "Let not the believers take the unbelievers for friends rather than believers; and whoever does this, he shall have nothing of (the guardianship of) Allah, but you should guard yourselves against them, guarding carefully; and Allah makes you cautious of (retribution from) Himself; and to Allah is the eventual coming"; 4:89: "They desire that you should disbelieve as they have disbelieved, so that you might be (all) alike; therefore take not from among them friends until they fly (their homes) in Allah's way; but if they turn back, then seize them and kill them wherever you find them, and take not from among them a friend or a helper"; and 5:51: "O you who believe! do not take the Jews and the Christians for friends; they are friends of each other; and whoever amongst you takes them for a friend, then surely he is one of them; surely Allah does not guide the unjust people."

Al-Wala' wa al-Bara' is extremely important for the jihadist use of takfir. David Cook explains: "*Al-Wala' wa al-Bara'* enables radical Muslims to assert control over the definitions of who is and who is not a Muslim and it forces those who would wish to challenge that control into silence or into being characterized as 'non-Muslims.'"[86] There are exceptions to *al-Wala' wa al-Bara'*: Al-Maqdisi wrote that open enmity toward infidels is not necessary in cases where secrecy is imperative to serve Islam—a principle that is obviously applicable to clandestine jihad operations.[87] Abd-al-Qadir Ibn Abd-al-Aziz, an influential Egyptian jihadist, wrote in his important book, *The Key Guide to Preparations*, that it is permissible to lie to the enemy in times of war. Ibn Abd-al-Aziz, also known as Dr. Fadl, was the original leader of Egyptian Islamic Jihad, later turning over leadership of the movement to al-Zawahiri. Ibn Abd-al-Aziz argued that unlike in *da'wah*—calling others to Islam—secrecy is a basic principle in military operations.[88]

The concepts of *taqiyyah* and *kitman* also provide theological justification for deception. Taqiyyah—most often used in Shi'ite history—allows a Muslim to conceal one's true religious or ideological beliefs if the expression of those beliefs could result in harm. In a 2006 article, for example, al-Qa'ida member Abu-Yahya al-Libi called taqiyyah Shi'ite "hypocrisy," which has allowed them to penetrate other countries and "carry out the most shameful and indecent acts while safe from suspicion and accusation." [89] Similarly, kitman allows one to conceal something that is in process until it is complete. One Islamic website gives the example of Muhammad and the earliest Muslim community in the early days of Islam: because the community of Muslims was small, there was a requirement for secrecy in preaching [da'wah] so as to protect the community from enemies; kitman was also practiced when Muhammad fled the city of Mecca for Medina—known as the *hijra*—which only two individuals other than the Prophet knew about. More applicable to al-Qa'ida and other jihadists, kitman can also be used during times of war when concealing malevolent intentions or as a way to compartmentalize information.[90]

COMMON GOALS, COMMON ENEMIES

Several shared themes emerge from the writings summarized above. The various authors concentrate on identifying a set of common goals for the ummah. They also focus on a common set of enemies who, they claim, aim to make it impossible for Muslims to attain those goals. Here we explore those common goals and common enemies.

A careful reading of the jihadist movement's literature reveals a set of shared pan-Islamic goals. The first—liberating all of Palestine from Zionist control—has been a rallying cry for Islamists since the founding of Israel in 1948. Restoring Jerusalem to Muslim rule is a goal that, no matter how unattainable under present circumstances, is impossible to abandon. It is one of the paramount symbolic issues for Arabs, and indeed for Muslims everywhere, as Jerusalem is the third holiest site in Islam. Hence, to abandon this cause would be political suicide for the radical organizations espousing violent jihad.

The establishment of an Islamic state based on Shari'ah is the second core goal shared by both the intellectual founders and adherents of the jihadist movement. Afghanistan under the Taliban and the Islamic regime in Iran offer examples of both Sunni and Shi'ite Islamic states respectively. With the fall of the Taliban, Iran moved even more aggressively to assert its position as a source of inspiration for radical Islamists. Shi'ite groups like Hizballah were encouraged to strengthen their political role in Lebanon. At the same time—and ironically for Sunnis—the Iranian regime was an example to Hamas, the Muslim Brotherhood, and al-Qa'ida that secular regimes could be toppled, even if the victorious forces were led (as in Iran) by Shi'ite clerics.

The removal of Western influence or foreign presence from Muslim territory is the third major goal. Reflecting the influence of Sayyid Qutb and Abu-al-A'la Mawdudi, the world is reduced to a collection of good and evil societies, with the former being only true Islamic societies following Shari'ah. Removing Western influence from the territory occupied by Muslims—ideally, an entire nation—is especially important. Even when the territory in question is not an Islamic state, this goal has been pursued by many Islamist groups. Similarly, when Iran formed its Islamic government after the 1979 revolution, there were crackdowns on secularism. New laws were instituted to limit what was seen as the decadent influence of Western society. Successfully ending Jahiliyah is extremely important to the contemporary Islamist movement.

Spreading the message beyond the borders of the Islamic state or territory is also very important. Many times, efforts to spread the Islamist message are coupled with measures designed to achieve the fifth goal, namely, of supporting the Muslim brethren on a worldwide basis. Much of Hizballah's support came from Iran, including money, arms, training, and security in the form of Iranian *Pasadran* guards. The spread of the message and support of Muslims is also carried out through large systems of social programs and activism on behalf of communities. Hamas and Hizballah have long been known for their public works projects, in which they provide welfare, housing, schools, social programs, summer camps for children, and other forms of support. Such social activism generates tremendous respect for Islamist groups within the general public. This increases their support base and gives the general population a rationale for not speaking out against violence.

Furthermore, there are a number of common enemies throughout the literature of the Islamists, especially Jews and Christians, who are intertwined in the minds of militants. Proximity to the refugees of Palestine and the way in which Israel handles its terrorism problem are major reasons why Jews are seen in a negative way by many Muslims in the Middle East. The brutality of the Crusades, which has faded from the minds of most Westerners, is still fresh in the minds of Muslims, and their heroes of that era, especially Salah ad-Din, are as admired today as ever. Present-day, nonviolent crusades in the form of evangelical efforts to convert people to Christianity are seen as actions designed to cause doubt, to cause confusion, and to discredit Islam. Islamist publications in Egypt have referred to "all Jews" as evil and to "most Christians" as evil.[91]

Secularism also is denounced as anathema, whether it is adopted by regimes in the Middle East or imposed by foreigners. The Soviet invasion of Afghanistan and its policy of imposing atheism within the Muslim republics of the USSR were viewed as heretical by Muslims worldwide. The influence of Western-inspired secularism similarly has been a source of major grievance for Islamists in countries like Algeria, Egypt, and Turkey. Indeed, as the internal conflict within the Palestinian community demonstrates, secular-based organizations like Fatah have been heavily criticized by Islamist groups like Hamas for neglecting the spiritual dimensions of the conflict.

These common enemies are frequently mentioned, and they have become major rallying points for Islamist organizations. The use of Crusader imagery also reminds history-conscious Muslims of the brutality of the Crusades against Muslims, makes the enemies of Islam look inhuman and dangerous, and focuses the Muslim world on one large target. The substantial involvement of the United States in the Middle East has fostered a series of Islamist grievances. First, opposition to U.S. support for Israel resonates not only with those who support al-Qa'ida, but within the whole of the Muslim world regardless of sectarian lines. Second, the mere presence of U.S. forces in Muslim lands is offensive to many Islamists. Third, they object to the use of U.S. power to thwart their efforts to replace existing regimes. Thus, after decades of fighting the near enemy (home-grown, foreign-influenced regimes), the fight is being brought to the far enemy (countries that support the regimes that keep Muslims disabled and prevent the destruction of Jahiliyah).

CONCLUSIONS

The philosophical foundations for the global jihad draw heavily on interpretations of the history and origins of Islam as grounded in takfiri ideology. Jihadist groups like al-Qa'ida depict themselves as a righteous vanguard seeking justice and retribution for past wrongs on behalf of Islam. Qutb and others popularized the theme of an Islamic vanguard, saying that "it is necessary that there should be a vanguard which sets out with this determination and then keeps walking on the path, marching through the vast ocean of *Jahiliyah* which has encompassed the entire world."[92] The idea of a revolutionary vanguard—frequently seen in the writings of many jihadist ideologues and Islamists—parallels that called for in Marxist-Leninist literature. As Miriam Abou Zahab and Olivier Roy note, "True internationalism therefore relates to circles which are already globalised, which are in search of roots or new identities, and which mobilise around the issues of *jihad* and the *umma*."[93]

Jihadists paint a picture of Islam under attack by the modern world and call for action. One commonly articulated theme essentially splits the world into good versus evil, creating a desperate spiritual struggle. Qur'anic verses are quoted out of context to support action against infidels, unbelievers, and pagans. This allows jihadists to portray their actions as a defensive jihad—one that offers religious legitimacy to a perceived obligation to defend the faith. To reinforce the sense that jihad is necessary, many radical Islamist writers proclaim that abstaining from the jihad is just as bad as, if not worse than, abstaining from prayer and fasting—two of the most basic religious obligations for Muslims.[94]

The argument that jihad must be waged is typically buttressed by assertions that only the violent manifestation of jihad is acceptable and virtuous, since the West is characterized as being implacably hostile to Islam. Portraying the struggle as a defensive one against an aggressive foe is a way to evoke religious sanction, appeal to the masses, and make violence morally acceptable. Using the rhetoric of defensive action also avoids criticism from those Islamic scholars who might object to an offensive jihad, since the Qu'ran states, "There is no compulsion in religion."[95] When action is taken against Muslims, Ibn-Taymiyyah is frequently referenced, since his fatwa effectively enables jihadists to excommunicate fellow Muslims as apostates, which in turn justifies attacking them.[96] In essence, by stipulating that the goal is to defend Islam, violence is both moral and necessary to defend "true" Muslims.

Parallels to the founding era of Islam also are frequently evoked. The jihadists deliberately portray themselves as the modern equivalents of Muhammad's companions. For many jihadists, bin Laden's flights to Sudan and, later, to Afghanistan parallel the movements of Muhammad when he fled from Mecca to Medina. The jihadists see themselves as fighting a similar battle against incredible odds on behalf of Allah and using modest weapons. For example, a set of instructions for the September 11 hijackers found in Muhammad Atta's delayed luggage afterwards illustrates the hijackers' belief that the path of the current jihadist movement parallels the path of Muhammad's fight against Jahiliyah. Symbolically, everyday occurrences such as getting dressed, bathing, or packing a suitcase have intense spiritual meaning as a way for al-Qa'ida to represent itself as the "most faithful heir to the Prophet and his original followers, and the implacable enemy of savage non-believers."[97] As a result, their adversaries are compared to the tribal enemies of the Prophet. For example, bin Laden stated in December 2004 that "the Iraqi who joins this renegade [Iraqi] government to fight against the mujahedeen who resist occupation, is considered a renegade and one of the infidels, even if he were an Arab from Rabi'ah or Mudar tribes."[98]

Similar historically based comparisons are present in statements by a number of jihadist leaders, when they refer to the conflicts in Iraq and Afghanistan as "new Crusades." Coalition personnel in Iraq are also frequently referred to as Crusaders in jihadist propaganda. The United States has been equated as the modern day Ad, an Arabian tribe destroyed by God, which, as Fawaz Gerges points out, is the Qur'anic equivalent of Sodom and Gomorrah.[99]

Jihadist ideology uses religious commonalities to emphasize the need not only for brotherhood in the face of a moral collapse of society, but also for action on behalf of Islam. This approach is illustrated in the writing of Abu-Mus'ab al-Suri, a Syrian al-Qa'ida strategist.[100] Al-Suri offers a number of justifications for jihad: to keep infidelity from prevailing; to make up for the lack of men ready to fight; the fear of Hell; to perform a duty and answer the divine call; to follow the worthy Salaf;[101] to establish a foundation as a starting point for an Islamic revival (usually, a state governed by Islamic law); to protect the weak; and to become a martyr.[102] These goals are not inherently violent. In fact, many are shared by a large number of nonviolent Islamist groups that believe that preaching is the way to reach a truly moral and Islamic society. However, for the intellectual fathers as well as for leaders and followers of the jihadist movement, violent action consistently forms the basis for defining and legitimizing the struggle.[103]

The ideology of the modern jihadist movement is a product of the merging of people and ideas in Afghanistan with Islamist political activists in Egypt and Salafis from the Arabian Peninsula, who have been profoundly influenced by Wahhabi notions of apostasy. Modern ideologues, many of whom were not Islamic scholars but rather teachers and journalists, set precedents for the "laymanization" of Islamic thought, opening the way for a new generation of jihadist activists to position themselves as voices of the new Islamic vanguard.

The philosophical foundations of the jihadist movement provide an ideological framework, grounded in shared beliefs, that fosters cohesion within groups and across the entire jihadist social movement. Its relative generality, especially concerning Jahiliyah, allows jihadists to tailor it to fit a wide range of military and civilian targets. Moreover, because the enemy is perceived as inherently evil, it readily supports justifications for attacks, since Jahiliyah is, in its most aggressive form, the embodiment of evil. According to Islamist ideology, the fight against Jahiliyah is a righteous and desperate struggle; therefore, extreme acts of terrorism are defensible. Viewed from this perspective, the ensuing violence can be seen as a product of political vision, specific conditions, and circumstances sanctioned by religious belief.[104]

2

STRATEGIC VISION

To kill the Americans and their allies—civilians and military—is an individual duty incumbent upon every Muslim in all countries, in order to liberate the al-Aqsa Mosque [in Jerusalem] and the Holy Mosque [in Mecca] from their grip, so that their armies leave all the territory of Islam, defeated, broken, and unable to threaten any Muslim. . . . With God's permission we call on everyone who believes in God and wants reward to comply with His will to kill the Americans and seize their money where ever and whenever they find them.

Usama bin Laden, 1998 fatwa

IN A 1998 FATWA, Usama bin Laden made clear his vision of individual obligation and declared war against the "Jews and Crusaders."[1] Although religious language such as bin Laden's typically is used to frame goals, those goals actually reflect political as well as religious aspirations. In fact, the overarching goal is creating Islamic "Emirates," which will later be tied together as a restored caliphate; ultimately, extending the caliphate's boundaries to encompass the world represents an overarching desire to inextricably unify the political and religious. This chapter examines continuity and change in the strategic vision guiding such calls for jihad.

CORE PRINCIPLES

At the core of the jihadists' strategic vision is a crucial concept: that jihad is an individual religious obligation in defense of Islam, and that it is a duty for every Muslim to play some part in war, whether by fighting, supporting, or promotion. Emphasizing that jihad is an individual obligation provides a powerful motivation for collective action, binding leaders and followers together to achieve the movement's goals.[2] By appealing to shared religious values, it also provides a mechanism for building popular support, appealing to the larger Muslim population, such as the frequently invoked "Arab street," beyond the movement's core activists. For example, in his 2001 autobiography, al-Zawahiri argues:

> The Islamic movement in general and the jihad movement in particular must launch a battle for orienting the nation by:
>
> - Exposing the rulers who are fighting Islam.
> - Highlighting the importance of loyalty to the faithful and relinquishment of the infidels in the Muslim creed.
> - Holding every Muslim responsible for defending Islam, its sanctities, nation, and homeland.
> - Cautioning against the ulema [Islamic scholars] of the sultan and reminding the nation of the virtues of the ulema of jihad and the imams of sacrifice and the need for the nation to defend, protect, honor, and follow them.
> - Exposing the extent of aggression against our creed and sanctities and the plundering of our wealth.[3]

In essence, the call to jihad becomes a vehicle for mobilizing combatants and solidifying popular support in order to achieve strategic goals. Al-Zawahiri has always emphasized the need for popular support: "An important point that must be underlined is that this battle . . . is a battle facing every Muslim. . . . In order for the masses to move, they need the following: 1. A leadership that they could trust, follow, and understand. 2. A clear enemy to strike at. 3. The shackles of fear and the impediments of weakness in the souls must be broken."[4]

A prolonged, constant state of warfare is a second core attribute of the radical Islamists' strategic vision. The operative timeframe for the struggle in the jihadists' minds is not months and years, but decades and centuries. Having portrayed the jihad as a cosmic struggle between good and evil, few jihadists envision a "short war," unless the enemy's will is broken through successful terrorist strikes involving martyrdom operations and mass-casualty attacks combined with a war of attrition. Instead, the jihadists envision a protracted and global conflict. The concept that the restoration of the caliphate through jihad is a long-term struggle is exemplified by this quote from al-Zawahiri:

> If our goal is comprehensive change and if our path, as the Qur'an and our history have shown us, is a long road of jihad and sacrifices, we must

not despair of repeated strikes and recurring calamities. We must never lay down our arms, regardless of the casualties or sacrifices.

We must realize that countries do not fall all of a sudden. They fall by pushing and overcoming.[5]

The jihadists' war should not only be prolonged, it should also reach outside of the Middle East and into the enemy territory: "The more diversified and distant the areas in which operations take place, the more exhausting it becomes for the enemy, the more he needs to stretch his resources, and the more he becomes terrified."[6]

The third core principle is that the jihadists represent a revolutionary vanguard and exemplar for the Muslim world. As Michael Scheuer notes, bin Laden has long intended that al-Qa'ida serve as the example. In fact, bin Laden wants others to see him as the "inciter-in-chief."[7] For example, bin Laden has declared: "I must say that my duty is just to awaken the Muslims, to tell them as to what is good for them." He wants his and the mujahidin's actions "to instigate the nation [ummah] to get up and liberate its land, to fight for the sake of God, and to make Islamic law, the highest law, and the word of God the highest word of all."[8] The idea of a vanguard is grounded in the concept that it is essential to create a critical mass of mujahidin within the Muslim world who will take the necessary actions to restore the caliphate. As noted previously, this is a recurring theme in jihadist literature and statements.

NEAR ENEMY, FAR ENEMY

While advocates of the jihad share a set of core principles, their strategic vision for implementing those principles has emerged from three some-times-competing elements in political Islamic movements. The first is composed of ethnic and territorial resistance movements that include the Chechens, Kashmiris, Palestinian Islamists such as Hamas, and Abu-Say-yaf in the Philippines. Each of these groups focuses inwardly with the strategic goal of creating ethnically based political states governed by religious precepts. The second element consists of religious nationalists such as Egyptian Islamic Jihad or the Algerian GIA—organizations that do not seek separation but instead focus on a violent "realignment" of governments that are seen as having strayed from a proper Islamic path. This second element—with its emphasis on the Near Enemy, secular "apostate" regimes in Muslim countries such as Egypt or Syria—was the dominant school of thought until the emergence of al-Qa'ida following the Afghan-Soviet War. Al-Qa'ida, with its emphasis on the Far Enemy, the Western governments that supported local regimes, represents the third and newest element in jihadist strategic thinking. Like the other two elements, this third one aims to establish a religiously based state, but it is much more radical and internationalist in scope. It seeks first to restore the caliphate within its original boundaries, and then to extend it to encompass the globe.

Depending on which time period one selects to delineate its geographical extent, even limiting reestablishment of the caliphate to its various historical boundaries would involve a fundamental reordering of the international system.[9] For example, figure 2.1 reveals that if one opts to use the geographical boundaries of the Muslim world during the time of Muhammad (ca. 632 CE), then the area is limited to the Arabian Peninsula. The era of the first four caliphs encompasses a much larger area.[10] By 750 CE, the Muslim world covered all of North Africa, Spain and Portugal, and the Middle East, as well as much of Southwest Asia. Subsequent expansions—especially by the Umayyads, the Abbasids, and the Ottomans from the eighth through the eighteenth centuries—brought additional areas under Muslim control. In the modern era, Muslims comprise a substantial percentage of the world's population. Figure 2.2 reveals that Muslims are the majority in "more than fifty nations, and they also constitute important minorities in many other countries. Muslims comprise at least 10 percent of the Russian Federation's population, 3 percent of China's population, and 3 to 4 percent of Europe's population."[11] Hence, the global presence of Muslims combined with religious zeal is used by adherents to the jihadist movement to justify a truly global insurgency that seeks regime change transcending existing nation states or even regions.

The shift from focusing on the Near Enemy to the Far Enemy signaled a fundamental change in strategic emphasis. A series of opportunistic attacks staged by al-Qa'ida against American targets overseas foreshadowed the shift to direct attacks on the U.S. homeland. Among others, these included the 1998 bombings of two U.S. embassies in East Africa, involvement in the 1993 Battle of Mogadishu in Somalia, and the October 2000 attack on the *USS Cole* (DDG 67) when that guided missile destroyer was making a port call at Aden in Yemen. When al-Qa'ida

Figure 2.1. Historical Muslim World

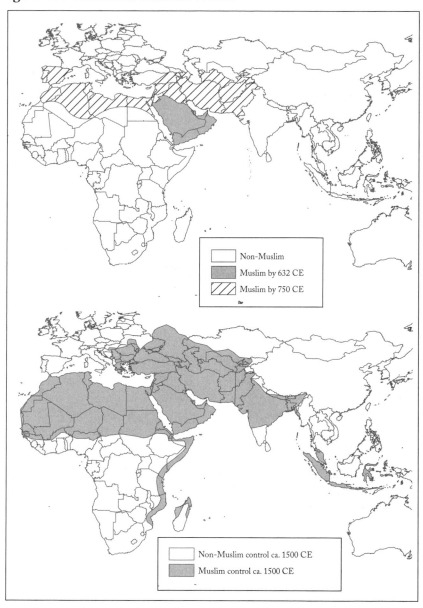

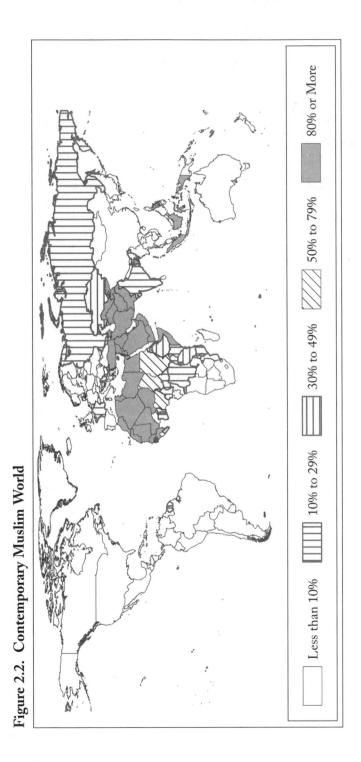

Figure 2.2. Contemporary Muslim World

Less than 10%   10% to 29%   30% to 49%   50% to 79%   80% or More

followed up those attacks and launched its successful attacks inside the United States on September 11, it provided dramatic evidence that the jihadists' reach had become truly global.

Al-Qa'ida's decision to attack the United States homeland, instead of U.S. interests overseas, was driven by the recognition that causing American support for existing Arab governments to evaporate was critical to achieving their goal of overthrowing those regimes. It also reflected deep-seated animosity towards the United States, stemming from U.S. support for Israel and the presence of American forces in Saudi Arabia. Nonetheless, the shift in emphasis required a number of al-Qa'ida's cadre to turn away from their primary emphasis on opposing Arab targets. For example, many of the senior leaders of al-Qa'ida were Egyptian militants who had a history of focusing on the Near Enemy, as a result of their opposition to the Egyptian government. The Egyptians who joined al-Qa'ida argued that it was necessary to shift from a local focus to the global focus that we are most familiar with today, when the Egyptian Islamic Jihad fractured after some elements reached a ceasefire agreement with the Egyptian government. The other elements sought to continue the jihad and became advocates of the Far Enemy approach. Furthermore, the shift in focus was born out of necessity. Many jihadists, who had been defeated by the security forces of their home countries, decided to change their religious-nationalist agenda as a way to remain active.

In essence, conditions on the ground made globalization of the jihad—with its corresponding shift to confronting the Far Enemy, especially the United States—unavoidable if the jihad was to continue. By shifting to focus on the United States and other Western democracies, the jihadists increased their access to extensive media coverage. The enhanced media coverage lessened the likelihood that their Far Enemy opponents would be able to resort to using proxies to conduct harsh campaigns of repression or could maintain necessary domestic political support to engage in prolonged conflict.

Additionally, the rise of a jihadist class of Afghan Arabs following their participation in the Afghan-Soviet war and the continuing repression of Islamist movements by pro-Western rulers in Muslim countries created a ready pool of recruits.[12] When bin Laden issued his 1998 fatwa creating the World Islamic Front for Jihad Against Jews and Crusaders—a fatwa dedicated to confronting the West—several militant leaders, including Ayman al-Zawahiri, one of the Egyptian Islamists who had focused on overthrowing the government of Egypt and installing a theocracy, opted to formally accept the Far Enemy strategy. This action forced the various groups of jihadists to decide whether to continue their ethno-religious nationalism campaigns, remain faithful to the Near Enemy strategy, or adopt the Far Enemy strategy advocated by bin Laden.

By acting to change his group's strategic doctrine without consulting his lieutenants and operators (most of them wanted to continue targeting the Near Enemy), al-Zawahiri had to confront criticism within his group. In response, Al-Zawahiri wrote a letter to his colleagues in Egyptian Islamic Jihad, describing the offer from the "Abdullah Contracting Company" [bin Laden and al-Qa'ida] and arguing in favor of the shift:

> Encourage commercial activities [jihad] in the village to face foreign investors; stimulate publicity; then agree on joint work to unify trade in our area. Close relations allowed for an open dialogue to solve our problems. Colleagues here believe that this is an excellent opportunity to encourage sales in general, and in the village in particular. They are keen on the success of the project. They are also hopeful that this may be a way out of the bottleneck to transfer our activities to the stage of multinationals and joint profit. We are negotiating the details with both sides.[13]

The initial reaction to al-Zawahiri's letter outlining the benefits of bin Laden's offer was negative. The unknown writer of one reply called the "profits" to be gained a "farce of compound losses," and said that such an endeavor would fail.[14] Ultimately, however, al-Zawahiri prevailed, became bin Laden's deputy, and formally merged his group with al-Qa'ida in 2001.[15]

Free to pursue any strategy dictated by its ideology, many of the mujahidin choose to shift attention from the Near Enemy to attack a shared and available target, the United States, in order to remain united. Although he largely has given up Near Enemy targeting, al-Zawahiri occasionally emphasizes the targeting of Near Enemy targets. However, in those instances, it is based primarily on pragmatic rather than ideological reasons. An example of this can be seen in messages urging violence against the Pakistani government, especially President Pervez Musharraf. [16] This shift in focus has been justified by al-Zawahiri, who asserts that attacking the Far Enemy will result in three victories for the jihadist movement: first, dealing a blow to the "great master" [the United States], which has been hiding behind its agents; second, winning over the [Islamic] nation by hitting a target it approves; third, exposing local regimes that "defend its U.S. and Jewish masters."[17] Discussing Far Enemy targeting as a way to bring about a direct, open confrontation between the West and Islam, or as a way to force new Western policies towards the Muslim world, al-Zawahiri continues:

> The Islamic movement and its jihad vanguards, and actually the entire Islamic nation, must involve the major criminals—the United States, Russia, and Israel—in the battle and not let them run the battle between the jihad movement and our governments in safety. . . . The masters in Washington and Tel Aviv are using the regimes to protect their interests and to fight the battle against the Muslims on their behalf. If the shrapnel from the battle reach their homes and bodies, they will trade accusations with their agents about who is responsible for this. In that case, they will face one of two bitter choices: Either personally wage the battle against the Muslims, which means that the battle will turn into clear-cut jihad against infidels, or they reconsider their plans after acknowledging the failure of the brute and violent confrontation against Muslims.[18]

Montasser al-Zayyat, a prominent Islamist lawyer who knew al-Zawahiri, wrote in his book about the al-Qa'ida deputy that al-Zawahiri's shift in focus was due to a number of reasons: the success of the Egyptian security forces in countering his ability to mount operations in Egypt; the extradition of a number of leading Islamists to Egypt; lack of financial resources; the arrest of a prominent aide; internal divisions; the influence of bin Laden; and the impact of the al-Gama'at al-Islamiyah's (Islamic Group, IG) initiative to cease armed operations both inside and outside of Egypt, since the IG was the most important and most active militant group opposing Egypt.[19]

A similar pattern of events happened in Algeria. Loss of popular support and counterterrorist success convinced some members of the Algerian Salafist Group for Preaching and Combat (known by its French initials, GSPC) to surrender and accept an amnesty deal offered by the Algerian government. The most radical elements chose to continue as jihadists. On the second anniversary of September 11, the group issued a statement in which it declared its allegiance to bin Laden and al-Qa'ida: "GSPC announces to the world in general and to Muslims in particular its allegiance to all Muslims and to fighting to the glory of God in Palestine and in Afghanistan under the direction of Mullah Omar . . . and of the al-Qaeda organization of Osama bin Laden."[20]

The carefully timed announcement did not appear to generate the publicity that the group had hoped to garner, and al-Qa'ida's leadership made no public statements acknowledging the GSPC. The lack of response, however, did not deter the GSPC from declaring war in 2004 on foreigners—both people and companies—in Algeria, a typical al-Qa'ida move. Finally, in a 2006 interview, al-Zawahiri announced that the GSPC had joined al-Qa'ida.[21] In the video, al-Zawahiri expressed hopes that the GSPC would attack not only "French Crusaders"—longtime enemies of the GSPC and other Algerian militants since Algeria's days as a colonial holding—but also the United States. Four months after its merger with al-Qa'ida, the GSPC formally announced that it was changing its name to the al-Qa'ida Organization in the Lands of the Islamic Maghreb. The name change symbolized a shift away from a narrow focus on Algeria to one that encompasses all of Northern Africa. This is consistent with other actions by the group, such as its targeting of Mauritanian military personnel in December 2007.[22]

The GSPC members who did not surrender have begun to strengthen international connections and expand international networks. They have sent foreign fighters to Iraq and issued messages of fraternal support to other jihadist groups. Recent operations that have been planned or carried out by GSPC personnel suggest an agenda to expand its operations outside of Algeria. This has included making threats against American military bases in Mali and Niger, with operational planning taking place in Algeria and Mauritania. In December 2006, the GSPC claimed responsibility for an attack on mostly Western employees of an affiliate of Halliburton, a U.S. multinational company. The GSPC warned Algerians to stay away from areas in which foreigners are present, a common warning issued by jihadist groups throughout the Middle East.

These apparent changes in the GSPC's strategic doctrine, however, are not as dramatic as al-Zawahiri's. The GSPC still identifies France and the Algerian government as its two top enemies. Including American targets or sending fighters to Iraq, where they could be fighting Shi'ites and Iraqi forces as well as Americans, represents an expansion of the group's target set instead of a complete change in strategy. The alliance with al-Qa'ida could indicate that the GSPC formally submits to al-Qa'ida's Far Enemy doctrine. Alternatively, it could mean that al-Qa'ida is willing to modify its own strategic doctrine in exchange for GSPC logistical support and fighters.[23] GSPC's training camps and well-established European support networks could help al-Qa'ida by expanding its operational capabilities.

Although the Far Enemy focus currently dominates al-Qa'ida Central's strategic doctrine, it has not been accepted by all jihadists. Islamists who emphasize religious nationalism still embrace the Near Enemy approach and stress local or regional issues. That approach is evident in conflicts where the Muslim Brotherhood, the most influential religious nationalist group in Egypt, exerts a strong influence, most notably with Hamas in Israel and the Occupied Territories. Religious nationalists are also prominent in Chechnya, Kashmir, Bosnia, and the Philippines. Although religious nationalists may have extreme anti-Western attitudes, they are less likely to directly target the Far Enemy than transnational jihadists such as al-Qa'ida and its affiliates. For example, until he shifted his target set to the Far Enemy, al-Zawahiri rejected any calls to internationalize the jihad, preferring to focus on the revolution at home. Al-Zawahiri's earlier position undoubtedly reflected the influence of his mentor, Abd-al-Qadir Ibn Abd-al-Aziz (or Dr. Fadl), a key Egyptian jihadist who once wrote that "it is obligatory to begin fighting the nearest enemy."[24] The Algerian Armed Islamic Group (GIA) followed a similar strategic evolution, whereby it shifted from attacking the Algerian regime early on to attacking France, the biggest supporter of the Algerian government.[25]

In the case of the Indonesian Jemaah Islamiya (JI), a shift from the Near Enemy to the Far Enemy may have resulted in a factional schism within JI. Some members believed that an escalation in violence would jeopardize the group's goals of expanding their constituency and establishing a secure base as their operational headquarters. For them, those goals were necessary preconditions that the group had to achieve before pursuing jihad in hopes of establishing an Islamic state. Disagreements over the increasing number of Muslim civilians killed and a changing political landscape, which made it possible for formerly clandestine activists to lobby publicly for nonviolent change, may have been other possible explanations for the split. It is also conceivable that JI's problems may have been more structural than ideological. The adoption of an al-Qa'ida strategy emphasizing mass-casualty attacks against soft Western targets inside Indonesia resulted in the Indonesian government's crackdown in the form of mass arrests. Counterterrorism victories against the group's cache of explosives and the death of the group's top bombmaker also may have forced JI to use much smaller bombs in its 2005 Bali attacks than it did in the 2002 Bali attacks. Additionally, because several key Jemaah

Islamiya leaders were arrested, the group has become more decentralized. As a result, it is entirely possible that the apparent rifts are due primarily to a combination of structural factors and a successful counterterrorism campaign rather than genuine splits attributable to disagreements over Near Enemy versus Far Enemy targeting.[26] In fact, the JI situation is likely to be due to a complex interplay of the factors summarized above.

Moreover, given the Wahhabi variant of the Salafi fundamentalist belief system to which most jihadists subscribe, the jihadists always will have Near Enemies to target. This is an inherent feature of their interpretation of Islam and is likely to lead to continued tensions involving Near Enemy versus Far Enemy strategies. For example, al-Qa'ida in Iraq under al-Zarqawi's leadership was firmly committed to a Near Enemy strategy, even though al-Zarqawi and his group were officially subordinate to bin Laden. Al-Zarqawi emphasized targeting the Jordanian government, Shi-'ites, and Iraqi forces as well as Americans. In a 2004 letter written before he officially merged with al-Qa'ida, al-Zarqawi declared the Near Enemy—apostates and Shi'ites—to be a greater and far more dangerous enemy than the United States.[27] In 2005, after the merger, Abu-Hamzah al-Baghdadi, the chief of al-Zarqawi's legal committee, renewed the group's commitment to the Near Enemy strategy by making a similar declaration.[28]

Although al-Zarqawi was seen as a representative of bin Laden in Iraq, there are noticeable differences in their choice of rhetoric and strategies. Those differences reflected the absence of coordination between bin Laden and al-Zarqawi early on in Iraq. Hillel Fradkin, director of the Center on Islam, Democracy, and the Future of the Muslim World, points out that bin Laden's description of the current jihad emphasizes a conflict between Islam and global heresy led by the United States and its Muslim apostate clients. On the other hand, al-Zarqawi's descriptions offer a stark contrast. They emphasize a conflict with Islam on one side and the heresy of liberal democracy on the other.[29]

For Far Enemy advocates, fighting the United States is the best way to affect local enemies by cutting off their funding and political support. Without the active involvement of the United States, bin Laden and al-Zawahiri believe, local enemies will collapse. The resulting chaos will provide the necessary conditions for the mujahidin to establish a theocratic state. An al-Qa'ida statement released in April 2002 used the metaphor of cutting down the entire tree instead of pulling leaves from a tree one at a time—leaves, of course, symbolizing apostate enemies in the

Muslim world—to place the Near Enemy–Far Enemy discussion in context and justify the September 11 attacks: "How can one permit the killing of the branch [Near Enemy "apostate" regimes] and not permit the killing of the supporting trunk [the United States and Western allies]?"[30] Jihadist writer Abu-Ubayd al-Qurashi explains further:

> Al-Qa'ida follows a clear strategy. The choice to target the United States from the beginning was a smart strategic choice for the global jihad movement. The struggle with the United States' hangers-on in the Islamic region has shown that these hangers-on cannot keep their tyrannical regimes going for a single minute without US help. This is why we must strike the head. When it falls, it will bring down the rest. The choice to target the United States is understood and accepted throughout the Islamic community because everybody knows the crimes the United States has committed against Islam and Muslims. This is what ensures popular sympathy and support.[31]

Disputes over the Near Enemy–Far Enemy divide persist within the ranks of the jihadists. A September 2007 interview with Abu-Yahya al-Libi, a senior al-Qa'ida Central official who gained importance in the group's propaganda after his 2005 escape from Afghanistan's Bagram prison, provides unambiguous evidence that disagreement over which enemy should be the priority has not been resolved. Al-Libi was interviewed by al-Qa'ida's al-Sahab Establishment for Media Production.[32] In the video, he attempts to clarify the importance of Far Enemy targeting. Al-Libi concedes that there are passages in the Qur'an as well as Muslim legal sources that stipulate that the nearest enemy should be given priority.

Al-Libi argues that these historical rulings do not apply to the current struggle for several reasons. First, the difference in the geographical reach of military technology today compared to the technology available during the time of Muhammad around the seventh century CE, when Muhammad and his followers first sought to spread Islam. Then the enemy was truly near in a physical sense (e.g., the distance that an arrow could fly after being shot by an archer). Now, distances of literally hundreds and even thousands of miles can separate combatants. Al-Libi observes that it is possible to wage war against Muslims from remote locations by pushing a button to launch a cruise missile from a naval vessel or by dropping munitions from manned or unmanned aircraft. Because of this change in the reach of military technology, al-Libi says that "nearness and farness in our modern age does not have the same significance it once had." Al-Libi also maintains that the distinction is moot because the Far Enemy supports the Near Enemy, using the Near Enemy as a proxy. This makes them a single entity confronting the jihadists. He argues that the relationship between jihadists and all non-Islamic sects (Jews, Christians, Shi'ites, Hindus, apostates, etc.) is the same, requiring "total separation, complete disloyalty, and open animosity," in accordance with *al-wala wa al-bara* (allegiance to what is pleasing to Allah and his Messenger and disavowal of what is displeasing). However, because he does not think it is "legally or rationally desirable" to wage war on these sects simultaneously, al-Libi maintains in the interview that the Far Enemy must take priority.

Al-Libi's comments during the interview undoubtedly reflect his recognition of the greater military capabilities and reach of the Far Enemy. The United States has substantial military power. Moreover, it can be supplemented by the resources of America's allies. If brought to bear in a sustained and focused fashion, those capabilities can frustrate the jihadists' ambitions and may stymie or prevent them from being successful.

LOCALIZED FAR ENEMY TARGETING

On May 12, 2003, suicide bombers detonated car bombs inside three Western housing compounds in Saudi Arabia, killing twenty-six and injuring hundreds. Both foreigners and Saudis were victims of the attack. These suicide bombings commonly are pointed to as the beginning of a jihadist insurgency and terror campaign in Saudi Arabia that lasted through 2004, leaving scores of Westerners and Arabs dead.

The Saudi branch of al-Qa'ida (Al-Qa'ida in the Arabian Peninsula, AQAP), which conducted the campaign, preferred to attack local targets—both Saudi and Western—in an effort to show that the Saudi regime is ineffective in providing security, and to rally support against the Saudi regime by forcing it to protect American interests in the Kingdom. Another ultimate goal—the overriding one—was to rid the Arabian Peninsula of foreign (and more specifically non-Islamic) presence; the words "Expel the polytheists from the Arabian Peninsula" were displayed beneath the group's logo. One of the campaign's leaders was Abu-Hajir Abd-al-Aziz al-Muqrin. [33] Al-Muqrin stated in an al-Qa'ida-affiliated magazine: "I did not go to Iraq, and I will not go to Iraq. I swore to clear the Arabian peninsula of polytheists. We were . . . born in this country so we will fight the Crusaders and Jews in it until we have expelled them."[34] Another example of AQAP's localism can be seen in a 2003 article in the group's popular *Sawt al-Jihad* magazine, titled "Do Not Go to Iraq," encouraging potential jihadists to stay in the Peninsula and carry out attacks on Americans instead of traveling to Iraq for jihad.[35] Over the next year and a half, several attacks like the one in Riyadh followed, as did a number of assassinations of foreigners in the Kingdom.[36]

Al-Qa'ida strategist Abu-Mus'ab al-Suri outlines in his 1600-page masterwork, *The Call to Global Islamic Resistance*, a pragmatic targeting system similar to the one adopted by AQAP before the book's release. The strategy al-Suri proposes combines elements from both the Near and Far Enemy positions. It represents a sort of localized or opportunistic Far Enemy targeting, in which the jihadist thinks globally but acts locally. His perspective on Far Enemy targeting is based more on abilities than intent. Individuals or groups following his recommended targeting strategy are likely to be limited in their geographical reach when it comes to operations. As a result, a local focus may not necessarily reflect the attacker's opinion of operations in the West.

The four strategic goals articulated in *The Call to Global Islamic Resistance* are as follows:

1. Expelling the Crusaders and Jewish campaigns under the leadership of America and its allies, and chasing its remnants from the Islamic world.
2. Eliminating the agent forces and hypocrites who work to achieve the goals of the invading campaigns.
3. Overthrowing the regimes of apostasy and betrayal in our country because they support these campaigns.
4. Establishing Shari'ah on the remnants of those apostate forces.[37]

Since he believes that the jihad is best fought by individuals and small cells instead of by bulky organizations, al-Suri places a great deal of importance on the ability to plan and execute operations in an environment in which the jihadist is unobtrusive and has the benefit of knowing the theater of operations from having lived there. While holding the United States and other Western countries to be the greater enemy (a Far Enemy concept), al-Suri believes that Muslim countries should be the primary theater for jihadist attacks (a Near Enemy concept). In al-Suri's "military theory," the jihad should be easy to join. Therefore, it should be

indigenous and operate locally as opposed to relying on attacks on diffi-
cult-to-reach sites in the West, which would necessitate traveling to conflicts in Iraq, Chechnya, Afghanistan, or elsewhere.[38]

In his September 2007 interview, Abu-Yahya al-Libi advocated the
localized Far Enemy approach in a similar way. Al-Libi portrayed it as
the path of least resistance:

> With our enemies today, their near is near and their far is near. The
> role the mujahidin play in choosing the time and place of the confronta-
> tion is to try and aim as much as they can to wage the decisive battle
> which suits their abilities, has factors for success, saves them from a
> great deal of effort, and leads to the elimination of the greater enemy
> [already specified as the Far Enemy earlier in the interview] which
> spreads corruption and ruin, and under whose wings the regimes of tyr-
> anny and torture develop and prosper."[39]

In terms of individual and small-cell terrorism, Abu-Mus'ab al-Suri
prioritizes the targets of the jihad in geographical terms. First, aspiring
jihadists should focus on attacking U.S. and Western interests—
economic, cultural, diplomatic, and military—in "our countries": the Arab
and Islamic world, specifically mentioning countries in the Arabian Peninsula and the Levant, in addition to Egypt, Iraq, North Africa, Turkey,
Pakistan, Central Asia, and "the remainder of the Islamic countries." Next
on the list would be "their countries": the United States and its allies in
the Third World and Europe. Third would be a generic category of "other
countries": those that have not been covered by the first two categories.[40]

Jihadist targets abroad—in the United States and Europe—are no surprise: political, economic, military, Jewish, and intelligence community
targets are all listed. Civilian populations are also targeted for attacks of
deterrence and reciprocity, though al-Suri cautions that killing women
and children should be avoided when they "are away from their men."
Targets in the third category—"other countries"—fall along the same
lines, with heavy emphasis on American and other Western nations' interests.[41] While al-Suri believes jihadists should focus on attacking Western
interests in the Arab world, he does not completely forgo the inclusion of
traditional "Near Enemy" targets: "apostate" governments, official groups
collaborating with the American "invasion" (security, military, and political forces), and official groups targeting jihadists, in addition to promoters
of imperialism, proponents of American-Zionist normalization, defamers
of Islam, and promoters of vice in general.[42]

AQAP's targeting agenda can be seen as a good example of a targeting system already applied by jihadists and that al-Suri later promoted in his book: focusing on local U.S. interests, and—to a lesser extent, in the case of AQAP—on Saudi "apostate" targets.[43] Although terrorists did attack a number of Saudi-national targets during the campaign, a quickly rising Saudi body count generated a negative backlash in popular opinion. Recognizing the need for popular support, al-Qa'ida responded by altering its targeting practices. The group decided to focus almost exclusively on targeting American and other Western targets.

In a May 2004 attack on another Western housing compound, this time in the eastern Saudi city of al-Khobar, militants killed twenty-two civilians, reportedly splitting their hostages according to nationality and religion. At the end of the day-long hostage crisis, several Westerners and Christians had their throats cut and others were shot. Muslims appear to have been spared deliberately by their captors. In a description of the assault posted to jihadist websites, the group highlighted its claim that the mujahidin "did not spill Muslim blood."[44] Such statements suggest that AQAP recognized the need to avoid attacks on targets within the Kingdom that might damage its image vis-à-vis public opinion. In essence, AQAP softened its Near Enemy position and adopted a more Far Enemy–based approach to expelling foreigners from the Peninsula. Presumably, such a focus would undermine the Saudi regime without making the regime itself the explicit focus for the majority of the group's attacks.

As the Saudi attacks illustrate, terrorism is in part a tactic for attempting to gain control over a geographical area. The choice of targets, according to al-Suri, is strategic and should reflect the global jihad's priorities, especially the need to ultimately control territory, if the caliphate is to be restored. The next section examines this issue.

THE NEED TO CONTROL TERRITORY

Unless the radical Islamists can exert control over territory, they will be limited to acts of terrorism but stymied in creating and maintaining an Islamic state. Moreover, the core strategic goal of restoring the caliphate is premised on establishing and extending physical control based on Islam: "The foremost duty of Islam in this world is to depose *Jahiliyah* from the leadership of man, and to take the leadership into its own hands and enforce the particular way of life which is its permanent feature."[45] To accomplish this sweeping objective, al-Zawahiri has emphasized the need to control territory from which the mujahidin can wage war as essential to restoring the caliphate: "A jihadist movement needs an arena that would act like an incubator where its seeds would grow and where it can acquire practical experience in combat, politics and organizational matters."[46] In a 2005 letter to al-Zarqawi, al-Zawahiri explains further:

> The jihad movement must adopt its plan on the basis of controlling a piece of land in the heart of the Islamic world on which it could establish and protect the state of Islam and launch its battle to restore the rational caliphate based on the traditions of the prophet. . . . Armies achieve victory only when the infantry takes hold of land. Likewise, the Mujahid Islamic movement will not triumph against the world coalition unless it possesses a fundamentalist base in the heart of the Islamic world.[47]

But where would this base be located? Like the caliphate, it is often based on available opportunities to exploit a power vacuum in a particular country with a chaotic security situation. Obviously, Iraq and Afghanistan are prime examples of countries where jihadists took advantage of violent conflict in an effort to further their strategic visions. These are not the only locations in which jihadists have taken an interest. For example, the Arabian Peninsula country of Yemen has long been a focal point for bin Laden's attention. He worked with Yemeni jihadists fighting Southern Yemeni communists in the 1980s, before the country's northern and southern regions were unified in 1990. Bin Laden, who is of Yemeni descent, hoped to facilitate the jihadist movement in the country. His fatwas incited at least 158 operations in Yemen between 1990 and 1994, mostly against "infidel communists."[48] The group also carried out attacks against Yemeni petroleum facilities, assassinated Yemeni socialist party officials, and, in 1992, bombed a hotel housing U.S. military personnel in transit to war-ravaged Somalia (a second bomb targeting another hotel exploded before reaching its target). In 1998, bin Laden explained that these attacks were a warning to the United States that it should not establish military bases in Yemen.

With the outbreak of Yemen's civil war in the summer of 1994, al-Qa'ida militants began to plan to take advantage of the conflict's chaos in hopes of expanding the jihad. A recently declassified letter written by an al-Qa'ida member identified only as "Hassan" to the group's "African

Corps" observes that "the events in Yemen provide an auspicious opportunity for declaring jihad in the Arabian Peninsula"; it argues that jihadist groups in the country should be established in an effort to rid the Peninsula of the un-Islamic influence of Jews, Crusaders, communists, secularists, and atheists.[49] Hassan continues:

> Now a new opportunity has appeared on the horizon. How suitable will it be for a new Islamic thrust, albeit limited in scope and results? It may not be possible for us to make Yemen leap from its present situation into a fully-integrated Islamic status through military jihad action. I believe that this is not possible, not in Yemen nor anywhere else. However, the alternative is not to stop the jihad but to carry out a phased advance through continuous jihad battles. As we push the enemy backward, we will gradually advance toward a position that presents us with a decisive and final battle at some time in the future.

Hassan suggests that the radio be used by militants to demand the evacuation of infidel forces from the Peninsula and to warn those who defend the infidels that they would be "treated as apostates"; in addition, he writes that wealth and property—especially petroleum—should be restored to Muslims in accordance with Islamic law. Hassan also underscored the geographic importance of Yemen. He notes that it "provides an excellent location for establishing Islamic jihad positions in the mountains to threaten the heartland and arouse terror in the hearts of the Jews and Christians."

Bin Laden was not alone in seeking to use Yemen as a base for operations. Ayman al-Zawahiri also hoped to use Yemen in the 1990s. Al-Zawahiri, who had not yet joined bin Laden's group, thought Yemen would be an ideal base from which Egyptian Islamic Jihad could launch attacks against the Egyptian regime. However, after a failed assassination attempt against a former Egyptian prime minister in 1993, pressure that the Egyptian government placed on Yemen's government forced al-Zawahiri to transfer his fighters from Yemen to Sudan.[50]

Clearly drawing on their personal experiences over several decades of being forced to move from country to country, the jihadists recognize the importance of sanctuaries and bases for training and staging operations. The jihadists have launched concerted efforts to establish dominion over "the vast ocean of *Jahiliyah* which has encompassed the entire world."[51] Afghanistan, Iraq, Somalia in the 1990s and perhaps again today, as well as Sudan (where bin Laden lived from 1991 to 1996) underscore the active efforts by radical Islamists to gain and keep control of territory. The 2020 Plan offers one possible roadmap for establishing such control.

THE 2020 PLAN

In 2005, Jordanian journalist Fu'ad Husayn published a biography of al-Zarqawi. Husayn got to know the al-Qa'ida in Iraq leader when he was sentenced to the same prison as al-Zarqawi and his mentor, Abu-Muhammad al-Maqdisi. Husayn acted as the mediator between al-Zarqawi's prison followers and the prison's warden during a riot that erupted after al-Zarqawi was placed in solitary confinement for a second time. Husayn's biography of al-Zarqawi presents a clear picture of a jihadist "master plan" to restore the caliphate starting in 2000 and ending in 2020. Husayn claims that his understanding of the plan is based on interviews with al-Zarqawi and al-Qa'ida security chief Sayf al-Adil. The 2020 Plan, Husayn says, is to be carried out in seven stages over a period of twenty years starting in 2000.[52]

Stage One—The Awakening: 2000–2003

This stage began with the planning for the September 11 attacks, which were carried out, according to Husayn, in an effort to trigger an American attack on the Islamic nation. Al-Qa'ida strategists, he argues, needed the United States to move away from its conventional bases and become a closer, easier target to strike. This stage ended with the U.S. occupation of Baghdad.

Stage Two—The Eye-Opening: 2003–2006

In this stage al-Qa'ida and the jihadist trend becomes popular. It is characterized by direct confrontations with Israel; the burning of Arab oil as a way to deprive the West and its proxies of revenues; electronic jihad; establishing centers of power; using Iraq as a base to build an Islamic army; and the preparation of Islamic law studies to steer Muslims toward offering the mujahidin financial and material support.

Stage Three—Reawakening and Standing Upright: 2007–2010

This stage will be one in which major transitions and changes will take place in the region surrounding Iraq. Husayn says that the mujahidin will focus their activities in the Levant and Turkey. Confrontations with Israel will begin and the mujahidin will attack the Jewish population in Turkey. After destroying what he asserts is Jewish control over the Turkish economy and military, the mujahidin will have obtained a large number of "trained and educated young men" to carry out the fourth stage.

Stage Four—Recuperation and Possession of Power: 2010–2013

The burning of Arab oil continues in an effort to undermine the economies of the United States and other enemy regimes around the world. Direct confrontations between the mujahidin and the regimes will ensue and these regimes will begin to fall.

Husayn claims that al-Qa'ida has recruited economists and researchers to refute the theory that what he terms American and Jewish economies can print money without needing to back currency up with precious metals. Al-Qa'ida ideologues will then disseminate ideas stressing the importance of backing up national currencies with gold. World markets will return to a gold standard, devaluing the dollar. Although not using economic terms to convey his ideas, Husayn then goes on to describe a currency crisis caused by the rapid devaluation of the American dollar due to the lack of gold, the lack of access to Arab oil, and exhaustion from constant battles. World-wide skepticism about the dollar will cause countries around the world to withdraw their investments from U.S. markets. Husayn claims that, because the American and Jewish economists who brought forth the printing-of-money theory actually bought precious metals as a precaution against economic depression, the American people will see that they have been duped, a "major transition" will take place, and American support for Israel will decrease.

Stage Five—Declaring an Islamic State: 2013–2016

Husayn says that Western power in the Arab world will fade during this period, and that China and India will become superpowers. The British, seeing Anglo-Saxon superiority decreasing, will halt the rising unity of

Europe. Israel will be weakened and unable to carry out any preemptive strikes. Finally, an Islamic caliphate will be established.

Stage Six—All-Out Confrontation: 2016–2020

The world will be divided into two camps. A final war between faith and atheism ensues, bringing about the seventh stage.

Stage Seven—Final Victory: 2020

The end of falsehood will be achieved. With final victory, the Islamic caliphate will once again lead humanity. In the words of Qutb, "The foremost duty of Islam in this world is to depose *Jahiliyah* from the leadership of man, and to take the leadership into its own hands and enforce the particular way of life which is its permanent feature."[53]

The scenario outlined in the 2020 Plan is apocalyptic; it enthusiastically embraces the idea of a massive clash of civilizations on a global basis. Whether an actual plan with a timetable exists may be largely irrelevant, because the so-called 2020 Plan has been widely disseminated in traditional media and on the Internet, exposing it to thousands of potential jihadists and sympathizers. The strong focus on economic issues and attacks on energy infrastructure in the Middle East may motivate these prospective jihadists to become activists. If this happens, a series of major attacks directed against oil facilities could destabilize the world's economies.

It is, of course, possible that al-Qa'ida does not have such a plan. However, Husayn's characterization is consistent with al-Zawahiri's assertion that

> armies achieve victory only when the infantry takes hold of land. Likewise, the mujahid Islamic movement will not triumph against the world coalition unless it possesses a fundamentalist base in the heart of the Islamic world. All the means and plans that we have reviewed for mobilizing the Ummah will remain up in the air without a tangible gain or benefit unless they lead to the establishment of the state of caliphate in the heart of the Islamic world.[54]

If the goal is simply to inspire action, then the 2020 Plan may already have accomplished that goal. However, if the goal is to gain and maintain control over one or more geographical areas, then the jihadists' timing, tactics, and choice of targets are likely to affect their ability to establish their vision of a caliphate restored. In essence, how they approach the management of savagery will influence their own actions, but it will also impact the preemptive actions and responses of the West and its allies within the Muslim world following terrorist incidents. We turn to a consideration of the jihadists' management of savagery in the next section.

THE MANAGEMENT OF SAVAGERY

Abu-Bakr Naji, a jihadist writer whose articles have appeared in the al-Qa'ida-affiliated *Sawt al-Jihad* magazine, advocates an approach very similar to al-Zawahiri and bin Laden's. In his 2004 book, *The Management of Savagery*, Naji asserts that jihadists should study the political, military, cultural, and management principles of the West in an effort to locate weaknesses and find strategies that could work for the jihadist movement.[55] Naji devotes much of his attention on the need to focus attacks on particular areas in an effort to "dislodge" regimes, creating a security vacuum, a concept that parallels al-Zawahiri's: "We must realize that countries do not fall all of a sudden. They fall by pushing and overcoming."[56] After creating a security vacuum, the jihadists would presumably take the necessary steps to exploit it, allowing them to move in and begin to build the foundation of a state by administering territory. Naji's book also sheds light on a general line of thought that is typical of al-Qa'ida, and that deals with basic strategy, targeting, and popular support.

Naji argues that because jihadists have been unsuccessful at toppling regimes that are proxies for superpowers, jihadists should provoke a superpower into invading the Middle East. He maintains that the jihadist movement can capitalize on the popular support for a war against an invader, and that it can convince the Islamic nation to rise up with them. One major objective in Naji's thinking is to expose the weaknesses of the United States in an effort to force it to abandon its "media psychological war and proxy war" on Islam, or to goad the United States into fighting Muslims directly.[57] This approach—forcing a strategic choice on the United States by confronting it directly—mirrors the argument advanced by al-Zawahiri. Jihadist writer Sayf al-Din al-Ansari explains the importance of forcing a direct conflict between the United States and Muslims:

Our Islamic community has been subjected to a dangerous process of narcosis. As a result, it has lost the vigilance that comes from faith and fallen into a deep slumber. The most dangerous consequence of this is that most Muslims can no longer distinguish between their enemies and their friends. The fallout from choosing the peace option and normalization [of relations with Israel] has caused a great confusion of ideas. The resultant situation poses a genuine threat to our very identity . . . The blessed raid [September 11 attacks] came to move this war from the shadows out into the open, to make the community aware of the enemy.[58]

In his book Naji advocates escalating the severity of operations and repeating attacks against the same targets, such as in the 1993 and 2001 attacks on the World Trade Center in New York, or the 2004, 2005, and 2006 attacks on mass transit in Madrid; London; and Mumbai, India. Naji believes that diversifying and widening violence is a way to force the enemy to disperse its efforts, and that economic and financial targets provide a good opportunity to do serious damage to the economies of the United States and other Western countries. Presumably, attacking such targets will force those countries to use their militaries to protect their homelands, leaving the peripheries unprotected and opening a security vacuum in these areas.[59]

Although he supports an overall escalation of operations and a diversification of violence, Naji believes that the mujahidin should stick to attacking targets that the leadership of the movement has already approved because the average jihadist may not be able to determine the political consequences of attacking new targets. Similarly, Naji proposes granting some autonomy to local leadership in conducting medium and small attacks, but he believes that the decision to carry out large-scale attacks, such as those on September 11, should be left up to the central leaders. Naji explains:

Of course there are classes of people who the mujahid-salafi movements, by means of their firmly-rooted ulama, have deemed to be permissible and necessary targets. I believe that this is sufficient at our current stage and the decision (to target others) at this time should be left to the High Command and the political leadership, who can determine the benefit of targeting them now or delaying that. This is to be done through consultation with the midlevel, learned cadres, at the very least. However, our words and our warning here concern what will come from (later) stages and what will be found among classes of people in the future or in the coming stages. The decision to target them or refrain from that is not only left to the learned cadres, but also to those firmly-rooted in knowledge from the beginning, just as we said.[60]

Naji goes even further by saying that every group should systematically weigh the possible political consequences of targeting different classes of enemies in order to determine which class is the most appropriate target:

> Among the most important benefits of political studies is defining the responses to any step which we plan to undertake and then either proceeding to take it or delaying it for an appropriate time or preparing circumstances in which it will be appropriate. From that, (we can) define who among the classes of people of the enemy we will begin (targeting). Therefore, every group should make a catalog of all of the targeted enemies in its scope, arranged according to the danger of each of them and the importance of putting them in a higher category of opposition. (Each group should also note) the anticipated response (which will come) once operations begin against each class among the enemies and how we can make the targeted class openly declare its crimes which it has concealed, which will justify targeting them to the masses.[61]

Naji's delineation of the target set and his underlying reasoning are very similar to the objections expressed by both bin Laden and al-Zawahiri in opposing al-Zarqawi and his followers' widespread targeting of the Shi'-ites in Iraq. Bin Laden and al-Zawahiri's concerns have not been driven by sympathies for the Shi'ites, but rather they have stemmed from the realization that attacking Shi'ites has diminished popular support for the insurgency.

Naji advocates other elements of the vision articulated by bin Laden and al-Zawahiri: unity, attention to popular support, and the strategy to be followed after the establishment of an Islamic state. As discussed previously, bin Laden and al-Zawahiri have both indicated that a primary element of their strategy involves emphasizing unity among the mujahidin to wage war against the West. Naji has addressed the issue of unity in a similar way, pointing out instances of respected Islamic scholars, such as Ibn-Taymiyyah, cooperating in jihad with rulers they undoubtedly considered to be heretics.[62]

Naji believes that until the goals of the mujahidin and the people are unified, the jihadist groups will never be successful. Naji encourages spreading awareness throughout the community, primarily by establishing media branches for jihadist groups, so that they can effectively communicate with the people. Media units are a widespread component to jihadist organizations. For example, al-Qa'ida has its al-Sahab Institute, and most insurgent groups in Iraq have a media department. Like many jihadists, Naji is concerned with motivating Muslims around the world to join the battle; what is important about Naji's approach is that it advocates polarizing the people and intensifying the violence of the battle. Making the battle even more violent, Naji says, will make the people believe that entering the battle will frequently lead to death. "That will be a powerful motive for the individual to choose to fight in the ranks of the people of truth in order to die well, which is better than dying for falsehood and losing both this world and the next."[63] Naji believes that the mujahidin must explain their attacks to the public in order not to fail, as so many have in the past, and that violence—not peaceful proselytizing—is the only way to force the Muslim masses to choose sides.

As we have seen, al-Zawahiri intends for Iraq and Afghanistan to become not only Islamic states but also the bases from which the mujahidin can spread their jihad to regional neighbors. In much the same vein, Naji writes:

> It is as if I see the mujahids given power in the countries of the Maghreb—especially in Algeria. If God were to grant them this, on the morning of the following day (by the permission of God) there would be no time for relaxation and none of them could pray the afternoon prayer except in Tunisia on the borders of Libya. On the following morning they would begin to prepare for conquering Libya and Egypt. . . . It is as if I see the mujahids given victory in the Arabian Peninsula. If God were to grant them this, on the following day (by the permission of God) they must prepare immediately to begin conquering the smaller states which these paltry regimes in Jordan and the Gulf rule.

The Islamic Army in Iraq

The global jihadist line of thought has undoubtedly had a profound impact on radical Muslims worldwide. There is no shortage of places that need liberating, at least in the minds of the jihadists. Pakistan, Syria, Saudi Arabia, Egypt, Jordan, and the rest of the Muslim world are all targets for the installation of an Islamic state. Given the global sweep of their strategic vision to restore and then extend the caliphate, the jihadist battle will not end with the establishment of an Islamic state in Somalia, Iraq, or Afghanistan.

The U.S. occupation of Iraq, typically portrayed in jihadist propaganda as a frontal assault on the Muslim world, has provided Islamists with the opportunity to fight for religious nationalist goals. It also has created an opportunity for adherents to its anti-Western ideology to direct the flow of violence towards American and coalition targets in Iraq. One of the leading jihadist groups in Iraq, the Islamic Army in Iraq (IAI), offers a less radical alternative to al-Qa'ida in Iraq (AQI). The Islamic Army in Iraq appears to be composed mostly of Iraqi nationals, many of whom have military or intelligence experience. Although many of the members appear to have served in the Iraqi services under Saddam, the group appears to harbor hostile opinions of Ba'athists and the former regime. The members of the IAI appear to be Islamists who were not especially vocal about their political and religious beliefs while Saddam was in power. The group's spokesman, Ibrahim al-Shammari, claims that all members of the IAI have met "Islamic criteria" before being selected for membership. The group's amir—literally "prince" but often used as commander—has stated that the group is composed exclusively of Sunnis and that the group has no Shi'ite members.[64]

The Islamic Army, like other global jihadists, characterizes the battle raging in Iraq in religious rather than political terms while pursuing the strategic goal of establishing rule by Islamic law in Iraq. Although the group has declared its admiration for bin Laden, it has refused to pledge allegiance to him or any other person. The official reason offered by the Islamic Army of Iraq is that its leadership and members believe that only God is worthy of allegiance.

The IAI—like bin Laden, al-Zawahiri, al-Suri and other prominent jihadists throughout the years—calls for unity among the mujahidin, urging jihadists to set aside partisan prejudice and to form a united front for opposing the occupation of Iraq. Despite these calls for unity, however, the group did not join the Mujahidin Shura Council or its successor organization, the Islamic State of Iraq—the leading al-Qa'ida-affiliated jihadist alliances in Iraq. At the same time, the group stresses that it is locally focused rather than preoccupied with larger geographic ambitions.[65] As a result, the IAI claims that it does not extend its operations outside the borders of Iraq, though it cautions people not to mistake this for patriotism and nationalism, since both concepts conflict with jihadist ideology, which the group says has become more transnational.

The group operates on the belief that Iraq is not under one occupation but two: an American occupation and an Iranian occupation; they see the latter occupation as much larger and more dangerous than the American. The IAI harbors obvious anti-Shi'ite tendencies, even though their anti-Shi'ism is motivated and promoted in a very different way than that of al-Qa'ida in Iraq. The group's anti-Shi'ism appears to be motivated by their suspicion of Iran, which they see as subversive and meddling in Iraqi affairs. The group justifies most of its anti-Shi'ite violence as defensive and confined to attacks on the Badr Corps and Muqtada al-Sadr's Mahdi Army, the two primary Shi'ite militias.[66] Ibrahim al-Shammari, the group's spokesman, has even declared that the IAI would welcome any Shi'ite resistance against the U.S. occupation.[67]

On numerous occasions, the IAI has made it clear that it views negotiations with U.S. and Iraqi authorities as permissible under Islamic law.[68] al-Shammari has stated on two different occasions that the group would be amenable to participating in negotiations, provided two conditions are met. First, Congress would enact legislation obligating the United States to withdraw all U.S. military forces from Iraq. Second, the U.S. government would "recognize the Iraqi resistance as the sole legitimate representative of the Iraqi people."[69] There are indications that, although these two conditions have not been met, the Islamic Army has been involved in informal negotiations with U.S. officials in Amman, although the IAI denies this.[70] Nonetheless, it seems plausible that the group considers such negotiations as integral parts of its strategy for liberating Iraq.

The Islamic Army's "Creed and Methodology," which expresses its strategic vision, states that the judgment of being takfir is not imposed on individuals unless that decision is determined by consensus of all Salafi scholars.[71] This represents a significant departure from al-Qa'ida in Iraq, which does not rely on such consensus. The IAI's semilenient position on Iraq's Shi'ites, coupled with the group's restrictions on martyrdom operations, openness to negotiations, and selective targeting doctrine have made it inevitable that the IAI would clash with al-Qa'ida in Iraq, which has a large number of foreign fighters and is one of the most radical jihadist groups in the movement's history.

In fact, starting in 2005 a number of battles erupted between largely indigenous insurgent groups and al-Qa'ida in Iraq. The battles were prompted by inter-insurgent murders by al-Qa'ida, as well as by many local groups' extreme religious goals, attempts to trigger a sectarian war, efforts to override Iraqi nationalist and tribal traditions, and uneasiness over the high civilian body count. All of this preceded the Anbar Awakening (Sahawah al Anbar), in which Sheikh Abdul Sattar al-Rishawi and other local Sunni leaders throughout the province began forming alliances in the spring and summer of 2006 to oppose AQI.[72] Initially, they formed the Jazeera Council in Ramadi, which worked closely with Coalition forces to defend the town against AQI. Building on that success, the former insurgents and other tribal elements announced the formal creation of the Anbar Awakening in October 2006 to oppose AQI. Similar Awakening groups were established in other provinces by the spring of 2007 to oppose AQI.

Following the October 2006 announcement of the creation of an Islamic state in Iraq by the Mujahidin Shura Council (MSC), the Islamic Army criticized the move and did not align itself with the MSC. The MSC was the main transnational jihadist umbrella organization in Iraq before it was dissolved upon the creation of the Islamic State of Iraq (ISI) umbrella group in October 2006. Al-Qa'ida in Iraq is the driving force behind both groups. MSC essentially announced a name change to the Islamic State of Iraq. Immediately afterwards, MSC was not used in AQI statements, and the group began referring to itself as ISI.

The IAI, on the other hand, declared publicly that the conditions for creating an Islamic state were not yet right.[73] Unlike the GSPC in Algeria or al-Qa'ida in Iraq, and because it appears to be pursuing broad public support within the Sunni Arab community, the Islamic Army in Iraq may be a model for future jihadist operations. This may be particularly the case when escalation of regional conflict, especially in regime-change situations, mobilizes jihadist groups to establish a religious-political system. The further alignment with al-Qa'ida-type values and goals—probably those of bin Laden instead of the now-deceased al-Zarqawi—might be sufficient to transform an entirely local force into a transnational actor that enthusiastically embraces the Far Enemy doctrine.[74]

THE SYRIAN CRITIQUE

In the late 1970s, the Syrian government engaged in intense, open warfare against Islamist and jihadist elements of the Muslim Brotherhood and other groups who viewed the secular Ba'athist regime as apostates. The Syrian government responded harshly and even leveled the city of Hama, where much of the opposition was based. Ultimately, the insurgency was crushed by Syrian security forces, traumatizing the Syrian people and preventing public demonstration and government opposition through to the present day. Al-Qa'ida strategist Abu-Mus'ab al-Suri is assumed to be the writer of a document examining the failures of guerrilla warfare, the media war, and the overall jihad in Syria.[75] This document provides a comprehensive look at jihadist self-criticism—and a glimpse of a jihadist understanding of insurgency that has changed over time. While there is no evidence to suggest that Iraqi insurgents are familiar with al-Suri's critique, insurgents appear to have learned the same lessons.

Al-Suri begins the document by discussing ways in which the general jihad movement in Syria failed, and then he looks at the individual failures of several groups involved in the movement. Many of the criticisms, especially those concerning the media and popular support, have been voiced many times by jihadist figures such as bin Laden, al-Zawahiri, and Naji. First, al-Suri claims that the jihad movement in Syria failed partially because it had no comprehensive strategy or plan for after the forecasted fall of the Syrian regime; concerns about the immediate aftermath and how to govern a state are similar to those voiced by Naji in *The Management of Savagery*. The movement failed, al-Suri insists, to explain its goals and to communicate those goals effectively to the people. This kept them from gaining the popular support of the Syrian people.

Low religious instruction and low political awareness were a hindrance to the movement (a topic covered by Naji), as were a lack of self-sufficient groups (many were receiving support from other countries, such as Iraq) and a focus on the quantity of operations over their quality. Al-Suri says that the movement did not benefit from the experiences of other Islamic and guerrilla groups, and he also notes that a temporary regrouping of the movement outside of Syria eventually became a permanent condition, as many fighters and leaders did not return to the nation. Another fault was operating in the open; these sorts of organizations, al-Suri says, should be secret.

Al-Suri believes that the Syrian jihad should have spread outside the borders of the country in an effort to distract the local foreign governments that were cooperating with the Syrians by arresting and monitoring militants. Staging strikes in Jordan, Iraq, and other countries could have dispersed the resources otherwise used by these countries to work against the jihadist movement. Also important to the failure of the Syrian jihad was the fact that the movement did not rally behind its Islamic scholars, and that the movement did not mobilize all sections of the population, such as tribal elements. Similar criticisms, as we have seen, were directed at al-Zarqawi for his isolation and disparagement of clerics who did not participate in jihad. It may have been due to his refusal to cooperate with Iraqi tribes too. Al-Suri also recommends a systematic approach to claiming responsibility for operations, something which has, to a large degree, been common practice in the Iraqi insurgency. Sunni insurgents in Iraq claimed hundreds of attacks each month prior to 2007. Although attacks have been claimed in other conflicts, attacks in Iraq were claimed much more frequently than elsewhere. Websites often grouped claims into specific sections where they could be easily found, and groups became adept at releasing claims soon after incidents.

Al-Suri compares two organizational structures—hierarchy and chain networks—and concludes that it is probably best to use a combination of the two. Similar comparisons were expanded in his major work, *The Call to Global Islamic Resistance*, where he compared sectional, pyramidal, and secret organizations to open-fronts and to individual- and small-cell terrorism. There he determined that terrorism by individuals and small, disconnected cells should be the base for jihadist military theory, in addition to cooperating in open-front warfare—as in Bosnia and Chechnya—when circumstances permit.

The contrast between this strategy and the statements by members of the al-Qa'ida leadership mentioned above, especially bin Laden and al-Zawahiri, is noteworthy. Instead of stressing the joining of forces and strict allegiance to leadership figures, al-Suri's strategy is suited for a clandestine, fragmented movement operating under extreme duress. Such conditions certainly apply to the situation of the jihadist movement after the U.S. invasion of Afghanistan. As a result, it is not surprising that al-Suri's strategy is enjoying a wide readership, since it better fits the current reality. The strategy also finds wide acceptance among supporters in Europe who are not attracted to a hierarchical system that binds them to distant leaders and requires the use of extensive communication media that represent a security threat to their operations.

Al-Suri embraces a number of familiar jihadist contentions: that the war between the jihadists and their opponents is a protracted conflict in which open confrontation must be avoided; that the struggle has a political core that should be stressed in communications with the people; and that the goal is to carry out "successive strategic military operations" in an effort to exhaust the regime. Urban guerrilla warfare, al-Suri says, was very successful until a series of arrests compromised the group's security, allowing the regime to effectively counter it. Al-Suri believes that the radical Islamists' focus on urban areas may have contributed to successful countermeasures by the security services. He suggests that instead of focusing solely on urban areas, the mujahidin should learn how to appropriately utilize rural areas. Al-Suri contends, in a similar vein as in his later work, that "to yield high dividends, the military high command managing this type of battle must have centralized planning and strategy, . . . [and that] on the other hand, the nature of this type of war requires that the regional and field commanders be awarded a high level of autonomy in planning and managing their own affairs."[76]

Unity—the longstanding approach advocated by bin Laden and al-Zawahiri—is also a major theme of *The Call to Global Islamic Resistance*. In fact, a lack of unity is listed among the major shortcomings of the jihadist movement. In his critique, al-Suri contends that there were simply too many groups acting independently of one another in the battle against the Syrian government. Each group had its own leader or set of leaders, which often resulted in the various groups pursuing contradictory objectives. Instead, al-Suri states that the jihadists must work against secular and "semi-Muslim" groups in a concerted campaign. Attacks should be constant so as to create a sense of unity:

> Any lull in the war puts the revolution at a dangerous cross road; the various ideological differences and allegiances would resurface, people will revert to their old ways and mentalities in addressing issues of the day, and since all are stubborn and armed revolutionaries, frictions and divisions—no matter how trivial—could escalate to an extremely dangerous level. This major problem should be addressed and corrected through proper instruction and education of members, through finding ideological and strategic common grounds, in addition to a wise and judicious leadership that keeps things in check.[77]

Not only is a sense of unity important to the movement, al-Suri contends, but a good and close relationship between leaders and fighters is also important. There appears to be, as in the Syrian jihadist case, "a growing gulf between the central al-Qa'ida leadership and those engaged in close combat," reducing al-Qa'ida's central authority to providing ideological leadership and some targeting guidance in the form of taped messages.[78]

It appears that jihadists have responded to these criticisms. A 2006 West Point study finds that many of the mistakes made during the Syrian experience have been avoided and corrected in the Iraqi insurgency, such as establishing media and political branches, coordinating military operations, and conducting strategic planning.[79] Although it is unclear whether insurgent leaders in Iraq or Afghanistan actually are familiar with al-Suri's examination of the Syrian jihad, it is apparent that those leaders have analyzed their own operational environment and strategy. This has resulted in significant improvements in the overall effectiveness of their campaigns. Al-Suri's critique of the Syrian jihad gives us a good picture of what many jihadists think are the appropriate modifications, based on their recognition of weaknesses in their capabilities, structures, or campaigns. Those insights also can assist counterterrorism and counterinsurgency authorities in designing their own efforts to defeat the jihadists.

ISLAMIC INSURGENCIES

Radicals around the world have long understood the principles of asymmetrical warfare. The current jihadist enemy is no different. With the exception of referring to the enemy as a Crusader, remarks made by bin Laden in 1996 could have easily been made by any number of insurgent leaders throughout time:

> It must be obvious to you that, [owing] to the imbalance of power between our armed forces and the enemy forces, a suitable means of fighting must be adopted, i.e. using fast-moving light forces that work under complete secrecy. In other words, to initiate a guerrilla warfare, where the sons of the nation, and not the military forces, take part in it. And as you know, it is wise in the present circumstances, for the armed military forces not to be engaged in conventional fighting with the forces of the crusader enemy . . . unless a big advantage is likely to be achieved; and great losses induced on the enemy side . . . that will help to expel the enemy defeated out of the country.[80]

Jihadist writer Abu-Ubayd al-Qurashi has been described as one of bin Laden's closest aides.[81] Al-Qurashi wrote for al-Qa'ida's popular *al-Ansar* magazine throughout its years of publication. His articles were part of the magazine's Strategic Studies section, making him one of the more prominent jihadist military thinkers. Al-Qurashi frequently cited works by strategic thinkers such as Sun Tzu and von Clausewitz. His writings often argue that the jihadists should learn from the experience of various insurgencies around the world. Yet as the following quote reveals, his actual knowledge of military doctrine and history is somewhat superficial:

> The time has come for the Islamic movements facing a general Crusader offensive to internalize the rules of fourth generation warfare. They must consolidate appropriate strategic thought, and make appropriate military preparedness. They must increase interest in da'wa [call to jihad], and recruit the people's public and political support. In addition to the religious obligation, this has become an integral part of the means to triumph in fourth-generation warfare. Old strategists, such as [von] Clausewitz and Mao Zedong, have already indicated this. Perhaps the best example is the phenomenon of the Intifada that wiped out the Zionist military's mighty superiority over the Muslim Palestinian people.[82]

Central to this strategy is the assumption that the jihadists are capable of sustaining a conflict in which the effectiveness of a much stronger enemy's technological advantages in conventional warfare is stymied. This is consistent with waging asymmetrical warfare in order to limit an adversary's ability to deploy its superior military technology, especially air power.

It is debatable whether these self-proclaimed strategists accurately interpret the lessons to be drawn from military history, especially the American experience. Instead, as the following quote from an al-Qa'ida article demonstrates, they seem to provide a strange reading of U.S. military history, even if one limits the analysis to Afghanistan and Iraq:

> Regarding the American army, the mujahidin have tested it in many fields. The mujahidin gained experience in fighting the biggest power in the world then, the army of the Soviet Union. Whoever was engaged in the two wars can confirm that there is no comparison between the two armies. The United States' superiority is in its air power only, and air power, as everyone knows cannot decide a war. Advancing in enemy territory is impossible without ground forces. Although the US ground forces are strong technologically and in air support, their strength is inconsistent with the power of the United States and its international reputation. In all its history, the United States has not waged a successful ground war and has not depended on ground forces in battles in a large way. Its greatest strength was air power.[83]

Unless this statement was meant only for propaganda purposes, its authors seem to have accepted unquestioningly several dubious assumptions. First, consistent with the founding myth of al-Qa'ida, it is true that the Red Army ultimately withdrew from Afghanistan. However, the United States played a direct role in that outcome by providing the mujahidin with highly lethal, man-portable, anti-aircraft missiles that ended the Soviet military's uncontested presence in the air. In addition, the superpower competition with the United States during the 1980s ultimately accelerated the collapse of the Soviet economy. These circumstances undermined the Soviet leadership's willingness to sustain its involvement in Afghanistan. Even after the Red Army left in 1989, the resounding mujahidin victory was delayed until 1992, when the Afghan regime collapsed.

Second, the authors of the quotation above seriously underestimate the past success of U.S. forces in ground combat engagements before and during the current battles in Afghanistan and Iraq. In reality, they conveniently ignore the fact that the jihadists have failed consistently to defeat American ground forces or counter U.S. airpower. For example, American troops successfully engaged in intense urban combat and killed a number of insurgents during the 2004 sieges of al-Fallujah and al-Najaf in Iraq.[84] And, they also fail to recognize that American manned and unmanned aircraft use precision-guided munitions with stand-off capabilities to provide close-air support to U.S. troops or attack individual targets as small as a single house in urban areas. To offer only one example, Abu Laith al-Libi, a senior al-Qa'ida leader who was field commander in Afghanistan, was killed along with other militants on January 29, 2008, in Pakistan's North Waziristan tribal area by a missile launched in a U.S. unmanned Predator air strike. As a result, this statement should be seen as propaganda for the unsophisticated. It does not constitute serious analysis of the strengths and limitations of U.S. military capabilities against the jihadists.

A similar but slightly more sophisticated appraisal is provided by Yusuf al-Ayiri. He too focuses on the prospects for limiting the use of airpower to counter the jihadists. Al-Ayiri argues that protracted, urban guerrilla warfare will "eliminate the Crusader enemy's" ability to utilize airpower and thwart its ability to locate guerrilla forces, making it the best way to defend the Ummah; he argues that it is "the method before which all disparities of armament and equipment with the invaders fade."[85] Al-Ayiri goes on to say that all Muslims, therefore, should concentrate on using protracted guerrilla warfare against the "Crusaders." He is correct in stating that urban guerilla warfare poses special problems for any military force, including the potential for increased casualties, collateral damage, and restricted fields of maneuver. In the past, because of these

problems, it was difficult for security forces to counter the guerrillas' operations unless those forces were willing to use force indiscriminately. Even
then, civilian casualties due to the indiscriminate use of force frequently
added to public support for the guerrillas. This was true for the French in
the Algerian War for Independence from 1954 to 1962, and for the Israelis in Lebanon in 1982. As noted above, the warfare capabilities of the
U.S. military are designed to minimize collateral as well as friendly forces
casualties. This does not totally undermine al-Ayiri's argument if the
jihadists succeed in sustaining protracted urban combat. However, both
Afghanistan and Iraq demonstrate that U.S. capabilities—including the
ability to deploy air assets—make it difficult for the jihadists to maintain
a high operational tempo against Western troops as opposed to suicide
bombings targeting civilians in urban areas.

Despite the shortcomings of the two approaches summarized above,
the ability to sustain an insurgency or terrorist campaign offers the jihadists a way to erode the political will of their adversaries. Seemingly endless
fluctuation between intense urban combat with its resulting casualties,
patrols, and garrison duty can wear down any military force. As numerous
cases from history demonstrate, prolonged conflict without a clear end-
point can diminish morale within the military, and it inevitably diminishes public support for military engagements in Western democracies.
Moreover, today's 24–7 global news cycle amplifies these impacts. Simply
put, democracies are willing to make great sacrifices in blood and treasure
but want—and politically may need—quick victories. Unfortunately, if
one examines their statements and behavior, the timeline for the jihadists
indicates it is likely to be a long war.

Abu-Hajir Abd-al-Aziz al-Muqrin, the slain al-Qa'ida in the Arabian
Peninsula leader, provides a guerrilla warfare strategy that is more sophisticated than the two summarized above. We describe it because his
approach is more suited to sustaining a long war. His proposed strategy
parallels the strategy used successfully by Mao Tse-Tung during the Chinese Civil War between the Communists and Nationalists from 1927 to
1948. Al-Muqrin, a Near Enemy jihadist, frequently wrote columns on
guerrilla warfare for the al-Qa'ida military magazine *al-Battar Camp*. Two
of these articles, published in January and February 2004, outline a three-
phase system for guerrilla warfare to be followed in the jihadist terrorist
campaign in Saudi Arabia and by Islamic insurgencies elsewhere.

Al-Muqrin calls his first phase "strategic defensive," and its characteristics are similar to those in Mao's first phase.[86] In this phase, al-Muqrin

says, operations must have great propaganda value.[87] Military operations are aimed at ruining the prestige of the regime, and they demonstrate to the nation that the regime is unable to protect against strikes, thereby undermining its legitimacy. Public relations and gaining allies are important during this phase while insurgents use small hit-and-run attacks to disperse enemy forces.

Al-Muqrin's second phase is called "strategic stalemate."[88] In it, the insurgents intensify their strikes and expand their media campaign to appeal to the people of neighboring countries. The insurgents initiate a foreign policy by sending "diplomatic messages, either through political statements or through the language of blood and fire" to foreign governments that support the enemy regime. The insurgents also set up administrative bases in liberated areas under the control of the mujahidin, building camps, hospitals, Shari'ah courts, and radio stations—an approach similar to that promoted by Naji in *The Management of Savagery*. These "liberated" bases will serve as staging areas for further military and political operations. Al-Muqrin adds that the mujahidin are able, in this phase, to set up negotiations, but only to discuss the terms of the enemy's surrender—not as a power-sharing arrangement.[89]

Al-Muqrin's third phase, the "decisive stage," entails the building up of semiregular and regular forces.[90] These forces will incorporate enemy deserters who have been rehabilitated. According to al-Muqrin, one goal of the offensive during the third phase is to build a military force that will become the nucleus of an army.[91] Al-Muqrin, however, argues that even after establishing regular military formations, guerrilla forces should remain intact after the decisive victory.[92] Al-Zawahiri has used similar language, referring to the Islamic state as being "a political endeavor in which the mujahedeen would be a nucleus around which would gather the tribes and their elders, and the people in positions, and scientists, and merchants, and people of opinion, and all the distinguished ones who were not sullied by appeasing the occupation and those who defended Islam."[93] This concept echoes the notion of an Islamic vanguard promoted by Qutb and others, which in turn parallels a similar concept in Marxist-Leninist ideology.

Abu-Mus'ab al-Suri, in *The Call to Global Islamic Resistance*, also outlines a three-stage theory of warfare. The first stage al-Suri describes, the "stage of attrition," involves small cells and "limited terrorist warfare," in which cells depend on simple operations to strain economies, force a "security collapse," and cause "political confusion." In the second stage, the "balancing stage," cells draw regular armed forces into battle and begin to establish control over territory. Al-Suri cautions that cells during this stage must not be centralized. In the third stage, "the stage of termination or liberation," guerrilla cells take control of more territory, often in open battles, and use captured ground as a base from which they can launch operations on remaining territory.[94] Other strategists, such as Yusuf al-Ayiri and Abu-Ubayd al-Qurashi, have also written extensively on three-stage theories.[95]

Part of the progression between stages in guerrilla wars hinges on the ability to gradually formalize the jihadist military presence, often by the deployment of regular military forces and engagement in more traditional, symmetrical battles with the enemy. Because the focus has been heavily on terrorism and guerrilla insurgency, there have been few examples of this later stage in the history of the global jihadist movement. One exception would be a highly structured April 2005 assault carried out by al-Zarqawi's group against U.S. forces at the infamous Abu-Ghurayb prison, twenty miles west of Baghdad. At least forty to fifty jihadist fighters attacked from several directions. They used a variety of weapons, including mortars, rockets, and car bombs, and retreated under covering fire. Insurgent reports of the assault indicated that the group carried out surveillance of the prison, and U.S. military officials called the assault one of the most sophisticated of the insurgency.[96]

In their writings, al-Muqrin, al-Suri, and Abu-Ubayd al-Qurashi refer to an analogy for guerrilla warfare popularized by the American historian Robert Taber. In this analogy, guerrilla warfare is likened to a flea that bites a dog's skin and flies away. The dog proceeds to scratch his skin raw, but the flea returns and bites the dog repeatedly. Over time, the dog dies. Their use of this analogy highlights one of the core principles of jihadist strategy: the goal is to prolong the war and exhaust the enemy, thereby weakening the legitimate government.[97] Moreover, their writings demonstrate that strategic thought is an active component of the jihadist movement and draws on the historical experience of other revolutionaries.

Conclusions

Al-Qa'ida and the overall jihadist movement have a genuine strategic vision. By carefully embedding their political goals within a religious context, the radical Islamists seek to mobilize broad-based public support throughout the Muslim world for their agenda.[98] This reflects recognition by the jihadists that they must obtain and maintain support from individuals who may only be tangentially connected to the struggle. Transforming the jihad into a global struggle offers the jihadists the chance to gain at least rhetorical, if not more tangible, support by invoking the imagery of Islam under attack by a hostile West. As a result, the shift from a Near Enemy to Far Enemy strategic emphasis reinforces the sense that the jihad is in defense of Islam.

The jihadists' various "strategic studies" serve two primary purposes. First, no matter how unrealistic scenarios such as the 2020 Plan may seem to us, these studies show potential sympathizers that the jihadist movement has a plan for victory. The importance of this in mobilizing and sustaining adherents to their cause should not be underestimated. Second, such studies make what is often opportunism in targeting seem more like a coherent strategy. In the end, however, the radical Islamist effort to restore the caliphate will depend on more than their ability to articulate a coherent strategy that does not garner widespread opposition within the broader Muslim community. Their ability to win will depend on whether they or their adversaries are more adept at engaging in military operations, mobilizing public support, utilizing intelligence, and persevering in the struggle—that is, on nonreligious factors.

3

ORGANIZATIONAL DYNAMICS

The need exists to preserve the religious, intellectual, and cultural identity of the ummah, and maintain the thought and methodology of the Islamic Awakening and its jihadist vanguard.

Due to these circumstances, I believe that there will arise—within this living ummah—the nuclei of resistance that will be strewn about with nothing to unite them in thought, methodology, or identity—except [the goal of] repelling the assault.

—Abu-Mus'ab al-Suri, *The Call to Global Islamic Resistance*

THE CALL TO GLOBAL JIHAD, which is embedded in a religious context, clearly has resonated among the Salafi mujahidin, forcing the West to confront a new challenge to its domestic security and the stability of the existing international order. Faced with a new and somewhat mysterious enemy who fights using terrorism as a tactic to advance its strategic vision, it becomes imperative to examine how the jihadist movement is organized and how it recruits followers, if we hope to understand this latest variant in the history of terrorism. Collecting empirical data on the organizational dynamics of the jihadist movement, however, is a highly challenging task. Our effort is hampered greatly by the fact that the jihadist movement generally—and al-Qa'ida in particular—is clandestine. Unlike open organizations, the internal organization and decision-making processes of such secretive organizations are, at best, opaque. Limited, and often highly selective, glimpses into the inner workings of the organizations can wrongly be assumed to be representative of organizational policies and practices. Moreover, when examining the global jihad, it is only prudent to exercise caution when describing its structure in order to avoid imposing a Western template for organizational behavior on a non-Western movement. With these considerations in mind, this chapter explores continuity and change in the approaches taken by radical Islamists in organizing for jihad.

TERRORIST NETWORKS

Traditionally, terrorist organizations have tended to organize into groups that can be conceptualized as constituting a network. A key goal of network design is to maximize network resiliency—the network's ability to withstand the loss of one or more elements but still be able to function and carry out assignments. A parallel goal in designing networks is to optimize capacity, which involves determining the ideal scale of operations for a network based on its size. Capacity reduces network resiliency because it brings part, or all, of the network into the open and exposes the network to observation and possible penetration by enemy forces. As a result, an inescapable trade-off exists between resiliency and capacity for all network structures. For example, the use of sleeper agents and cut-outs typically results in more resilience, since the sleeper or cut-out typically is not as deeply embedded in the network. This may enhance network security because information about the network is compartmentalized in a "need to know" fashion, which makes penetration more difficult. For this reason, the loss of a sleeper or cut-out may not degrade substantially the resiliency of the network as a whole.

John Arquilla and David Ronfeldt found that terrorist networks can be classified into four possible structures: hierarchical, chain networks, hub networks, and all-channel networks.[1] Their structural classifications are generally accepted by terrorism experts and include: chain networks (in which information is passed from node to node); star or hub networks (in which a central node connects individually to the other nodes); and all-channel networks (in which all nodes are connected to each other). Each network structure has advantages and disadvantages depending on the situation. Moreover, sometimes an organization may choose to mix and match network models to accomplish tasks.

In analyzing networks, the term "node" refers to one or more people in the network who act as a transfer point for information. Within a network, the individuals who function as bridges and hub nodes are recognizable because of the large amount of communications that pass through them. Because they engage in intensive interaction with others, they are often charismatic, affable personalities who act as midlevel managers for the jihadist organization.

The hierarchical model is undoubtedly the most readily recognizable structure for a network. Numerous revolutionary and guerrilla organizations throughout time have used this model with varying degrees of success. Common in military organizations, hierarchical networks follow the standard "organization tree" shape for command-and-control, with a leader at the top level, lieutenants at the second level, and so on. Orders travel down the hierarchy from the highest level until reaching the individual field operators. Because this type of network is easiest for security services to penetrate, hierarchies are difficult for terrorist organizations to maintain over long distances or extended periods of time while trying to stay clandestine. By their very nature, hierarchical structures require information hand-off so that some level of intelligence can be gathered from any member once orders have been issued. Hierarchical networks also are vulnerable to attack because removing the top leader can mean the destruction of the group or, at the very least, cause confusion and possible in-fighting. Therefore, hierarchical networks are generally used in insurgencies and for organizational militias such as the 055 Brigade—Al-Qa'ida's pre-9/11 guerrilla force in Afghanistan.

Chain networks are used mostly in smuggling as well as in courier operations and travel facilitation. In his writings, Yusuf al-Ayiri advises the jihadists to use chain networks to bring foreign fighters into Iraq from bordering countries (which he does not name, for security reasons).[2] Information passes from node to node to node in a form of end-to-end communication. Like hierarchies, this type of network structure is relatively easy to attack once identified. As figure 3.1 illustrates, the removal of one or more of the intermediate nodes in the chain may cause the network to cease functioning. For example, the leftwing American Weather Underground, which operated during the 1970s, used a version of a chain network when it shifted to operating as a totally clandestine terrorist group. Weather Underground members reported losing contact with their associates when a member of the chain quit or was apprehended. As a result, they became isolated and effectively were cut off from the group, thereby reducing the organization's ability to sustain coordinated operations.

The hub network, also called a wheel or star network, illustrated by figure 3.2, puts the leadership, sometimes called the central node of the

Figure 3.1. Chain Network

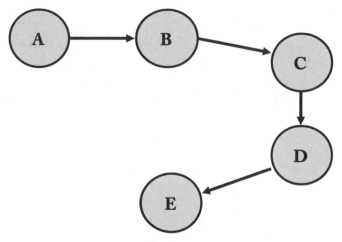

Figure 3.2. Star or Hub and Spoke Network

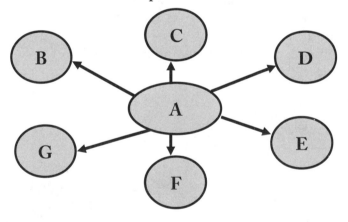

organization, at the center of the network. The second-level leadership, field commanders, and even the individual field operators receive orders directly from the leadership or central node. This type of organizational structure is similar to the model typically used by drug cartels. The individual nodes must use the central node as a bridge to communicate with the leadership. Removal of the central node can mean the destruction of the hub network. This vulnerability exists because the individual nodes are isolated from each other and lack a way to communicate, since all information is passed through the central node.

With the advent of widespread access to computers and the Internet, the all-channel network illustrated by figure 3.3 is the newest variant suggested for terrorist networking. The all-channel network presumably combines decentralization with the ability to be highly focused through shared communications. In theory, an all-channel network is quite possibly the hardest to attack and defend against because every node is connected to all other nodes in this structure. Universal connectivity automatically creates a tremendous amount of data duplication and information redundancy, since localized and network-wide data are contained in each node. Moreover, because every node is connected to all other nodes in the network, a potential strength of an all-channel network lies in the fact that the ability and channels are in place in case the nodes need to communicate. This does not mean they are automatically communicating with each other. To achieve this capability, all-channel networks require dense communications that are enhanced by the use of advanced technology. The overall number of nodes and volume of communications within an all-channel network can be a source of potential vulnerability. If the network becomes too big it can become bogged down in heavy communications, causing confusion or greater susceptibility to penetration by intercepting communications.

Figure 3.3. All-Channel Network

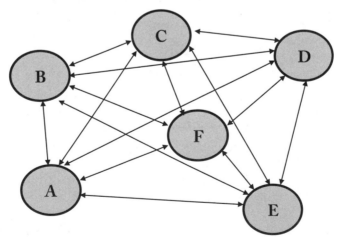

Based on his study of terrorist network dynamics, Marc Sageman asserts that in attacking an all-channel network, at least 5 to 15 percent of major hub nodes must be destroyed in order to isolate the secondary and tertiary nodes into smaller noncommunicating islands of nodes, which are less likely to be able to coordinate an operation while maintaining clandestine status.[3] However, it is difficult to determine whether this would be a successful strategy in dismantling an all-channel network, primarily because social ties between cells are often clandestine and based on shared past experiences, such as training camps.[4]

If the major visible hub nodes are destroyed, there is still the risk of the emergency activation of these previous ties, which would immediately "heal" the network and allow the small noncommunicating islands to begin to communicate and operate. Another difficulty in dismantling covert networks, as opposed to open social networks, is the fact that strong ties may be made to look like weak ties and that covert groups may not interact with outside elements, which makes spotting them even more difficult.

Valdis Krebs's analysis, although done after the fact and therefore enjoying the benefits of hindsight, makes an excellent point about clandestine operational groups. They tend to avoid outside contact because they do not trust outsiders, and they know instinctively that discovery by the opposition is made much easier anytime a group member provides a link to a nonmember. The requirement to avoid entanglements, even while ostensibly living as a normal member of society, is a hallmark of the terrorist, spy, or subversive operator. The most disciplined operators will adhere strictly to the rules and avoid calls home, email contacts, or any other linkage that will draw attention to themselves.

The all-channel network, while often the most effective, is the hardest to organize and sustain. The organizational design is flat and must be self-organizing, something that takes a great deal of time and patience. The all-channel network relies on quick and broad dissemination of information among the nodes, which is accomplished through dense, technologically fueled communications. In all-channel networks, there is ideally no central leadership, command, or headquarters, which makes it difficult to decapitate the network in the style of a hierarchical network. In all-channel networks, there is little to no hierarchy, and multiple leaders are possible. Local initiative and autonomy is encouraged as decision making and operations are decentralized, leaving the original leadership, such as

Usama bin Laden and the Central Staff cluster, free of blame for an operation.[5]

The outcome when groups like al-Qa'ida organize themselves as all-channel networks is that the organization itself is transformed into a loosely networked entity that may lack a clear command-and-control structure. The name "Al-Qa'ida" is likely to be increasingly used by start-up networks of radical Islamists as a brand name with which to label and attribute operations. These start-up networks and nodes are likely to emerge sporadically, depending on their resources and motivations as well as domestic politics. Start-up networks assume the mantel of the "brand name" group as a way of instantaneously gaining credibility for their actions, as a way of adopting a political stance with a minimum of words, and as a way of giving themselves an image of being larger than they really are. Under the self-starting model, the central staff or core leadership cluster, most notably bin Laden and his deputy Ayman al-Zawahiri, can honestly distance themselves from direct blame—or they can claim credit—for an operation. They become inspirational leaders with no direct involvement in decision making, target selection, or choice of tactics employed. The name al-Qa'ida more and more often refers to an ideology and not simply to an organization. This essentially puts into practice the "Leaderless Resistance" terrorist model attributed to Louis Beam. In this model, cells operate independently without any centralized guidance, command, or control from a leader, while still pursuing a common objective. The parallel to Abu-Mus'ab al-Suri's model of independent jihadist groups that emerge autonomously in various locations, taking actions without the need for central direction or control, is also noteworthy.

Although very appealing in theory, the all-channel network at this point in time is primarily a theoretical structure. It does not appear to be used widely by actual terrorist organizations. The inherent lack of operational security that is part and parcel of such a highly connected structure would argue against using an all-channel network as the exclusive or primary organizational structure for a clandestine group. Instead, it appears suitable for more limited and specialized applications involving less than total connectivity across all nodes. In fact, elements of the all-channel network without total connectivity can be seen in exposed terrorist organizations.

Studies on al-Qa'ida and a number of affiliated jihadist organizations indicate that the tendency has been to organize along geographic lines (which often results in emphasis in ethnicity or nationality). Al-Qa'ida, following the model of the two major Egyptian groups—the Islamic Group and al-Zawahiri's Egyptian Islamic Jihad—frequently organized different geographical branches into a number of self-contained cells, called *anqud*, the Arabic word for a cluster of grapes. Operational (cell) leaders were connected to the central leadership through lieutenant hubs that oversaw major clusters. Often, cell leaders were given considerable autonomy during the attack preparation stage, receiving logistical, financial, and other assistance from their connections to the central staff but left to determine methods of weapons acquisition and the timing of the attacks on their own, such as in the September 11 attacks, the disrupted millennial Los Angeles plot, the Indonesian Jemaah Islamiya's 2002 Bali bombing, and others.[6]

Similarly, the Algerian GSPC divides Algeria into nine zones with a GSPC-appointed amir heading each zone. Jemaah Islamiya organizes its operations into four zones—called *mantiqis*—with several subcells, all headed by a number of lieutenants subordinate to the overall amir of the group. In all three cases—al-Qa'ida, GSPC, and JI—geographic branches often had different responsibilities and functions, ranging from smuggling, financing (often through criminal means such as credit card fraud), travel and other facilitation functions, training, and a variety of other tasks. In al-Zarqawi's Tawhid wa al-Jihad group (a moniker used before the group adopted the al-Qa'ida name in October 2004), which consisted primarily of Levantine Arabs, the Sunni Triangle area of Iraq was divided into nine autonomous zones with varying numbers of fighters.[7] The division of labor in this network is unclear, probably because it differed from al-Qa'ida, GSPC, and JI in that its operations were more guerrilla than they were conspiratorial.

Pre-9/11 Al-Qa'ida

Following bin Laden's return to Afghanistan, the al-Qa'ida organization was able to operate from 1997 to 2002 from a secure location without fear of undue observation by or interference from their opponents. The Taliban regime in Afghanistan permitted the operation of jihadist training camps, allowed free communication flow from the makeshift headquarters, and interposed no objection to the travel in and out of Afghanistan of recruits, operatives, interested parties, and supporters of al-Qa'ida.

During this time period, the movement was able to operate as a more or less formal organization. This was consistent with al-Zawahiri's assertion that "a jihadist movement needs an arena that would act like an incubator where its seeds would grow and where it can acquire practical experience in combat, politics and organizational matters."[8]

Several attempts were made to describe the organizational structure of al-Qa'ida during this period. The 9/11 Commission noted that al-Qa'ida essentially functioned as a hierarchical network with a more or less formal chain of command. Figure 3.4 illustrates the structure prior to the U.S. invasion of Afghanistan that resulted in the removal of the Taliban regime. It indicates that al-Qa'ida, at least formally, was operating like a traditional centrally directed organization. Following the overthrow of the Taliban regime, al-Qa'ida went into hiding and its formal organization was largely abandoned. A number of its senior officers were captured and probably compromised details of the organization.

Under the structure outlined above, the actual operational work, such as the September 11 attack, was done by clandestine cells. The cells operated under the direction of al-Qa'ida's advisory council and its military committee. Individual cells were organized in an ad hoc fashion, depending on the location, mission, and other circumstances unique to each operation. Figure 3.5 illustrates the structure used by a simple support cell that provides refuge in safe houses for traveling clandestine operatives.

In this cell structure, the leader was allowed to know a number of operatives who visited his area for rest and recuperation following operational missions. Owners of safe houses knew the appearances of operatives staying with them, but they were usually content to just call their guests by their *nom de guerre* and not to ask too many questions. The operatives and the cell leader were careful not to break any laws or do anything to give the local authorities cause for moving against them.

Other operational cells were more complicated, as befitted their role. Figure 3.6 provides an example of the organizational structure for a cell that was set up to make and place explosives in public places. This cell was made up of five terrorists under the command of the lead operative. The cell's leader was the only member who had any contact outside the cell because he knew the operational control located abroad. The lead operative also met with other people, who apparently were innocent, in order to confuse possible surveillance by local security services as to his intentions. In this case, like many al-Qa'ida missions such as the U.S. Embassy bombings in East Africa, the plan was for the lead operative to

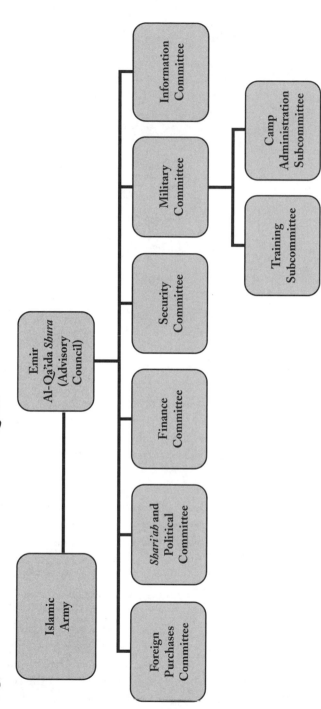

Figure 3.4. The Pre–9/11 Structure of Al-Qaʾida

Figure 3.5. Support Cell Structure

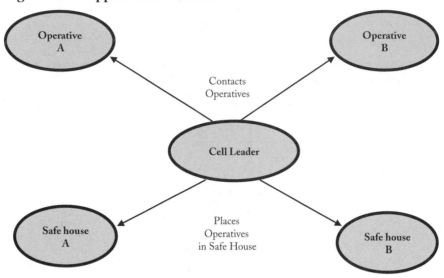

depart the area prior to the action taking place. The five cell members were to place the bomb and then escape. This type of cell exemplifies a classic, hierarchical model. Other than the leader, individual cell members know at most the target and the names of other members of their specific cell. If captured and interrogated, they could identify the lead operative but would be unable to provide information about higher echelons of the organization.

In each of the cases above, there was clear contact and direction from higher authorities in al-Qa'ida. The cell members may have had considerable latitude as to how they would accomplish their missions, such as the September 11 attacks, but their function was dictated from outside. It was this type of careful control by bin Laden and the senior leadership cadre that allowed al-Qa'ida to orchestrate its most sensational attacks and to conduct a program of steadily increasing violence and shock value in its operations.

Recruitment into the various al-Qa'ida cells was primarily a top-down activity. The operational control officer directed the lead operative to carry out a mission. The lead operative recruited within his circle of friends and coworkers, inviting them into the group and revealing the plan to them in stages. The cell leader had to approve the addition of any new members.

Figure 3.6. Field Operations Cell Structure

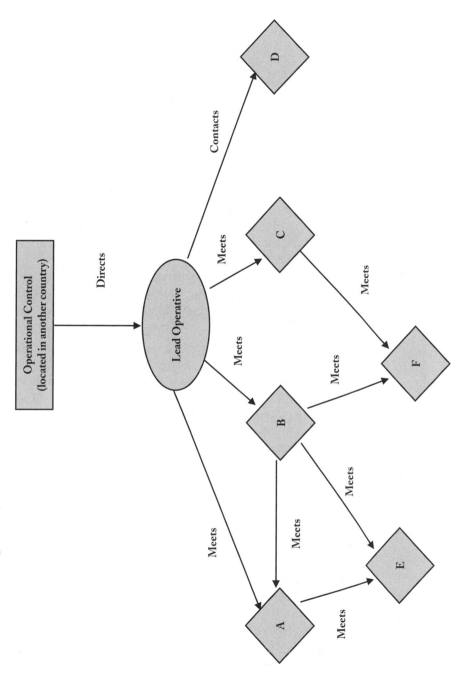

After the Fall of the Taliban

Since the post-9/11 losses sustained by al-Qa'ida, the group—and indeed the jihadist movement as a whole—has made changes in its organizational structure in order to maintain operational capacity. The loss of the Afghanistan base and the capture, death, and fragmentation of the cadre around bin Laden in the wake of the U.S. response to September 11 accelerated a tendency that was already developing in the jihadist movement towards a decentralized structure, or what has been called a "leaderless resistance."[9] Under a leaderless resistance scheme, individuals create small groups that engage in activity without central direction but follow a common inspiration that serves as their motivational ideal. For example, while many jihadists will claim they are following bin Laden, they are really following the idea of global jihad that bin Laden so effectively articulated.

Abu-Mus'ab al-Suri, who was arrested in Pakistan in 2005, has become one of the most prominent proponents of a decentralized strategy. Al-Suri's decentralization theory was published and widely disseminated via jihadist websites in late 2004 and early 2005 and in *The Call for a Global Islamic Resistance*. The doctrine of leaderless resistance is a central theme:

> In time, it was proven that the armed endeavors of the jihadist movements and organizations that were carried out on the basis of the sectionalized-secret-pyramidal framework leads to a path of annihilation and failure, because they were unable to prevent the global transformation that took place with the launching of the new world order, and because they did not understand its political and security dimensions and their impact on them. The leaders and their supporters—they were the cream of the ummah's youth at that time—did not have the required strength of motivation, loyalty, and dedication to avoid their fate, of which the signs were apparent to those who could observe them.[10]

While adhering to the underlying ideology of the global jihad, according to the doctrine of leaderless resistance, groups form from the bottom up with friends talking among themselves and, when necessary, expanding the group by carefully choosing other contacts to participate.

In a 2002 high-level al-Qa'ida Shura Council meeting that bin Laden did not attend, al-Suri allegedly led a discussion on how al-Qa'ida can effectively operate within the new restraints and confinements imposed by counterterrorism efforts. Al-Suri had studied Western counterterrorism strategy in an effort to look for weaknesses and areas that could be exploited.[11] According to Spanish counterterrorism judge Baltasar Garzon, al-Suri "told the shura that al-Qa'ida could no longer exist as a hierarchy, an organization, but instead would have to become a network and move its operations out over the entire world."[12] Although al-Suri presents his decentralization concept as a response to these key elements of Western counterterrorism policy since before September 11, he adopted decentralization as early as 1991 in a much shorter version of 2004's *The Call to Global Islamic Resistance*. In his 2004 book, he said that direct military confrontations with the United States after September 11 in Afghanistan, Pakistan, Iraq, and even in Yemen reaffirmed his previous ideas regarding decentralization and individual resistance. Al-Suri's decentralization model is designed to respond to key elements in Western counterterrorism policy:

1. drying up of financial sources;
2. systematic targeting of jihadist leaders and cadres for killing and capturing by counterterrorist forces coupled with multinational agreements for handing over and exchanging criminals and terrorists (jihadists);
3. eliminating refuges and safe havens for the mujahidin;
4. moving the fields of security cooperation from regional to international;
5. expanding counterterrorism legislation.[13]

Believing that decentralization can make these policies less effective, al-Suri advocates relying on independent terrorist action undertaken by individuals or small groups of individuals inspired and influenced by operations and propaganda. He maintains that moving away from a more traditional network structure maximizes effectiveness and geographical dispersion. In order to make such an approach work, al-Suri notes that propaganda efforts need to emphasize the importance of individual action without group affiliation and be broad enough to have mass appeal.

This new, highly decentralized model has some distinct advantages over the former hierarchical model, especially for jihadists operating outside their home countries. While foreigners may be subjected to more scrutiny by security services, their meetings are usually limited to known colleagues or co-religionists, making it very difficult for the security services to penetrate the group. For example, the Madrid cell that conducted the 2004 train bombings reportedly met clandestinely, with no fixed meeting site and on a constantly changing schedule that was communicated to participants orally. Small home-grown groups may even be capable of autonomous action. Operational cells organized using this model require little, if any, contact with other operational cells or communications with external leaders, which makes them less visible to the security services, especially the signals intelligence community, thereby lessening the risk of discovery.

People join the jihad primarily as a result of strong personal bonds, such as kinship and friendship. In fact, even for the pre-9/11 version of al-Qa'ida, data from Marc Sageman's study of terrorist networks, which focuses exclusively on the Salafi jihadists, reveals that individuals joined the movement through friendship with a person who was already involved rather than through a formal organizational process of recruitment.[14] Because jihadist groups or individual cells based on kinship or friendship are likely to be tightly knit, outsiders would find it difficult to penetrate such groups: the vetting process for nonkinsmen literally takes years of friendship as a minimum requirement to join. In his remarks about a leaderless resistance model, al-Suri notes the advantages of

> calling the youth and the Muslim masses to practicing individual resistance, so that the resistance does not depend on pyramidal and cell-based organizations and structures where the arrest of some of its individuals leads to the annihilation and arrest of all its individuals. That happens by selecting a system of work and not an organization in the traditional sense of the word, so that everyone participating in resistance works—that is, all Muslims, fall under one designation: The Global Islamic Resistance. The work of the collective maximizes the benefit, so that the arrest of one does not lead to the arrest of all, because there is no connection between any of them.[15]

Attacks on formal leadership structures inside jihadist organizations have little effect on the formation of leaderless cells. Actions such as the invasion of Iraq or security service successes in capturing key leaders of jihadist groups may actually stimulate the formation of new cells. For example, the Southeast Asian Jemaah Islamiya (JI) group started life as a hierarchical organization. The group's guiding document outlines a "top-down chain of command and meticulously defined objectives and activities," and it "exhibits clear military overtones at the level of planning and launching terrorist attacks."[16] However, the group has evolved into a leaderless resistance model following the success of the region's governments in capturing its leaders and thwarting planned operations. Security service officials in the region believe that when JI became defunct, the actual number of new jihadist cells increased as sympathetic Muslims who did not approve of the actions around the world against jihadists formed their own personalized cells to discuss the problem—and in some cases to move into action.

Finally, unlike more traditionally organized groups, the leaderless model of small self-directed, and probably self-financed, cells can profit greatly from the use of virtual resources available on the Internet. Such a group can obtain training information through the web. Its members also can validate their belief system by reading jihadist literature that contains the same ideas as they embrace. As is the case with larger groups, these autonomous cells can announce their presence by claiming credit for acts of terrorism at times of their choosing.

DECENTRALIZATION AND INCITEMENT CAMPAIGNS

If individual obligation actually is sufficient to motivate radical Islamists to participate actively in the jihad, extended networks are unnecessary and decentralization becomes viable as an organizing principle for incitement campaigns. With decentralization, the mujahidin are guided solely by the goal of resisting the enemy. Under a decentralized system, the vow of allegiance, or *bay'ah*, is made not to a leader, such as Usama bin Laden; instead, it is between God and the individual jihadist. For al-Qa'ida, the *bay'ah* is central in cementing the group's command and control basis and structure. Al-Suri's efforts to redirect *bay'ah* to God seek to reorient and expand the jihad, making it more resilient and more easily self-initiated, and it may prevent struggles over succession upon the death of major leaders.[17] This represents a deliberate shift in emphasis away from the establishment of an Islamic state, using the pre-9/11 model of al-Qa'ida in an effort to maximize mass appeal. The focus on mobilizing resistance avoids potential disputes over the appropriate geographical location for initially establishing an Islamic state. It also avoids having to choose between the Near Enemy or Far Enemy strategy, since one merely needs to pursue jihad wherever the opportunity arises and emphasizes the need for what is essentially a global insurgency carried out by small cells and individuals.

Studying the experiences of jihadists over the last forty years, al-Suri concludes that "sectional, secret, and pyramidal" organizations have been "a complete failure on all fronts"—military, organizational security, preaching, educational, and political. Open, "exposed" fronts, such as in Bosnia, Chechnya, and Afghanistan, have generally been successes, and in the case of Afghanistan (against the Soviets) a complete success. Al-Suri continues by saying that individual terrorism, and terrorism carried out by small, disconnected cells, has been a success in confusing the enemy and arousing the Islamic Nation. Al-Suri's conclusion is that the jihad must rely on terrorism by individuals and small, disconnected cells, and—when circumstances permit—on more traditional guerrilla action in open fronts.[18]

A decentralization strategy like al-Suri's seems to have been accepted and followed in the 2003 Casablanca, the 2004 Madrid, and the 2005 London terrorist bombings. In each of those attacks, the perpetrators organized themselves into local, self-sustaining cells. It appears that each of the cells functioned as a self-contained network but also probably accepted guidance from visiting emissaries of the global movement. More recently, the same strategy appears to have been used by radical Muslims whose planned attacks were foiled in Toronto and London in 2006. The same pattern emerged in the 2007 Glasgow airport attack.

Other jihadists have advocated an approach similar to the one outlined in great detail by al-Suri. For example, in 2006 Egyptian jihadist Muhammad Khalil al-Hakaymah—who publicly joined al-Qa'ida in the same year—published a number of books and essays. His writings included instructions for lone-wolf jihadists titled *How to Kill Alone* and a compilation of jihadist writings from al-Suri, al-Zawahiri, and others, which emphasized the need for jihadist decentralization and increased attention to maintaining public support for jihadist groups.[19]

Prominent Saudi jihadist Yusuf al-Ayiri in 2002—two years before the release of al-Suri's masterwork—promoted decentralization, especially in urban guerrilla warfare. He argued that pyramid and chain structure groups are extremely dangerous and urged jihadist guerrillas to decentralize cells.[20] More specifically, al-Ayiri suggests that jihadists divide their cells into four groups: the leadership group (2–4 people), the reconnaissance/information group (4 people), the equipment group (2–4 people), and the operation execution group (undefined number of personnel). Al-Ayiri and al-Suri both advise jihadists to build small cells of around twelve people. It is unknown to what extent—if any—al-Ayiri's work influenced al-Suri, but there are certainly interesting parallels. According to al-Ayiri, cells should avoid centralization, but a "general command" can exist as long as it is located in a safe area "far from the field," and as long as the command does not know several important details of the cells, such as the number of personnel, their location, or their leader. Cells are connected to the general command by a cell member anonymously acting as a "coordinator," whose identity must remain unknown to other cell members.

Although reliance on semicentralized guerrilla warfare is given less importance by al-Suri than many of his colleagues, al-Suri believes that in addition to what he calls "popular resistance" brigades, the resistance will also make use of "general military brigades" and "specialized resistance brigades." The latter types of units will have more training and capabilities than the popular resistance. They also will be the base of secret work and guerrilla operations. So-called "strategic operations brigades" will be utilized too. These units will consist of jihadists with some strategic vision and will have "knowledge and operational capabilities in obtaining and using weapons of mass destruction when necessary."[21] However, because individual obligation on a mass basis is the key to decentralization, these other brigades are of limited importance in al-Suri's writings.

Table 3.1 compares al-Suri's model and "traditional" models for organizing the global jihad. Al-Suri, in effect, is calling for jihadist leadership to relinquish its role as guiding the movement. Instead, he advocates action of any kind on the individual level. His model, grounded in bin Laden's 1998 fatwa asserting that jihad is an individual duty, essentially calls for the simplification of jihadist ideology in the hopes of more effectively rallying the masses to battle. Al-Suri says in his book that the resistance must become a "strategic phenomenon, following the model of the Palestinian Intifada against occupation forces, settlers, and all who aid them," and that the resistance should be broadened to "embrace all corners of the Islamic world."[22] The result is a more goal-oriented al-Qa'ida, following Mao Tse-Tung's concept of strategic centralization and tactical decentralization.

Al-Suri acknowledges the effects of decentralization on the overall movement's ideology. He recognizes that attrition of jihadists and their leadership will deprive the movement of an institutional memory for its "education, political, legal, and intellectual methodology." Lacking an

Table 3.1. Al-Suri's Comparison of Decentralized Resistance and Traditional Organizations

	Decentralized Resistance	Traditional Organizations
Goal	Resistance for the sake of defending [against] the aggressors and their intermediaries	Toppling the government and establishing a Shari'ah government
Program	Program of the Global Islamic Resistance	Agenda of the jihadist organization
Leadership	General guidance for the global brigades and a special amir for the brigade	Central amir and leadership
Plan	Resistance of occupation and striking it everywhere	Work agenda of the organization
Financing	Special financing by the brigade by theft and donations	Financing by donations
Al-Bay'ah wa al-Ahad [Allegiance and Covenant]	Vow with God about jihad and resistance, and a vow to obey the amir of the brigade	Central bay'ah to the amir

Source: Table translated from Arabic. Abu-Mus'ab al-Suri, *The Call to Global Islamic Resistance*, 1403.

established structure to facilitate operations and organizational learning is likely to leave new recruits without a fixed identity and ways of resolving group conflicts. Recognizing that this potentially creates operational and morale problems, al-Suri advocates maintaining organizational learning structures, especially outlets for jihadist publications, in order to provide technical and operational information as well as to foster group cohesion and sustain morale. Moreover, under a decentralized system, the loss of technical and operational information could decrease capability to initiate successful operations, especially complex or large-scale ones.

Before the American military response to September 11 in Afghanistan, al-Qa'ida used a system of training camps to transmit operational experience to recruits. Currently, in response to Western counterterrorism efforts to deny terrorists safe havens, jihadists are trying to meet these needs by publishing online operational training materials, such as bomb-making tutorials, secure communications procedures, instructions on assassination techniques, and broader strategic studies. Why operate from the mountains of Afghanistan when one can easily disseminate training materials on the Internet? Although online training will not produce the professionalism of physical training camps, it makes training readily available for radicalized Muslims who want to plan and execute attacks.

Mirroring his goal-oriented operational decentralization theory, al-Suri calls for goal-oriented media and incitement campaigns designed to support recruitment, spread the ideology of the jihadist movement, and win popular support. Successful incitement is crucial to the decentralized, leaderless resistance model; al-Suri explains:

> The goal is to unite the efforts of the resisters from the ranks of the individual jihad, the remnants of the jihadist current, its supporters, and its new sympathizers who are resentful of the American invasion and those desiring to take action from the different parts of the Islamic nation on all of its levels, and to control it in common type and method in order to reach the goal, altering the individual jihad into a phenomenon that combines the group's effort under one designation and symbol, disciplined by one political, education, and legal program.[23]

Al-Suri also focuses on presenting religious justifications and rulings for the global jihad.[24] In his book, al-Suri presents a comprehensive guide to jihadist thought and practice, covering every subject an aspiring jihadist would need to know to begin the struggle. Al-Suri notes that all jihadist groups in the past failed partially because they lacked a common intellectual and strategic curriculum; with its scope and wide applicability to potential jihadists worldwide, *The Call to Global Islamic Resistance* aims to fill that gap.

His writings emphasize themes of glory earned through combat, especially the Crusades from the eleventh through the thirteenth centuries.[25] The medieval Crusades were a series of military campaigns conducted from 1095 until 1272 in the name of Christianity and sanctioned by the Pope. Their original aim was to recapture Jerusalem and the Holy Land from the Muslims while supporting the Byzantine Empire against the Turkish Muslim expansion into Anatolia. The immediate cause of the First Crusade was Alexius I's appeal to Pope Urban II for mercenaries to help him resist Muslim advances into territory of the Byzantine Empire.

However, the First Crusade represented a response to larger resentments in Western Europe directed against the Muslim world. In 1009, the Fatimid Caliph al-Hakim Abi-Amr Allah destroyed the Church of the Holy Sepulchre. Al-Hakim's successors allowed it to be rebuilt later by the Byzantine emperor and pilgrimage was again permitted, but many reports began to circulate in the West about the cruelty of Muslims toward Christian pilgrims. In 1063, Pope Alexander II gave papal blessing to Iberian Christians in their wars against the Muslims, granting both a papal standard (*vexillum sancti Petri*) and an indulgence to those who were killed in battle. By the late eleventh century, the concept of Christendom as a political and religious entity had emerged; combined with a resurgence of religious zeal, this made the West receptive to Pope Urban II's call for the First Crusade to recapture the Holy Land in 1095. Subsequent crusades were less motivated by religious zeal.

Although the Crusades have faded into the mists of history for the West, the term still has substantial symbolic resonance within the Muslim world, especially when combined with the legacy of colonialism. As a result, al-Suri portrays the War on Terror and the Iraqi conflict as the "Third Crusade" and appeals to anti-American and anti-Israeli sentiments by "exposing" the American and Jewish conspiracies against the Islamic world in an effort to mobilize popular support for the jihadists' cause.[26] His analysis stresses the importance of tailoring the jihadist message's style, content, and means of delivery to specific audiences to maximize the message's impact on the target audience.[27]

CONSOLIDATION AND RELIANCE ON ADVISORS

At the other end of the spectrum from al-Suri's argument for decentralization, some within the jihadist movement have called for relying on centralization. They advocate the consolidation of groups and leaders and the reliance on advisors to define policies. Often, group consolidation can be traced to Qur'anic and other Islamic injunctions for unity among Islamic groups. For example, verses 3:103, 3:104, and 3:105 all stress the importance of unity and the concept of an Islamic vanguard:

> 3:103: And hold fast, all together, by the Rope which Allah (stretches out for you), and be not divided among yourselves; and remember with gratitude Allah's favor on you; for you were enemies and He joined your

hearts in love, so that by His Grace, you became brethren; and you were on the brink of the Pit of Fire, and He saved you from it. Thus Allah makes His Signs clear to you: that you may be guided.

3:104: Let there arise out of you a band of people inviting to all that is good, enjoining what is right, and forbidding what is wrong; they are the ones to attain felicity.

3:105: Be not like those who are divided among themselves and fall into disputations after receiving Clear Signs: for them is a dreadful Penalty.

Another oft-cited injunction for unity is found in verse 8:73: "The Unbelievers are protectors, one of another: Unless ye do this, (protect each other), there would be tumult and oppression on earth, and great mischief." The Hadith also provide further grounding for the promotion of unity. For example, Sahih Muslim 18:4255: "He [God] is pleased with you that you worship Him and associate not anything with Him, that you hold fast the rope of Allah, and be not scattered."

In keeping with these religious injunctions, evidence culled from bin Laden's statements points to a conscious strategy of inclusion and unity. As early as his 1996 fatwa, bin Laden spoke against divisions among the mujahidin, saying that "an internal war is a great mistake, no matter what reasons are there for it. The presence of the occupier—the USA—forces will control the outcome of the battle for the benefit of the international Kufir."[28] Qur'anic injunctions on unity among Islamic groups also have been used by jihadists to promote unity within the ranks of a particular group, and not just among the various like-minded jihadist organizations and movements. For example, al-Qa'ida training materials urge teamwork. Nonetheless, one of bin Laden's former Yemeni bodyguards, Abu-Jandal, has alleged that rivalries within the ranks of al-Qa'ida existed along regional and nationalist lines fostering intergroup tensions. Abu-Jandal says members boasted about being of a particular nationality, such as Egyptians, Saudis, Yemenis, Sudanese, or Arab Maghreb citizens of particular nationalities. The national and geographic divides also impacted the structure of al-Qa'ida, with the Egyptian contingent providing much of its early leadership and doctrine and young Saudis and Yemenis primarily carrying out the military operations. Similarly, in his letter to al-Zarqawi, "Atiyah" advised the al-Qa'ida in Iraq leader not to kill Sunni leaders in Iraq; he also advised al-Zarqawi to build strategic relationships with tribal and religious leaders in Iraq who may not necessarily subscribe to his position.[29]

This potential for internal divisions to weaken the jihadist movement may account for bin Laden's frequent emphasis on unity. Using Iraq to illustrate this point, bin Laden has elaborated on this theme of unity by stating: "the Iraqi who is waging jihad against the infidel Americans or Allawi's [former Iraqi Prime Minister Ayad Allawi] renegade government is our brother and companion, even if he was of Persian, Kurdish, or Turkomen origin."[30] In a written message prepared by the Islamic Studies and Research Center, an al-Qa'ida mouthpiece, bin Laden discouraged disunity among Muslims, regardless of different views and interpretations of Islam.[31]

Al-Zawahiri shares bin Laden's concern about the need for unity under the aegis of al-Qa'ida. Discussing the importance of unity among the mujahidin, he explains: "The jihad movement must realize that half the road to victory is attained through its unity, rise above trivial matters, gratitude, and glorification of the interests of Islam above personal whims. . . . The importance of the unity of the Mujahid Islamic movement is perhaps clear now more than anytime before. The movement must seek this unity as soon as possible if it is serious in its quest for victory."[32] In a 2006 interview, al-Zawahiri even went a step further than just promoting unity among the mujahidin. He promoted unity, albeit temporary, among jihadists and non-Muslim enemies of the United States:

> I invite all of America's victims to Islam, the religion which rejects injustice and treachery. If they don't convert to Islam, then they should at least take advantage of the Muslims' defensive campaign to repel America's aggression against them and overcome them [the Americans], each in his own way, under his own banner, and with whatever is at his disposal. This is their historic chance because America is reeling from the blows of the mujahideen in Iraq and Afghanistan, thanks to God.[33]

Similarly, although he did not cite Qur'anic examples, Abu-Mus'ab al-Suri—in his writings on jihad in Syria—emphasized the importance of pan-Sunni unity when fighting: "We must concentrate on the internal cohesion of the Sunni sect. We must abandon any form of theological dispute and controversy over the interpretation of Islamic law, and internal controversy of any kind within the Sunni sect at this stage."[34]

Writing to al-Zarqawi, "Atiyah," a senior al-Qa'ida figure believed to be Atiyah Abd-Al-Rahman,[35] promotes the same basic unity strategy that bin Laden, al-Zawahiri, and al-Suri advocate: "So, strive in this, my brother, with all of the people around you who are Sunnis, even with the derelict ones and those who are not without sin or immorality, as long as they are prominent individuals and influential in their communities; indeed even the ones who are hypocrites."[36]

Consolidation can also represent a group's reaction to the post-9/11 era, especially the situation in Iraq after the fall of Saddam Hussein's Ba'athist regime. For example, disagreements over tactics and targeting between the late al-Zarqawi's group and other insurgents in Iraq may have led to the formation of the Mujahidin Shura Council (MSC), an umbrella body composed of at least seven jihadist insurgent groups. According to Stephen Ulph, "Disagreements over tactics, rumors of groups holding discussions with the U.S. military and outright internecine confrontations have progressively destroyed the 'enemy of my enemy' consensus within the resistance"; the announcement of the formation of this council came after "a period of increasingly open disaffection between the 'nationalist' and Islamist groups of the insurgency."[37]

The groups who have signed onto the MSC all share a similar, if not identical, jihadist perspective with respect to the situation in Iraq. After the formation of the MSC, the participating groups ceased claiming responsibility for attacks under their original names, opting instead to use the name of the Mujahidin Shura Council. In the statement announcing the creation of the MSC, a number of purposes were listed. Most concerned management of the battle and unification of the mujahidin, but one of them dealt with determining a "clear position" for the insurgency and communicating that position to the people to win public support.[38]

The need to maintain popular support and ameliorate tensions between religious nationalist and global jihadist groups is consistent with bin Laden's unity statements. As a result, formation of the Mujahidin Shura Council may have been a response to concerns like those expressed by al-Zawahiri in a 2005 letter to al-Zarqawi that was captured and released by U.S. authorities. One of the four issues al-Zawahiri addressed in this letter involved unifying the jihadist groups and placing them under a single leader. Al-Zawahiri asserted that this leader should be Iraqi because local sensitivities to foreign leadership could fragment and factionalize the jihad. Although al-Zarqawi retained a significant leadership position in the MSC until his death, media reports claimed that he had been replaced or demoted as the Council's political leader (while remaining a major military leader) as the "result of several mistakes he made," including tak-ing "the liberty of speaking in the name of the Iraqi people" and "targeting the Islamic states neighboring Iraq, particularly Jordan."[39] Al-Zarqawi's replacement as the Council's political head is rumored to be an Iraqi named Abdullah bin Rashid al-Baghdadi.

The reports of al-Zarqawi's demotion prior to his death are consistent with al-Zawahiri's efforts to unify the jihadist groups in Iraq. The appar-ent wish to have an Iraqi lead the jihad in Iraq demonstrates recognition of nationalism's role in generating popular support. As Michael Scheuer notes, al-Qa'ida's willingness to contribute valued resources without replacing existing leadership allowed it to be accepted in a number of insurgencies around the world where jihadists were active.[40] Efforts to replace al-Zarqawi with Iraqi leadership may represent a return to the historical al-Qaeda insurgency model, as opposed to a model in which an al-Qa'ida representative takes a more active role in the leadership of the insurgency.

On balance, the MSC failed to become the success that its leaders surely hoped it would be. The Council attracted few new member-organi-zations after its inception. Most important, the other major insurgent groups in Iraq did not join the MSC, including Ansar al-Sunnah and the Islamic Army in Iraq. The Council's failure may have been the impetus for a second attempt to achieve consolidation. In October 2006, the MSC announced the formation of a new alliance between a number of groups and tribes in Iraq. Subsequently, it announced the formation of the Islamic State of Iraq, proclaiming the majority of Iraq's land under the banner of the new "state," apparently in anticipation of a possible division of Iraqi territory between the Kurds and the Shi'ites: the statement in which its establishment was announced started off by presenting the Islamic State of Iraq as the only home for Iraqi Sunnis. However, like the MSC before it, the Islamic State of Iraq proved to be a harder sell to the Iraqi public, including the major indigenous Sunni insurgent groups, than its creators likely anticipated.

Outside Iraq, the Islamic State's announcement was met with evenly divided support and criticism from the jihadist Internet masses around the world, many of whom believed that an Islamic state could not be established in an area of continued conflict still under occupation by the enemy. Forum participants asked questions like, "Shouldn't they have waited until the Americans left before they announced an Islamic state?" Influential jihadist cleric Hamid al-Ali and the Islamic Army in Iraq—an insurgent rival of al-Qa'ida in Iraq—voiced similar concerns, saying that because the mujahidin are part of a resistance movement and do not have the authority to establish a state, the conditions for creating an emirate are not right.[41]

The Islamic State of Iraq later attempted to respond to such criticisms by publishing a book titled *Informing People of the Birth of the Islamic State*.[42] In it, the group asserted that defending the Islamic State, like carrying out the jihad, is an individual obligation—*fard ayn*—that applies to all Muslims. Subsequently, the self-proclaimed Islamic State of Iraq announced the formation of a cabinet in April 2007. This declaration was intended to convey the impression that it actually has a functioning bureaucracy and is not simply a collection of insurgents.[43] The Islamic State, however, is more an exercise in al-Qa'ida propaganda than a real polity. The charade surrounding the naming of its amir graphically illustrates this point. Abu-Umar al-Baghdadi, presumably an Iraqi, instead of Abu-Ayyub al-Masri, who was the late al-Zarqawi's Egyptian-born successor as leader of AQI, was proclaimed amir following the 2006 dissolution of the MSC and the creation of the al-Qa'ida-backed Islamic State of Iraq.

FITNAH IN IRAQ

As the Bush administration floundered without a coherent strategy and the insurgency grew, American involvement in Iraq became increasingly unpopular. Fighting dragged on with no viable end in sight, and the consensus among experts about the situation on the ground was bleak. By early 2007 the prospects of a U.S. foreign policy debacle loomed as a geopolitical defeat in the heart of the Middle East seemed to be inevitably replacing what had been a quick military victory over Saddam Hussein's forces in 2003.

The year 2007 was an exceedingly chaotic one for the Iraqi insurgency. The U.S. military was engaged in executing its "surge" strategy under the leadership of General David Petraeus, who assumed command of the Multi-National Force-Iraq on February 10, 2007. At the same time, Iraqis who previously had taken up arms as part of the insurgency fought against al-Qa'ida as a part of the al-Anbar Awakening Council, a collection of tribal militias led by Sunni sheikhs. In addition, the earlier unity among the jihadists in Iraq was called into question by internal disputes. Disagreements between al-Qa'ida and other groups led to violent clashes, leading to the splintering of several groups and the creation of other new groups. The apparent chaos among Iraqi insurgents was denounced by members of the online jihadist community as *fitnah*, a reference to sedition between Muslims that threatens the unity and foundation of Islam.

By late 2008 the situation was transformed dramatically, and in retrospect it appears likely that the year 2007 was a genuine break from the past. The insurgency in Iraq is not over by any means, and the security gains flowing from the surge are reversible, but it appears as if a general reduction in violence was attributable to the combined effects of the surge and to many Iraqi Sunnis opting to join the Awakening Council, even though al-Qa'ida and other insurgent groups once again sought to escalate violence in early 2008.

The Islamic Army in Iraq

Several events happened in early April 2007 that demonstrated the emerging schisms and shifting alliances that continued to evolve throughout the year. Kuwaiti jihadist cleric Hamid al-Ali issued a controversial fatwa asserting that the declaration of the Islamic State of Iraq should be retracted. His fatwa also stated that al-Qa'ida in Iraq should revert to being one group among many within the insurgency.

In response to this public criticism of AQI, the Islamic Army in Iraq released an open letter to the ISI's fictional Amir, Abu-Umar al-Baghdadi, attacking the actions of AQI and the ISI. Having refused to pledge its loyalty to bin Laden, IAI accused its rivals of "transgressing Islamic law."[44] The Islamic Army listed a number of grievances in the letter. Those complaints were based on the Islamic State's actions and the statements of Abu-Umar. Table 3.2 reveals that the litany of grievances with al-Qa'ida in Iraq and its Islamic State of Iraq was both factual and ideological. For example, the IAI letter complained of AQI: "Indeed, Sunnis in general have become a legitimate target for them, especially the wealthy: either he pays them what they want or they kill him. They try to kill anyone who criticizes them or goes against them and shows their error in such actions." The characterization of allegiance to the ISI as the "duty of the age" mirrors the fatwa issued by Hamid al-Ali, in which he urged retraction of the Islamic State.

Table 3.2. Islamic Army in Iraq's List of Grievances with Al-Qa'ida in Iraq and the Islamic State of Iraq

Factual Grievances	Ideological Grievances
AQI/ISI has leveled false charges against IAI, such as affiliation with the Ba'ath Party	Abu-Umar holds all lands of Islam to be lands of disbelief
AQI/ISI has threatened mujahidin from other groups with death if they did not pledge *bay'ah* to Al-Qa'ida and its other names	Abu-Umar said that the duty to fight Arab governments is greater than the duty to fight the "occupiers"
AQI/ISI wrongly killed over 30 fighters from other insurgent groups in Iraq	Abu-Umar said that jihad has been *fard ayn* since the loss of Muslim control in Spain; the IAI contends that this is opinion and has never been set down in writing
AQI/ISI kills any Sunni seen as being against the group, including religious figures and unarmed people; extortion of wealthy Sunnis	Abu-Umar stated that Ahl al-Kitab [people of the book; Jews and Christians] are belligerent and hold no right to protection
AQI/ISI has permitted attacks on peoples' houses and theft of their property	Abu-Umar referred to other jihad groups as "subversive"
AQI/ISI makes "widespread" use of takfir	Abu-Umar said that giving allegiance to the ISI is the "duty of the age" and not doing so is a sin
Abu-Umar made remarks belittling the jihad of non AQI/ISI groups	According to Abu-Umar, the permission of the Islamic State must be given before negotiating with the enemy

Source: Translated from Arabic. Letter published by the Combating Terrorism Center at West Point, http://ctc.usma.edu (accessed February 25, 2007).

In addition to outlining its grievances, the IAI also used the open letter to appeal simultaneously to several audiences. Each of the audiences was asked to respond with one or more specific actions. For example, Islamic scholars were asked to address IAI's unresolved ideological grievances, while al-Qa'ida leaders—especially bin Laden—were urged to take responsibility for IAI's multiple factual grievances against al-Qa'ida in

Iraq. Table 3.3 shows the audiences to whom IAI's open letter was directed and the responses sought from each audience.

Jihadist reaction to the Islamic Army's letter was explosive and highly negative. Jihadist website visitors vehemently criticized the Islamic Army for releasing the letter on the Internet. Instead of rallying the masses to IAI's side in its disputes with Al-Qa'ida in Iraq and the Islamic State, the IAI was accused of undermining the jihadist cause by fostering sedition—*fitnah*—within the ranks of the mujahidin. The use of the word *fitnah*, a term of extremely powerful religious overtones, was significant. Just as there are many Qur'anic injunctions for unity between Islamic groups, many of those same injunctions warn Muslims to avoid *fitnah*, which weakens the Muslim community. Accusations of weakening the community, especially during a time of war, are extremely serious.

A number of battles and hostile messages between the Islamic Army and al-Qa'ida in Iraq followed. Although the factual grievances listed by the Islamic Army—such as those involving extortion and bullying other jihad groups into pledging allegiance to al-Qa'ida—are certainly powerful arguments on the ground, they do not appear to have resonated well with the broader audience that follows jihadist websites on the Internet. In fact, most of the Internet audience is outside of Iraq. As a result, because groups such as the Islamic Army in Iraq have a national or local focus, their appeal is limited to a single country, or is subnational. This inevitably tends to make them less popular, and open to more criticism, than

Table 3.3. Islamic Army in Iraq's Target Audiences for and Desired Responses to April 2007 Open Letter

Audience	Desired Response
Islamic scholars	Issue legal rulings on unanswered or controversial issues; do not remain silent
Al-Qa'ida leaders (specifically, Usama bin Laden)	Take "legal and organizational" responsibility; "It is not enough to disown actions—the course must be corrected."
People affiliated with AQI	If you have done something wrong, repent to God
Other jihadist groups	Give "sincere advice" to AQI

groups such as al-Qa'ida that express an emphatic pan-Islamic agenda. Moreover, the Islamic Army's public image took a serious hit when several important jihadist websites began to refuse to carry the group's statements. A website closely aligned with AQI/ISI issued a statement condemning the IAI letter, eventually joined the boycott of the Islamic Army's statements, and began to prominently display the logo of the Islamic State of Iraq. Abu-Umar and the Islamic State's reaction to the IAI letter was notably lukewarm. Due to the widespread show of support for AQI and the Islamic State, no strong reaction was required on their part.

Ansar al-Sunnah

The announcement of the splintering of the Shari'ah Committee of the Ansar al-Sunnah Group was also made in April 2007. A statement signed by Abd-al-Wahhab Ibn-Muhammad al-Sultan, referred to as the "Chief of the Shari'ah Council and Judge of the Group," described the danger of division between the various insurgent groups in Iraq. He went on to express frustration with efforts to unify them. According to al-Sultan, the Shari'ah Council had been working for over two years to finalize the unification of insurgent groups. Such unification was seen as necessary in order to facilitate accomplishing four key objectives of the insurgency:

1. create a common, moderate approach, "without excess or abuse in seeking the approval of God";
2. increase religious education among insurgents, which had been lacking and in turn "deepened the mujahidin's dangerous behavioral and intellectual deviations";
3. strengthen ties between the insurgents and the Sunni populace and tribes; and
4. unite against common challenges.[45]

According to al-Sultan's statement, the unification initiative was coldly received by Abu-Abdullah, who was the amir of the Ansar al-Sunnah Group. Instead, the amir repeatedly put off discussion of the matter. Finally, much to the surprise of the Shari'ah Council, the amir issued a statement in which he attacked the goals of the unification plan and those who supported it.

This announcement came in the midst of a period marked by an unusually high volume of statements from the leadership and Ansar al-Sunnah Group's (ASG) amir, Abu-Abdullah. Beginning in March, ASG issued a number of statements alleging that the Coalition and the Iraqi government were engaging in a "media war" designed to confuse Muslims and create chaos in the ranks of the mujahidin in Iraq. For their part, ASG leaders denied that they had participated in talks with American forces, who were then attempting to reach out to a number of insurgent groups. In late March, Abu-Abdullah released a statement describing a recent meeting between jihadist groups in Iraq to discuss unification. Abu-Abdullah admitted that two ASG leaders, Abu-Sajjad and Shaykh Abu-Hind, had attended the meeting. In his statement, he claimed that they had not been asked to go and did not represent the official views of the group. Abu-Abdullah denied that ASG's Shari'ah Council had splintered, and he maintained that the two men left the ASG because of personal *ijtihad*, or legal interpretations. As part of his statement, Abu-Abdullah said that ASG believed that unification of groups is a religious duty, but one of the groups did not adhere to the Shari'ah and "causes problems."[46]

The first two points of al-Sultan's April 2007 announcement about the splintering of ASG closely resembled what was published on a private jihadist website by the Shari'ah and Judiciary Office of the Ansar al-Sunnah Group earlier that same year. That message also urged the jihadists to create a common, moderate approach and to increase religious education among the insurgents. In a message to Abu-Hamzah al-Muhajir, the amir of AQI, ASG's Shari'ah and Judiciary Office berated Abu-Hamzah for the kidnapping, torture, and killing of ASG personnel, allegedly by AQI members:

> You have been warned before about the behavior of some of your members who have reached the point of ill-thinking in an astonishing amount in accusing the Muslim who disputes with you of being a non-believer, and to regard blood feud (killing) him as lawful; meaning that the one who disputes you, it is permissible to shed his blood, and who-ever does not give authority to your Imam and group, it is permissible to (shed his blood), as well.[47]

The letter notes that ASG leaders have had a difficult time contacting Abu-Hamzah to discuss their concerns, and after a lack of response from the AQI leader, ASG posted the letter—originally a private communication—to a password-protected jihadist website. ASG noted in the letter that if it received no response from Abu-Hamzah on that site, it would post it to a publicly accessible website.

Other parts of the message to Abu-Hamzah pointed out that Shari'ah rulings are what keep Muslims from committing intellectual and conceptual mistakes and used different but similar words to allude to behavioral and intellectual deviations by mujahidin that were not specified in the Shari'ah Council announcement. Both statements also refer to abductions and killings between jihadist groups. Although it is difficult to tell for sure, it is possible that the Shari'ah Council that split away from the Ansar al-Sunnah Group wrote this letter to Abu-Hamzah. At the very least, the letter to Abu-Hamzah demonstrates that by early 2007 there was growing frustration and concern among Iraqi jihadists stemming from the fratricidal consequences of an increasingly aggressive brand of takfir that targeted even fellow insurgents.

Later that year, in December 2007, Ansar al-Sunnah announced that it was changing its name back to Ansar al-Islam, the name under which many ASG members operated until 2004. This move was probably intended to distance ASG from the Shari'ah Council splinter group.

The Jihad and Reform Front

Less than a month after its April letter, the Islamic Army in Iraq made another attempt to gather support against the Islamic State of Iraq. In early May, jihadist websites carried a message announcing the creation of the Jihad and Reform Front (JRF). The JRF claimed to unite the Islamic Army, Mujahidin Army, and the Shari'ah Council of the Ansar al-Sunnah Group. The al-Fatihin Army later joined the JRF on June 20, 2007. Abu-Abdullah, the amir of the Ansar al-Sunnah Group, issued a denial that it had joined, clarifying that the Shari'ah Council of the Ansar al-Sunnah Group is a splinter and does not represent ASG.[48]

The JRF's announcement included a description of the group's methodology and general policies. Not surprising, given the JRF's origins, its stated aims were very similar to the grievances outlined in the earlier letter issued by the Islamic Army.[49] Basically, the overall thrust of the JRF announcement was to present the group as a more flexible and moderate alternative to al-Qa'ida and the Islamic State. The JRF promised to focus its attacks on the "occupiers and their agents" instead of on innocents (i.e., presumably other insurgents). Among the other policies listed in its posting on the Internet, the JRF declared that it would forgive the "minor mistakes" of good people, spare the "blood, property, and honor of Muslims," and refrain from engaging in "side battles."[50]

Subsequent events demonstrated that the JRF was unable to accomplish the initial objectives outlined in its May 2007 announcement, despite the high hopes of the Islamic Army and those who hoped to use the JRF to combat al-Qa'ida in Iraq. The JRF failed from the beginning to create a large insurgent coalition to counter al-Qa'ida's influence in Iraq. At least publicly, the Islamic Army in Iraq abandoned its campaign against the Islamic State in June 2007, when IAI announced an agreement with ISI to stop the "escalation" of the military and media conflict between the two groups and form a committee to rule in all "cases" involving disputes between the two groups.[51] The JRF suffered further erosion of its power base in January 2008 when the al-Fatihin Army, which had joined the JRF in June 2007, withdrew. This apparently happened after al-Fatihin became convinced of the JRF's inability to reach what al-Fatihin termed "our intended goal"; the al-Fatihin statement simply said that the JRF's approach failed to meet the "realities of the arena of jihad," but did not offer additional details.[52]

Hamas-Iraq

Of all of the divisions and confrontations between jihadists in Iraq, the split of the 1920 Revolution Brigades was the cleanest. In March 2007, a statement was posted to jihadist websites announcing that the 1920 Revolution Brigades would be dividing into two distinct groups. The statement outlined the geographical division of Iraq's territory between the two groups, and it included provisions mandating the sovereignty of both. Both groups had agreed to share the name 1920 Revolutions Brigade, but also agreed that directly after this name would be the name of one of the two groups: Islamic Jihad Corps or Islamic Conquest Corps. This name-sharing agreement proved to be short-lived. Less than two weeks after making the agreement, the two groups changed their names again. The Islamic Jihad Corps reclaimed the name 1920 Revolution Brigades. The Islamic Conquest Corps announced it had adopted the name of the Islamic Resistance Movement in Iraq—Hamas-Iraq for short.[53]

In subsequent statements from the two groups, it became clear that the major difference between them was their willingness to participate in some sort of a political process inside Iraq. The 1920 Revolution Brigades issued statements reiterating their insurgent and jihadist credentials. The group proclaimed its disinterest in politics and negotiations with Iraqi or Coalition officials. As a result, the 1920 Revolution Brigades' rhetoric did not significantly shift, and the group appears to have continued on its original path. Hamas-Iraq also continued to engage in insurgent operations. At the same time, parallel to its activities supporting the military insurgency, Hamas-Iraq issued a number of statements underscoring the importance of the political process. Unlike the 1920 Revolution Brigades, Hamas-Iraq left the door to negotiations somewhat open by stating that negotiations could take place, but only with agreement from the "Iraqi resistance."[54]

Hamas-Iraq has portrayed itself as a moderate, centrist Islamist group. It claims to follow the ideology of Hasan al-Banna and Sayid Qutb and is comprised of Muslim Brotherhood adherents, while also including some Salafis and Sufis within its ranks. In its public statements, Hamas-Iraq also dismisses the idea that sectarian conflict between Iraq's Sunnis and Shiites is inevitable, saying that the two sects have lived and continue to live together in peace. The group further states that it is impermissible to use weapons to resolve "religious, sectarian, or racial disputes." Although it retains the name Hamas, the group denies any connection to the well-known Palestinian group, although it says that it agrees with Palestinian Hamas's goals and methods.[55]

CONCLUSIONS

The organizational dynamics of the global jihadist movement appear to be relatively fluid over time. In part, as the Algerian and Egyptian experiences demonstrate, this flexibility stems from pragmatic decisions made by individual leaders and their followers, who have had to respond to specific historical circumstances. It also is a by-product of the fact that global jihad is a mass movement. As Faisal Devji argues in his book *Landscapes of the Jihad*, the jihadist movement is similar to ethics-based social movements, such as the antiglobalization movement, in which largely autonomous action is often taken by individuals on their own initiative or in small groups because it is simply "the right thing to do."[56] Not surprisingly, the assumption of moral superiority embedded in a shared ideology creates powerful motivations for those individuals to act. At the same time, divergent priorities and varying local circumstances can create strong pressures for autonomy and decentralization within the mass movement, especially if it is widely dispersed geographically.[57]

The shift to a more decentralized organization has both benefits and costs for the jihadists. Bard O'Neill points out that it may undercut organizational efforts by fostering conflicting political and military policies, especially if rival groups are struggling for primacy in terms of resources and public support.[58] Decentralization also constrains the ability to plan, conduct, and support multiple operations simultaneously. Decentralization, however, may decrease the ability of security services to penetrate and eliminate jihadist groups and increase the ability of those groups to sustain prolonged underground operations.

Particularly in Iraq, insurgent groups have recently begun to shift away from staging entirely independent operations. The various groups have attempted—and with varying degrees of success—to operate under the auspices of an alliance or umbrella group. AQI's Mujahidin Shura Council and the Islamic State of Iraq illustrate this development. Additionally, locally focused insurgents created the Jihad and Reform Front as a more moderate approach to waging the insurgency and improving its relations with the Iraqi people. Another similar alliance, the Jihad and Change Front, appeared in the summer of 2007.[59] Hamas-Iraq and the Islamic Front for Iraqi Resistance forged an alliance in May 2007.[60] Each of these alliances is based, in part, on ideological similarities. Each also allows the various participants to retain their own autonomy while providing some protection in the face of increasing hostility between insurgent groups.

In many respects, the shifting patterns of organization reflect adaptive learning. Such adaptation has driven changes in response to successful countermeasures by security services combined with internal pressures to maintain the organizational status quo ante. The evolution of al-Qa'ida provides an example of this dynamic. The pre-9/11 era can be characterized by reliance on a traditional, hierarchically based structure that stressed a top-down leadership model, mirroring the approach followed by other militant groups. The post-9/11 era, especially since the fall of the Taliban regime in Afghanistan, offers evidence that al-Qa'ida has pursued a dual track. The original concept of top-down leadership flowing from bin Laden and al-Zawahiri remains, although their roles may have evolved into more symbolic, rather than decision-making, forms. At the same time, organizational decentralization has emerged, especially on the decision-making and operational levels. The ongoing insurgency in Iraq and the series of successful and unsuccessful terrorist bombings in Western Europe illustrate this new reality.

4

RECRUITMENT AND TRAINING

It is necessary that there should be a vanguard which sets out with this determination and then keeps walking on the path, marching through the vast ocean of *Jahiliyah* which has encompassed the entire world.

Sayyid Qutb, *Milestones*

LIKE ANY OTHER GROUP, the jihadist movement cannot survive without regularly adding to its membership through recruitment, radicalization, and training. Over time, it is essential to attract new members who are committed to the jihad to replace individuals who drop out, die, or are arrested by security forces. Without an ongoing stream of new adherents who become activists, instead of merely passive supporters, it is impossible for social movements—especially clandestine ones—to sustain operations, grow, and extend their reach.

This chapter examines how jihadist organizations like al-Qa'ida recruit and train members. It also explores the emerging, and more analytically challenging, question of how self-generating groups of activists may be inspired by the actions and rhetoric of larger umbrella organizations such as al-Qa'ida, or by the underlying philosophical foundations of the global jihad, to become jihadists.[1] The self-generating groups, which we refer to as "freelance" jihadists, are often no more than a small circle of friends who decide to join forces on their own. Once mobilized, they pursue violent jihad where they live. Although such groups share common attributes with larger organized groups like al-Qa'ida, the self-generating cells have significant differences that make them very difficult for security forces around the world to counter. Moreover, the emergence of these cells may well signal increasing reliance on the leaderless resistance model to wage the global jihad. Signs of the occurrence of this phenomenon are already evident. One need only look at the 2005 bombings in London or the 2007 attacks on Glasgow airport for examples.

Because this chapter focuses on a historical overview of recruitment by various groups making up the jihadist movement, it is important to understand that radicalization—while often an important part of recruitment—is a separate phenomenon. Radicalization, unlike traditional recruitment, can take place without a group. According to Marc Sageman, however, the transition from being radicalized to joining a terrorist group is a collective rather than individual process.[2] Many Muslims have developed a sense of moral outrage over the suffering of fellow Muslims in Chechnya, Iraq, or Palestine. Still others think that such incidents are indicative of Western assaults on Islam. For some Muslims, personal experiences and geopolitical grievances fuse into a general receptivity to jihadist interpretations of the world. At this point, the individual has become fully radicalized but has not actually become a jihadist. Those who take the next step and join a terrorist group or cell have embraced fully the jihadist movement.

Given the ever-increasing importance of the Internet as a vehicle for jihadist propaganda—much of which is an abstract form of recruitment in which the group has less contact with the individual and, therefore, less ability to customize the message for the potential recruit—radicalization certainly poses a significant threat to countries worldwide. This does not mean that structured recruitment will become irrelevant for jihadists: groups will continue to exist, and as such they will need at least some form of recruitment to continue to exist. Instead, it underscores that individuals join the jihad through a complex interplay of self-radicalization and formal recruitment processes that cultivate and reinforce radicalization. The two occur simultaneously, with some individuals choosing to join the jihad after being influenced primarily by self-radicalization, while others become jihadists after exposure to more formal recruitment. As a result, both a grassroots bottom-up approach and a more structured top-down dynamic influence radicalization and the transition to terrorism. The actual influence of those factors varies from individual to individual as well as over time because the movement continues to evolve.

THE RECRUITMENT CYCLE

For jihadist groups ranging from the Egyptian Islamic Jihad and Algerian GSPC to al-Qa'ida or Abu Sayayf, adding new members is fraught with danger. The safest course of action for any conspiratorial organization, taken in order to minimize the chances of discovery and disruption, is to limit the number of people knowledgeable about and/or involved in what is happening. To maximize operational security, the safest conspiracies rarely—indeed, if possible, never—add new members. Each person who is approached, and who ultimately decides to accept or reject recruitment, may compromise the group's security. Recruitment is, therefore, a sensitive act and must be undertaken with great care. Intelligence officers talk about a cycle of recruitment that convinces an individual to join a conspiratorial relationship or group. We summarize that process in this section but readily concede that the actual dynamics of recruitment will vary for specific groups as well as by context. Nonetheless, the basic elements of the process outlined in figure 4.1 apply, whether one is joining a large established organization or a small group of friends or relatives.

The first step in recruiting someone involves identifying a potential candidate who seems to meet the requirements for membership in the group. Identifying individuals who accept or at least respond to an ideology at some level, even if only to a rudimentary degree, is extremely important for recruiters in the early stages of the recruitment cycle. As Quintan Wiktorowicz points out, "Ideological affinity may predispose an individual to join, but friends and social connections tend to pull the individual toward participation. People make decisions, especially important ones, in a social context by discussing them with trusted others."[3] A primary goal for a jihadist recruiter is to become that "trusted other."[4]

Regardless of whether the candidate is seen as a potential fighter, logistical asset, or investigative or intelligence gathering asset, making the decision to bring the person into the group is fraught with danger. During this spotting period, the group will attempt to confirm the person's identity, making sure they know who he is before proceeding any further. Group members will undertake any investigation that is within their power in order to get as full a picture of the candidate as possible, and they will also decide how best to approach and engage that person.

The second stage in the process involves meeting and having one or more conversations with the person in order to assess a series of key factors: What motivates this person? What needs does he or she have? Are there issues that are of prime importance to the individual, and, if so, why? What about energy level? Does this person seem like the type to join the group in its mission? Another question that is often asked is whether or not the candidate can be visualized as taking part in the

Figure 4.1. The Recruitment Cycle

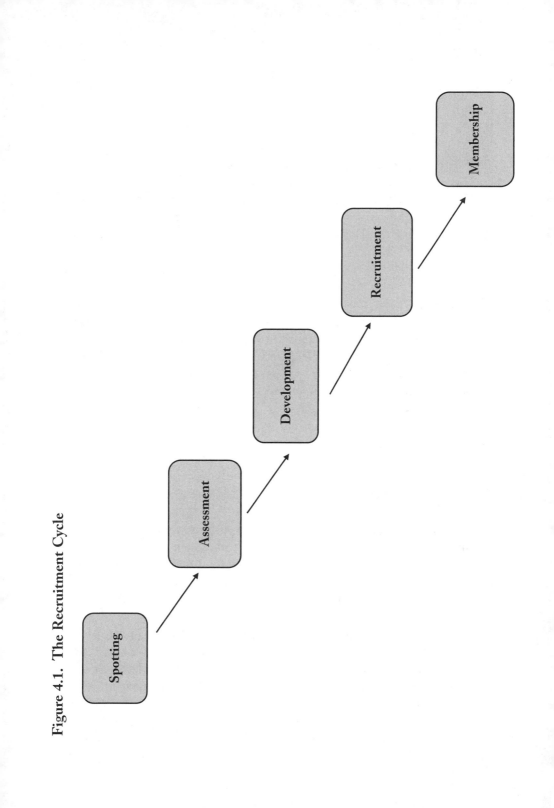

desired activity, or becoming a committed member of the group. Recruiters are asked, "Can you see this person taking action?" The assessment outlined above can be one-on-one, with the candidate interacting with a single recruiter, or the candidate may be brought before several members of the group who are acting as a recruitment team.

If the assessment is positive, the recruiter moves into high gear, building an in-depth relationship with the person. This stage in the process can have a fairly short time span or can take an extended amount of time, depending on the candidate and the circumstances. Most recruiters usually proceed with considerable caution in order to avoid tipping their hand too quickly. At each step in the development of an in-depth relationship, the recruiter is constantly reevaluating the candidate and judging the candidate's reaction to their evolving personal relationship. How skeptical is the target? Does the person seem to be wary? Or is the individual moving along with you intellectually, "getting it" as the relationship deepens? A primary goal of the development stage is to decide whether the candidate will agree if asked to join the group. If there is much doubt, then it is safer to stop the approach before anything harmful is revealed. The recruiter must evaluate one's own impact on the target; if they are not hitting it off, then perhaps another group member can be introduced who will be more appealing.

If the development stage proceeds satisfactorily and the person seems ready, then the candidate will be asked to join. Most recruiters will ask the question gingerly, creeping up on the big question by getting the candidate to agree to intermediate steps. In his case study of the U.K.-based al-Muhajiroun movement, an Islamic activist movement dedicated to establishing a caliphate wherever members live, Quintan Wiktorowicz says that the group's objective in the early stages of recruitment is to have the prospective jihadist assume personal ownership for the choice to delve more deeply into Islam. Conditioning the individual to take this step is done through a structured and intensive socialization process in which religious lessons and study groups are a central element. Jihadist recruiters employ this approach to identify "issues that are personally relevant to the individual to open a discussion about Islam and hopefully foster a cognitive opening," which helps facilitate possible receptivity to the movement's ideology; movement activists do not start off with discussions of reestablishing the caliphate.[5] Once a potential recruit shows signs of accepting a group or movement's worldview, the candidate is asked to do things that will perhaps demonstrate a willingness to enter into a full relationship with the group. If all signs are positive, the recruitment is attempted. If not, the process is stopped before the ultimate goal of the new relationship is revealed.

Once a candidate agrees to join, the process of actually admitting the person to the group is determined by group policies, the operational situation, the degree of secrecy under which the group operates, and the degree of trust the group has in the candidate. Usually, new members must further prove themselves by particular actions, or they must go through some sort of apprenticeship period before being allowed full membership in the group.

Each stage of the recruitment cycle poses risks to groups seeking to recruit new adherents to the jihadist cause. Numerous front organizations and false names may be used by radical Islamist groups to confuse authorities, and to divert credit for actions that the public may not approve of. The activist recruiter or front may also decide to conceal its true identity until after the potential recruit has made the decision to accept the ideology. Following this approach is a rational move for the jihadists, since merely approaching an individual may expose a previously unknown group's existence to discovery by the security services. For covert networks, each person approached is a potential informant who may decide to betray the group. Nonetheless, underground groups engaged in terrorism or insurrections must add new members to sustain their existence.[6] New recruits are also needed to expand capabilities to conduct simultaneous operations across multiple geographical areas, create a more visible presence, or enhance political influence. Even when jihadist groups are operating in an environment where the public generally is supportive, recruiting new members is still a risky endeavor. The more public their recruitment efforts, the easier it may be for opposition intelligence or security services to penetrate and place their agents inside the group. Hence, like covert groups, more open groups need to exercise caution when recruiting new members. As a result, even though the group may be working in a relatively supportive environment, recruitment of new members must still involve careful checking of the bona fides of each candidate, assessment of the candidate's suitability, and testing before allowing the candidate to know operational secrets or to get too close to other members.

This underscores the importance of vetting to test the loyalty of a new recruit. Vetting is the investigative process used by an organization to verify whether a candidate for membership should be allowed to join the group. The time required for a potential new member to complete the vetting process depends on the operational situation in which the organization finds itself. For jihadist groups, in the case of an open insurgency, new members can be put to the test quickly. They may be offered the chance to place a bomb, to shoot a person, or to take some other action that will promptly verify their sincerity about joining. Refugee camps also offer a venue for quickly vetting recruits, especially when the individual has regular contact with people outside the camp or an extended family within the refugee community who can be virtual hostages to ensure faithfulness to the cause. The recruitment opportunities offered by refugee camps are evident in the cases of Palestinian militant groups. Lebanon's twelve Palestinian refugee camps, for example, have long been lawless, and turf battles between various militant groups have plagued them for decades.[7]

For groups operating in complete secrecy, the process of accepting a new member is inevitably more complicated and lengthy. Entering a covert group is akin to entering into an espionage relationship or joining an ongoing criminal enterprise. Such groups seek to hide all their actions, conceal the names and faces of group members, and conduct meetings in secret locations in order to stymie opposition intelligence and security forces. Survival requires clandestine behavior, limiting knowledge of plans even among trusted members, a cell structure of some sort, and discipline. Mistakes can literally lead to the destruction of the group. Misjudgments may result in severe punishments. As a result, decisions are double-checked and assimilation of a new person is incremental, with testing conducted at each stage of the process.

It is important to understand, however, that recruitment as described above is not the only method by which the jihadist movement is supplied with new members to replace those killed or captured. Recruitment is largely an organizational function, driven by group representatives who guide the recruit's radicalization and provide contacts for further integration into the group.

Radicalization is not a synonym for recruitment. Formal recruitment does produce individuals who are radicalized prior to becoming full-fledged members of the group. Radicalization also can take place outside of the confines of the formal organization. Individuals can, in effect, radicalize themselves. The person who has acted as a "self-selector," like a traditional recruit, accepts the jihadist worldview and may act on violent impulses. It is plausible that self-selection will continue to occur, because the guidance and context for radicalization that were once provided by a traditional recruiter are now readily accessible on the Internet. As a result, there is an increased probability of what the Dutch government and others have labeled "local autonomous networks," which lack direct links to al-Qa'ida Central but rely on the same overall strategy and shared goals. The growth of these networks and the further radicalization of their members, who make the decision to engage in violence, is often triggered by events, such as the war in Iraq, that receive significant media attention.[8]

THE IMPORTANCE OF OPERATIONAL ENVIRONMENT

As noted above, the recruitment methods used to bring new members into jihadist groups reflect the operational environment in which the group finds itself. That environment ranges from highly covert, which mirrors the historical experience of terrorist groups, to open insurgency or insurrection bordering on civil war. Jihadists involved in an open insurgency, or operating in a setting where there is general support within the public for their goals, can recruit more or less openly. The open operational environment often is referred to as an "open front."

On the other hand, when the operational environment requires a high degree of secrecy, then recruitment activities necessarily are less transparent in order to avoid easy penetration by intelligence and counterterrorism forces.

When the operational environment is open or semi-open, recruitment efforts are both top-down and multifaceted. New recruits typically are solicited actively in a variety of contexts, including religious settings, school situations, and community activities. Individuals who already are jihadists can encourage their friends and relatives in a more or less open fashion to join in the movement. A 2007 West Point analysis of a list of over six hundred foreign fighter recruits for al-Qa'ida in Iraq found that many foreign fighters entering the country arrived with a group from their hometown, which indicates that AQI recruiters are likely to make a conscious effort to "try to attract groups of friends simultaneously."[9] The insurgent and refuge camp situations both lend themselves to open or semi-open recruitment. In an insurgent situation, jihadist militants may be seen by the community from which they are drawn as similar to an army fighting to protect their lands or people from an occupying force. In such an environment, although security is certainly a concern, new members may be invited to join in just about any setting in which people interact. A decision to participate in the movement is the stuff of patriots, lacks any hint of moral or ethical conflict, and requires little explanation other than an obvious willingness to fight for the cause. Open insurgency situations remove the ambiguity of affiliation for new recruits. After joining, new members can be quickly put to the test and may find themselves fully indoctrinated and deployed in very short order. While the insurgents may be condemned by the occupying nation as terrorists or criminals, their countrymen will generally view the fighters as sacrificing to protect others, much as recruits for any national army are viewed.

In refugee settings, or when a specific group clearly identifies itself as being persecuted, new members may be added to underground groups with less openness, but still in a manner that takes advantage of general social acceptance and support. If the refugees are under scrutiny by the local security service, joining must be accomplished in such a way as to preclude the immediate identification of new members. The group moves amid the refugee society, its activities cloaked from outside eyes but somewhat visible to trusted people inside the community. Fully supportive community members may provide hideouts, meeting sites, logistical support, or other assistance. Less supportive community members can generally be trusted to remain silent about what is going on, even if they do not fully endorse it. An example would be the recruitment of young people as suicide bombers in Palestinian settlements for actions in Israel. The news that someone has joined is not broadcast; in fact it is usually hidden from the recruit's family prior to the attack. However, immediately following the attack, there is general societal praise for the action, and an aura of religious and patriotic duty surrounds the bomber. This, at least indirectly, encourages others to follow in the same path.

In a clandestine group—or a group engaged in illegal, revolutionary, or terrorist acts—recruitment is equally vital if the group is to continue and flourish. Adding new members, however, inevitably poses a security risk to such a group's survival. It is not enough to merely assess the candidate to see if he or she appears to agree with the group's goals. It is also necessary to evaluate the proposed new member on a variety of other criteria. These include the individual's suitability for clandestine life; his or her willingness to take action, including committing violence against the group's opponents; his or her ability to submit to the operational discipline of the group, which may be harsh and involve limiting or ending social interaction with individuals outside the group; and the likelihood that the new member will not betray the group even if he or she makes the decision not to join. Covert groups are extremely likely to seek recruits among individuals who are well known to existing members, have backgrounds that are verifiable, or have some type of pre-existing relationship with one or more current members of the group.

Motivations for Radicalization and Recruitment

Why do people agree to join a conspiracy, an insurgency, or a terrorist group? Various theories have been advanced, all of which seem to explain some cases, but not others.[10] Indeed, numerous studies have been conducted attempting to describe or explain terrorist motivations. Some are individually based, with psychological constructs aimed at identifying personality characteristics that predispose a person to join a terrorist group. Others have focused on rational choice models, whereby the individual makes a decision to join based on group dynamics or as a result of an individual assessment of the situation. For example, according to Wiktorowicz, Islamic activists are less "grief-stricken reactionaries" than they are strategic thinkers acting rationally.[11] Political or sociological influences also may result in people joining a movement and continuing to play a role inside the organization. Those studies look at larger political, social, or economic pressures that influence people to join. For example, in some instances, individuals join because they are living in an occupied land or are part of a minority that is being subjected to harsh persecution. The terrorist group offers a means to resist. In other cases, individuals may be motivated to join because they have a predisposition to anger and violence.[12] For them, joining the terrorist group offers an attractive outlet for violent behavior. The motivating factors that lead other individuals to join the group may seem far less obvious. They may be leaving behind a privileged background, abandoning a family, or opting to cut short a life that seems filled with promise. The more contact we have with terrorist group members, the more apparent it is that there is no universal factor that motivates individuals to become terrorists or that accounts for terrorist behavior.[13]

Recruitment patterns in which social context functions to define one's identity and leads to involvement in Islamic radicalism are evident among jihadists. Numerous jihadist operatives have been converted to a life of jihad as a result of highly selective instruction by religious mentors. Looking for answers to personal problems, or to shortcomings in society generally, the recruits are given "the answer" and "the method" by which they can find personal fulfillment and undo perceived wrongs. The biographies of the bombers who attacked the London subway system in 2005 show young men who were dissatisfied with the tenor of the preaching at their mosques, and who came under the spell of a mentor who guided their further development and integration into a clandestine cell.[14]

Individual appraisals of self-interest can serve to motivate acts of terrorism too. An interesting study by Thomas Hegghammer on members of the group al-Qa'ida in the Arabian Peninsula offers insights into why individual members joined that group. Most were alumni of the battles in Afghanistan who had returned home to Saudi Arabia. As "Afghan Arabs," some of them experienced difficulty fitting back into society and thus gravitated to other former fighters who had shared their experiences. As their group evolved into an activist unit, members discussed harsh treatments and arrests they had suffered, and then agreed to take action. Some cited religious reasons for their actions, asserting that, because it was unacceptable for them as devout Muslims to have two religions on the peninsula, they had sworn personal oaths to fight polytheists (a term used by jihadists to refer derogatively to Christians, due to their belief in the Holy Trinity) and to get them out of the region. Others articulated political rationales, such as getting the United States to withdraw military forces from Saudi Arabia, or changing the current government. The group recruited from the top. Private discussions led to invitations to attend small group meetings. Some people were attracted by media campaigns on the Internet, but mutual affection was more important in bringing people into the group than was any formal recruitment process.[15]

Being involved in tense, high-stakes activities like terrorism or revolution is an addictive activity. Former revolutionaries will often speak with great nostalgia about their days as activists; younger people who leave the life will often seek a way to return to it, as was the case with many of the Afghan Arabs. The allure of action is a motivator for some recruits to terrorist organizations. One need only look at Internet websites that promote lengthy discussions of weapons and tactics, or at notebooks recovered on the battlefield that are adorned with drawings of Kalashnikovs, machine pistols, and similar weaponry. Al-Qa'ida videos of bin Laden or subordinates feature prominently displayed weapons, often in counterpoint to highly philosophical language.

In fact, the jihadists base their recruitment appeals on the lure of religion, combat, and being a revolutionary vanguard. For example, the author al-Suri lists the major reasons cited by jihadists in calling Muslims to fight:

1. So that infidelity does not prevail.
2. That men who are willing to fight are scarce.
3. Fear of damnation.
4. Performing a duty that is an answer to a divine call.
5. Following the teaching of the worthy ancestors.
6. Establishing a firm base for the development of real Islam.
7. Protection of the weak.
8. In hope of martyrdom.[16]

We note that this list is heavily oriented towards religious justifications, starting with the need to prevent infidels from prevailing. At the same time, although the religious underpinnings of jihad dominate al-Suri's litany, it is impossible to miss an implicit concern with acquiring and exercising political power.

The Appeal of Religion

For most individuals who become jihadists, joining a jihadist group is a direct outgrowth of their personal involvement in fundamentalist religious activity. Although fundamentalism is not a sufficient cause, it is a necessary precondition for making some individuals receptive to the jihadist message. In essence, devout Muslims are recruited or seek recruitment based on their piety and willingness to meet the demands of strict religious observance.

Because active engagement in the jihad is portrayed as a religious duty, joining a jihadist group provides tangible proof through deeds of the dedication to Allah that is expected of one who wishes to erase sin and enter into paradise. For the religiously motivated, justification of the actions to be undertaken depends heavily on selective quoting and interpretation of scripture, willful distortion of religious teachings, and demonization of opposing groups as enemies of God.[17] The concept of the "other" as totally evil and prepared to do harm to the truly faithful is key to explaining the legitimacy of the violent actions taken against them.

For the call of religion to resonate strongly enough for some Muslims to turn to violent jihad, religion needs to be the primary factor in defining one's identity. In addition, perceiving Islam as under attack or viewing one's religion as setting the individual apart from the larger society may contribute to radicalizing those Muslims for whom Islam defines their identity. Moreover, for Muslims living in countries beyond the borders of the traditional Muslim world, incomplete assimilation or acculturation—whether due to lack of acceptance by the dominant culture or unwilling-ness to achieve social integration—may contribute to some Muslims becoming receptive to answering the call to global jihad.

Data collected in a series of worldwide surveys conducted by the Pew Global Attitudes Project during the period from 2002 to 2006 can help illuminate the potential appeal of the call to religion.[18] We report the results of those surveys because they asked comparable questions over time, drew upon large samples of Muslims and non-Muslims, and were broadly inclusive from a geographical standpoint. The surveys were con-ducted in nonmajority Muslim countries in North America, Europe, and Asia, as well as in majority Muslim countries. Results for the surveys are based on telephone and face-to-face interviews of adults aged eighteen and older, using national samples, except in China, India, Morocco, and Pakistan, where the samples are disproportionately or exclusively drawn from urban areas.

The surveys reveal that large numbers of Muslims in predominately Muslim countries think it is very important for Islam to have a more influential role than it currently does in world affairs, and many of them believe that Islam faces serious threats.[19] Moreover, the significance attributed to Islam in the political life of many countries where it is the dominant religion is reflected in the large numbers of respondents who identify themselves first as Muslims and only secondarily by their nation-ality. Large majorities of Pakistanis (79%), Moroccans (70%), and Jorda-nians (63%) consider themselves to be Muslims first; a substantial percentage similarly identify primarily with their religion even in more secular countries like Turkey (43%) or Indonesia (39%).

At the same time, many European Muslims think that Europeans are hostile to Muslims even if they have had no negative personal experiences. The percentage of Muslims indicating that they think many or most Europeans are hostile to Muslims included 39% in France, 51% in Ger-many, 31% in Spain, and 42% in the United Kingdom. The perception that many Europeans are hostile towards Muslims is also held by many of their co-religionists in the Middle East, Sub-Saharan Africa, and Asia. For Muslims outside Europe, the percentages were 63% in Egypt, 36% in Indonesia, 50% in Jordan, 50% in Nigeria, 61% in Pakistan, and 57% in and Turkey.

Most European Muslims are generally satisfied with the direction that the country in which they live is moving. This is a positive outcome, especially since Muslim alienation from (as opposed to integration into) European society is a legitimate cause for concern. Nonetheless, Muslims' sense of belonging to the countries making up the European Union (EU) may be tenuous. A 2008 report by the European Monitoring Centre on Racism and Xenophobia (EUMC) says that it has documented a wide range of anti-Muslim or Islamophobic abuse across the EU's twenty-five member states.[20] The report warns that alienation and radicalization are likely unless EU governments and their Muslim populations work together to foster integration. The EUMC report is not surprising, since large majorities within the Muslim community voiced concerns about the future well-being of Muslims living in their respective countries. This angst ranged from as high as 80% of Muslims who participated in the surveys while living in the United Kingdom, 72% in France, and 69% in Spain, to as low as 59% in Germany.

This concern about belonging and integration mirrors a split between Muslims and non-Muslims in the United States and Europe in terms of opinions about whether Muslims want to assimilate. Large majorities of non-Muslim EU citizens, and also of Russians (perhaps not surprising given the ongoing conflict in Chechnya), expressed doubts about Muslims' desire to assimilate. For example, in 2005, majorities of non-Muslims in France (53%), Germany (76%), Russia (69%), Spain (67%), and the UK (64%) thought Muslim immigrants do not want to adopt their national customs and way of life. Even in the United States, a country whose civic culture traditionally has valued assimilating immigrants, a plurality expressed that opinion (44%), probably reflecting concerns in the aftermath of September 11. Muslims, on the other hand, were divided between those who sought to maintain separation from the larger society and those willing to adopt national customs after immigrating. The percentage of Muslims who expressed willingness to assimilate ranged from as high as 78% in France and 53% in the U.K. to as low as 41% in Spain or 30% in Germany. However, a sizeable segment of the Muslim population in each country thought Muslims coming to Europe today want to remain distinct from the larger, non-Muslim European society. This ranged from a majority of German Muslims (52%) to 35% of British Muslims, 27% of Spanish Muslims, and 21% of French Muslims.

And, even if assimilation and integration occur, there is clear disagreement between Muslims and non-Muslims over whether increasing a distinct sense of Islamic identity is desirable. Among both Muslims and non-Muslims, substantial majorities of Americans and Europeans thought by 2006 that the sense of a distinct Islamic identify among Muslims was growing in their country. Most Muslims agreed that this is a good thing. Most Westerners and Indians viewed the strengthening of Islamic identity as a negative, primarily stemming from concerns that it may lead to violence. The percentage of non-Muslims indicating that they thought a growing sense of Islamic identity in their country is a bad thing included 87% in France, 83% in Germany, 78% in India, 54% in Russia, 82% in Spain, 59% in the United Kingdom, and 46% in the United States.

The data summarized above underscore why the call to religion is likely to resonate among some Muslims, leading them to embrace violent jihad, especially if their religion serves as the locus for defining their personal identity and they think that that religion is under attack. Moreover, such attitudes are likely to persist unless the pattern of disgruntlement with current conditions and the bleakness of political prospects is transformed—especially in the Arab world.

The Call to Battle

For jihadists, the idea of rallying to the cause of restoring the caliphate and the preeminence of Islam provides a second powerful inducement. In the case of the global jihad, the call to battle resonates with people from all walks of life who agree that there is a common threat to their vision of the Muslim world. It combines religious fundamentalism with appeals to defend Islam against clearly defined, historical enemies—the West, Zionism, and apostates. Moreover, grounding recruitment in appeals to defend Muslims against attacks or perceived injustices can enhance the attractiveness of the cause, thereby facilitating recruiting. This type of recruiting is public and broad-based while also selectively narrow in focus.

The American-led coalition's invasion of Iraq has made possible relatively public and fairly broad-based recruiting for the insurgency among jihadist groups, especially within the Sunni population of Iraq and neighboring countries such as Saudi Arabia.[21] Examination of jihadist websites reveals that, consistent with the jihadist worldview, the overthrow of the Ba'athist regime and occupation of Iraq is constantly depicted in propaganda as a strike against Islam. Moreover, as with Afghanistan in the 1980s, a general call could be made to the Muslim public to support the new mujahidin in a struggle against a superpower. Again, this supports their propaganda efforts by making it possible for jihadists to invoke the powerful symbolic imagery of the fight against the Soviet Union in Afghanistan, where co-religionists came to the aid of fellow Muslims to defeat the invader. Those recruiting efforts have been extended to Muslims beyond the Middle East through the revolution in access to mass communications, especially the Internet and such satellite television networks as al-Jazeera, which conveys images of the insurgency to all corners of the globe.

At the same time, while also sometimes public or quasipublic, more narrowly focused recruiting efforts have been made in parallel to the broad-based, open appeals and occur in more controlled environments. These efforts concentrate on more circumspect solicitation and emphasize enlisting the help of selected individuals who could bring critical skills to the jihadist cause. For example, people with a particular ethnic background, language skills, or technical expertise might be needed to attack specific targets. Recruiting them in carefully chosen settings facilitates greater control over who actually knows an individual is being recruited to join the jihad.

The Lure of Conspiracy

Jihadist groups operating in areas where there has been no defining act, such as an invasion, and where the general populace may not be in agreement with their stated goals are forced to forego most public recruitment in favor of private activities. In discussing this recruitment mode, we need to note the following caveat: our information is limited to published accounts and to our own experiences dealing with people who are involved in clandestine groups generally and terrorist groups specifically. Although outside observers cannot acquire full details about the actual recruitment process of a secret organization, it is possible to look at published accounts of individuals who joined jihadist groups to discern patterns and similar processes at work. In addition, because we have worked directly with hundreds of people involved in clandestine work, we can make some generalizations about the nature of the decision to join a secret relationship.

Adding people to an existing secret organization involves modifying the recruitment approaches described in the "open front" setting. A group like al-Qa'ida that has clearly defined itself, and that has name or "brand" recognition, can do some recruiting in a public manner, even though the group itself is in hiding. Al-Qa'ida has done public recruiting through published statements, video exhortations released to the media, online magazines and websites, and Internet discussion groups. Such activity aims to keep the message in front of potential recruits, but it obviously stops short of telling the reader how to make contact and to join.

Clandestine organizations typically use as recruiters those members who are skillful in interpersonal relations and who have the ability to make accurate assessments of others. The successful recruiter will combine some of the skills of the salesman, gambler, and evangelist, along with an ability to discuss religion, politics, or both. The recruiter must be able to identify and gain access to groups that are likely pools of candidates. Once in the group, the recruiter skillfully adapts his sales pitch to fit the needs and beliefs of the people being targeted.

Joining an organization that operates in secrecy typically involves some sort of introduction of the candidate to the group in suitably secure surroundings. People attending religious functions aimed at the most fanatical believers, students in religious schools, followers of religious leaders who are openly radical, prisoners who share a religious orientation, and exiles, refugees and Diaspora members huddled in big city ghettos are all potentially of interest. Approaches to these people must be private and discreet but can be made in carefully selected groupings. These "private, group" recruitment pitches have the advantage of drawing on peer pressure from others in the group to encourage joining. Martial arts groups, sports clubs, and similar social settings may be ideal for a private group approach.

Other potential recruits must be approached one by one. These candidates may be deemed too sensitive for any contact in public because of the mission planned for them, or the recruiter may believe that, in order to secure the target's cooperation, only a private discussion will work. In some cases, the candidate may not be active in an organization that lends itself to contacting him in a group setting. For whatever reason, some people will be asked to join in a "private, single" setting. Some of these recruits may never acknowledge membership and are destined for undercover missions or for collecting intelligence. Others recruited singly will be assimilated into the group in exactly the same fashion as new members acquired via recruitment through group or general appeals.

PSYCHOLOGICAL CATALYSTS FOR VIOLENCE

People join a movement for various reasons, including a belief that membership can satisfy personal psychological needs. In addition to ideology, a variety of psychological factors can function as catalysts to change or modify the level and type of violence associated with the jihadist movement. The jihadist movement affects each of the primary situational variables that, Dave Grossman argues, are likely to influence or enable people to kill others: authority, group absolution, and social distance from the victim.[22] The leadership of the jihadist movement combines an ideology that provides an overarching motive with a framework for action couched in religious authority. This fosters acceptance of terror as a moral imperative, which allow terrorists to transfer responsibility for their actions onto others.

Group absolution similarly exerts a more powerful influence as identification with the group, proximity of the group, intensity of the group's support for killing, size of the immediate group, and the legitimacy of the group increase, and as it becomes more salient as a primary reference point. "Group think" and social conformity diffuse responsibility and enable people to act harshly as they conform to group norms. Moreover, the dynamics of prolonged clandestine operations magnifies the centrality of the group as the primary source of information, confirmation, and security.[23] The intense "hot house" environment of an active group operating clandestinely translates and intensifies highly subjective group interpretations of options and events. The probability that individuals will participate in killing significantly increases as jihadists bond with their comrades; this is partially due to a need not to let them down, and partially due to the sense of anonymity given to individuals in groups, which can contribute further to a willingness to commit acts of violence.[24]

Not surprisingly, dehumanization of victims through increased cultural, religious, or social distance removes moral constraints against killing.[25] For terrorist groups to be effective in reaching their violent goals, recruits must be converted into dedicated combatants who are committed to the groups' success. In the jihadist movement, much of this process of psychological transformation takes place even before actual recruitment; it is part of the vetting exercise and is nurtured through the consumption of ideological propaganda. The goal of this process, as with most other terrorist groups, is to cognitively restructure "the moral value of killing, so that the killing can be done free from self-censuring restraints," with the end-goal being that the recruit takes pride in destructive accomplishments.[26]

The concept of eighteenth-century theologian Ibn-Abd-al-Wahhab, for whom "Wahhabi" Islam is named—"whoever does not do *takfir* of the disbeliever is a disbeliever himself" (*takfir* being the Arabic word for declaring a Muslim to be an apostate)—is a strong incentive to fall in line with the thinking of the overall group. Declaring an individual takfir is somewhat analogous to excommunication in the Christian sense; however, in the jihadist mind, to be an apostate is punishable by death.

Although group dynamics can affect cognitive processes, strong individual motivations also exist to encourage terrorists to commit violent acts. As Marc Sageman notes, most jihadists are enthusiastic about killing and not just responding "to social pressures and group dynamics."[27] Indeed, in the current environment, a jihadist recruiter need not explicitly spell out the need to be prepared to kill, since it is generally assumed by all.

Lengthy and painful prison terms in a variety of Muslim countries, especially those that involve abuse and torture, exact a psychological toll and have also fostered increased support for violent jihad. Because so many of the leading figures, such as Qutb and al-Zawahiri, who have shaped the jihadist ideology once were imprisoned, prison radicalization and recruitment into Islamic militant groups is an issue that warrants serious thought and attention.[28] The humiliation and trauma of torture becomes a useful propaganda tool for many militant groups, spawning a rationale for revenge.[29] Al-Zawahiri's own prison and torture experience is said to have radicalized him greatly, as was the case with many other Egyptian militants who subsequently joined al-Qa'ida. In Egypt, imprisonment created a stream of recruits and training centers for radicalism. Ironically, given the regime's desire to suppress radical Islam, harsh prison conditions actually accelerated radicalization and provided the prisoners with the opportunity to discuss their plans and ideology. The shared prison experience, especially in Egypt from the 1950s to the 1970s, altered the future path of Islamist militancy. The prisons turned out to be effective networks that hardened the resolve of many militants, who emerged from prison far more dangerous and much more committed to actively waging jihad than when they went in.[30]

The Egyptian case is not unique. Other nations have also witnessed how prisons can serve as incubators for the radicalization and recruitment of new adherents to the jihadist cause. For instance, in 2005 a group arrested in the United States on charges of plotting terrorist actions was entirely made up of prisoners and ex-convicts who had joined together in a jihadist cause while in prison. This suggests that a variety of factors, potentially involving the interplay of individual attributes and group dynamics as well as environmental factors, account for the willingness of individuals to join the jihad and engage in acts of terrorism.

Training for Violent Jihad

Once recruited for the cause by an organization, new members have to undergo training if they are to be effective, trusted, and valuable to the jihad. The type of training a new member receives is directly linked to the job or jobs the individual is destined to perform inside the movement. Where and when he receives training is similarly dependent on what role he will play. Regardless of the new member's ultimate role within the movement, a key element typically is basic paramilitary training in the same skills taught to other insurgents and even to trainees in regular armies. What sets jihadist training apart from simple insurgent training is the possibility of further training in terrorist tactics, assassination, kidnapping, and similar nontraditional military skills.

For jihadist groups, religious training is paramount. Although the new recruit or volunteer has almost certainly been indoctrinated to some extent in the Salafist interpretation of Islam, becoming an active jihadist requires unwavering acceptance of the worldview outlined in chapter 1. By infusing religious dogma into the training regimen, the new recruit is immersed in the thinking of those Islamic theoreticians whose writings serve as guides to the jihad (and who have been discussed earlier in this book). Indoctrination in the religious dimension underlying the jihad is augmented during training by drawing on illustrations of attacks on believers and threats to the Islamic faith around the world. For example, in early 2007 jihadist training focused on the attacks against the Islamic Courts Council in Somalia; on the role of the United States in supporting the Ethiopian military, which ousted the Islamists from power; and on the ongoing insurgencies in Afghanistan and Iraq.[31] Depending on the setting and the group involved, the actual teaching of this religious element may vary from straightforward indoctrination to a more sophisticated approach, in which ongoing discussions that promote some element of self-discovery are encouraged. The religious element of the training is designed to produce doctrinal and intellectual preparation in the new member that will translate into a willingness to fight, a clear identification with the jihad, and the moral strength required.[32] In addition to traditional paper copies of jihadist texts, the Internet has become a source of jihadist religious training materials, which are readily available on Arabic-language websites sympathetic to the cause.

Like other organizations, jihadist groups have to introduce new members to the mores of their society. Who is in charge? What are the requirements of membership? How does one progress in the organization? All these elements of "joining" must be explained along with the unwritten rules of fitting into the new social structure. In most cases, new members are also introduced to some level of clandestine behavior. This indoctrination will proceed according to the operational milieu in which the group operates. Like espionage operations, it may be as simple as using "war names" for members and introducing the "need to know" concept; or it may require a more comprehensive immersion in conspiratorial behavior, clandestine communication, and tradecraft.

The training experience also includes some sort of introduction to the operational environment of the struggle. In his definitive work, *The Call to Global Islamic Resistance*, al-Suri refers to this type of training as preparing the candidate in combat capabilities and developing him for joining in the battle. For example, if the group is involved in an ongoing insurgency, training will be provided on the differences between urban and rural operations, the fundamentals of guerrilla activity, and insurgent organization and goals. This type of training is excellent for members who will take part in the "battle in the first stage of guerrilla warfare, especially urban combat," according to al-Suri.[33] Similarly, if the goal is to create terrorist operatives, then training must stress the role of terrorism as a tool in the arsenal available to the jihad.

More advanced operational training will depend on the role of the candidate. He may be given explosives, small arms, communication, or logistical training as required. If the new member is in a training camp environment, he will likely be given a version of basic training that will emphasize physical fitness, intellectual orientation, an introduction to tactics, and a basic familiarization with weaponry. If the training is being conducted secretly in homes or similar locations, there will be obvious constraints on how much of this gets done. Specialized advanced training will build on the basic instruction and will be designed to provide skills needed for the planned mission.

Large-scale Training Camps

Training camps require space and security to operate. In terms of building a network of individuals who share common bonds, it is impossible to overstate the value of having a secure site in which to conduct the training of jihadist operatives. Whether one thinks of religious indoctrination or realistic hands-on explosives training, having a safe spot where the training can be conducted without interruption is extremely beneficial. Training camps provide more than seclusion and security. They also allow for the creation of a controlled environment where the recruits can be immersed fully in the new group, continually evaluated and tested, and gradually initiated into the organization.

Prior to the fall of the Taliban and the removal of al-Qa'ida from Afghanistan, the Taliban government served in the role of a state sponsor, allowing al-Qa'ida to operate freely in its territory. Al-Qa'ida operated a network of secure and secluded training camps that were dedicated to converting recruits into trained jihadists prepared for active service. Other camps existed outside Afghanistan. Those camps were equally effective in the training they provided. However, they were forced to operate with considerably more circumspection than were the camps in Afghanistan. As a result, the loss of the Afghan sanctuary was a major victory for counterterrorism forces, but it has not amounted to the final defeat of the global jihad that some hoped for in 2002.

When al-Qa'ida had its training camps in Afghanistan, those sites were ideal for the full spectrum of training. The isolation of the Afghan training camps effectively removed the recruits from external influences or sources of information that might conflict with or moderate al-Qa'ida's socialization processes. Instead, the recruits found themselves embedded in an intense social setting where everyone was engaged actively in discussing and thinking about the global jihad. The total control that the camps had over recruits' activities made it possible to combine religious indoctrination with operational training. Not unlike basic training in the military, by removing the recruits from their previous civilian settings, it was possible to put recruits into stressful situations and then evaluate their performance and suitability for intended missions. Real or artificial stressors could be placed on the trainees to give their instructors chances to evaluate their suitability for the intended missions. Moreover, the ability to alternate one type of training in the camps with another—for instance, having a religious session following time on the shooting range—allowed recruits to easily infer the connection between the philosophy and practice of the movement.

We know that most people who went through al-Qa'ida training camps were exposed to the idea of jihad, to religious instruction, and to basic military skills. They did not, however, become full-fledged members of al-Qa'ida. A smaller number of recruits who passed through the camps, however, did become al-Qa'ida operatives. For example, the September 11 hijack teams were given intensive training apart from other trainees. The pilots were given different training than the "muscle" teams. As a covert operation, we can be certain that the identities of the September 11 hijackers were well protected and kept secret from others who might be in and around the camps.

The initial course was more basic insurgency training than any sort of effective preparation for life as a terrorist. Testimony from graduates indicates that the first two months or so of training were heavily focused on weapons handling (rifles, handguns, light antitank weapons, surface to air missiles), religious indoctrination in the afternoons, and sports or physical training.[34] After finishing their basic training, the majority of the recruits were not accepted into the al-Qa'ida movement; instead, they were sent home to return to their normal lives. Some trainees, who came to the camps seeking adventure, went back to their homes bragging about learning to fire Kalashnikovs, but they were well aware of the fact that they wanted nothing further to do with the dedicated fanatics who ran the camps. Still other trainees, who were interested in going further in the organization, were told to go home and await further contact. Most of these graduates were not really "sleepers" so much as they were partially trained volunteers who might someday prove valuable to the organization, but for whom there was no pressing need for service. For example, Khalfan Khamis Mohammed, a support asset who eventually played a logistical role in the bombing of the U.S. Embassy in Tanzania, went through basic training and was sent home. He was later asked to go to Somalia to be an instructor there. Following that stint, he was again dropped from active service and only later reactivated by al-Qa'ida when his nationality and language skills became important for the embassy bombing operation.[35]

Selected trainees who seemed most suited for use as operatives were given specialized training following the standard basic sessions. The Darunta training camp west of Jalalabad in Afghanistan was used by al-Qa'ida for training in the fabrication and deployment of high explosives. Students there were graduates of basic training at other camps and were exposed to more than basic military explosive training. The Darunta trainees were also taught how to fabricate explosives and detonators from scratch. A number of recruits who were destined to undertake terrorist missions received training at this camp, including Ramzi Yousef (planner of the 1993 World Trade Center attack) and Ahmed Ressam (who planned the attack on the Los Angeles airport). This was also the camp where experiments were conducted in the use of chemical and biological weapons.

Training camps can also operate in areas where an active insurgency is under way. Alternately, in some countries it may be possible to run a training camp in an area that is outside governmental control. In insurgent situations, although the camps may be forced to be mobile or more hidden, they have the advantage of completely immersing the recruit in the real world of insurgent tactics from the very beginning of the training process. Trainees in such camps may be used as insurgents upon graduation or, if they are from other countries, may be sent home to carry out missions there.

Al-Suri writes about the effectiveness of training in camps and suggests that small groups of 5–12 people are the ideal class size.[36] Al-Suri goes on to assert that, while organized camps provide the best possible venue for training, they also offer a target for penetration and monitoring by security forces. He also worries that having different groups in the camps may lead to competition between the groups, especially if some groups are singled out as special. Acknowledging that the primary function of the camps is to provide basic training, he laments that some opportunities for "methodological" (i.e., ideological) instruction are lost in these settings.

While training camps have definite advantages, there are some downsides to their use. Trainees are often brought in from some distance and the costs in money and supporting manpower are significant. To avoid undue attention from hostile forces, the jihadists have to use clandestine networks to move the trainees into the camps so that their identities do not become known before they ever begin. Alliances will form in the camps among trainees that may result in later contacts among camp alumni that negate attempts to keep people in tightly controlled cells.

Training without Large Camps

Since the 2001 American invasion of Afghanistan and overthrow of the Taliban regime, maintaining large training camps has become more difficult for jihadist groups. There are still countries where such camps can operate in an open or quasi-open mode, but the number of suitable sites is constantly dropping. As a result, more training must now be conducted in ways that permit instruction of new recruits even if there is active opposition from security forces. In his writings, al-Suri proposes a possible solution to this problem. He points out that in the Algerian insurrection a great deal of training was done successfully in private homes. Instead of sending recruits to a camp, al-Suri advocates having jihadist trainers work among the population by conducting training in private homes or comparable locales. Given the demand among radical Islamists for training, if security services prevent camps from operating, in-home or similarly private settings may be the most viable option for training volunteers.

Although it typically is not feasible to practice shooting or small unit tactics in homes or apartments, it is entirely feasible to train recruits in a variety of topics, such as light weapons familiarization, physical fitness, and the fabrication and deployment of explosive devices.[37] Such locations are also convenient venues for providing intelligence collection, surveillance detection, and conspiratorial communications training. Numerous jihadist websites include extensive collections of training manuals that can be downloaded and used by individuals or by groups at their leisure; *al-Battar Camp*, the premier jihadist training magazine published by al-Qa'ida in the Arabian Peninsula for nearly a year, was hugely popular and covered everything from instruction in using weapons to case studies for assassinations and ambushes. Military manuals are also available on the web and from book dealers; they teach weapons disassembly, explosives, wireless communications, military topography, encryption, operational security, and movement and surveillance. For example, the radical Islamists who carried out the July 7, 2005, attacks in London used homemade organic peroxide-based devices that are easily fabricated from readily available materials.[38] Instruction for making such devices can be found in various publications and websites.

Some jihadist groups have used recreational activities at public venues, such as white water rafting, laser tag, and paintball shooting games, as means of imparting skills, forming bonds among members, and allowing recruits to test themselves. Skills required for conspiratorial behavior, such as identifying surveillance and conducting activities without notice in public places, can similarly be taught out in the open without much risk of discovery. Trainees can be sent out to conduct mock target studies of given installations to allow them to gain experience prior to attempting the real thing.

Training of volunteers will be determined by the role envisioned for them. Support assets, who will be used to do things like acquire safe sites, vehicles, and supplies, need not have the same level of training as support assets who will be used to gather materials for improvised explosive devices. Candidates who will be used to do target studies or casings will require a different set of skills than either of the categories of trainees mentioned above. Central to all levels of operatives is a basic introduction to conspiratorial behavior, or what intelligence services call clandestine communications or "tradecraft." This instruction prepares the candidate for life as an operative, focusing on things like being aware of one's surroundings and having an explanation for why the candidate is in a particular place or engaged in a particular activity. Methods of conducting secret meetings, passing messages, and identifying hostile surveillance must be taught. This type of training lends itself very well to instruction in private homes or similar settings. The candidate is first sensitized to the problem, then given an intellectual understanding of the techniques, and finally taken out on the street to simulate making meetings, conduct observation tasks, and spot potential problems. The skills learned in this type of training provide a basis for any type of conspiratorial work, and they provide the basic indoctrination any future operative will require.

Advanced forms of conspiratorial training include techniques like the use of encryption in messages, how to use the Internet for communication without being discovered, secret writing techniques, and the use of false documents.[39] Just as was the case with the basic military training, conspiratorial training provides an excellent means of assessing the candidate and evaluating his or her potential for future work. Candidates who adapt well to the training are more likely to be successful than are less skilled trainees who fail to catch on to the concepts being taught.

Depending on the location where the training must occur, even some basic firearms instruction can be conducted. At a minimum, recruits can be exposed to weapons manipulation, use of sights, trigger control exercises, and emergency action drills that can be conducted without the need to actually fire any weapons. If recreational target shooting is permitted, then actual experience with weapons can be gained under cover of sport. Even if such shooting is discouraged or illegal, it may be possible to find out-of-the-way locations that will permit some weapons use. Jihadists in New York State, one of the most restrictive environments in terms of regulating private ownership of firearms in the United States, were able to conduct weapons training with highly illegal automatic weapons in remote areas prior to the first World Trade Center bombing.

In spite of our focus on training, it must be remembered that much of what a terrorist might be asked to do can be done with almost no real preparation. Suicide bombers seldom receive any real instruction. Many bombers have been recruited to simply drop off the devices in target locations without knowing anything about explosives. Spontaneously emerging groups that lack contact with any established terrorist network may be able to get all the materials they need from the local library, the Internet, or via mail order book services. Groups that arise from the indigenous population have far less need for the trappings of clandestine communication and conspiratorial behavior than do groups of "outsiders" who are under more scrutiny. The practice of broadcasting material suitable for the training and preparation of terrorist operatives through the Internet is an alarming—and probably unstoppable—threat to counterterror forces. In many ways, the specter of would-be jihadists training on their own is more of a challenge to security forces than the idea of centralized training by organized groups in camps, even though training camps can produce much more capable fighters.

PORTRAIT OF THE JIHADISTS

Who then has responded to those recruiting and training efforts? In order to develop a portrait of the jihadists, we turn to three databases: the list of Guantánamo detainees, the martyrs list of insurgents who died in Iraq, and the al-Qa'ida in Iraq/Mujahidin Shura Council list of eminent martyrs. When analyzed as a set, the three databases provide information about where the jihadists actually come from as well as whether the over-whelming number of recruits are young.

The Guantánamo list consists of 759 individuals detained from January 2002 through May 2006; they were processed through the Combatant Status Review Tribunal (CSRT) process conducted by the U.S. Department of Defense (DoD) to determine whether the detainees had been correctly classified as illegal enemy combatants. Because the nationality of the detainees was recorded, the Guantánamo list released by the DoD provides a sense of the international appeal of the jihad prior to the fall of the Taliban in Afghanistan. Most, but not all, of the detainees were captured in Afghanistan after September 11. Following capture, they were denied prisoner of war status by the Bush administration and declared to be "unlawful combatants" in a foreign theater of conflict.

After the U.S. Supreme Court's *Hamdi v. Rumsfeld* (452 US 507) ruling in November 2004, the Bush administration began using the CSRT process to determine the status of detainees held at Guantánamo Bay, Cuba, as possible enemy belligerents under Article 5 of the Third Geneva Convention.[40] The use of the CSRT is based on the Bush administration's position that the tribunals fulfill the obligations of Article 5, which entered into force on October 21, 1950. Each tribunal is composed of three U.S. military officers who were not involved previously with the detainee. One of the officers is a judge advocate (i.e., attorney). Detainees have the right to testify before the tribunal, call witnesses, and introduce any other evidence. Following the hearing of testimony and other evidence, the tribunal determines in a closed-door session whether the detainee is being properly held as an enemy combatant. Any detainee determined not to be an enemy combatant is supposed to be transferred to their country of citizenship or receive other disposition consistent with domestic and international obligations and U.S. foreign policy. Detainees also are supposed to be notified of their right to seek a writ of habeas corpus for relief in the federal courts of the United States.

The other two databases—the martyrs list and the AQI/MSC Eminent Martyrs list—are compilations of individuals identified as martyrs during the ongoing insurgency in Iraq. Each list is more recent than the Guantánamo list, and both lists were posted on the web. Because foreign fighters dominate both lists, they provide insights into where the call to global jihad resonates most strongly. The martyrs list was compiled and released by Moheb al-Jihad (Jihad Lover) in May 2005. Moheb al-Jihad claims that he is not part of any jihad group, and that he compiled the names and information for his list from jihadist websites. Al-Jihad also apologizes for the shortage of Iraqi names on the list; he says that information on them is more difficult to find. His list consists of 395 individuals, and all but six of them are identified by name. The cause and location of death are not always obvious from the list, although the most frequent location listed when one was given was al-Fallujah, so many of them probably were killed during the sieges of that city.

The AQI/MSC Eminent Martyrs list contains twenty-seven names. It was complied from the *Biographies of Eminent Martyrs,* which was released by AQI/MSC starting in October 2005 and generally was published every one to three weeks until October 2006. Each publication usually covered one martyr. Sometimes two or three were included if all of them were killed in the same operation. The publications provided individual biographies of about ten pages. Unlike the martyrs list, the AQI/MSC Eminent Martyrs list indicates the cause of death for twenty-six of them. Eight died in suicide operations, while eighteen were reported killed in combat.

The Guantánamo Detainees

The overwhelming majority of the Guantánamo detainees (68%) were not released after undergoing the CSRT process.[41] Not surprisingly, because most of the detainees were captured in Afghanistan, table 4.1 reveals that almost 29% of the prisoners who completed the CSRT process are Afghans. The Afghans were captured while active military operations were ongoing against the Taliban. Almost half of them subsequently

Table 4.1. Region of Origin for the Guantánamo Detainees

Region	% (n)
Afghanistan	28.6 (217)
Neighboring Countries	12.3 (93)
Core Arabs	39.9 (303)
Maghreb Arabs	8.7 (66)
Sub-Saharan Africa	2.2 (17)
Europe	3.7 (28)
Other	4.6 (35)

were released from detention at Guantánamo Bay (48%). Another 12% of the prisoners came from neighboring countries.[42] Approximately 9% are Pakistani (79% released) and 3% are other Central or South Asians (30% released).[43] For those Afghans and their neighbors—the "locals"—who were not released, the jihad in Afghanistan was essentially a local effort.

However, the remaining 59% of the detainees, whom we call "travelers," made a conscious decision to travel often long distances to Afghanistan. In fact, as of mid-May 2006, only 21% of the "travelers" were released after going through the CSRT process. Hence, for "travelers" the choice is a clear sign of a personal commitment motivated by religious zeal or a sense of adventure to engage in a global jihad.[44] They can be viewed as representative of the hardcore jihadists.

In analyzing the Guantánamo list, we have chosen not to focus on the Afghan, Pakistani, or other Central or South Asians. By concentrating primarily on the "travelers," we can develop a reasonable sense of the extent to which al-Qa'ida had a broad appeal within radical Islamist circles prior to September 11. Table 4.1 reveals that the Afghan camps attracted radical Islamists from literally all corners of the globe. Muslims from the core Arab countries of the Middle East—especially Saudi Arabia (18%) and Yemen (14%)—make up almost 40% of the detainees.[45] Each of the other core Arab countries account for only a handful of the "travelers" who became detainees. For example, although Egyptians such as Qutb have played a major role in shaping the ideology of the global jihad, and others like al-Zawahiri have played key roles in leading al-Qa'ida, very few of the detainees are Egyptians (approximately 1%). Not surprisingly, given the ongoing conflict between the Israelis and Palestinians, very few Palestinians became detainees (less than 1%). Arabs from the Maghreb nations of North Africa account for almost 9% of the detainees.[46] Algerians constitute the largest contingent (38%) of the Maghreb Arabs, with detainees coming from throughout North Africa. The rest of the detainees came from Sub-Saharan Africa, Asia, Australia, Europe, and North America.[47] Interestingly enough, radical Islamists from Europe—especially France, the United Kingdom, and Russia, with approximately one percent from each country—are the next largest contingent. The sole American detainee—Himdy Yasser, who was born in Baton Rouge, Louisiana—had dual U.S.–Saudi citizenship. Three of the detainees are Iranian citizens. These results are consistent with Marc

Sageman's finding that core Arabs dominate the terrorist network that makes up the global jihadist movement.

In addition to citizenship, the Guantánamo list provides the place and date of birth for all but nineteen (less than 3%) of the detainees. This makes it possible to determine whether jihadists are primarily young males. The age profile is similar for both sets of jihadists. Not surprisingly, the Guantánamo list demonstrates that waging violent jihad—as has been historically true for warfare in general—draws primarily on younger males. Table 4.2 indicates that the overwhelming majority of "travelers," as well as the Afghans and other "locals," were younger than forty years old (79.7%) as of May 2006, which was the cut-off date for the Guantánamo list.[48] Several of the detainees were teenagers when they were captured, with the youngest being two Afghans and one Pakistani who were born in 1988. Detainees in their twenties make up the largest group (41.8%), while those in their thirties are the next largest group (37.9%). Very few of the prisoners are fifty or older (4.9%), and less than a quarter of them are "travelers." Only a handful of the detainees whose birthdates are known were sixty years or older (less than 3%). Only two of the older detainees are not Afghans, and they are "locals" who were born in Afghanistan but no longer lived there prior to returning and being captured. The two oldest detainees were Afghans too. One was born in 1935 in Kabul (71 years old) and the other was born in 1913 (93 years old). These results reinforce the conclusion that young Muslim males, if radicalized, are the most likely to become active jihadists, especially if the arena for conflict requires foreign travel.

Table 4.2. Age Distribution for Travelers Compared to Afghans and Locals

Age Group	Travelers % (n)	Afghans and Locals % (n)
29 or under	43.9 (197)	38.7 (120)
30–39	40.3 (181)	34.5 (107)
40–49	2.2 (55)	13.9 (43)
50 or over	1.8 (8)	9.4 (29)
Unknown	1.8 (8)	3.5 (11)
Total	100.0 (449)	100.0 (310)

The Iraq Insurgency

First, we examine the martyrs list compiled and released by Moheb al-Jihad in May 2005. Like the Guantánamo list, foreign fighters—especially core Arabs—dominate his list of names, with only a little more than 7% of the individuals named being identified as Iraqis. As noted earlier, the shortage of Iraqi names on the martyrs list stems from the fact that Moheb al-Jihad discovered that information on Iraqi insurgents was more difficult to find. In fact, table 4.3 underscores the fact that establishing nationality was not always possible. The nationality of almost 25% of the individuals on this list is unknown, making that category the second largest on the list. Core Arabs make up the overwhelming majority of the individuals whose nationality can be identified. Saudi Arabia (36.2%, or 143 in all) followed by Syria (10.4%, or 41 in all) are the primary countries that have contributed foreign fighters to the Iraq insurgency. As is the case with the Guantánamo detainees, radical Islamists who are known to be Egyptians (1.3%, or 5 in all) or Palestinians (1.8%, or 7 in all) make up a relatively small percentage of the core Arabs who have died in Iraq. Among the Maghreb Arabs, Libyans (3.3%, or 13) are the largest contingent.[49] Only a few of the jihadists who have been identified come from areas other than Iraq, the Middle East, or North Africa.[50]

We now turn to examining the AQI/MSC Eminent Martyrs list. Although limited to only twenty-seven names, table 4.4 reveals that two distinct and largely separate groups—Iraqis and foreign fighters—acting largely autonomously from one another, have been fighting in Iraq against the American-led coalition.[51] Not surprisingly, because the list was released by AQI and the MSC in a series of communiqués between October 2005 and October 2006, core Arabs are most prominent, which is consistent with their salience within al-Qa'ida. The fact that Iraqi names

Table 4.3.   Region of Origin for Individuals on the Martyrs List

Region	% (n)
Iraq	7.3 (29)
Core Arabs	60.0 (237)
Maghreb Arabs	6.3 (25)
Other	1.8 (7)
Unknown	24.6 (97)

Table 4.4.   Region of Origin for Individuals on the AQI/MSC Martyrs List

Region	% (n)
Iraq	14.8 (4)
Core Arabs	48.1 (13)
Maghreb Arabs	24.8 (4)
Other	3.7 (1)
Unknown	18.5 (5)

make up less than 20% of the list reinforces the finding, based on the larger martyrs list described above, that Iraqi insurgents who are Sunnis have chosen to operate separately from al-Qa'ida. Few Iraqis have decided to cast their lot with foreign-fighter-dominated jihadist groups such as AQI. Instead, Iraqis primarily have joined or renewed allegiance to local insurgent groups, which operate in a classical insurgent role to repel invading forces or to settle age-old scores among different factions. Non-Iraqis, on the other hand, rallied to al-Qa'ida or its affiliates—groups that could transport foreign volunteers to the war zone and give them a mission.

The AQI/MSC list also provides information about the cause of death for twenty-six of the twenty-seven people identified as "eminent martyrs." Most of them were killed in combat operations instead of suicide bombings (67%, or 18 in all). The others typically died in suicide attacks (30%, or 8 in all). Given the dates for the death notices, this is not surprising: it suggests that most of them died during the sieges of al-Fallujah in the Sunni Triangle's al-Anbar province. The fact that all of the Iraqis and most of the foreign fighters on the AQI/MSC list are reported as having been killed in action further suggests that the deaths were tied to the insurgency rather than to sectarian violence.

"Freelance" Jihad

Since the U.S. attack on al-Qa'ida strongholds in Afghanistan and the subsequent fragmentation of the organization's safe haven and headquarters, terrorist attacks carried out by small, seemingly independent groups, or small cells, have been on the rise. Particularly in Europe, successful attacks have been made by individuals who live in the country and who come together for the express purpose of carrying out jihad. Prior to the invasion of Afghanistan, most groups that formed on their own would reach out to al-Qa'ida and would seek contact, funding, training, or all three. With the loss of the base in Afghanistan, groups that form in areas outside the region, where the influence of terrorist groups is small and their members are well hidden, find it difficult to make contact. In fact, from an operational security standpoint, their attempts to make contact are one of their greatest vulnerabilities.

Groups that are genuinely pursuing "freelance" jihad emerge from pre-existing relationships that draw on personal bonds. In essence, they embody the buddy approach to radicalization, in which friendship and kinship are key features. They are self-supporting in terms of getting funding and supplies, and they have no real need to reach out to anyone outside their group. Instructions on how to fabricate weapons are not difficult to obtain. The cost of putting together improvised explosive devices is not prohibitively high and can be funded from personal funds or petty crime. If the groups intend to operate locally—and most do—target selection is simple. Group members have probably observed the target in the course of their normal lives, and they need only to look at the target again as an attacker to come up with an operational plan. If the group wishes to adopt the mantle of a larger movement, there is no problem in assuming the name of al-Qa'ida or another group and then simply acting. Al-Suri's book clearly addresses these homegrown groups in many of its suggestions.

The recruitment techniques we have already discussed that are used to entice people to affiliate with an existing jihadist group are recognizable also in the formation of independent groups, but they are highly modified to suit the group being formed. The process of joining such a group will be as unique as the individuals within the group. Obviously, all contacts are personal and based on some sort of existing bonds. It would be expected that such groups would start meeting and talking, slowly ratcheting up their discussions to the point of deciding to take action. How they conduct their business will be a reflection of the intelligence, maturity, training, experience, and professionalism of the members. If the group is not serious or is composed of incompetents, its members may look for people they do not know to help them. Groups that survey the market looking for help usually quickly run into the security services and are quickly identified, infiltrated, and disbanded. The serious groups will understand that maintaining security is paramount and will find ways of doing things themselves and limiting knowledge of their activities to group members.

Self-generating groups often follow an inspirational leader or read texts that motivate them to action. Less thoughtful members are guided in their decision-making process by more capable members, who explain the steps they are taking and provide as much or as little context as necessary for actions that are undertaken. We need only look at the lively conversations in jihadist web forums, or the similar discussions that occur among far rightwing groups in this country, to see how much material is available to people who want to get organized and take action. Many of the sources of motivational material for jihadists are also sources of training materials. Although there are limits to the military skills that can be learned without actual practice, the minimal skills required for making and placing explosives are easily acquired through reading instruction manuals or through distance education methods. As a result, terrorism initiated by "freelance" jihadists is possible.

Conclusions

Although an individual's decision to respond to the call to jihad is an intensely personal choice, some common themes emerge when one examines those who have been recruited to the cause. Our analysis demonstrates that young Muslim males, especially individuals from the core and Maghreb regions of the Arab world, make up the majority of those who join the jihad. While the decision to join a jihadist group like al-Qa'ida is individual-specific, the appeal of adventure or the pressure of the group should not be discounted. Young people may be especially vulnerable to such suasion. They often make the decision together and respond to private group approaches from older, highly persuasive leaders who can identify the uncertainties of youth and who offer a seemingly ideal solution to their problems. For example, the fact that Saudis and other core Arabs tend to cluster together in the jihadist movement, while Iraqis have joined their own sectarian groups, is an indication of how recruiting for such organizations tends to rely heavily on shared backgrounds, such as nationality, tribe, or clan membership. Analysis of fighters in the Iraqi insurgency shows that, while Iraqi nationals tended to join homegrown insurgent or terrorist groups, large numbers of foreign fighters came into the country to provide support under the direction of external organizations like al-Qa'ida. In essence, while a recruit may be going off to fight for someone else, he goes to battle with people like himself.

The teachings and issues that motivate jihadists to join the movement will, to some extent, resonate with individuals at considerable distance from the main battles. While the call to defend one's homeland or immediate neighbors obviously resonates most strongly, appeals to global jihad resonate outside the political boundaries of the traditional Muslim world; therefore, radical Islamist groups willing to engage in acts of terrorism are likely to be the major threat facing the United States and Europe in the coming years. If this happens, the Afghanistan and Iraq experiences suggest that young Muslim males who become radicalized are the most likely targets for recruitment and training, followed by attempts to incite them to violence. Some of these groups, which we have labeled "freelance" jihadists, may recruit their members from exile or immigrant communities, particularly if Muslim youths in those communities perceive themselves to be ostracized as outsiders or treated as foreigners. Other jihadist groups, similar to the cell that conducted the London bombings in early July 2005, may be organized by citizens who are angered by government policies that they consider to be anti-Muslim, who have not assimilated Western values, or who are sympathetic to the plight of their co-religionists in other countries. Unlike transnational groups, such as al-Qa'ida, which have widely publicized their efforts, such homegrown groups are likely to fly well below the radar and conduct their recruitment and training in secrecy.

5

OPERATIONS AND TACTICS

The mujahid Islamic movement must escalate its methods of strikes and tools of resisting the enemies to keep up with the tremendous increase in the number of its enemies, the quality of their weapons, their destructive powers, their disregard for all taboos, and disrespect for the customs of wars and conflicts. In this regard, we concentrate on . . . the method of martyrdom operations as the most successful way of inflicting damage against the opponent and the least costly for the Mujahidin in terms of casualties.

Ayman al-Zawahiri, *Knights under the Prophet's Banner*

THE OPERATIONS CONDUCTED and tactics used by jihadist groups (as well as by other insurgent and terrorist groups) are diverse, ranging from assassinations to sabotage.[1] However, some have become widely recognized as classic al-Qa'ida hallmarks, carefully chosen to maximize their effects in terms of destruction, loss of life, and psychological trauma. They emphasize reliance on suicide attacks, commonly called martyrdom operations in jihadist statements and literature and often carried out simultaneously in multiple locations, and on mass-casualty operations. The ritual beheading of captives, accompanied by graphic videos, recently saw an upsurge in popularity, most notably in Iraq, but use of this tactic has fallen off recently. Al-Qa'ida also has expressed a highly publicized desire to obtain and use weapons of mass destruction (WMD). This chapter examines continuity and change in the operations and tactics favored by those calling for global jihad.

TARGETING

Jihadist groups, including those outside of the broader al-Qa'ida movement, show the greatest amount of variation and dissent over targeting doctrine. Targeting doctrine forces us to confront two central questions: Who is an acceptable target for violent action? And what is an acceptable target? The answer to those questions, according to C. M. J. Drake, is "determined by a number of factors, and the terrorists' ideology is central to this process, not only because it provides the initial dynamic for the terrorists' actions, but because it sets out the moral framework within which they operate."[2] As a result, the guidance offered to jihadists ranges from extremely general to very specific admonitions.[3] Targeting guidance is also based on a number of nonideological factors, such as available resources, target availability, and target security.

Jihadist ideology provides the philosophical foundation for radical Islamists to define targets and justify their elimination. Violent jihad, or *jihad bil-saif*, is justified by the intellectual architects of the global Salafi jihad through selective citation of Islamic laws and traditions, which are twisted to support an agenda of hate and murder for political purposes.[4] For the jihadists, flexible target definitions are the norm. Typically, only the mujahidin's supporters are considered to be innocents and, hence, off-limits as potential targets.

Abu-Hajir Abd-al-Aziz al-Muqrin, the now-deceased leader of al-Qa'ida operations in Saudi Arabia, wrote a March 2004 article outlining acceptable targets for the mujahidin. Target attractiveness revolves around three elements: available tactics for attacking the target, the importance of the target, and the presumed payoff from operations against the target (essentially the jihadists' gain and the enemy's loss).[5] Al-Muqrin maintains that the payoff of operations against the jihadist movement's adversaries consists of the following factors: (1) to stress the struggle of the faiths; (2) to show who the main enemy is; (3) to get rid of the renegades and purify the lands as an example for others; (4) to spread fear in the enemy lines; (5) to lift the morale of the Islamic nation; (6) to destroy the image and stature of the targeted governments; (7) to obstruct political projects of the infidels and renegades; and (8) to retaliate for the killing of Muslims.[6]

Influential al-Qa'ida figure Yusuf al-Ayiri provided a similar list in his defense of a 2002 hostage situation at a Moscow theater, which was carried out by Chechen militants and in which 129 hostages were killed: (1) to move the battle into the heart of Russia; (2) to increase stress on Russian security; (3) to add strain to the Russian war in Chechnya; (4) to terrorize the Russian people who support their government; (5) to highlight "the reality" of the war, so that people will reconsider the conflict;

(6) to lift the spirits of Chechens; and (7) to bring Chechnya to the fore-front of people's minds worldwide. Al-Ayiri, writing that five of these objectives were met in one way or another, defends the operation.[7]

In his writings, al-Muqrin also grouped the potential targets that he identified into three categories, which are ranked by their importance: faith (i.e., religious), economic, and human. Table 5.1 summarizes al-Muqrin's perspective about the relevance of these target categories in light of the advantages and disadvantages of operations inside cities.[8] Al-Muq-rin viewed what he termed faith targets as being the most important. They include places used by missionaries, covert intelligence operatives, and attackers of Islam and Muslims, and by financial, military, or moral supporters of attacks against Muslims. Economic targets were defined as any infrastructure target whose destruction supports destabilization of the overall situation, hinders economic recovery of an area, or causes with-drawal of foreign investments from local markets.[9] Examples included housing compounds for foreigners and petroleum-related facilities.

Human targets were identified in some cases by nationality, with prior-ity given to targets in specific countries in which the jihadists operate. In Saudi Arabia, al-Muqrin identified Americans as the most important targets, then British, and so on. In Iraq and Afghanistan, the most impor-tant human targets were, again, Americans. In Algeria, the French were the most important targets. In Indonesia, the Australians were most important. After ranking human targets by nationality, al-Muqrin turned to grouping targets by religion, starting with Jews, then Christians, and then apostates. In the Jewish category, in descending order of importance, are American and Israeli Jews, followed by British Jews, and then French Jews. In the Christian category, the rank order of targets is American, British, Spanish, Australian, Canadian, and lastly Italian. Al-Muqrin argued that any Muslim who is close to Jewish or Christian governments was a renegade, making them an acceptable target. He also identifies sec-ularists and those who mock Islam as well as intelligence agents as targets.[10]

The various categories of human targets in al-Muqrin's typology are then given values according to profession. Businessmen, bankers, econo-mists are in the first tier of targets. Diplomats, politicians, scholars, ana-lysts, and diplomatic missions are in the second tier. Scientists, "associates," and experts are below them. Military commanders and sol-diers make up the fourth tier. Finally, non-Muslim tourists, and anyone

Table 5.1. Advantages and Disadvantages of Jihadist Operations in Cities

Advantages	Disadvantages
To lift morale of the mujahidin and the nation, and to lower (but not destroy) the morale of the enemy	The killing of mujahidin and its leaders when operations are discovered
To prove the truthfulness of the group	Big material and human losses
To punish the ruling government and limit its power	If the operation fails, morale of the mujahidin is lowered
To show the meaning of the *shahada* and to achieve belief in God	The target government is given an excuse for action against innocent citizens
To make government and other main figures lose popular support	The morale of the target government and its supporters can be lifted if a victory over the mujahidin is won
To affect the economy of the target country	The arrest of mujahidin fighters affects security negatively
To help the mujahidin gain experience to lead nations later	If many operations fail, there is a loss of confidence in the mujahidin among the people and group members
To study and analyze operational mistakes for future operations	
To prepare the nation and its members for future battles of which the Prophet spoke	
To gain support through successful operations	
To force governments to change policies	
To cause infighting in the target's military and political establishments	

who has been warned not to enter the territory of Muslims, are acceptable targets.[11]

Abu Mus'ab al-Suri has provided similar targeting guidance to jihadists. He identifies six categories of targets: (1) missionary centers and cultural missions; (2) foreign companies and employees; (3) diplomatic facilities; (4) military facilities; (5) foreign security operations; and (6) tourists. Al-Suri asserts that all "Western teachers and doctors are actually in disguise and are spies," opening medical and educational personnel up for attack.[12] In his discussion of acceptable targets, al-Suri explicitly warns potential mujahidin that Islamic scholars and clerics should never be targets of violence, regardless of how much they may have "deviated from their course." Such scholars should be confronted through proof, evidence, and political rebuttal, and "not through weapons or the sword, even though many of them deserve the sword," since to attack scholars could turn the Muslim masses against the jihadists. In a similar fashion, al-Zawahiri advised al-Zarqawi in a 2005 letter: "The ulema [scholars] among the general public are, as well, the symbol of Islam and its emblem. Their disparagement may lead to the general public deeming religion and its adherents as being unimportant. This is a greater injury than the benefit of criticizing a theologian on a heresy or an issue."[13]

Al-Qa'ida's leadership periodically calls for attacks against very specific targets. For example, shortly before the March 2003 invasion of Iraq, bin Laden claimed that, aside from Iraq, "the areas most in need of liberation" from "oppressive, tyrannical, apostate ruling regimes" are Jordan, Morocco, Nigeria, Pakistan, Saudi Arabia, and Yemen.[14] Tirades against the Saudi ruling family are a frequent theme in bin Laden's public and private statements. Al-Zawahiri has issued other statements, declaring that the Saudi royalty and other rulers have become traitors to their religion, even if they dress as Muslims, have Muslim names, grow beards, wear turbans, or claim noble descent.[15] Al-Zawahiri also has issued a number of statements in which he encourages the Pakistani Army to disobey orders. He has urged Muslims in Pakistan to rise up and topple Pakistani President Pervez Musharraf. In those statements, he consistently uses highly inflammatory words such as *treason, infidel, killer,* and *traitor* to describe Musharraf's actions.[16] It is likely that al-Zawahiri's words have influenced the Pakistani population. Ever since he joined the American-led War on Terror in 2001, Musharraf has been the target of numerous assassination attempts by jihadist sympathizers.[17]

Bin Laden also has spoken about the "theft of our oil" by the West, and he has called for attacks to "stop the biggest plundering operation in history."[18] Following encouragement from al-Zawahiri in late 2005, al-Qa'ida members attempted a suicide attack against a Saudi oil facility in February 2006.[19]

Regime Officials versus Civilians

As we noted above, the decision to target individuals forces jihadist groups to confront a second question: "Are civilians legitimate targets?" Some radical Islamist groups have been extremely reluctant to expand the range of human targets beyond security forces, government officials, and their supporters. For example, Egyptian religious nationalists were reluctant to attack nonregime targets because they thought that maintaining support from the general population was essential for a revolution to happen.[20] Others, especially the more radical Salafi elements, have failed to draw such distinctions, making the experience of the GIA more typical of the trajectory followed by jihadists. While the GIA in Algeria initially limited its attacks to governmental targets, it exhibited no reluctance to expand its attacks to include civilians. The Algerian case, however, is complicated, since Algeria was embroiled at the time in a bloody civil war in which neither the government nor the GIA observed any limits causing extensive civilian casualties. Nonetheless, the decision to target civilians cost the GIA public support. Ultimately, it was eclipsed by a new jihadist group, the Salafist Group for Preaching and Combat (GSPC), which promised to avoid civilian casualties. Eventually, the GSPC began to target civilians, and disagreements over targeting resulted in what Stephen Ulph called "a serious ideological hemorrhage and collapse of morale in the GSPC."[21]

Al-Qa'ida, in its formal statements, maintained that it initially chose to limit its targets to regime officials. In a 1997 interview with CNN journalist Peter Arnett, bin Laden stated that the focus of al-Qa'ida's declaration of jihad was on soldiers in Saudi Arabia and that "American civilians are not targeted in our plan," although he advised them to leave the country. Bin Laden also said that he would not rule out a future policy of targeting American civilians in reaction to the "U.S. government's targeting of Muslim civilians" by enforcing sanctions against Iraq, which he claimed was an attack on Muslim civilians, and for which, he indicated, the American public bears some responsibility since the nation chooses its leaders freely.[22]

In reality, prior to September 11, al-Qa'ida made no distinction among its targets, as demonstrated by its 1993 attack on the World Trade Center in New York or the failed 1995 Bojinka plot to destroy twelve commercial airlines—eleven of which were American—over the Pacific Ocean. The disconnect between al-Qa'ida's rhetoric and the reality of its actions was removed in 1998, when bin Laden announced the creation of the World Islamic Front and issued his fatwa declaring, "To kill the Americans and their allies—civilian and military—is an individual duty incumbent upon every Muslim."[23]

The debate over whether to target civilians is often framed by specific terms that are easy to tailor for justifications of violence. Many jihadists claim that, under Islamic law, there is no such thing as a "civilian." Al-Zawahiri explains how the simple act of paying taxes in a Western country can open a person up to legitimate targeting:

> There is no difference in the Shari'ah between civilians and soldiers. The Shari'ah divides people into combatant or non-combatant. A combatant person is one who supports the fighting with his life, money, or opinion. According to this criterion, all Western peoples are combatant because they have willingly elected their leaders and representatives in parliaments, which draw up the policies that call for killing our sons, occupying our lands, and plundering our resources. Western peoples pay taxes, which fund these policies, and provide troops, support, and backing for the armies, which attack us. We are obliged to defend our faith, children, and resources. America and the West attack our cities with seven-ton bombs, carpet-bombing, and chemical weapons. Then they demand that we confront them with light weapons only. This is impossible. As they bomb us, they will be bombed, and as they kill us, they will be killed.[24]

Civilian Casualties and Collateral Damage

After the 1998 attacks on the American embassies in Kenya and Tanzania, which killed a number of non-Americans including Muslims, al-Qa'ida became worried that inflicting such heavy civilian casualties might lessen popular support for the jihadist cause. The group sought opinions from Islamic scholars that would justify inflicting civilian casualties. Alan Cullison, a journalist who purchased two computers previously owned by al-Qa'ida leadership during the 2001 Afghanistan invasion, provides a typical letter:

> Dear highly respected _____,
> . . . I present this to you as your humble brother . . . concerning the preparation of the lawful study that I am doing on the killing of civilians. This is a very sensitive case—as you know—especially these days . . . .

It is very important that you provide your opinion of this matter, which has been forced upon us as an essential issue in the course and ideology of the Muslim movement. . . .

[Our] questions are:

1. Since you are the representative of the Islamic Jihad group, what is your lawful stand on the killing of civilians, specifically when women and children are included? And please explain the legitimate law concerning those who are deliberately killed.
2. According to your law, how can you justify the killing of innocent victims because of a claim of oppression?
3. What is your stand concerning a group that supports the killing of civilians, including women and children?

With our prayers, wishing you success and stability.[25]

Seized al-Qa'ida documents suggest al-Qa'ida was able to obtain a positive response to this inquiry. For example, Ramzi bin-al-Shibh who with Khalid Shaykh Muhammad masterminded the September 11 attacks, wrote: "In killing Americans who are ordinarily off limits, Muslims should not exceed four million non-combatants, or render more than ten million of them homeless. We should avoid this, to make sure the penalty [that we are inflicting] is no more than reciprocal."[26]

Drawing on this religious cover for engaging in acts of terrorism, al-Qa'ida has a set of conditions legalizing operations in which civilians are killed, regardless of whether or not they are the primary targets. These conditions similarly make it acceptable to kill fellow Muslims, who are part of the "collateral damage" in attacks on the infidels. Only one of the following conditions must be observed in order for civilian casualties to be permissible: (1) the enemy has purposefully killed Muslim civilians; (2) civilians have assisted the enemy in "deed, word, or mind"; (3) Islamic fighters cannot distinguish between combatants and noncombatants; (4) there is a need to burn enemy strongholds or fields where there are civilians; (5) heavy weaponry needs to be used; (6) the enemy uses civilians as human shields; or (7) the enemy violates a treaty with the Muslims, and therefore civilians must be killed as a lesson.[27]

Events in Iraq reinforce the importance that jihadist circles attach to having a religious justification for inflicting civilian casualties. Prior to his own death, al-Zarqawi spent a great deal of time attempting to establish a complex theological basis for allowing the deaths of civilians. For example, al-Zarqawi's now-deceased advisor, Abu-Anas al-Shami, argued that civilian deaths are acceptable if those civilians are being used by the enemy as human shields or if the alternative to killing civilians is not fighting at all.[28] The position advocated by al-Shami is grounded in an argument commonly known as *al-Tatarrus*, derived from the Arabic word for shield, *turs*.

Al-Zarqawi took even further the concept that inflicting civilian casualties, including deaths, is a legitimate part of the jihad. He maintained that the mujahidin are required under Islamic law to use the most lethal weapons whenever possible, regardless of civilian casualties. Consistent with his unwillingness to differentiate between civilian and noncivilian targets, al-Zarqawi rejected making any distinction between civilians and combatants as legitimate targets, saying that, under Islamic law, "every infidel on the face of the earth, who does not make peace with Islam and Muslim through custody, truce, or safe conduct, is a warrior infidel. There is absolutely no protection for him, unless his killing is forbidden to start with, such as women and children."[29] Attacks on civilians reflect the very loosely defined political goals of al-Zarqawi's group. According to a U.S. Military Academy study, while he was alive, al-Zarqawi's ambitions appeared "to extend little beyond driving out the United States and preventing a political settlement. Given their objectives do not hinge on winning broad based popular support, Zarqawi's group does not need to be as careful about whom they inflict casualties upon."[30]

Nonetheless, despite the willingness of jihadists to treat noncombatants as legitimate targets, the killing of civilians has caused a severe backlash against al-Qa'ida in Iraq in the form of losses in popular and tribal support. This negative reaction has compelled the al-Qa'ida leadership and other influential radical Islamists to at least attempt to limit the targeting of noncombatants. Several exchanges illustrate this shift in rhetoric. For example, in videotaped lectures dated August 2000, al-Suri encourages jihadists to "kill wherever and don't make a distinction between men, women, and children."[31] Softening his position in *The Call to Global Islamic Resistance*, al-Suri advises jihadists to avoid targeting women and children "when they are away from their men."[32] Abd-al-Qadir Ibn Abd-al-Aziz wrote in his *Key Guide to Preparations* that if it is impossible to strike an unbeliever without killing women and children, it is permissible to kill the women and children, "even if they do not fight or assist them," but only if their deaths are not intended.[33]

Similarly, in a captured al-Zarqawi network letter, an anonymous author writes to "Abu-Usamah" a series of instructions regarding a particular cell's operations in Iraq. The author, in one of his points, writes: "Stop the killing of people unless they are spying, military, or police officers. We have to find a secure method because if we continue using the same method, people will start fighting us in the streets."[34]

Like al-Zawahiri's 2005 letter to al-Zarqawi, in which he reproached the al-Qa'ida in Iraq leader for his tactics and targeting, a December 2005 letter to al-Zarqawi from "Atiyah" cautions against "things that are perilous and ruinous."[35] Much like al-Zawahiri, Atiyah is worried about the alienation of Sunnis caused by attacks on civilians, especially in the 2005 Amman hotel bombings carried out by al-Zarqawi's group. He urges al-Zarqawi to avoid "the mistake of lack of precision in execution" in this attack. Atiyah instructs al-Zarqawi not to expand his reach beyond Iraq and to remember that "policy must be dominant over militarism." In short, theology should rule al-Qa'ida and its war. Atiyah explains: "unless our military actions are servant to our judicious shari'ah policy, and unless our short-term goals and successes are servant to our ultimate goal and highest aim, then they will be akin to exhaustion, strain, and illusion."[36]

Much like al-Zawahiri, Atiyah is very concerned with popular support and public perceptions of the jihadists in Iraq. He urges al-Zarqawi to win over the people and not to alienate them. In addition to urging him to pay attention to religious scholars, he urges al-Zarqawi to respect them and not oppose any of them in spite of any disagreements with them. Atiyah also instructs al-Zarqawi strictly to refrain from killing any religious or tribal leader. Atiyah tells al-Zarqawi that, because he is operating under the name al-Qa'ida, he must be cautious and not be overzealous in targeting and operations. The Atiyah letter shows the dissent within al-Qa'ida about the methods and strategy of al-Zarqawi.[37]

Similar criticism, this time of the GSPC/Al-Qa'ida in the Lands of the Islamic Maghreb, was revealed within the organization's ranks in May 2007. After a number of violent attacks in public places, several prominent members voiced their reservations about the group's choice of tactics. One member who renounced militant activities after the April 2007 bombings in Algiers said he did so in response to some members' complaints about "carrying out of suicide operations, shedding the blood of innocents in public places, setting up fake checkpoints in order to rob Muslims of their money, and abducting and terrorizing innocents in order to receive money." Another member, a Shari'ah officer in the group's second district, opposed the use of Iraq- and Afghanistan-style tactics, because Algeria is Dar al-Islam (the house of Muslims) and not occupied by the United States or Britain, saying that such tactics are "not permissible by Shari'ah."[38]

Such objections reflect reservations about killing or wounding fellow Muslims. According to recent analysis of suicide bombings in Afghanistan from 2001 to 2007, civilians were involved in the attacks 5 percent of the time. In all but two of these attacks, civilian casualties appeared to be unintentional. Several of these attacks targeted military convoys or official personnel, and in a few instances Taliban officials publicly apologized for the deaths or completely denied responsibility. This avoidance of targeting areas with high civilian concentrations and low security—that is, soft targets—is likely a side effect of the Taliban's desire to employ Iraqi insurgency-style tactics while retaining its base of popular support by keeping civilian casualties to a minimum. A shift toward hard targets—official targets with much higher security—has negatively affected the number of kills per Taliban suicide attack, yielding much lower kill statistics than attacks by jihadists in Iraq.

MARTYRDOM OPERATIONS

Since September 11, the mass media has reported numerous incidents of suicide bombers (*shuhada,* plural of *shahid*), commonly referred to as "martyrdom operations" by the jihadists, and for which they anticipate heavenly rewards.[39] Individuals who become martyrs, according to the jihadist concept of martyrdom, accrue numerous benefits, ranging from the well-publicized seventy-two virgins in heaven to lesser-known benefits, such as dying without pain and having blood that smells like incense. In some cases, martyrs are said to be spared "the torments of the grave," so that their bodies will not decompose after death. Perhaps most important, because of the religious implications of suicide, one of the biggest benefits promised is that martyrdom erases prior sins. A person can be considered a martyr even if he or she never prays or performs any of the Islamic rituals.[40]

The use of suicide bombings, according to Fawaz Gerges, "represents a rupture, not continuity, with classical Islamic political thought and practice."[41] Although suicide (*qatlu nafsi-hi*) is not referred to in the Qur'an,

it is forbidden in the Hadith, the collected statements and actions attributed to the Prophet Muhammad and traced back to him through the
accounts of presumed witnesses. The Hadith include things done in the
Prophet Muhammad's presence that he did not forbid, as well as the
authoritative statements and acts of his companions.

Abu-Muhammad al-Maqdisi, al-Zarqawi's former mentor and one of
the most influential figures in the jihadist movement, dismisses the potential religious conflict posed by having individuals engage in suicide attacks.
He maintains that the prohibition against suicide does not apply. His case
rests on the premise that suicide is motivated by fear and desperation, and
that it is an inherently selfish act; martyrdom operations, on the other
hand, cannot be considered suicides because they have altruistic intentions.[42] Although suicide is prohibited in Islam, martyrdom is consistently
praised in both the Qur'an and the Hadith.[43] According to Hadith: "The
Prophet said, 'Nobody who enters Paradise will ever like to return to this
world even if he were offered everything, except the martyr who will
desire to return to this world and be killed 10 times for the sake of the
great honor that has been bestowed upon him.'"[44] By defining suicide
bombing as martyrdom, radical Islamists have succeeded in providing a
religious justification for their use of the tactic.[45] Moreover, reliance on
the tactic has fostered images of self-sacrifice and heroism among jihadists, which are essential to sustaining martyrdom operations.[46]

By enveloping suicide terrorism in an aura of religious legitimacy, the
jihadists are able to pursue their strategic goal of compelling Western
democracies to withdraw military forces from areas of conflict. Robert
Pape, drawing on data from suicide terrorist incidents around the world
(including some that are not connected to jihadism), has concluded that
the status of suicide terrorists who are reacting to shared religious and
ideological motives is elevated among the broader community.[47] This is
consistent with al-Qa'ida doctrine. In a 2004 statement, bin Laden
instructed the mujahidin to "become diligent in carrying out martyrdom
operations," due to their effect on the enemy. Bin Laden continued by
saying, "These are the most important operations."[48] In an article about
the importance of the September 11 "raids," Abu-Ubayd al-Qurashi
explains the centrality of martyrdom operations to al-Qa'ida's strategy:

> The asymmetric strategy that Al-Qa'ida is pursuing entails the use of
> means and methods that the defender cannot use, recognize, or avoid.

They rendered the United States' tremendous military superiority useless and reduced the effectiveness of U.S. military deterrence internationally. The proliferation of the "martyrdom bomb" and its expansion beyond Palestine to U.S. targets has thrown off U.S. calculations and caused the United States' sense of security to evaporate.[49]

In the past, martyrdom operations were conducted by men only. Although martyrdom operations involving women are still fairly rare events within the context of the global jihad, women recently have conducted a series of highly publicized suicide terrorist acts. Examples that received extensive coverage in Western media include the Chechen "Black Widow" attacks in Russia, the Amman hotel bombings in 2005, an attack in Uzbekistan, and at least two attacks in Iraq.[50] The increase in female suicide bombers, according to Saad al-Faqih, a Saudi Islamist reformer, does not signal an evolution in the tactic's perceived permissibility by jihadist groups. Instead, al-Faqih attributes the increase to more women being willing to join the jihad, the desire for revenge following assaults on themselves and their families, and the elevated social position of women in some tribes.[51] Occasionally, the motivation may be to restore family honor and avoid a shameful death in instances where women had prohibited sexual contacts outside of marriage. Attempts to recruit Muslim women to participate in suicide terrorism have occurred in recent jihadist propaganda efforts that directly targeted women.[52] At least one women's organization has been created to carry out operations against the United States.[53]

Mass-Casualty Operations and Weapons of Mass Destruction

Al-Qa'ida and other militant organizations have emphasized mass-casualty operations, including efforts to obtain WMDs. Al-Suri, for example, advocates targeting densely populated centers, since "the target which deters countries and topples governments is mass human slaughter."[54] Mass-casualty operations, especially ones using WMDs, would be the most effective—and perhaps the most psychologically destructive—way to achieve this objective. Al-Zawahiri has explained the strategic rationale for this tactic by arguing that the mujahidin must concentrate on "the need to inflict the maximum casualties against the opponent, for this is the language understood by the West, no matter how much time and effort such operations take."[55] For Abu-Mus'ab al-Suri, "the aim of resistance missions and the jihad of individual terrorism is to inflict the largest human and material losses possible on American interests and allied countries, making them recognize that the resistance has transformed to an intifadah [literally uprising—the same term used in two Palestinian popular resistances against the Israelis] phenomenon against them as a result of their aggression."[56]

The jihadists have turned to the rulings of radical Islamic scholars to justify conducting mass-casualty operations, including the use of WMDs if they can acquire them. The rulings cited by the jihadists rely on the principle of retaliation to justify indiscriminately murdering millions of people. Suliman Abu Ghaith, a prominent al-Qa'ida spokesman, issued a statement in late 2001 declaring that al-Qa'ida's war with the United States would not be over until Muslims have fulfilled their "right to kill four million Americans—two million of them children—and to exile twice as many and wound and cripple hundreds of thousands."[57] He went on to say that al-Qa'ida would displace eight million Americans and cripple hundreds of thousands more. Abu Ghaith asserted that those actions would be in retaliation for what he called the "crimes" of the United States against the Arab and Muslim world. In order to justify his own numbers, he claimed that the United States is responsible directly and indirectly for the death of four million Muslims. Not surprisingly, his total is tied to a series of conflicts that have strong emotional resonance within the Muslim world: 1.2 million Iraqis (presumably from the 1990 Gulf War and subsequent UN sanctions); 260,000 Palestinians due to U.S. support for Israel; 12,000 Afghans and Arab fighters; and 13,000 Somalis. For good measure, he also alleges that millions of other Muslims have been killed throughout the world due to America. His total for Muslim deaths is simply an assertion, without credible independent documentation, which he and other jihadists treat as factual. It is best viewed as propaganda designed to legitimate acts of mass terrorism, including the use of WMDs if they can be obtained.

As noted above, al-Qa'ida leaders have long sought WMDs in order to advance the jihadist agenda. Abu Ghaith, for example, declared that "it is our right to fight them with chemical and biological weapons, so as to afflict them with the fatal maladies that have afflicted the Muslims because of the [Americans'] chemical and biological weapons."[58] Letters written by al-Zawahiri to Muhammad Atef, a key al-Qa'ida military commander, similarly underscore the group's interest in obtaining chemical and biological weapons. Al-Zawahiri, drawing on his training as a physician, emphasizes that chemical or biological attacks are extremely destructive and very hard to defend against.[59] Al-Zarqawi's successor, Abu-Ayyub al-Masri, has also called for the use of WMDs against Americans, urging those with the scientific expertise to create such weapons to assist the mujahidin and to use U.S. military camps in Iraq as "test sites" for chemical, biological, or radiological weapons.[60]

Abu-Mus'ab al-Suri has also devoted considerable attention to the possible use of WMDs to advance the global jihad. In a 2004 statement, al-Suri wrote:

> [One] option was to destroy the United States by means of decisive strategic operations with weapons of mass destruction including nuclear, chemical, or biological weapons if mujahidin are able to obtain them in cooperation with those who possess them, purchase them—or manufacture and use primitive atomic bombs or so-called dirty bombs. I believe that the adoption of the slogan dirty bombs for a dirty nation is not free of justice. Let the radiation harm the American people who vote for the killing, destruction and expropriation of the people's resources, and [the] malignant narcissism to control others. After all, we will just say that we regret the radiation.[61]

Later, in 2005, al-Suri wrote of two ways to defeat the United States. The first option was through protracted guerrilla warfare. The second involved using weapons of mass destruction. Al-Suri argued that the first option, while possible, "seems distant at the present in light of the silence and submission of the Islamic people"; the second option, though—destroying the United States by using WMD—would be a short-term solution to the conflict.[62]

Furthermore, bin Laden has declared the acquisition of WMDs to be a religious duty.[63] In May 2003, a young Saudi cleric named Shaykh Nasir bin Hamid al-Fahd provided a formal religious justification to al-Qa'ida and the rest of the global jihadist movement for using WMDs.[64] In *A Treatise on the Legal Status of Using Weapons of Mass Destruction against Infidels*, al-Fahd cited Qur'anic examples of acceptable forms of reciprocal violence and argued that WMDs were consistent with those examples. His argument also justified killing ten million women and children, including Muslims, in such attacks.[65] As a result, although there is no definitive evidence that al-Qa'ida has attempted to launch a WMD operation, the will to do so is evident and the necessary theological justifications have been framed for such action. Whether a successful WMD operation occurs in the future is likely to be contingent on the ability of al-Qa'ida or other jihadist groups to acquire sufficient materials and thwart Western measures to prevent their use.

ABDUCTIONS AND EXECUTIONS

Taking and killing hostages are not new terrorist tactics. In fact, they represent classic terrorist tactics dating back to People's Will (*Narodnaya Volya*) in Czarist Russia during the nineteenth century. In the intervening years, kidnapping campaigns for ransom or to kill victims have been carried out by terrorists in Western Europe, North and South America, the Middle East, and Asia. In the last several years, kidnapping and execution operations conducted by jihadist organizations around the world have become more frequent, more lethal, and more public.

Algeria

Kidnapping and execution has been used by jihadist groups in Algeria for a number of years. The early nineties witnessed a brutal campaign of abductions by the Armed Islamic Group (GIA), a jihadist organization aiming to replace the secular Algerian government with an Islamic state that later aligned with al-Qa'ida. According to the U.S. State Department's *Patterns of Global Terrorism Report—2000*, the GIA began to carry out violent operations against both Algerians and foreigners after the Algerian government voided the victory of the Islamic Salvation Front (FIS) in the country's legislative elections in December 1991.[66] The GIA focused its operations (including assassinations, abductions, car bombings, and other kinds of attacks) on both Algerian civilian and government targets until 1993, when it announced its campaign to rid Algeria of foreigners. In that year, the GIA abducted three French consular workers, demanding that all foreigners leave the country. Although the three consular workers were released unharmed after a week, the GIA issued an ultimatum, via one of the hostages, to the French residents of Algeria, ordering them to leave the country within a month. The *Le Figaro* newspaper also received a video cassette from the kidnappers showing the hostages and ordering all foreigners, French or otherwise, to leave the country immediately. The hostages, upon their release, claimed to have been treated well, but offered no other details of the abduction.

Other abductions followed the expiration of the GIA's one-month ultimatum, including the kidnapping and subsequent executions of three employees of an Italian pipeline company in October 1993. In 1994, the group transmitted another message, this time to the Algerian government, offering to cease the killing of foreigners in exchange for the release of one of the group's founders, Abd-al-Haq Layada, who had been sentenced to death by an Algerian court. Like the prior ultimatum, the method of transmission was the same: the group released two hostages, diplomats from Yemen and Oman, who then carried the message to authorities. Layada was not released.

Numerous other kidnappings and executions followed, including several targeting French citizens. In August 1994 the GIA threatened to take "dissuasive" measures against teachers and students who frequent government-run educational establishments because the curriculum is "contrary to the rules of Islam."[67] In 1996 the group abducted seven French monks, demanding that France release jailed Algerian militants. After two months the GIA announced that all seven monks had been executed.

The Salafist Group for Preaching and Combat (GSPC), a splinter group of the GIA, eclipsed the GIA in 1998 as the most effective terrorist group in Algeria. The GSPC also eclipsed the GIA in popular support, largely because of its pledge to avoid attacks on civilians in Algeria. Nonetheless, while the GSPC has mostly focused its attacks on government and military targets, there have been occasional civilian casualties.[68] Despite differences with the GIA concerning civilian targeting, the GSPC continued the GIA's tradition of kidnapping and execution; in mid-February 2003 the GSPC abducted thirty-two European tourists in several kidnapping operations, attempting to ransom them. The hostages were mixed together. In May 2003 seventeen of the tourists were released amid uncertain circumstances. Some reports claim that the release of the hostages was the result of a rescue operation by the Algerian army. Other reports claim that the ransom was paid.[69] One of the remaining hostages died of heatstroke in July 2004. The other hostages were later released by the GSPC in northern Mali in August. Press reports cited a ransom of 4.6 million euros paid to the GSPC for their freedom.[70]

The GIA seems to have favored kidnappings and executions more than its successor, the GSPC. Differences can be found in the demands of both groups during hostage situations: while demands in the GSPC's one major kidnapping event were monetary, the GIA's demands most often focused on the release of comrades, the expulsion of foreigners, and, in the case of threats to students and teachers, the introduction of Islamic curricula in Algerian schools. In most of the cases where the hostage died, the GIA preferred to execute the hostage by cutting the throat. The GSPC executed no hostages. Both groups, according to released hostages, treated the captives well.

Yemen

Kidnappings of tourists have become a routine occurrence in Yemen. Most victims are taken not by jihadists, but by tribesmen who use the hostages to pressure the government into providing the tribes with new roads, water, and clinics. The hostages are generally treated as guests and later released unharmed. The kidnapping of sixteen Western tourists in 1998, however, was much different. While religious ideology has not been the motive in tribal hostage taking, it appears to have played a major part in the 1998 operation that left four hostages dead. This incident was the first time kidnapping was used by Islamic extremists in Yemen.

During his trial, one of the kidnappers—Abu-al-Hassan, leader of the Islamic Army of Aden-Abyan—referred to the December 1998 American and British bombings of Iraq to justify the abductions. He said the kidnappings were justified because the United States and the United Kingdom attacked Muslims indiscriminately and killed old men, women, and children. Abu-al-Hassan claimed that he instructed his comrades to use hostages as human shields during a raid by Yemeni authorities, which perhaps led to their deaths. He later told the court of a plan to "liquidate" U.S. nationals in Yemen and bomb a church after the kidnapping: "Two religions (Christianity and Islam)," he insisted, "cannot unite and a church bell cannot sound in the Arabian Peninsula."[71] The kidnappers ran a military camp in southern Yemen and demanded the release of two of their leaders, according to Yemeni security officials, in addition to demanding that UN sanctions against Iraq be lifted.

Although the group did not have a chance to execute their hostages (if that was their intent) before the raid by Yemeni authorities, the group did display several ideological tendencies, exemplified by Abu-al-Hassan's statements, which are similar to those of al-Qa'ida. The demands regarding the UN sanctions on Iraq directly echo remarks by Usama bin Laden, who began referencing the sanctions in 1996, claiming that they had resulted in the deaths of 600,000 innocent children.[72] Actual links are uncertain, but it is reasonable to suspect that the kidnappers were at least familiar with bin Laden and his statements. After all, bin Laden had, in the same year as the kidnapping operation, issued his famous World Islamic Front fatwa, which received widespread coverage throughout the Muslim world. In his fatwa, he declared it was the duty of every Muslim to kill Americans and their allies. The hostages would have well fit this target profile. The sixteen tourists included twelve Britons, two Americans, and two Australians, so bin Laden's fatwa may have inspired this incident.

Daniel Pearl in Pakistan

In January 2002, *Wall Street Journal* reporter Daniel Pearl was kidnapped and, a week later, beheaded, video of which was widely circulated on the Internet, to the dismay of Pearl's family and the international community. Pearl was kidnapped by a previously unknown group calling itself "The National Movement of Restoration of Pakistani Society" while on his way to meet with a suspected terrorist leader. The group sent the U.S. government its demands via email. It demanded that the U.S. release detainees in Guantánamo, lift a ban on the sale of F-16 fighters to Pakistan, return the Taliban ambassador to Pakistan to Pakistani custody, and give access to lawyers and their families for any Pakistani citizens detained in the United States due to terrorism investigations. The group also accused Pearl of being a CIA employee, a claim that both the agency and *The Wall Street Journal* denied.

The previously unknown group that claimed responsibility for the kidnapping is thought to be a part of Jaish-e-Mohammad, an organization closely associated with Harakat-ul-Mujahidin, a terrorist organization with connections to the Pakistani intelligence service.[73] Fahad Naseem, one of the suspects in the kidnapping and subsequent murder of Pearl, alleged that Omar Saeed Sheikh, a British-Pakistani militant and the chief suspect in the crime, said that Pearl was "anti-Islam and a Jew" and that he was to be kidnapped.

Although the motives behind the conspiracy remain unclear, it is reasonable to suggest that Pearl was killed in part because he was an American, Jewish, and a reporter.[74] In the Pearl video, just before his gruesome execution, he seemingly reads from a script and says, "I am a Jew, my mother is a Jew."[75] Other references to Judaism appear on the tape. If Pearl was reading from a script, as many people believe to have been the case, then these references to Judaism may signal that his religion provided some motivation for his having been targeted. Alternatively, it is possible that the fact that Pearl was Jewish helped his abductors and killers assuage any sense of guilt about committing murder. Regardless of their actual motivations, the references to Judaism were transmitted around the world as part of his ritual execution. Presumably, the video created a highly charged and very graphic example of what many jihadists accept as the best way to treat a Jew or to terrorize the United States.

Saudi Arabia

In mid-2004, Saudi Arabia was the target of a destructive terror campaign by the Saudi wing of al-Qa'ida (al-Qa'ida in the Arabian Peninsula, AQAP), led by Abd-al-Aziz al-Muqrin. AQAP issued a series of statements vowing to hunt down and kill Westerners in order to cleanse the Arabian Peninsula of infidels.[76] Statements like this have been made by nearly every major jihadist group in the past several years, making the idea of cleansing the Peninsula a recurrent theme in jihadist ideology.

The statements were followed by violent actions. In late May the group staged a shooting and hostage-taking rampage in al-Khobar that resulted in the deaths of twenty-two people, including four Westerners. The attackers sorted out the Muslims from the non-Muslims before the Saudi authorities descended upon the hotel where the attackers and hostages were located. In June, al-Muqrin appeared on a video released via jihadist websites behind an American aviation engineer, Paul Johnson, who was bound and blindfolded. Al-Muqrin read a lengthy statement in which he declared that the hostage would be executed within seventy-two hours unless AQAP militants detained in Saudi Arabia were freed. Upon the expiration of the deadline, a set of pictures began to circulate on jihadist websites showing Paul Johnson's body lying in a pool of blood with his severed head placed on his back. Al-Muqrin was killed by Saudi forces on the same day. Nonetheless, while AQAP has been disabled, it has not been destroyed. Its 2004 attacks may inspire future generations of militants who wish to cleanse the Peninsula in much the same fashion as that attempted by al-Muqrin and AQAP.

Iraq

Since American-led forces entered Iraq in 2003, kidnapping and murder has become increasingly common. As Iraq has spiraled downward into full-scale civil war along sectarian lines between the Sunnis and Shi'ites, the country—especially Baghdad—has become the modern-day equivalent of war-torn Beirut during the Western Hostage Crisis of the 1980s. In fact, in terms of the scale of abductions and killings, Iraq has surpassed Beirut in its hostage crisis.

It is impossible to come up with a precise estimate for the death toll of Iraqi civilians from the insurgency and sectarian violence. Verifiable statistics are extremely difficult to obtain. As a result, figures for civilian casualties since the March 2003 invasion of Iraq are highly controversial. Those estimates range from as few as 43,491 killed to a high of 793,663 violent deaths due to the war.[77] Wide variation exists in estimates provided by different sources, and lack of consensus is not surprising given the chaotic situation on the ground. Reliable time series data from national mortality records are nonexistent, since official statistics are not released by the Iraqi government on a regular basis. Instead, Iraq's Ministry of Health periodically reports estimates of the number of bodies brought to hospitals. Iraq's Medico-Legal Institute, located in Baghdad, similarly provides occasional updates of the number of unidentified bodies it receives. And, while the United States and the UN Assistance Mission for Iraq (UNAMI) as well as nongovernmental organizations such as the Iraq Body Count have released estimates of the number of civilian casualties, those reports are incomplete, based on different methodologies and on varying time periods, so that the final number is likely to remain indeterminate.[78]

As a result, it is only prudent to exercise extreme caution when considering estimates of Iraqi civilian casualties. It is clear, nonetheless, that the toll undoubtedly has been tens of thousands of people. For example, UNAMI released a report in early 2007 that estimated that 34,452 civilians—an average of 94 people each day—were killed, and that 36,685 were wounded in 2006 by the ongoing insurgency and sectarian violence.[79] In fact, the level of violence during the last six months of 2006 reached an all-time high.

The data for 2007 and early 2008 indicate a general decline in the overall level of violence, although very lethal individual events, especially bombings, continued to happen throughout this period. UNAMI released a follow-up report on November 13, 2007, that concluded, "Conservatively, it is estimated that since January 2007 over 10,000 civilians have been killed and a further 21,000 plus injured."[80] The first six months of 2007, which coincided with the U.S. military's ramp-up for the surge, remained deadly for Iraqi civilians; this period was followed by overall improvements in the level of violence.[81] It remains an open question, however, whether a downward trajectory in civilian casualties can be sustained as the Iraqi government assumes more responsibility for the security situation and containing sectarian violence.

Insurgent and terrorist groups are not the only ones that are taking part in hostage-taking and killings. Evidence exists that criminal gangs abduct foreigners and sell them to the highest bidder, regardless of what that bidder intends to do with the hostage. These gangs, according to a spokesman for Iraq's Ministry of the Interior, "have turned [kidnapping] into a cottage industry."[82] Through 2005, at least 425 foreigners and countless numbers of civilians were abducted by insurgent groups, 18 percent of whom were killed. The numbers for Iraqis kidnapped are uncertain. Iraqi officials estimate that as many as thirty are kidnapped each day, but only 5 to 10 percent of Iraqi cases are reported.[83] The groups involved in kidnappings are as diverse ideologically as they are numerous, spanning the spectrum from jihadists to religious-nationalists to Ba'athist remnants and those referred to as Sodalists. Demands are also extremely diverse. They include the release of female prisoners, the rebuilding of houses destroyed by military operations, the withdrawal of foreign forces and companies, or the withdrawal of diplomatic missions.

Treatment of hostages differs by the group. Some hostages have reported being treated well. Others, as is evident from videos released by the kidnappers, have been treated harshly. For example, al-Zarqawi's Tawhid wa al-Jihad group—which later changed its name to al-Qa'ida in Iraq—has been known to torture hostages.[84] The various organizations do not appear to adhere to any defined and common targeting doctrine. However, there are some hints about the targeting doctrines of individual groups. The Jihad Brigades in Iraq, for example, published a statement in 2004 saying that women, children, and hired individuals would not be killed.[85]

Although economic incentives play an important role in domestic kidnappings, sectarian clashes appear to be a primary motivation.[86] Several hard-line jihadist groups have displayed anti-Shi'ite tendencies; the most active in pursuing an anti-Shi'ite campaign has been the now deceased

Abu-Mus'ab al-Zarqawi and his al-Qa'ida in Iraq organization. For example, in 2005, allegations of sectarian enmity swirled in Salman Pak, Iraq, where as many as one hundred Shi'ites were said to have been kidnapped. Reports indicated that the kidnappers demanded that all of the Shi'ites in the area leave immediately or else the hostages would be executed. Shortly thereafter, fifty bodies were found in the Tigris River. Many believe these victims came from Salman Pak and that a mass attack on Shi'ites had taken place. Other mass graves have been found, one of which contained the bodies of thirty-six Baghdad Police Academy applicants. Abductions and murders have continued unabated in Iraq at a steadily growing pace, fueled in large part by sectarian conflict with Shi'ites and Sunnis both committing atrocities.

While some kidnappings include demands, with promises of the subsequent release of hostages, al-Qa'ida in Iraq does not always offer demands. For example, when two Moroccan diplomats were kidnapped and executed in 2005, no demands were issued before the diplomats' executions were announced nearly two weeks after the abductions.[87] The same scenario played out when the Egyptian ambassador to Iraq was abducted in 2005. In this case, the group released two statements and video of the ambassador's forced "confessions." A lengthy notice of his execution was released to jihadist websites within a week. A substantial portion of the statement focused on accusations against the Egyptian government, concerning its apostasy and counterterrorism campaign against radical elements in the country.[88]

In late 2005, after al-Zarqawi's group issued a direct threat to diplomatic missions in Iraq, the group abducted six Sudanese nationals, including five diplomats.[89] In a video released on jihadist websites, the group threatened to execute them in forty-eight hours unless Sudan ended diplomatic relations with the new Iraqi government, closed the embassy, and withdrew Sudanese officials from Iraq. Sudan closed its embassy and withdrew its diplomatic staff.[90] In mid-January, another video was posted to jihadist websites in which al-Zarqawi's group showed the release of the hostages. In the video, the group reiterated its threat to countries that recognize the occupation and the new Iraqi government by keeping a diplomatic mission in Iraq.[91]

In July 2005 al-Zarqawi's group abducted two Algerian diplomats and claimed responsibility for the abductions through jihadist websites. Several days later, the GSPC issued a statement on jihadist websites congratulating al-Zarqawi's group. The GSPC asked al-Qa'ida in Iraq to interrogate and post the confessions of the two diplomats. According to the GSPC, the confessions would be to involvement in two massacres of Algerian Muslims. Shortly afterwards, al-Zarqawi's group claimed to have executed the two diplomats. Subsequent statements from the group responded to those who denounced the killings and confirmed responsibility for killing the two "apostates."[92]

Efforts to build or sustain public support appear to be a frequent tactic of al-Qa'ida in Iraq and other insurgent groups.. Before executing a hostage, al-Qa'ida in Iraq typically issues a statement saying that the hostage has been turned over to the group's Legal Council to "enforce the rule of God" or "enforce the ruling of the Legal Court." This framing of the execution in legalistic terms is meant to increase credibility and legitimacy in the eyes of the public. Other groups have also published guidelines for hostage-takers and the treatment of prisoners in an effort to standardize their practices and reduce chaos and public revulsion.[93] Part of this effort involves the use of videos. While video footage of hostages has appeared in other areas of the world, groups in Iraq have popularized it and standardized the practice. Videos are edited and released, often with Arabic subtitles if the hostage is speaking in another language. In several al-Qa'ida in Iraq videos, the hostage is wearing an orange jumpsuit, meant to signify the reversal of roles by evoking the similar jumpsuits worn by detainees held in Guantánamo. Additionally, the hostage's personal items may be videotaped in front of the kneeling hostage; identification documents are often spread out among these items. Identification documents frequently appear on the Internet accompanying a claim of responsibility for abductions, even if no video accompanies it. Groups may also digitally insert their logos in the corners of the hostage video, much like a network television station. Music is sometimes playing during the video.

BEHEADINGS

Beheading has been acceptable throughout Islamic history as a method of execution, but never in the way that some contemporary jihadists use it. The practice is rooted in the forty-seventh sura of the Qur'an: "When you encounter the unbelievers on the battlefield, strike off their heads until you have crushed them completely; then, bind the prisoners tightly." Also, according to Muhammad's earliest biographer, the Prophet "ordered the decapitation of 700 men of the Jewish Banu Qurayza tribe in Medina for plotting against him," giving the practice "the aura of authenticity."[94]

While the videos of Daniel Pearl's and Paul Johnson's grisly murders offered graphic evidence of the use of beheadings, the practice became routine in Iraq. For instance, in March 2006 authorities discovered thirty beheaded bodies near Baqubah. Although the identity of the executioners remains unknown, such discoveries, combined with executions where specific groups—especially al-Qa'ida in Iraq while under al-Zarqawi's leadership—claimed credit, became an all too common event. The fact that al-Zarqawi did the beheadings personally is a departure from ancient practice, when executioners were usually hired, reinforcing its role as a terrorist tactic.

For the jihadists, the act itself has become imbued with imagery and symbolism that have no historical antecedents. A primary example involves the use of language. Initially, on videotaped executions al-Zarqawi and other jihadists used the Arabic word meaning "beheading," but later they began to use the word for "slaughter." This same word is normally used to describe the act of slaughtering a lamb for the Hajj, implying that the victims are themselves animals, since the Arabic word for beheading implies that the victim was human. Adding to this animal imagery is symbolism that accompanies the knife that is used in such executions. While executions were traditionally carried out with a large sword, today's jihadist executions are usually carried out with a small knife. In fact, the knife itself is the same kind that is used to slaughter lambs. The symbolism behind the act functions to transform it into a ritual, especially in Iraq. Videos of beheadings typically follow a set format: first showing the victim kneeling in front of a number of masked jihadists and their flag, then the "confessions" of the victim, and finally the execution.

Beheading as a tactic has been met with criticism from both inside and outside of the jihadist movement in Iraq. This practice was addressed by al-Zawahiri in a 2005 letter to al-Zarqawi that was captured and released by American authorities. Al-Zawahiri wrote that ordinary Muslims did not find the videotaped decapitation of hostages palatable and asked al-Zarqawi to discontinue these actions, due to its effect on popular support:

> However . . . I say to you: that we are in a battle, and that more than half of this battle is taking place in the battlefield of the media. And that we are in a battle for the hearts and minds of our Umma [Islamic

community]. . . . And that we can kill the captives by bullet. That would achieve that which is most sought after without exposing ourselves to the questions and answering to doubts. We don't need this.[95]

Internal criticisms of this sort may have caused al-Zarqawi and other jihadists to stop releasing videos of beheadings. Such videos, formerly widespread, virtually disappeared during 2005 and 2006, and beheadings were allegedly restricted to members of the Badr Corps,[96] the Shi'ite militia organization that is the primary target of the Umar Brigade, a section of al-Zarqawi's group. Moreover, captured al-Zarqawi network letters from Iraq indicate that there were restrictions placed on beheadings of Islamic Party members, tribal shaykhs, and "renegades" by al-Qa'ida in Iraq and the umbrella organization Mujahidin Shura Council in Iraq.[97]

ECONOMIC TARGETING

Discussion of economic warfare as a tactic, especially against the West, is a recurrent theme in jihadist statements and publications. The actual choice of economic targets for terrorist attacks has varied by country, based on the relative centrality of the target to that country's economy as well as its symbolic value. The successful destruction of the twin towers at New York's World Trade Center and the consequent impact on the airline industry offer dramatic evidence of the jihadists' use of economic targeting. Regardless of the actual magnitude of the economic damages, claims that the September 11 attacks caused massive loses to U.S. gross domestic product also provided al-Qa'ida with valuable propaganda.[98] The dual economic disruption and propaganda windfall explain why reliance on economic targeting, especially against the United States, is a central element of al-Qa'ida's operations. In fact, bin Laden's personal correspondence to Taliban leader Mullah Omar demonstrates that it was a deliberate strategic decision to carry out attacks on the American economy:

> A campaign against Afghanistan will impose great long-term economic burdens, leading to further economic collapse, which will force America, God willing, to resort to the former Soviet Union's only option: withdrawal from Afghanistan, disintegration, and contraction.
>
> Thus our plan in the face of this campaign should focus on the following:

—Serving a blow to the American economy, which will lead to:
a) Further weakening of the American economy
b) Shaking the confidence in the American economy. This will lead investors to refrain from investing in America or participating in American companies, thus accelerating the fall of the American economy.[99]

Numerous other statements emphasize the need to bankrupt the United States. Those statements typically assert that the mujahidin bankrupted the Soviet Union in Afghanistan.[100]

Western Europe also has been a focal point for economic targeting. For example, both the 2004 Madrid and 2005 London bombings involved attacks against mass transit systems that are critical components of each city's infrastructure. The Madrid and London bombings were particularly lethal. The March 11, 2004, bombing of packed commuter trains during the Madrid rush hour killed 191 people and injured more than 1,000 others. It also was instrumental in leading to the electoral defeat of the conservatives, and to the withdrawal of Spanish troops from the American-led coalition forces in Iraq following the Socialist party's victory in elections that were held three days later. The July 7, 2005, coordinated attacks on the underground and one bus in central London during the morning rush hour killed 52 people and injured 770 others. Similarly, the thwarted 1995 Bojinka and 2006 United Kingdom plots to destroy commercial airliners were directed against key elements of the West's economy and could have killed hundreds of people had either been successful.

Radical Islamist groups have selectively targeted the tourism industry in South Asian and African countries. Indonesia, in particular, has been the scene of a series of bombings since 2000. For example, the Bali bombings in Indonesia targeted areas frequented by Australians and other Western tourists. The October 12, 2002, attack in the tourist district of Kuta was the deadliest act of terrorism in the history of Indonesia, killing 202 people, 164 of whom were foreign nationals, including 88 Australians, and 38 Indonesian citizens. In addition, 209 people were injured. The October 1, 2005, Bali bombings involved a series of explosions at two sites in Jimbaran and Kuta, killing about twenty people, including four Australians and one Japanese national, and wounding more than one hundred people.

Within the Middle East, the jihadists have emphasized attacks on petroleum-related targets that allow them to hit at both the Near Enemy and the Far Enemy simultaneously. Like other tactics, economic targeting of the energy industry has received a theological blessing in least one publication, *The Religious Rule on Targeting Oil Interests*.[101] Those who advocate using this tactic argue that it will cause oil prices to go up, damaging Western economies, forcing foreign multinationals to withdraw investments, and increasing the cost of occupying Iraq. These themes have found a receptive audience within the jihadist movement. In an October 2005 article titled "Al-Qa'ida's Battle Is Economic, Not Military," Abu-Mus'ab al-Najdi, a senior member of al-Qa'ida in the Arabian Peninsula who was killed in a confrontation with Saudi security forces in December 2005, explained the importance and effectiveness of attacking economic targets as part of waging a war of economic attrition against the United States.[102]

Jihadists inspired by al-Qa'ida have a history of attacking oil targets, including attacks on industry personnel in Saudi Arabia, the 2002 attack on a French oil tanker, a failed 2006 attack on a major Saudi oil facility, and the frequent attacks on pipelines in Iraq that began in June 2003. By mid-July 2003, there were over 250 recorded oil-related attacks, and similar attacks have continued in the years since then. Such attacks reflect recognition by the jihadists that increasing the costs associated with protecting Iraq's petroleum infrastructure increases the costs to the United States and its coalition partners for military operations in Iraq.[103] It is interesting to note, however, that while attacks on oil facilities and pipelines in Iraq are quite frequent, they are rarely claimed by the numerous insurgent groups operating in Iraq. This could be in recognition that doing so could decrease the Iraqi public's support for the resistance because low levels of oil production make the everyday Iraqi's life more difficult, since oil revenues are an important source for funding the reconstruction effort.

Perhaps to counterbalance such concerns, it is not surprising that the "theft" of Muslim oil by the United States is a recurrent theme emphasized in bin Laden's statements. For example, twice in December 2004 he directly urged Muslims to target oil facilities in Iraq and the Gulf in response to such theft. Bin Laden urged the mujahidin to strike supply routes and oil lines, to plant mines, and to assassinate company owners who provide the enemy with supplies. Such statements also demonstrate that bin Laden understands the central role that oil plays in the global economy. Al-Suri similarly argues for targeting major sea lanes, especially those used for transporting oil and natural gas to the West. He specifically mentions the Persian Gulf's Strait of Hormuz, the Suez Canal, the Bab al-Mendeb strait between Yemen and the Horn of Africa, and the Strait of Gibraltar.[104]

The pattern of a warning from al-Qa'ida and an attack on an oil facility has been repeated throughout the Gulf. In February 2006 an attempted suicide attack on a Saudi oil facility occurred following encouragement from al-Zawahiri in 2005.[105] Days after Ayman al-Zawahiri's September 2006 warning that al-Qa'ida's next round of attacks would be against economic targets in the Gulf, two suicide attacks on oil facilities in Yemen were foiled by authorities.[106]

TERRORISM AS DETERRENCE

In December 2003 an anonymously authored document called *Jihad in Iraq: Hopes and Dangers* began to circulate on jihadist websites.[107] It provides an analysis of the effects of the war in Iraq on the American economy and a strategy for action. A number of goals and plans of action are laid out, addressing military, information, internal, and security aspects of the war. It is notable that, given the preceding section's discussion of targeting oil-related facilities in Iraq, the anonymous writer lists strikes against oil facilities and initiating conflicts with the Shi'ites as important military objectives. The unification of the mujahidin and attempts to gain popular support by explaining the conflict to the masses are identified as important information objectives. Internal objectives include gathering fatwas in support of jihad and unification of the mujahidin, and—as a last resort—bringing the Shi'ites into the fight if possible. These ideas are neither new nor surprising.

The last half of the document, however, is innovative as far as jihadist open-source propaganda is concerned. It outlines a strategy for insurgency in Iraq, based on the central thesis that an Islamic resistance could not defeat the United States and its Coalition partners militarily. However, if the jihadist movement could remove America's European allies from the equation, the war would become a protracted and costly conflict for the United States to bear in isolation. Given this objective, the author turns to a discussion of the political and economic positions of Britain, Poland, and Spain in order to determine which one might be most vulnerable to pressure from the jihadists to force its withdrawal from Iraq. Spain is determined to be the most vulnerable. In a passage bolded and underlined in the original document, the anonymous author writes:

> We say that in order to force the Spanish government to withdraw from Iraq the resistance should deal painful blows to its forces. This should be accompanied by an information campaign clarifying the truth of the matter inside Iraq. It is necessary to make utmost use of the upcoming general election in Spain in March next year.
>
> We think that the Spanish government could not tolerate more than two, maximum three blows, after which it will have to withdraw as a result of popular pressure. If its troops still remain in Iraq after these blows, then the victory of the Socialist Party is almost secured, and the withdrawal of the Spanish forces will be on its electoral programme.[108]

This passage was especially prescient. The March 2004 terrorist attacks, coming just seventy-two hours before the polls opened in Spain, produced the predicted outcome. The attacks were perceived by a large portion of the public to be retaliation for Spanish involvement in the war. The Spanish Socialist Party won the election, campaigning heavily on a platform of withdrawing Spanish military forces from Iraq. After the Socialist victory, those forces were indeed withdrawn.

Analysts are divided over whether or not the Madrid bombers were familiar with *Jihad in Iraq,* but there is some evidence that suggests that they could have come in contact with the document. In April 2006 Spanish authorities released an indictment of the surviving members of the Madrid cell, stating that two of the plot's key planners had extensively visited a jihadist website on which the document was posted.[109] Thus, while there is ample evidence that the cell was not formally affiliated with al-Qa'ida, bin Laden's ideas may have inspired its members to launch the simultaneous mass-casualty attacks.

Even if the Madrid bombings were not explicitly designed to affect the outcome of the Spanish parliamentary election, the desire to influence European electoral outcomes by enhancing the chances of parties that are less receptive to committing military forces to support American foreign policy has obvious appeal. In at least one instance, there may have been an attempt to achieve that objective. According to an Italian Interior Ministry document, which was described by the Italian newspaper *La Repubblica,* an informant working for Italian authorities met with a number of foreign citizens in Milan in January 2006. The purported meetings involved discussions about plans to detonate two explosive charges in a

Milan train station thirty minutes apart in March in an effort to influence the outcome of Italy's April 9, 2006, general elections (however, no attack actually occurred at that time). In 2007, the Arabic-language paper *al-Hayat* reported that a French government report warned of attacks timed to influence the presidential elections in France, citing al-Qa'ida's desire to repeat the "Spanish scenario."[110]

If the political consequences of the terrorist attacks in Madrid are applicable to other countries, especially Western European democracies, attacking American allies appears to be a successful tactic for the jihadists. Certainly, radical Islamists have concluded that such inferences are warranted. Abu-Mus'ab al-Suri, in *The Call to Global Islamic Resistance*, argues that terrorist acts like the Madrid train bombings deter any nation from considering an alliance with the United States in Iraq or participation in the broader War on Terror. Al-Suri extends the notion of terrorism as deterrence even further. He advocates making any country (even if it is not an American ally) that pursues the mujahidin and jihadists "subject to an immediate operation of deterrence" by any Muslim or jihadist group capable of launching attacks.[111]

CONCLUSIONS

The choice of tactics and the types of terrorist operations conducted to advance the global jihad force radical Islamists to balance competing, and sometimes conflicting, priorities. Risks to the group's long-term survival, effects on recruitment, the effectiveness of security service countermeasures, and the ability to sustain public support from fellow Muslims are important considerations that either facilitate or constrain their flexibility in pursuing specific actions. In essence, the jihadists confront a variety of internal and external pressures, especially the need to make their actions acceptable to the Islamic community, that influence tactics and target selection.

As Peter Chalk explains, terrorist groups "are constrained by ceilings in operational finance and skill sets, [and] most have deliberately chosen to follow the course of least resistance," choosing tactics that "offer a reasonably high chance of success and whose consequences can be relatively easily predicted."[112] Moreover, al-Zawahiri has emphasized the need for the mujahidin to communicate their message in simple terms and to have a clear, understandable slogan in order to reach the people and win their "confidence, respect and affection."[113] The only absolute condition in jihadist targeting guidance is that the target and weapon chosen must have the maximum possible effect. Consequently, the choice of tactics and the scale of operations largely reflect capabilities interacting with the desire to maximize media coverage and erode the confidence of opposing regimes in their ability to provide effective security against terrorism. Simply put, the jihadists want to convey the message that they cannot be stopped.

Our review of operations and tactics demonstrates that the jihadists are very adept at social learning. Tactics and operations have been tested in one arena of conflict. Lessons are drawn from successes and failures. Successful ones subsequently are adopted for use elsewhere. The suicide bombings by Hamas and Hizballah are apt examples. For these reasons, there has been a dramatic increase in operations designed to achieve extensive media coverage, especially in the Western and Arab markets, and to exert maximum psychological impact.

It is not surprising that, with their imagery of martyrdom combined with the horror they inspire, suicide attacks that aim for mass casualties have become a favorite tactic of Islamic radicals. The series of martyrdom operations conducted in the Middle East, America, and Europe have generated massive media coverage in the United States and Western Europe. As a result, the jihadists believe that suicide attacks offer a proven way to communicate their message to a broad audience of potential recruits and sympathizers while instilling fear in their adversaries.

Kidnapping and assassinations also have a long history of being used by terrorists to convey political messages and provoke fear, so it is not surprising that the radical Islamists have adopted this tactic as well. Lebanon, Algeria, and Iraq offer classic examples of the use of this tactic. Reliance on kidnapping and assassinations is likely to continue for several reasons. Kidnappings produce intense media coverage when Westerners are taken hostage. They demonstrate the inability of security services to ensure personal safety. Finally, kidnapping can foster intense turmoil and exacerbate existing tensions. For example, the mass abductions of Shi'ites in Iraq, such as those in the Salman Pak region, or of Sunnis in Baghdad are partly intended to spur sectarian relocation.[114]

The ongoing insurgency in Iraq offers a large-scale, real-world laboratory in which the jihadists can learn. Tactics tested in Iraq—especially more advanced urban warfare and the use of improvised explosive devices

(IEDs)—have been transferred to the resurgent Taliban in Afghanistan and other radical Islamist groups.

Selective economic targeting of highly visible or strategically important sectors also offers the jihadists an opportunity to gain extensive publicity and exert a large psychological impact on their enemies. In fact, undermining the stability of Western economies, as well as the economies of pro-Western regimes in Muslim countries, is one of the most effective ways for the jihadists to attack their adversaries. Despite the rhetoric of being willing to engage military forces, attacking economic targets such as oil facilities or tourist hotels poses far less risk and offers a greater likelihood of success than facing Western troops in battle. This makes economic targeting both attractive and likely to continue.

6

FUTURE DIRECTIONS

It is a mistake to try to look too far ahead. The chain of destiny can only be grasped one link at a time. . . .

Never, never, never believe any war will be smooth and easy, or that anyone who embarks on the strange voyage can measure the tides and hurricanes he will encounter. The statesman who yields to war fever must realize that once the signal is given, he is no longer the master of policy but the slave of unforeseeable and uncontrollable events.

Sir Winston Churchill, various speeches

ONCE LAUNCHED, there are some ideas and political movements that are unlikely to ever go away. There are movements whose ideas find resonance with a sufficient number of people to practically guarantee that they will live on in some manner or another. The global jihadist movement is quite likely to be such a phenomenon. In large measure, this stems from the fact that the evolving global jihadist movement, like the al-Qa'ida group that gave it its impetus and that focused world attention on it, is motivated by long-term strategic goals.[1] Those ambitions are captured in Qutb's declaration that the movement's "foremost objective is to change the practices of this society."[2] Because the jihad is portrayed to its adherents as a long-term struggle, the success of the jihad for some Islamic militants is based on simply *working* to reach the movement's goals and to fulfill divine duties—not by achieving victory.[3] The result is a movement not easily deterred by a lack of tangible evidence that its strategic vision is being achieved.

Interestingly, modern communications technology, especially the Internet, is likely to reinforce the jihadists' resilience. Access to the Internet as a venue for propaganda, the essential lifeblood of the jihadist movement, has been a critical element in advancing the Islamic extremists' cause. The use of websites has allowed jihadists to widely and rapidly disseminate materials meant to indoctrinate and inspire. Terrorist groups often employ various formats when releasing video statements—including videos formatted for mobile phone use—that allow messages to reach exceptionally large audiences. Instead of relying on regional markets of varying size for the transmission of such materials (such as relying on one particular bookstore in one city, or relying on a particular group of individuals for ideological preparation), the Internet provides a vast "home market" for jihadists, allowing for the diversification of ideas, which in turn broadens the movement's appeal. The result is that the movement becomes more capable of reaching critical mass and creating a self-sustaining ideology. There is no small irony in this: although the jihadist movement appears to be a reaction to globalization, it is also exploiting one of globalization's primary tools.[4]

A pragmatic willingness to modify its organizational dynamics and tactical doctrine in pursuit of its underlying strategic vision of restoring the caliphate is a major key to the movement's ideological evolution and diversification. In essence, the jihadist movement is likely to remain dynamic, constantly recreating and adjusting organizational characteristics as it seeks to unify religious and political authority. Its leadership—whether al-Qa'ida or other groups that may emerge—will continue to capitalize on preexisting feelings of marginalization and anger within the Muslim community, stressing political issues such as the Israeli-Palestinian conflict, the war in Iraq, or perceptions that Islam is under attack to attract new recruits and to inspire violence; this will likely be effective as long as such appeals appear to be on behalf of Islam.

As a result, if the West is to maintain its values while simultaneously coexisting with or countering members of the global jihad, it must understand the jihadists' ideology and motivations. If the West oversimplifies the jihadists' cause and finds it more comforting to pigeonhole them in some pejorative category, it will actually play into the hands of the most fanatic jihadists. Similarly, if the West tries to negotiate with or use military force against radical Islamists based on a belief that its religious position is correct and Islam's is fundamentally evil, then it will again be fulfilling the expectations of its adversaries and fueling the disagreement without advancing national security. Instead, no matter how much Westerners legitimately disagree with the jihadists' cause, they must analyze and understand the jihadists' beliefs, the resulting motivations, and the interpretations that individual group members make of these fundamental positions. Without dispassionate insights of these sorts, it will be impossible to find potential allies within the Muslim world or identify adversaries willing to listen to Western arguments.

What then is likely to be the future direction of the jihadist movement over the next several years? In order to provide plausible answers to the question of the jihadist movement's future direction, this chapter focuses on the likelihood of continuity and change in its strategic vision. We also examine whether the jihadists are likely to continue to evolve in how they organize and operate.

PROSPECTS FOR CONTINUITY OR CHANGE IN STRATEGY

A common theme underlying the strategic vision of the jihadist movement, as we have seen, is the need for popular support from the Muslim masses. This is not surprising. The leaders of al-Qa'ida recognize that sustaining popular support is critical to the long-term success of most insurgencies and terrorist groups. Messages aimed at the Muslim public or key elements within that public also can provide insights into debates over appropriate strategies to pursue in order for the jihadists to succeed.

We have provided ample evidence that the leadership of al-Qa'ida recognizes the importance of shaping and responding to popular sentiment. Bin Laden, al-Zawahiri, and other senior leaders have all been extremely concerned with whether the Muslim public perceives al-Qa'ida's actions as consistent with the tenets of Islam, especially Muhammad's guidance for providing clear warning and giving infidels an opportunity to convert before they are attacked. For example, bin Laden released messages offering a truce to Europe in April 2004 and to the United States in January 2006. In those messages, he explicitly warned of continued attacks if these populations did not convert to Islam.[5] The offers and their rejection have allowed al-Qa'ida to preempt, or at least blunt, assertions that the jihadists' campaign against the United States and its allies is inconsistent with Islamic theology. In effect, the primary audience for these offers was not the West, but rather the Muslim world.

Recognizing the importance within the Muslim world of having theological sanction for their actions, bin Laden and al-Zawahiri have shifted the focus in their statements over the last several years. They and other senior leaders of al-Qa'ida now prefer to speak to the Muslim world more frequently. Their messages are used to rally support and establish the theological basis for future major attacks. This campaign became more visible in September 2006, when al-Zawahiri and an American Muslim convert named Adam Gadhan—also known as Azzam al-Amriki—appeared on a video that invited Americans to convert to Islam. Even earlier, in a 2006 video statement, al-Zawahiri invited President Bush to convert to Islam, stating that if Bush did convert, "we will forget all the harm and crimes you committed against us and against our brothers and our people." Al-Zawahiri continued:

> You have provided us with all the legal and rational reasons to fight you and punish you. You have committed ugly crimes, breached treaties that you used to impose on others to abide by. For our part, we have repeatedly warned you and repeatedly offered a truce with you. So, we now have legal and rational justifications to continue fighting you until your power is destroyed or you give in and surrender.

Given its centrality to the movement's overall prospects for success, establishing and maintaining public support for the jihad will remain a major priority. Debate within the movement, however, is likely to center on how best to build and keep public support for violent jihad. Resolving this question has been and is likely to continue to be a source of intergroup—and possibly, intragroup—tensions that may foster changes in strategy. There are two contentious issues that are likely to shape the outcome of that tension: first, disagreements between radical Islamists about the proper application of takfir doctrine; and second, tensions created by the Near Enemy/Far Enemy divide. The later issue, however, is less likely to create as much tension within the jihadist movement as takfiri ideology, primarily because bin Laden and his colleagues have adopted various Near Enemy jihadist groups under the banner of the World Islamic Front.[6] Moreover, the new jihadist battlefield in Iraq not only provided al-Qa'ida with a way to stay relevant and continue strikes against the United States, but also provided it with the opportunity to begin the military groundwork for creating an Islamic state close to Israel and the "apostate" regimes of the Middle East. In many ways, the American-led invasion of Iraq, with participation by other Western countries, provided a nearly ideal situation for the global jihadist movement to grow and prosper. It simultaneously offered an opportunity to join the jihad to Muslim militants from Saudi Arabia and other Arab countries who want to fight for an Islamic state close to home, as well as to foreign fighters willing to travel greater distances to strike the United States.

Another factor that may foster strategic evolution is the movement's inherently expansionist intentions. While many mujahidin may give up the fight once an Islamic state becomes a reality, the jihad's strategic leadership is committed to expanding the jihad beyond the borders of their Islamic states, in efforts to regain control of the Middle East and beyond, creating one Islamic state after another.[7] Still another important objective of global jihadist strategy is to compel Western security forces to operate in multiple, remote arenas simultaneously, thereby exhausting their resources and diluting their ability to bring to bear overwhelming military superiority.[8] Also important to note is that, more often than not, jihadist strategy is dependent on creating and filling a security vacuum in the Islamic world. Afghanistan, Iraq, Saudi Arabia, and Egypt have all been targeted as parts of this strategy in the last fifty years, by both Near and Far Enemy advocates and with varying degrees of success.

As a West Point study of al-Qa'ida's history in the Horn of Africa shows, al-Qa'ida—often in complex tribal or political situations—has had problems utilizing overly chaotic states as bases from which it can launch attacks (Somalia being the example cited in the study).[9] Training camps and other critical terrorist infrastructure in states with no central authority present easier targets for counterterrorist or military operations than in states with weak—but existent—authority. This is essentially the case with Iraq. No external attacks have been successfully executed by AQI, with the exception of the 2005 Amman hotel bombings and a rocket attack on U.S. naval vessels docked in Aqaba, Jordan.[10]

States with weak authority allow terror groups to operate with some level of protection (diplomatic or otherwise)—like that provided al-Qa'ida by the Taliban—giving the terrorist group sufficient comfort to set up its infrastructure and mount a greater number of successful external operations. For al-Qa'ida Central, a safe haven, much like it had in pre-9/11 Afghanistan, significantly increased its ability to plan and carry out successful external operations. It is conceivable that the group may have already found a comparable safe haven in Pakistan's Federally Administered Tribal Areas (FATA). Aside from finding a new safe haven, the other potential option would be to create one by establishing a security vacuum and then filling it by controlling the territory. This is what Naji proposes. Al-Zawahiri also advocates this approach, specifically for Iraq and Afghanistan: "And from this, the critical importance of the Jihad in Iraq and Afghanistan becomes clear, because the defeat of the Crusaders there—soon, Allah permitting—will lead to the setting up of two

Mujahid Emirates which will be launch pads for the liberation of the Islamic lands and the establishment of the Caliphate, with Allah's permission."[11]

The denial of opportunities to create and fill security vacuums must be crucial in Western counterterrorism policy. Al-Suri's decentralization argument is partially in response to policies designed to do just that. By taking away the short-term goal of establishing an Islamic state, and replacing it with a new goal of simple resistance, al-Suri hopes to move the jihad away from relying on security vacuums and create a sustainable pulsation of violence (swarming doctrine), all in an effort to weaken and exhaust the enemy.[12]

As we have seen in Naji's *The Management of Savagery*, whenever the jihadists believe that they are getting closer to attaining their goals, the more they discuss maintaining—and not just creating—a viable Islamic state.[13] This may result in a constant escalation of violence as a strategic deterrent for keeping governments from retaliating against the families of the mujahidin—and as a deterrent for keeping other nations from attempting to remove an Islamic regime from power, as the United States and its allies did in Afghanistan. Thus, escalating violence as a strategic choice is likely, especially if it seems to advance the jihadists' ability to achieve their goals. Daniel Benjamin and Steve Simon point out that, "in the view of its practitioners, violence is sanctified, and therefore the more, the better."[14]

Given the West's dependence on oil and natural gas imports, the jihadists are likely to attempt to expand attacks against the energy industry. Targeting oil and gas production facilities in the Middle East is likely to be a focal point for such attacks as long as they do not undercut public support for the jihad. It also is likely that jihadist concepts of economic warfare will become increasingly sophisticated. Possible strategies include efforts to force the withdrawal of foreign investment from Muslim countries governed by secular regimes, or attempts to trigger a currency crisis in the United States, the United Kingdom, or the European Union.

America's dependence on imported oil, however, is the most strategically important target for the jihadists.[15] The brutal reality is that total energy independence, while a constant in the rhetoric of American politicians since the 1973 Arab oil embargo, is an illusion. Specifically with respect to petroleum, there has been no realistic hope of attaining it for decades. One need only look at the dramatic gap between projected goals and actual oil imports to realize that the United States is incapable of meeting all of its energy needs for liquid fuels. Such dependence may ultimately leave U.S. foreign policy and its domestic economy highly vulnerable to economic warfare. Moreover, unlike the energy autarky that existed prior to World War II, when the United States economy was self-sufficient in terms of its oil supplies and needs, oil today is a global rather than segmented market. It seems doubtful that al-Qa'ida or other adherents to the global jihad will fail to try to exploit this vulnerability in the coming years.

PROSPECTS FOR ORGANIZATIONAL EVOLUTION

Just as the strategy pursued by radical Islamists is likely to adapt to changing circumstances, the ways in which the jihadist movement organizes and operates is evolving. In the near term, it is likely to become more rather than less decentralized, emulating many of the attributes described in al-Suri's model.[16] Al-Suri has said in public statements and interviews that it would be a mistake to pin the hopes of the global movement on a single group or set of leaders. Moving to a more decentralized structure, inspired by an ideal and lacking any fixed lines of authority, may well result in an expansion of "freelance" jihad, relying on local initiative and entrepreneurship. If this happens, then countermeasures that focus exclusively on identifying and removing leaders as a means of fighting the jihad are unlikely to be effective, and their shortcomings may actually accelerate the evolution of the jihadist movement into the fragmented, leaderless model discussed above. Such a development would be a major setback for counterterrorism efforts.

Evidence exists that al-Qa'ida increasingly is taking the group and the jihadist movement back to an even less complex mode of operation than the group operated under in the 1990s, when they displayed a tendency to work with local militants. Since the September 11 attacks, al-Qa'ida has pursued a dual track approach. It has aggressively sought engagement in the activities of local militants. At the same time, it has attempted to inspire the various "grassroots" networks of jihadists without offering any direct guidance, support, or contact. This is a new operational model for the jihadist movement, with various grassroots groups appearing to have no direct links to al-Qa'ida proper. Instead, at best, they seem to be only loosely coordinated, if at all, by al-Qa'ida proper as they engage in operations. The reliance on small, regional networks is likely to increase and thereby lead al-Qa'ida to more frequent emphasis on local grievances and Near Enemy targeting.

Al-Qa'ida already has solidified preexisting connections with other jihadist networks by formally merging with them. It merged with al-Zarqawi's Tawhid wa al-Jihad network, later becoming known as al-Qa'ida in Iraq. Subsequently, it brought the Algerian GSPC under the al-Qa'ida label. In January 2007 the GSPC changed its name to the al-Qa'ida Organization in the Lands of the Islamic Maghreb.[17] Similarly, in November 2007 al-Qa'ida announced a merger with the Libyan Islamic Fighting Group (LIFG). That group and al-Qa'ida leaders have had a longstanding relationship. In fact, some senior LIFG members appear to have belonged to al-Qa'ida's senior command structure and assisted with attacks.[18]

Achieving mergers with other jihadist groups under the al-Qa'ida umbrella has long been a part of al-Qa'ida's overall strategy to sustain the global jihad. Its bylaws state that it aims to create a "united global jihad movement," and that al-Qa'ida will continue attempts to merge with "true" jihadist groups.[19] Although these mergers certainly extend the operational reach of al-Qa'ida, it is possible they could work against the parent group if those mergers force al-Qa'ida's leadership to divert scarce resources to support the adopted organizations.

Mergers could also seriously impact the groups that join al-Qa'ida. For example, in reports that surfaced less than a year after the September 2006 announcement of the merger between the GSPC and al-Qa'ida that created al-Qa'ida in the Lands of the Islamic Maghreb, there were indications of internal disagreements within the GSPC about the decision to merge. Some critics alleged the decision to merge was made unilaterally by Abu-Mus'ab Abd-al-Wadud, also known as Abdelmalek Droukdel, the future AQLIM amir. In addition to being upset over the lack of consultation, some AQLIM members were also upset with the escalation in violence against targets in locations frequented by civilians. The escalation of violence represented a reversal of the GSPC's previous position, which emphasized trying to avoid indiscriminate violence in order to generate public support.

The more al-Qa'ida relies on small local networks instead of larger, more centralized networks, the better its operational security will become. In essence, al-Qa'ida will be trading tactical control for operational security. The smaller decentralized networks will still need operational expertise, gained either by connections to experienced jihadists or through the

Internet. The recent focus by the jihadists on decentralization may help the movement evade counterterrorism authorities. It certainly will provide more autonomy to individual units. This could lead to more opportunities for the jihadists to experiment and innovate at the tactical level. Al-Suri's decentralization theory, if fully utilized, will present serious challenges to counterterrorism efforts for some time to come.

Although killing the movement's leadership will not likely end the organization, the death of bin Laden and al-Zawahiri could do serious damage to the "unity first" jihadist crowd; as a declassified National Intelligence Estimate released in September 2006 says, their deaths (if they happened in quick succession) could "exacerbate strains and disagreements" that, in turn, could cause al-Qa'ida to fracture into smaller groups. The estimate concludes that the resulting "splinter groups" would initially pose a less serious threat to the United States than al-Qa'ida before such fractures, but that this would likely be temporary.[20] In fact, the resulting splinter groups might eventually pose a larger threat, over a more extensive operational area, with far less chance of discovery through data mining of communications intelligence and similar techniques.

An increase in freelance jihadist groups, which maintain only loose ties to any central leadership, probably will help the movement not only to evade counterterrorism authorities but also to provide individual units with more autonomy, and it will likely lead to more opportunities to experiment and innovate at the tactical level. However, this will also make it more difficult for jihadist leaders to implement a coherent overall strategy.[21] Hence, the simplification of the strategic vision by strategists such as Abu-Mus'ab al-Suri, who, by erasing the need for any deep philosophical thinking that goes beyond attacking the West, Israel, "apostates," and "renegades" in defense of Islam, are attempting to maintain operational momentum and initiative. This approach makes sense because, while bin Laden and al-Zawahiri are both hugely popular in jihadist circles, al-Qa'ida's leadership seems limited at this time to inspiring, influencing, and occasionally pushing a specific targeting agenda.[22] Since these two leaders are currently the most hunted men in the world, it is likely that incitement and inspiration is all they can do without posing a threat to operational security. Moreover, if decentralization accelerates, these and other prominent figures will be needed less and less to guide the movement and to provide the inspiration for attacks, as al-Qa'ida becomes a self-sustaining movement.

Although the global jihad is a religious-based movement, not all of those who identify themselves as jihadists turn to religion as the primary driving force behind their willingness to continue to take action. Among trainees in the Afghan camps, Nasiri found a wide variation in the degree of religious devotion.[23] Thus, when considering continuity and change in terms of the global jihad's organizational dynamics, it is essential that we understand the differing types of individuals and groups that form what is loosely labeled the global jihadist movement. We believe there are at least four different types of individuals and groups that make up the overall movement: religious fundamentalists, geopolitical strategists, national insurgents, and terrorists. Each has its own organizational attributes: primary motivation for participating in violent jihad, loyalty, cognitive openness, negotiation style, and responsiveness to outside leadership. Table 6.1 summarizes our classification system. We readily concede that our schema is imperfect and do not mean to assert that any individual jihadist can be placed in one of the four categories mentioned above with absolute certainty. Instead, our goal is to create starting points for assessing the future evolution of the jihadist movement. Moreover, because we think that genuine differences among the various radical Islamist groups (and among individual militants) are based on their organizational attributes, such understanding can provide the basis for defining the parameters of the threat they pose and determining whether they are truly implacable foes bent on winning a clash of civilizations.

Religious Fundamentalists

The most obvious set of individuals who become active in the global jihad are religious fundamentalists, who are motivated by their desire to bring about a society ruled by Islamic law and custom.[24] While all jihadists share a belief that an Islamic society is the goal, religious fundamentalists who become sufficiently radicalized become jihadists to transform their belief into reality. In their efforts to accomplish that objective, some fundamentalists would like to restore the caliphate or recapture any lands that were ever ruled by Muslims. Others believe in "evangelism at gun point," and they talk about forcing the conversion of the unbelievers or eliminating them through combat. Fundamentalists are followers of the theoreticians we have identified in preceding chapters. Their personal knowledge of the scriptures and of the theological basis for their beliefs may vary from

Table 6.1. Organizational Attributes by Type of Radical Islamist Group

Organizational Attributes	Religious Fundamentalists	Geopolitical Strategists	National Insurgents	Hard-Core Terrorists
Primary Motivation	Religion	Large-scale political transformation	Domestic regime change	Violent action, revenge
Principal Loyalty	Religious beliefs	Transnational or national cause	Nation, ethnic group, tribe	Flexible, often immediate colleagues
Cognitive Openness	Rigid viewpoint; believe divinely inspired	May be flexible; goal and long-term orientation	May be flexible; goal and victory orientation	Rigid viewpoint; goals may be unclear
Negotiation Style	Not interested in negotiation; may expect "magical" solution	May be interested in and understand negotiation; logical and may be good negotiators	May be interested in negotiation; logical but may be poor negotiators	Not interested in negotiation
Responsiveness to Outside Leadership	May follow religious leader; not responsive to political leadership	Follows rules; may respond to outside leaders	Recognizes victory, may respond to outside leaders	Unlikely to respond to outside leaders

encyclopedic to hazy understandings based on the explanations of fire-brand preachers. Fundamentalists are not open to much discussion of contrary views, since they believe their mission is God-given, and hence that it is not to be questioned. In fact, any among them who might challenge the mission run the risk of being branded as apostates. As a result, while Islamic fundamentalists may talk about political goals and appeal to the desires of their listeners for self-rule or the return of lost lands, this appeal is actually a mask for their religious work. Their interest in political power is as a facilitator for their larger goals of accomplishing what they see as divinely ordered missions on earth. Hence, appeals to fundamentalists that offer political gains will only be of limited interest.

Islamic fundamentalists who have accepted the view that violent jihad is a requirement, and who have committed themselves to this course, are not easily dissuaded. Political concessions, economic incentives, or cease-fire accords are not likely to be heeded. There is some doubt that even an authoritative religious instruction issued by their own religious leaders would be judged valid by all members of the movement. This is not to say that there are not fundamentalists who can change their minds—clearly there are—but as true believers, fundamentalists will not easily abandon their dedication to the movement.[25] Therefore, we think the weight of evidence indicates fundamentalists are likely to continue to make up the hard nucleus of the jihadist movement regardless of how world events evolve over the coming years. Their religious views allow them to ignore logic and what others perceive as facts in favor of a type of magical thinking. They may see "signs" in events that outsiders would perceive quite differently and continue to fight for—or dogmatically cling to—their views in spite of losses, even crushing defeats.

Geopolitical Strategists

Some Islamic geopolitical strategists have embraced the global jihad as a means to reach their goals, since it is a potent political weapon within the Muslim world. Activists or groups in this category are more political than religious in orientation. However, because they come from a highly religious society and share a common religious heritage with other Muslims, they cloak much of their activity in the verbiage of fundamentalism and religious fervor. Motivated by readily identifiable political and economic goals, some individuals or groups will be highly nationalistic—primarily concerned with their own nation or ethnic group—while others may be motivated by broader goals such as regional independence, control of natural resources, or reuniting fractured national groupings. This is not to say that many of these politically motivated adherents are not religious. Indeed, they often share to some extent the fundamentalist world view. However, for geopolitical strategists religious considerations are less salient than questions of a more mundane, earthly nature. If, for example, control of the Saudi Arabian area could be wrested from its current rulers and turned over to a religious government, there is no doubt that considerable wealth would be at play. There are jihadists who would like to participate in its reallocation, and who have participated in the jihad as a way to position themselves to take advantage of the opportunity that victory would present. Adherents of this stripe may be as fanatic and as devoted to the cause as any jihadist, but there is an underlying flexibility that puts them at odds with the true religious fundamentalists. Individuals and groups in this category can be reasoned with provided they perceive a clear gain coming their way, and so long as the solution does not present an untenable conflict between religious views and geopolitical goals.

Western political leaders can more easily understand and deal with this faction of the jihadist movement. Negotiators who correctly identify geopolitical strategists across the table have a far greater chance of reaching agreement. The problem is that the geopolitical strategist is not likely to identify himself as such, but must be recognized by a skillful teasing out of real motives from a barrage of covering language. The politically motivated jihadist must still pay homage to the movement and cannot be expected to abandon that movement's requirements, even if he sees the chance to obtain some of his other, unstated goals. To properly identify these people, and to work with them, the negotiators on the other side must know a great deal about jihadist ideology, be able to understand the language they use, and be sensitive to variations in meaning that might well elude even a highly skilled listener less versed in this culture and system of belief.

Sincere efforts to defuse the hatred seen in the jihadist movement will only succeed if some of the strategic thinkers in the movement can be allowed to win certain of their points. Only when these strategists see a clear gain can we expect to see them return to their base and explain why negotiation is required and compromise is good. Not all followers will agree, but some will, and the trajectory of the movement will be altered. In the near term, it remains questionable whether geopolitical strategists are likely to constitute more than a small, if not negligible, percentage of the overall movement. For this somewhat bleak prognosis to alter, transforming conditions would need to be met, such as the ascendancy of leaders who can negotiate workable agreements with the West (the history of the Middle East peace process underscores the difficulty of meeting this condition) or fundamental changes in U.S. foreign policy.

National Insurgents

Related to the geopolitical strategists but more limited in the scope of their objectives are those individuals and groups who see the jihadist movement as a means for removing an objectionable government in their country and replacing it with an Islamic one. Like insurgents anywhere, these jihadists want to replace an existing regime with one more to their liking. As a result, they are highly nationalistic and see their efforts as primarily directed at aiding their own nation or ethnic group. As a result, these individuals and groups are less dogmatic than religious fundamentalists. While their rhetoric and activities are conducted under the banner of religion, national insurgents are primarily intent upon regime change and the installation of their own group in power. In spite of their strong religious convictions, national insurgents will respond to opportunities to achieve their goals even if some compromises are required. When national insurgents are leading the jihadist group, negotiations that offer hope of achieving the focused political goals of the insurgents will be most productive. Insurgents may well decide to live alongside enemies and to abandon attacks on nonbelievers if they can gain control of their territory and attain a reasonable level of security. Like geopolitical strategists, national insurgents are goal-oriented, but their requirements for success are more limited in scope and may require a smaller group to lose for them to be successful.

National insurgents are relatively easy to identify among their jihadist associates. Careful listeners will detect their primary political interests fairly easily among the barrage of religious fundamentalist language. While it would be a mistake to discount the importance of their religious views, nationalist insurgents will be more open to discussions and compromises that offer the hope of attaining the political outcomes they seek. If the interlocutors on the other side are religious fundamentalists in their own right, it is unlikely that any real communications will ever occur. In a dialogue where either side is counting on divine intervention, inclined to a form of magical thinking, or absolutely opposed to any compromise that might lessen the importance and reach of their religious views, there is unlikely to be a successful outcome.

Depending on circumstances in the country in question, these national insurgents may create a guerrilla group on their own or affiliate themselves with some other group inside their borders. In cases where action within their own land still seems impossible, they may join a nearby insurgency or fight with co-religionists elsewhere as a first step towards taking the war home. Many of these insurgents are quite sophisticated and have long-range perspectives, and they are willing to support groups unrelated to their own as a means of getting training, preparing the environment, and creating a mass organization that can eventually be expected to bring about the changes dearest to them. The near-term growth of this component of the jihad is likely to ebb and flow depending on the extent to which the security forces of local regimes are weak and outside powers intervene as occupiers or provide direct military support to those regimes.

Hard-core Terrorists

Inside the global jihad, as in any group that encourages violence as a tactic, some individuals will be attracted to the movement simply because it gives them the opportunity to engage in violent behavior. Since being a jihadist makes it possible to participate in sanctioned acts of terrorism, the appeal of the movement increases among those attracted to violence. Some hard-core terrorists (or even terrorist groups as a whole) thrive on action. These individuals fill the pages of captured notebooks with poorly absorbed political lessons but festoon every page with detailed drawings of weapons. Others are the unfortunate losers in the global struggle, desperate souls who see no chance of winning in the battles raging about them. In return, they want to extract revenge on someone from the other side. Still others are professional fighters who wish to put their skills to work. For example, some "Afghan Arabs" who returned home after successfully defeating the invading Soviet forces in Afghanistan found it impossible or undesirable to reenter society. Instead, they congregated with other veterans. They easily slid back into violent activity against new targets that had little to do with the cause that initially took them to war. Motivational flexibility is apparent with these individuals so long as there is the possibility of participating in the behaviors that they find rewarding.

What makes hard-core terrorists particularly important is their contribution to the use of terrorist tactics by the global jihad. For them, the results of terrorism are particularly rewarding. The amount of damage that can be inflicted through terrorist tactics is several orders of magnitude greater than that from normal combat. The hard-core terrorists within the ranks of angry jihadists are incorrigibles. They want to punish their enemies and seek compensation for perceived wrongs done to themselves or fellow Muslims. It is questionable whether they will be satisfied with outcomes limited to political gains or strategic victories. They are also unlikely to be happy with any outcomes that promote religious goals without a corresponding price being paid by the losers in the struggle.

Hard-core terrorists who find their way on to negotiating teams will be as intransigent in their views as the most fanatical religious fundamentalists. They have little interest in compromise, no patience for the infinite series of adjustments that make up diplomatic maneuver, and may even secretly resist complete victory. The battle is an end in itself, and they are not in a hurry to see it end. Outsiders seldom come into contact with hard-core terrorists. Among themselves, hard-core terrorist fighters may be quite open in their views and willing to admit their motivations. Very sophisticated members of this persuasion—terrorists who may be chosen to meet with outsiders—are almost never willing to give voice to their true feelings. Negotiators will have to spot this tendency through a lack of internal consistency in their arguments or by evaluating their unwillingness to agree even to highly favorable offers.

Hard-core terrorists probably cannot "win" regardless of the outcome of the struggle. They will not easily abandon the global jihad even if national insurgents and geopolitical strategists decide to do so. Some may adopt the rhetoric of the true religious fundamentalists to stay active in the fight, or they may simply join any similar group that is still in conflict. Should peace break out all around them, they will likely go underground and continue to take actions against their enemies in violation of religious or political orders. Other than the religious fundamentalists, the hard-core terrorists are most likely to dominant the jihadist movement in the near term.

Conclusions

The more politically sophisticated among the jihadists recognize the importance of sustaining popular support for their strategic vision. Messages released to the media are aimed primarily at the Muslim public or key elements within that public. Bin Laden, al-Zawahiri, and others draw heavily on allusions to Islamic history and portray al-Qa'ida as a vanguard defending the faith against infidels. Those messages can also be analyzed (assuming it is not systematic disinformation) to reveal the jihadists' perceptions of their vulnerabilities. Those messages can provide insights into internal debates about doctrine, strategy, or tactics within the jihadist movement. As a result, the jihadists' own communications may be valuable assets for intelligence collection and analysis in order to counter their ambitions.

Although the global jihad is a religious-based movement, as is reflected in the use of religious rhetoric to legitimate its actions, the movement is not monolithic. Careful examination of its adherents reveals that it functions much like a "large umbrella" covering a wide array of radical Islamists. The jihadist movement includes religious fundamentalists, geopolitical strategists, national insurgents, and hard-core terrorists within its ranks. As a result, because they share a common underlying ideology, the jihadists display a pragmatic willingness to modify organizational dynamics and tactics. Careful monitoring of the evolution and diversification of the movement is central to thwarting its efforts to restore the caliphate.

Predictions of continuity and change in the future doctrine, strategy, and tactics of an adversary are inherently uncertain. They become even more tenuous when that adversary operates clandestinely. Reducing those uncertainties requires asking the right questions, collecting reliable information, and doing good analysis. Simply put, credible intelligence is a critical element in forging a winning strategy to counter the global jihad. In the next chapter we turn to a discussion of that challenge.

7

THE CHALLENGE OF CREDIBLE INTELLIGENCE

The greatest enemy of knowledge is not ignorance, it is the illusion of knowledge.

Stephen Hawking

There are two ways to be fooled: One is to believe what isn't so; the other is to refuse to believe what is so.

Soren Kierkegaard

The search for truth implies a duty. One must not conceal any part of what one has recognized to be true.

Albert Einstein

The greatest derangement of the mind is to believe in something because one wishes it to be so.

Louis Pasteur

By design, intelligence work usually goes on out of public view. However, as long as radical Islamists who answer the call to global jihad embrace terrorism as one of the chosen tools to achieve their strategic vision, intelligence collection will be a topic of major concern to the public as well as to government. In part, this reflects the fact that successful terrorist incidents—after they occur—are frequently attributed to perceived intelligence failures. Naturally, this causes a spike in media attention to, and public interest in, the subject of intelligence collection and analysis. In this chapter, we consider the prospects for acquiring credible intelligence about the movement, and the implications of that challenge for understanding and countering radical Islamists in the future.

There is no question that there were serious lessons to be learned from September 11 and the performance of American and foreign security services. Indeed, the 9/11 Commission devoted many pages of its report to ideas for changing intelligence gathering. Those ideas were presented as necessary to correct perceived mistakes that allowed the al-Qa'ida terrorists to enter the United States and carry out their attacks inside our borders. Several unstated assumptions are implicit in the 9/11 Commission's report. First, because a terrorist attack occurred, then by definition some mistakes had to have been made. Second, something had to be changed or someone held accountable. Both assumptions are plausible starting points for any lessons-learned exercise. However, assumptions are not the same as facts, which can only be discovered after careful and thorough review of available evidence. Moreover, changing wiring diagrams for agencies is not the same as holding individuals accountable if they have committed otherwise avoidable, demonstrable errors of judgment.

As is too often the case, much of the material in the Commission's report focused on bureaucratic fixes. *The 9/11 Commission Report* called for a major reorganization of the U.S. intelligence community. The creation of a new intelligence "czar" was one of its central recommendations. This individual, according to the Commission, would force the various elements of the intelligence community to work together. To ensure that this would happen, new "centers" for intelligence collection and analysis would be established. Although there is no credible proof that the attacks occurred because of some deficiency in the way the U.S. intelligence community was organized, the thrust of the 9/11 Commission's report was that an organizational fix would somehow remedy the situation. Recommending organizational changes is always popular because such suggestions give the impression to the public that a new organization chart will somehow "fix the problem" and make another attack impossible, or at least unlikely. Changing organizational structures, however, does not automatically lead to producing credible intelligence. The latter is inevitably dependent on the quality of collection and analysis, as well as on its comprehension by decision makers who choose to use it to inform action.

While the verdict remains out on the organizational changes, it is clear that *The 9/11 Commission Report* does contain many good ideas about intelligence collection. Unfortunately, those ideas were buried in a barrage of Washington-focused thinking about intelligence. Panel members tended to focus on how things work in Washington more than on how intelligence is actually collected in the field. This probably reflected the fact that there were so few panel members with any recent intelligence collection or analysis experience. As a result, many of the suggestions resulted in more bureaucracy. Redundancy was heaped upon redundancy, without really looking at structural fixes that would involve dramatic redistribution and focusing of the intelligence workload. Typical was the idea of adding a layer of supervision to the intelligence community, creating yet another center (actually renaming an existing center and moving people from one location to another), and creating a number of groups that would all look at the same raw information in the hopes that such redundancies would prevent any terrorists from slipping through the security net.

The 2003 invasion of Iraq offers additional insights into the challenges of producing credible intelligence to support decision making. President Bush's decision to invade Iraq was initially based, at least according to the administration's public statements, on a search for WMDs that were allegedly in the hands of Saddam Hussein. The available intelligence on the existence of such weapons was mixed, as it so often is, resulting in a very unclear picture prior to the American-led coalition's launch of "Operation Iraqi Freedom" to overthrow the Baathist regime.

In an interview broadcast on the CBS program *Sixty Minutes* on January 14, 2007, President Bush referred to the intelligence that he relied on prior to the 2003 invasion as an "intelligence failure." It will be some time before we know the entire story about this "intelligence failure." However, bits and pieces are starting to be revealed. The resulting picture is disturbing. It reveals mistakes and serious errors of judgment by a number of key players inside and outside the nation's intelligence community. Attempts to draw lessons inevitably will play out against a backdrop of claims that the Bush administration subverted the intelligence process to augment its case for invasion and regime change in Iraq. Attempts to understand what happened to the intelligence process would be aided by looking honestly at the effects of replacing career intelligence officers, known for their desire to discover and report the truth, with political operatives, known for their desire to make their superiors happy.

In the wake of the resulting deadly insurgency against American troops in Iraq, the Bush administration, rather than looking at the real problems of collecting intelligence against an active insurgency, has focused on the idea that outside terrorists—mainly foreign fighters tied to al-Qa'ida— rather than Iraqis have fomented the insurgency. Similarly, prior to the early 2007 appointment of General David Petraeus to command U.S.

troops in Iraq, public statements by the Bush administration focused primarily on outside support for the foreign fighters—especially from Syria and Iran—rather than the Iraqi insurgents. While grounded in facts, such statements gloss over the larger question of what our invasion means in terms of the global jihad and whether a successful counterinsurgency effort can be sustained.

More misleading, although politically useful to the Bush administration, are the oft-repeated assertions that Iraq is the central front in the war on terror, and that the insurgents in Iraq would somehow move the fight to the United States if America were not engaging them there. These statements confuse two very real, but quite different, problems. The first involves successfully executing a strategy for dealing with an insurgency and thereby stabilizing Iraq. The second is how to deal with terrorism, including how to prevent jihadists who have gained experience in Iraq from attacking the American homeland.

These examples underscore the importance of considering the intelligence challenge facing the West—especially the United States—as a result of the global jihad. Such an appraisal must attempt to gauge America's current level of success against the jihadists. It also should attempt to provide an assessment of what the future may hold. It is our assertion that the global jihad will manifest itself in more than one form in the future, and that each of these entities will require its own type of intelligence collection and analysis. This is not good news, since we have not done well against the single entity known as al-Qa'ida. To support our assertion, we turn to a review of collection and analysis before September 11, followed by an overview of collection and analysis today.

COLLECTION AND ANALYSIS BEFORE SEPTEMBER 11

Prior to the events of September 2001, al-Qa'ida was a different organization structurally. It operated as a fairly formal, hierarchical organization. It was managed top-down, with a central command structure largely located in Afghanistan. Its training infrastructure was located near its command-and-control centers, and al-Qa'ida counted upon fairly dependable communications as well as the ability to have personal meetings among its members as required. Because it operated as a clandestine group, al-Qa'ida was quite security-conscious. Al-Qa'ida practiced good tradecraft to hide its movements and to protect its personnel. Their extensive use of the base in Afghanistan, however, gave some advantages to Western intelligence services attempting to monitor the organization.

One of the first jobs facing any intelligence collector is the problem of locating the target so that an intelligence collection plan can be formulated. Having the al-Qa'ida leadership in Afghanistan provided the collectors with a fixed point on which to focus while still maintaining interest in other areas. Communications coming from around the world into Afghanistan—especially those directed to the sanctuary areas where the terrorists operated—resulted in the identification of suspected collaborators, operatives, and contacts. Afghanistan had limited advanced communications technology even before much of it was destroyed by the American bombing campaign that supported the overthrow of the Taliban after September 11. The number of communication circuits flowing into the country was, and remains, considerably less than one finds in more advanced nations. As a result, the requirement to scan all of these circuits in search of intelligence was manageable. Intercepted conversations provided occasional insights into the terrorists' plans.

Analysis of traffic patterns and careful exploitation of all messages to identify both senders and receivers made it possible for intelligence analysts to discover linkages between people. Such network analysis was even more valuable. While clever and cunning, the terrorists probably underestimated the degree of risk they were running as they directed their worldwide networks from their base in Afghanistan.[1] For a time, the al-Qa'ida leadership used a particularly flexible and handy form of communications for much of their work—a form that was highly susceptible to intercept by signals collectors. As *The 9/11 Commission Report* states, a leak that identified this particular vulnerability resulted in the loss of a great deal of valuable information. However, it is reasonable to assume that the paucity of alternative means of communications into and out of the country (and nearby Pakistan) meant that at least some of their messages continued to be intercepted and exploited.[2]

Many key decisions were made by the al-Qa'ida leadership following meetings held in Afghanistan. Travel by operatives into the areas where al-Qa'ida maintained training camps was another source of vulnerability. The ability to monitor the travel of persons of interest is greatly aided by having some idea of where they might be heading. At the same time, previously unknown people who traveled into the area were placed on suspect lists as a result of that travel. The primary travel routes to the camps passed through countries where the United States had existing intelligence exchanges, although that did not automatically guarantee the travel would be monitored.

Having a fixed, identified location meant that overhead reconnaissance methods could be used to monitor the al-Qa'ida training camps, equipment depots, and personnel movements. This type of imagery collection from satellites, unmanned aerial vehicles, and aircraft allowed the United States to designate targets for attack when the decision was made to oust al-Qa'ida from its Afghan sanctuary.

The operation of fairly well-known training camps for the instruction and assessment of recruits was also of value to the intelligence collector and analyst. It seems probable that some of the intelligence services around the world were successful in placing agents in the camps.[3] People who attended the camps—regardless of whether or not they were later affiliated with any terrorist group—could be identified as suspects. Many of these camp graduates were arrested or otherwise detained following the September 11 attacks in New York and Washington. Some of these camp graduates are still imprisoned. Other people who went to the camps were certainly recruited by security services and used as sources following their graduation.

The operational management methods used by al-Qa'ida prior to September 11 were also a point of vulnerability. The group's leadership liked to pass judgment on proposed operations. Al-Qa'ida leaders also wanted to be consulted as plans unfolded. Communications, both personal and electronic, increased as plans developed. The technique of monitoring the level of "chatter" was used as an analytical tool to predict attacks. Micromanagement of any sort of clandestine or conspiratorial behavior is a definite risk to the group's security. Experienced conspirators know that fewer face-to-face meetings decrease the likelihood of detection. They also realize that larger meetings should be even rarer occurrences. Financial support was given to promising groups, and the money was distributed using international financial channels that were subject to discovery and monitoring. The more control the leadership wielded, the more risk they ran of having their plans and operations detected by the U.S. intelligence community or other security services that opposed the jihadists. Yet al-Qa'ida opted to run those risks, since the group's desire to ratchet up the violence and destruction of their operations in order to capture headlines required coordination and communications.

However, none of these advantages was sufficient to generate satisfactory intelligence collection against al-Qa'ida. Al-Qa'ida was always a very tough target prior to September 11. Although many operations were uncovered and neutralized, there was never any delusion on the part of the various security services that they were covering everything.[4] Many of the operatives fielded by al-Qa'ida were solid performers with highly developed professional skills. The September 11 hijackers' ability to live in the United States and yet to avoid any lessening of their operational motivation is noteworthy. Most professional agent handlers would have assumed that several members of such a team, exposed to the temptations of American culture and with access to funds to enjoy themselves, would have opted out of the plan over the extended period that they remained in the country. Their firm commitment to their mission is testimony to the degree of dedication to the cause that each had. It underscores the importance of ideology as a key driving force behind the global jihad.

COLLECTION AND ANALYSIS TODAY

The damage done to al-Qa'ida by the U.S. attacks on Afghanistan is highly significant. Command and control of their operatives around the world was inevitably impaired to a great extent. Forcing the senior leadership into hiding, restricting their ability to meet contacts easily, and blanketing their communications have all been serious blows to the functioning of the organization. The loss of the training camps—and, consequently, the sanctuary where equipment could be stockpiled—was a significant blow. One has to wonder how much control of far-flung operatives is even possible now, given the realities facing the current al-Qa'ida leadership.

The downside of Western successes is that intelligence collectors and analysts now have to work against a highly fragmented target that has been driven deeply underground. Political realities of the region mean that the hidden leadership is basically out of reach, enjoying the hospitality of war lords hostile to Western interests. They have also learned from past mistakes and have greatly strengthened their operational security by increased use of couriers, by learning how to hide in the ocean of Internet communications, and by more astutely exploiting the modern technology available to everyone.

A heavy focus on increased signals and communications intelligence has been the result. On the one hand, traditional intelligence techniques like direction finding, signal identification, and traffic analysis have been used to guide both technical and human attacks against leadership targets. At the same time, widespread use of systems-level integrated collection techniques to scoop up more and more data, then attempting to use artificial intelligence to sort that data and identify terrorist activity, has had questionable results, even while such techniques have greatly eroded personal privacy for millions of innocent people.

The inability of military and security forces to capture all the most wanted targets in spite of a huge commitment of manpower and support is but a symptom of the complexity of the intelligence problem facing the West. Terrorist leaders have abandoned the idea of staying up to date with the movements of all their colleagues in favor of methods that allow them to make public pronouncements on occasion but that provide few clues as to their location. Carefully coordinated, highly theatrical operations that were the al-Qa'ida trademark are definitely more difficult now, since they require too much planning and communication and require constant approval from the movement's leadership. While we can only speculate on recent changes in the management of terrorist operatives, it seems reasonable to assume that centralized control has been dropped in favor of activities that are more locally driven.

The dispersed organizational model that has been evolving presents a daunting challenge to security services. Those services now must attempt to root out small, insular groups that do not raise their profiles enough to be spotted by classic collection techniques. Human intelligence would clearly be ideal, but our intelligence collectors find it difficult to infiltrate the target groups. In addition, our international reputation has made some previously friendly foreign services, with personnel who can blend with the targets, unwilling to work with us.

Terrorist attacks that occur daily in Iraq and Afghanistan have multiple authors. There is no doubt that people loyal to international terrorist movements are using Iraq and Afghanistan as a locale to attack U.S. forces and as a site for on-the-job training of people who will be the operatives of the future. It would be unwise, however, to attribute all of the violence in these locations to al-Qa'ida terrorists, since many of the attacks are clearly from insurgents interested only in claiming power in their own countries.

Terrorist attacks outside the war zone—like those in Madrid, London, and Glasgow—are especially troubling from the standpoint of getting credible intelligence. Each of those attacks was undertaken by individuals living in Spain and the United Kingdom, respectively. Although the people who conducted the attacks had linkages to external groups, they apparently did not require much, if any, outside support to stage their attacks. The participants in the Spanish and British cells were primarily Muslim immigrants who were angry about the treatment of Muslim populations around the world, and who had specific complaints against the governments of the countries in which they resided. Publicly available evidence indicates that, while some of the participants had contact with outside organizations, the terrorist incidents in London, Madrid, and Glasgow from 2004 to 2007 were not controlled in the same way or to the same extent as the September 11 attacks, which were clearly planned and managed by central al-Qa'ida leadership.

CONCLUSIONS

The intelligence community faces a serious but not insurmountable challenge with respect to generating credible information about al-Qa'ida and the other radical Islamic groups seeking to wage global jihad. Asking questions about their doctrine, strategy, and tactics is relatively straightforward. Getting accurate answers, however, in order to thwart their actions is often easier said than done.

In part, collection and analysis are difficult tasks because the jihadist movement is a complex and highly resilient adversary. Extremists are not welcoming to outsiders; this makes it hard to penetrate the radical Islamist groups espousing global jihad. Many of the terrorist networks only allow people who they know, who live around them, and who are easily evaluated to join. Self-generating terrorist groups engaging in freelance jihad are likely to become more prevalent in the future. If this happens, such groups will inevitably pose an even more difficult intelligence target than more readily identifiable targets like al-Qa'ida or its affiliates. At the same time, al-Qa'ida continues active operations, especially in Iraq, Afghanistan, and in Pakistan's North Waziristan tribal area. As a result, success in meeting the challenge of credible intelligence is critical to forging a winning strategy to counter the global jihad.

CONCLUSION: FORGING A WINNING STRATEGY TO COUNTER THE GLOBAL JIHAD

> Calling this struggle a war accurately describes the use of American and allied armed forces in the field, notably in Afghanistan. The language of war also evokes the mobilization for a national effort. Yet the strategy should be balanced. . . . Long-term success demands the use of all elements of national power.
>
> *The 9/11 Commission Report*

W E CONCLUDE with our perspective on forging a winning strategy to counter the global jihad. The United States has focused much of its attention on counterterrorism since the tragic events of September 11 with mixed results. Certainly, there have been public successes as of late 2008. The Taliban regime was deposed in Afghanistan, al-Qa'ida was forced to abandon its training camps after losing its Afghan sanctuary, repeats of the September 11 attacks on the American homeland have not happened, and—more recently—the attempt of the Islamic Courts to control Somalia was thwarted. At the same time, there have been conspicuous failures. Usama bin Laden, Ayman al-Zawahiri, and Mullah Omar remain at large more than seven years after September 11, al-Qa'ida and its affiliates continue to wage jihad against American interests, Taliban attacks in Afghanistan are increasing, a new generation of Sunni jihadists is gaining on-the-ground experience as foreign fighters waging insurgency and sectarian violence in Iraq, and the jihadist cause has been embraced by home-grown radical Islamists in Europe. Somber public reports from American and British intelligence chiefs about the threats posed by terrorism point to al-Qa'ida being resilient and cultivating stronger operational connections and relationships with groups in Africa, Europe, and the Middle East; such reports also point to the growing numbers of home-grown extremists. As a result, given the continuing reminders of the toll in blood and treasure from terrorism and insurgency waged by radical Islamists, it seems only prudent to ask: What viable options exist for forging a winning strategy that has some genuine prospects of countering the global jihad? Answering that question in order to provide a realistic path forward has become a necessity, as responding to the challenge posed by radical Islam has moved to the center of political debate in the United States.

The path forward we outline is premised on several key assumptions. First, the United States is not likely to alter its foreign policy—especially its support for Israel—enough to satisfy all segments of the jihadist movement. Second, the United States is likely to continue to perceive the rise of political Islam in its more radical variants—especially the restoration of an Islamic state encompassing most, if not all, of the historical Muslim world—as a significant threat to long-term American national interests. Third, it is likely to be a long war—with dramatic successes and failures intertwined—the duration of which is impossible to predict accurately. In essence, barring a major transformation of America's sense of its own strategic vision, these are boundary conditions that constrain feasible options for countering the global jihad. Because these assumptions mirror the constraints that governed U.S. foreign policy throughout the long decades of the Cold War, our proposed strategy looks to that era for lessons learned to frame a response to the global jihad.

Moving beyond Rhetoric

The first element of our proposed strategy emphasizes the necessity to move beyond the rhetoric of a clash of civilizations, emotions, or values. Similarly, while recognizing that some of our adversaries are genuinely evil, casting the current conflict as a struggle between good and evil fails to illuminate how we can emerge from the struggle both successful and with our core values intact. Instead, it is essential to acquire a genuine understanding of what, for want of a better phrase, "makes jihadists tick." In order to make informed decisions in confronting jihadism, we need to take a comprehensive look at this information so we can understand their belief structures and how their decision making responds to pressure. To achieve this, we need to allocate serious analytical effort to understanding the ideological underpinnings of the jihad as well as how their ideology is translated into practice. The volume of jihadist literature available through open sources is immense. Only by sustaining a real-time analysis of the content and evolution of the jihadist ideology can we hope to succeed in applying appropriate pressures to counter those individuals and groups that perpetuate the belief that violence is the only logical choice. After studying the ideology, we must put our understanding of it to use. Our diplomatic, military, and intelligence communities must be conversant with jihadist ideology if they are to have any success in interpersonal dealings with individuals involved in the movement.

UNDERSTANDING JIHADIST VULNERABILITIES

The second element of our proposed strategy emphasizes the necessity of gaining a coherent and actionable understanding of the jihadist movement's vulnerabilities. Because we argue that radical Islam is not monolithic, attempts to counter the threat posed by the jihadists will have to reflect the reality that the jihadist movement is a complicated political force made up of disparate elements—despite the fact that it is united by a common ideology. For example, as Michael Doran explains, "Al Qaeda's long-term goals are set by its fervent devotion to a radical religious ideology, but in its short-term behavior, it is a rational political actor operating according to the dictates of realpolitik."[1] We need to field an array of measures that are tailored to exploit potential divisions among the various personality types and radical Islamist groups that make up the jihadist movement. By doing so, it becomes possible to contain expansion of the most radical elements' political power in order to thwart their ambitions to establish a universal theocracy. To enact this approach, it is crucial to identify points of disagreement in their ranks and differing strategic goals.

One of the most substantial areas of disagreement within the ranks of the jihadists is over the use of takfir and the legality of using violence against Muslims, especially civilians. Although most Muslims reject the use of takfir, the concept has largely been accepted by jihadists.[2] Disagreements exist, however, over how to apply it, since most jihadists appear to believe that secular regimes, Muslims who violate *al-Wala' wa al-Bara'*, and Shi'ites are indeed infidels worthy of punishment.[3] This underscores that the global jihad essentially is a movement inspired, led, and conducted by Sunni extremists. The primary point of contention is over whether it is prudent to act on impulses for violence against these potential targets.[4] The gradual decentralization of takfir—the making of declarations of takfir by those without sufficient religious expertise and evidence—poses a significant threat to the Muslim public because takfir is increasingly declared not only against regimes but against entire societies.[5] This gap between the views of the vast majority of Muslims and some of the jihadists should be exploited to lessen public support for their cause. This decentralization also poses a threat to jihadist group relations. This has been clearly demonstrated by the Islamic Army in Iraq's letter to the Islamic State of Iraq, and in a similar letter from Ansar al-Sunnah to al-Qa'ida in Iraq leader Abu-Ayyub al-Masri, which accused AQI members of kidnapping, torturing, and killing Ansar al-Sunnah members.[6]

In addition to factional disputes and potential internal schisms, the jihadists may be vulnerable to Western countermeasures aimed at undermining their ideological confidence—especially sophisticated campaigns designed to raise questions about whether their actions conform to core Islamic tenants. This potential vulnerability has been recognized by al-Qa'ida. For example, Abu-Yahya al-Libi was asked in a 2007 interview with al-Qa'ida's media wing, al-Sahab, to discuss the tactics used by the West in the "war of ideas." Abu-Yahya noted the importance of the ideological battle, and went on to observe that the West

> realized that the greatest part of the battle lies in the well-founded convictions and doctrinal-methodological principles which the mujahidin adopt . . . and thus, they thought, calculated, looked around, and came to the conclusion that a large part of the battle depends on shaking the convictions on which the mujahidin build their march and casting doubts on the doctrinal principles they consider indisputable, in which case there will occur a splitting or perhaps collapse of the basic foundations and fundamentals on which the jihadist methodology stands.[7]

Having conceded the existence of potential vulnerabilities, Abu-Yahya proceeded to list six ways in which the West is attempting to attack the jihadist movement's ideology. First, he said, the West and its allies have announced that some imprisoned jihadist leaders have disavowed their previous positions. This was an obvious reference to former Egyptian jihadists in the Islamic Group and to Dr. Fadl, al-Zawahiri's one-time mentor.[8] They have rejected their earlier statements and spoken out publicly against al-Qa'ida. Based on their interpretation of Shari'ah, these IG leaders and Dr. Fadl, a former leader of the Egyptian Islamic Jihad, have spent considerable time attacking al-Qa'ida's philosophical justifications for violent jihad and its choice of tactics. They have cited the Qur'an and

Hadith references to support their assertions that, while jihad is a legitimate part of Islam, al-Qa'ida and similar groups misunderstand the tradition and are carrying out an unjust war.

Second, Abu-Yahya says that the West has fabricated lies and has exaggerated mistakes made in jihadist battle zones. He notes distorted claims, for example, that the mujahidin hold "the nation and its scholars to be infidel," or that they call for the killing of anyone who breaks away from al-Qa'ida, as examples of Western misrepresentations.

Third, Abu-Yahya describes Saudi tactics such as drawing on Islamic historical allusions to refer to the jihadists as modern-day Kharijites and issuing fatwas against jihadists and violence. Equating jihadists to the Kharijites, a seventh-century C.E. sectarian group that declared large sections of the Muslim community apostate, is extremely worrisome for al-Qa'ida, since most Muslims consider the Kharijites to have been extremists; such references can therefore be used as pressure points. Fourth, Abu-Yahya alleges that the West backs and portrays as "moderate" Islamic groups that follow a democratic approach and agree with the West. He says that the West uses those groups to foster conflict with the jihadists, keep them occupied, and isolate the mujahidin. Traditional counterterrorism measures designed to kill, capture, incapacitate, or defame prominent jihadists and leaders to deprive the mujahidin of a guiding authority are the fifth Western tactic he mentions. Abu-Yahya says that the West's sixth tactic involves "blowing out of proportion some of the minor, interpretive disputes, which might occur among the mujahidin," by portraying them as major doctrinal and methodological disputes. This tactic attempts to foster schisms and is used as a way to "fan the flames of difference" between groups, leading to infighting. In this case, Abu-Yahya probably is alluding to Iraq and the conflicts between al-Qa'ida and other Sunni insurgents, such as the Islamic Army in Iraq.

The fact that Abu-Yahya took the time to discuss these tactics in the war of ideas is significant. It underscores that the jihadists have real vulnerabilities, and that they can result in situations that force jihadists to respond and go on the defensive. Most of these tactics go beyond fairly ineffectual steps like simply calling bin Laden a bad Muslim or attacking Abdullah Azzam's defensive jihadist writings. Instead, they involve substantive matters that have the potential to isolate jihadists from the larger community of Muslims, whom they wish to rally to the jihadist cause. Although none of these tactics is likely to reverse the commitments of those who fully support jihadist violence, they can confuse potential sympathizers and those whose commitment is wavering. This may lead them to question what jihadists portray as benevolent intentions.

It is important to note that these tactics do not attempt to invalidate the litany of grievances perceived by potential supporters of the global jihad. Instead, they concentrate on attacking the justifications upon which groups like al-Qa'ida base violent action, on highlighting the violence that al-Qa'ida has perpetrated against other Muslims, and on using al-Qa'ida's historical-religious narrative to chip away at the group's pool of sympathizers. This underscores the importance of words and deeds in the ongoing struggle against Islamic radicalism. If we are to understand the vulnerabilities of the jihadists, we must listen to them and study their statements. Their geographic spread requires them to hold open discussions, often in semipublic settings accessible to those who understand the language. We need to promote the widest possibly study of jihadist statements by intelligence, diplomatic, and scholarly readers.

Intelligence collection will increasingly have to focus on the self-generating freelance groups of Islamic extremists that continue to emerge around the world. Because so many of these groups will be local in scope, efforts to find them will very often fall upon internal security services and police forces. We recommend enhancing our ongoing training of police, both in the United States and abroad, to sensitize patrol officers to the threat of local, freelance jihadists. It may be necessary to make some minor adjustments to the regulations covering intelligence collection by police forces in order to provide the tools required to those charged with staying alert to this threat. Our discussion of local collection requirements should not be interpreted as calling for any lessening of worldwide intelligence collection. We believe there will be a continual international attempt to coordinate action, to share resources, and to exchange information.

UNDERSTANDING OUR OWN VULNERABILITIES

The third element of our proposed strategy emphasizes the necessity of gaining a coherent and actionable understanding of our own vulnerabilities. In a geopolitical sense, we think three primary vulnerabilities exist. The first, as noted above, is America's commitment, spanning over sixty years and every president since Harry Truman, to maintaining the existence of Israel. We do not argue that that commitment should be abrogated. However, the United States needs to approach its relationship with Israel by focusing on what makes strategic sense for America rather than by being uncritically supportive of Israel. We think it is essential to recognize how U.S. support for Israel provides an ample source of propaganda for the jihadists' efforts to portray the United States as an enemy of Islam. To counter this, we think it imperative that the United States balance its support for Israel with serious efforts to move the Israeli-Palestinian peace process forward in order to achieve a viable two-state solution that does not undermine legitimate American national security interests in the region.

Given past history, we have no illusions that this can be easily accomplished, nor do we think the failure thus far of the peace process is the primary driving force behind the global jihad. However, if for no other reason than that it is of paramount symbolic importance within the Muslim world, moving the Palestinian problem off the table is critical to America's long-term strategic interests in the region. Although it is unlikely to alter the demands of all jihadists, it may reduce the appeal of violent jihad for some, especially those for whom the Israeli-Palestinian conflict is a fundamental issue. Furthermore, it would offer tangible proof to national insurgent and geopolitical strategist elements within the larger jihadist movement that diplomatic negotiations—under the right conditions—are the only realistic ways in which they can hope to achieve acceptable outcomes. It is a gamble, but if it works, it offers the potential to fragment the existing jihadist network. Reducing the number of adversaries we confront diminishes our own vulnerability.

Our second primary vulnerability is our lack of a sound energy policy for the present or the future. After more than thirty-five years, starting with Richard Nixon, the series of calls for "energy independence" that echo each January from one State of the Union address to another are sirens' songs devoid of any realistic acknowledgment of the impossibility of cutting America off from global energy markets or the nature of our own energy supply-and-demand system. Instead of pursuing a hollow policy doomed to failure, the United States needs to move aggressively towards adopting and implementing a robust strategy of energy security that reduces the nation's vulnerability to supply disruptions and that fosters the continuing availability of energy resources at prices that sustain economic growth. It is sensitivity to world market interruptions—

especially of oil that can be refined into liquid fuels for our transportation sector—that makes the United States vulnerable to energy shortfalls.

Relying on flexible markets and resisting the temptation for government to try to micromanage energy supply and demand is critical. There simply are no quick technological fixes, and structural relationships with energy suppliers can shift dramatically from being reliable to threatening. One need only look at the complexities of expanding the use of renewable energy, enhancing energy efficiency, and the emergence of Hugo Chávez in Venezuela to grasp these realities. At its core, energy security for America will require a real and continuing commitment to diversify the nation's fuel mix, maintain reliable supply sources, enhance energy end-use efficiencies, and reduce consumption. This cannot be accomplished solely by government fiat or by national economies acting alone. Instead, it requires a consistent commitment to building and maintaining a robust, open global energy market. Creating energy security makes good economic sense for America; it is attainable and will reduce the likelihood that current or future adversaries will be able to wage successful economic warfare against the United States.

It also is essential to recognize that, while establishing greater energy security is desirable for a variety of reasons, it is unlikely to cut off substantially the availability of funds for Islamic terrorism. Suggestions to the contrary—such as switching to alternative fuels in order to drive down oil prices, thereby cutting off funds for the jihadists—may make for politically appealing rhetoric, but ultimately they are not supported by facts. Most of the revenue from petrodollars does not finance terrorism, and conducting terrorist operations has proven to be fairly inexpensive. Simply put, Islamic terrorism has not been dependent on large outlays of capital, nor has it been reliant on high oil prices. One only needs to examine history to see that al-Qa'ida had no problems launching its attacks when the nominal world market price for a barrel of crude oil averaged just $32.32; indeed, the nominal average U.S. price was just $23.89 in the days immediately before September 11.[9] Therefore, while desirable in its own right, energy security can lessen the West's vulnerabilities but is unlikely to signal the end of Islamic terrorism.

Our third primary vulnerability is fundamentally a question of political commitment. Simply put, will the United States sustain a campaign aimed at countering the jihadist movement whose outcome is likely to be in doubt for years? Waging war is never easy, given its inescapable toll in lives and treasure. And waging a long war—which is inevitable, given the deep-seated commitment of our adversaries to global jihad—is especially difficult. It is impossible without a coherent strategy and the support of reliable allies. The verdict on this question is out, and—as was true in the Cold War with the former Soviet Union—definitive knowledge can only be known retrospectively.

EFFECTIVE USE OF NATIONAL SECURITY RESOURCES

The fourth element of our proposed strategy emphasizes the need to reassess how we can best utilize the full array of our national security resources—diplomacy, intelligence, and military assets—to confront the challenges posed by the jihadist movement. In other words, how can we best attack their weaknesses? First, and foremost, the United States needs to develop and implement a coherent strategy.[10] In doing so, it is essential to examine what can be accomplished—based on a ruthless critique of attainable goals, our own shortcomings and capabilities, and the time and money necessary to achieve those goals—instead of merely articulating a laundry list of amorphous aims and disjointed actions.

Diplomatic efforts will be required to open dialogues with more moderate members of the jihadist movement, paying special attention to those elements that are not totally driven by religious fundamentalist or terrorist motivations. Geopolitical strategists and national insurgents in the movement represent elements of the jihad that we can and should target diplomatically. Moreover, by focusing on jihadist brutality against some of the less extremist groups, such initiatives can be used selectively to take advantage of potential schisms within the movement. Focusing the debate on the jihadists' acts of savagery against fellow Muslims, instead of on America's image, is the key to success in the struggle for Muslim hearts and minds. The Anbar Awakening in Iraq offers evidence that such approaches can work. The underlying strategic goal of our diplomacy should be to prevent the most radical elements in the jihadist movement from succeeding in making their cause universally applicable to all Muslims. Instead, the United States needs to frame as many as possible of the jihadist causes as narrow regional or local issues. At the same time, America's efforts at public diplomacy need to focus on the disagreements and inconsistencies within the jihadist movement in order to sow doubts within the broader Muslim community. Narrowing the focus will make it more possible for us to deal with issues that might have solutions and that allow for compromises that might be acceptable.

Much of the attention of public diplomacy has focused on countries with Muslim majorities. This is understandable because the jihadist movement's origins and core support are in those areas. As a result, efforts in majority Muslim countries—especially the Middle East, North Africa, and Pakistan—are vitally important. From a strategic standpoint, however, the Muslim community in Europe is likely to be the principal battleground in the war for hearts and minds. Those countries already are democratic and offer far more promise for demonstrating that Muslims can simultaneously practice their religion and thrive in the modern world. Success will depend heavily on the EU's ability to integrate Muslims into European society and to address legitimate grievances while remaining vigilant against Islamic radicalism.

The application of diplomacy also means the United States inevitably will be compelled to take sides in disputes within the Muslim world. Increasingly, the contending sides are struggling over who will govern rather than how a country will be governed. The ongoing sectarian violence between Sunnis and Shi'ites in Iraq is the most visible, but by no means an isolated, case. Numerous other examples come readily to mind such as the struggle for political power between Hamas and Fatah in Palestine, the Islamic Courts and the interim government in Somalia, or Hizballah and their opponents in Lebanon. If past history serves as a guide, while temporary truces can be negotiated, the United States is unlikely to succeed in brokering enduring power-sharing agreements between the warring parties that really stop sectarian conflicts or civil wars. Instead, if long-term American interests genuinely can be affected by who rules, then it will become necessary to take sides definitively by providing diplomatic support to a preferred victor. Simply put, while it is a noble goal, democratization per se is of questionable value in countering the global jihad. Who governs and what actions those governments take really matter.

In tandem with diplomacy, intelligence special operations will continue to have an important role in this fight to counter radical Islam and the global jihad. It is naïve to think that diplomatic or open methods alone will prevail against such a determined and violent foe. The most violent members of the jihad will have to be neutralized by all necessary means, and sometimes that will require covert action. What we should avoid is the mindless application of these techniques to the jihad generally.

Because the use of these techniques can never remain secret for long, we must employ these methods only when failing to do so might have truly devastating consequences for America's national security. Moreover, when resorting to these techniques, it is important not to compromise the core values—particularly individual liberty and the rule of law—that have served America well since its founding.

Similarly, because the most hard-core among the Islamic extremists almost certainly will have to be confronted in battle, the use of the American military will be necessary in some cases. Committing U.S. armed forces to combat should be done sparingly, but it should be done decisively in those situations where there exists no other way to protect America's national security and advance our interests. On those occasions where the use of military force is deemed necessary, it is essential to have a coherent and attainable strategy for victory. America's political leaders, in both the White House and the Congress, have a moral as well as constitutional responsibility to the public—especially to the men and women who are asked to fight and die, and to their families—to develop and sustain a clear and compelling case for the selective use of military force.

In closing, we readily concede that moving forward to execute our proposed strategy is a daunting task. It is also an achievable task. First and foremost, it requires a truly dispassionate appraisal of our adversaries and the nature of the struggle we confront. It also is essential to assess realistically what we merely desire and what is genuinely critical for us to attain in a complex and dynamic international environment. This inevitably forces us to recognize that America's strategic interests, its capabilities, and the limitations on its ability to advance those interests are fluid. It also compels us to understand and accept the reality that ending all acts of Islamic terrorism or sectarian violence is highly unlikely, at least in the near term. However, for the foreseeable future—assuming adequate political will to use American power judiciously—the United States has more than ample ability to thwart the widespread restoration of the caliphate. We are convinced that success in the latter endeavor represents the true strategic challenge facing America and its allies. As long as we have sufficient patience and perseverance, combined with the always desirable element of good fortune, there is every reason to be confident that the challenge posed by Islamic radicalism and the global jihad can be met.

NOTES

Introduction

1. All dates used for this book are expressed using the Common Era. The Common Era, abbreviated CE, corresponds to and is an alternative to *ano domini* (i.e., AD or Christian Era) as a method of historical dating. The Muslim era begins in 622 CE, which corresponds to 1 AH (after *hijra*).

2. Aslan, *No god but God*. For examples of characterizing the West's battle with terrorism as part of a "Crusader campaign" against Islam, see Yusuf al-Ayiri, *The Crusaders' War on Iraq* and *The Future of Iraq and the Arabian Peninsula*, both posted to jihadist websites.

3. We use the following working definition of terrorism in this book: premeditated use or threatened use of violence as a means of achieving political objectives in which nonstate actors target noncombatants to influence the behavior of governments and cause them to acquiesce to the terrorists' demands.

4. Kennedy, *The Prophet and the Age of the Caliphates*.

5. Atatürk (1881–1938) was the founder of the Republic of Turkey and its first President. Originally named Mustafa Kemal, he was given the title Atatürk—which means "Father of the Turks"—by the Grand National Assembly. Atatürk abolished Islamic laws as the basis of the Turkish legal system between 1926 and 1930. The creation of a modern, secular, democratized state was the underlying goal of his cultural, economic, and political reforms.

6. See Roy, *The Failure of Political Islam*, 42–43; Roy, *Globalized Islam*, 238; and Kennedy, *The Prophet and the Age of the Caliphates*.

7. The elements of mythic war include: (1) the enemy embodies evil, and if he were defeated, the world would become paradise; (2) taking action against the enemy is the path to glory and to legendary heights of existence; and (3) anyone who does not agree with this accepted wisdom is a traitor. This transforms war into a struggle between good and evil, in which the good will prevail and the evil will perish. LeShan, *The Psychology of War*, 30.

8. Generally, the more combat a soldier sees, the more his viewpoint shifts from mythic to sensory (or realistic). When the mujahidin make the shift toward the sensory mode, they will be more likely to see flaws in the overall jihadist strategy and leadership. Recent reports of low morale in the Iraqi insurgency could be the first signs of a mythic-to-sensory shift. LeShan, *The Psychology of War*, 68.

9. Gerges, *Journey of the Jihadist*, 144.

10. Drake, "The Role of Ideology in Terrorists' Target Selection."

11. Gunaratna, *Inside Al Qaeda*, 12.

12. Freeman, *Arts of Power*, 13.

13. Fuller, *The Future of Political Islam*. Fuller identifies four types of Islamist groups. Traditionalists accept Islam as it has evolved historically in each local culture but will adapt to conditions; they are primarily concerned with preservation and conservation. Fundamentalists go further, opposing the status quo and promoting a conservative, literal reading of Islamic texts. Reformists attempt to renew the original (more correct) understanding of Islam and are interested in reforming society in an Islamic context. Modernists attempt to provide a contemporary interpretation of Islam. In essence, modernists attempt to infer how Muhammad would act today rather than in sixth-century Arabia. See also Mandaville, *Global Political Islam*.

14. The ulema are regarded as the leading thinkers in Islam. They are trained in theology at various Islamic institutions.

15. Fuller, *The Future of Political Islam*, 176. In many states, Islamist groups may choose to organize along sectarian (Sunni or Shi'a or tribal) lines, as is the case in Lebanon, Afghanistan, Turkey, Iran, and Pakistan.

16. Political Islam also has foreign policy objectives. Fuller observes that "nearly every Islamist movement maintains ties with others, compares notes on tactics, and discusses ideological and strategic issues" (*The Future of Political Islam*, 41).

17. Harmony document AFGP-2002–600048, provided by the Combating Terrorism Center at West Point (www.ctc.usma.edu).

18. Gunaratna, *Inside Al Qaeda*, 240.

19. Fox, "Do Religious Institutions Support Violence or the Status Quo?". Fox offers a series of reasons for why religious institutions can be used to facilitate violent action: (1) churches, mosques, and temples provide convenient places to meet; (2) it is often safer to organize within the context of religious institutions, since such institutions are less likely to be targeted by the opposing group or government; (3) religious institutions often have extensive access to the media, which can be vital to any opposition movement because church media is often the only uncensored media under authoritarian regimes; (4) religious institutions can provide legitimacy to a movement; (5) religious institutions can provide a unifying effect, serving as a common ground or a bridge between groups that would otherwise be at odds; (6) religious institutions often provide social services at little or no cost to the beneficiaries of these services, which strengthens the role of these organizations in the community, increasing their ability to mobilize the populace for political action; and (7) political, social, and economic hardships often lead the clergy to assume the leadership of a political protest movement.

20. The "5 Pillars of Islam" are the obligations that a Muslim must undertake: prayer five times a day, fasting during Ramadan, charitable donation, at least one pilgrimage if able to the Holy Sites in Mecca, and recitation of the Shahada—a proclamation that confirms the belief that Allah is the only god and that Muhammad is his messenger.

21. Sageman, *Understanding Terror Networks*, 114.

22. Mayer, "Cults, Violence and Religious Terrorism," 369.

23. See Hoffman, *Al Qaeda, Trends in Terrorism, and Future Potentialities*.

24. Hammes, *The Sling and the Stone*, 214.

25. The long-standing enmity between the Sunnis and Shi'ites reaches back to the original Caliphate and the defeat of Husayn ibn 'Ali ibn Abi Talib (Muhammad's grandson) at the battle of Karbala in 680 CE by the forces of Yazid.

26. National Commission on Terrorist Attacks upon the United States, *The 9/11 Commission Report*, 86–90.

27. Ibid., 99.

28. World Islamic Front statement, February 23, 1998; quoted in Lawrence, *Messages to the World*, 61.

29. Enders and Sandler, *The Political Economy of Terrorism*; Horgan, *The Psychology of Terrorism*.

Chapter 1

1. Esposito, *Unholy War*, 35. For example, Surah 9:5 states: "But when the forbidden months are past, then fight and slay the Pagans wherever you find them, and seize them, beleaguer them and lie in wait for them in every stratagem (of war); but if they repent, and establish regular prayers and practice regular charity, then open the way for them: for Allah is Oft-forgiving, Most Merciful." Also, Surah 9:29: "Fight those who do not believe in Allah nor the Last Day, nor hold that forbidden which has been forbidden by Allah and His Messenger, nor acknowledge the Religion of Truth, (even if they are) of the People of the Book, until they pay the Jizya [essentially a military service exemption tax for Christians and Jews unwilling to convert to Islam] with willing submission, and feel themselves subdued."

2. These movements are not a new phenomenon. A reclusive Shi'ite sect called the Assassins carried out a number of political assassinations of Muslim and Christian enemies during the Crusades.

3. Oren, *Power, Faith, and Fantasy*.

4. Esposito, *Unholy War*, 83.

5. Although there is no accepted definition of who can be considered a Palestinian refugee for legal purposes, United Nations Relief and Works Agency for Palestine Refugees in the Near East (UNRWA) defines them as "persons whose normal place of residence was Palestine between June 1946 and May 1948, who lost both their homes and means of livelihood as a result of the 1948 Arab-Israeli conflict." UNRWA's definition of a refugee also covers the descendants of persons who became refugees in 1948. The final 1951 UN estimate of Palestinian refugees was 711,000 people; the number is estimated to exceed four million people as of 2004.

6. Kepel, *Muslim Extremism in Egypt*, 26–27.

7. Benjamin and Simon, *The Age of Sacred Terror*, 196.

8. Kepel, *Jihad*, 257.

9. Ibid., 260.

10. Ibid., 266.

11. Abu-Mus'ab al-Suri was one of the two jihadist editors of this publication, not distributed on jihadist websites.

12. Kepel, *Jihad*, 272.

13. Wright, *The Looming Tower*, 190.

14. Letter found at http://dni.gov/press_releases/20051011_release.htm (accessed August 22, 2006).

15. Letter released by Iraqi National Security Advisor on September 18, 2006. English translation provided by the Combating Terrorism Center at West Point, www.ctc.usma.edu.

16. Ibid.

17. Ibid.

18. Abu Mus'ab al-Suri is the *nom de guerre* for Mustafa Setmariam Nasar. Al-Suri, a Syrian with Spanish citizenship, was arrested by Pakistani police in 2005 in Quetta. See Cruickshank and Ali, "Abu Musab Al Suri."

19. Abu-Mus'ab al-Suri, *The Call to Global Islamic Resistance*, 56, distributed on jihadist websites.

20. Ibid., 1501.

21. National Commission on Terrorist Attacks upon the United States, *The 9/11 Commission Report*, 53–54.

22. Kepel, *The War for Muslim Minds*, 181.

23. For a comprehensive treatment of their ideas in Arabic, see al-Musali, "Musu'ah Al-Harakat Al-Islamiyah fil-Watan Al-Arabi wa Iran wa Turkiyah"; Abd-al-Mun'im Al-Hafani, *Musu'ah Al-Farq wa Al-Jama'at wa Al-Madhahib wa Al-Ahzab wa Al-Harakat Al-Islamiyah.*

24. It is always challenging to summarize the writings of influential figures. The natural tendency is to oversimplify and ignore the intricacies of their worldviews. For a more detailed review of the ideological influences on the jihadist movement based on citation analysis, see McCants, *Militant Ideology Atlas: research compendium.*

25. Esposito, *Unholy War*, 46.

26. Benjamin and Simon, *The Age of Sacred Terror*, 43–52.

27. Ibn-Taymiyyah, *Majmua al-Fatwa* 28/358, quoted in Azzam, *Join the Caravan.* See http://www.islamistwatch.org/texts/azzam/caravan/caravan.html (accessed October 16, 2006).

28. Ibn-Taymiyyah, *Majmua al-Fatwa* 28/537, quoted in Azzam, *Defense of Muslim Lands*, http://www.religioscope.com/info/doc/jihad/azzam_defence_3_chap1.htm (accessed October 16, 2006).

29. Esposito, *Unholy War*, 47.

30. Stern, *Terror in the Name of God*, 68.

31. Zeidan, "The Islamic Fundamentalist View of Life as a Perennial Battle."

32. Kepel, *Jihad*, 31.

33. Wiktorowicz, "A Genealogy of Radical Islam," 81.

34. Benjamin and Simon, *The Age of Sacred Terror*, 56.

35. Ibid., 56–57.

36. Esposito, *Unholy War*, 53.

37. Benjamin and Simon, *The Age of Sacred Terror*, 53.

38. Abu-al-A'la Maududi, "Jihad fi-Sabil Allah," quoted in Zeidan, "The Islamic Fundamentalist View of Life as a Perennial Battle."

39. Maududi, *Toward Understanding Islam*, 94.

40. Kepel, *Muslim Extremism in Egypt*, 36–43.

41. Qutb, *Milestones*, 80–82.

42. Ibid., 57.

43. Benjamin and Simon, *The Age of Sacred Terror*, 68.

44. Qutb, *Milestones*, 70.

45. Ibid., 70.

46. Zeidan, "The Islamic Fundamentalist View of Life as a Perennial Battle."

47. Qutb, *Milestones*, 82.

48. Conroy, *Unspeakable Acts, Ordinary People*, 172.

49. Kepel, *Muslim Extremism in Egypt*, 74–89.

50. Benjamin and Simon, *The Age of Sacred Terror*, 72.

51. Faraj, *The Neglected Duty*, 67.

52. Zeidan, "The Islamic Fundamentalist View of Life as a Perennial Battle."

53. Faraj, *The Neglected Duty*, 24.

54. Ibid., 49.

55. Ibid., 48.

56. Ibid., 49.

57. Benjamin and Simon, *The Age of Sacred Terror*, 77–81.

58. Faraj, *Jihad—The Absent Obligation*.

59. Shaykh Ali Khudayr Al-Khudayr, "Who has a right to do takfeer?" posted to jihadist websites (accessed August 2006).

60. Faraj, *The Neglected Duty*, 49.

61. Esposito, *Unholy War*, 7.

62. Gunaratna, *Inside Al Qaeda*, 3–4.

63. Abdullah Azzam, *Defense of Muslim Lands*, http://www.religioscope.com/info/doc/jihad/azzam_defence_3_chap1.htm (accessed October 16, 2006).

64. Azzam, *Join the Caravan*, 33–34.

65. Abdullah Azzam, *Defense of Muslim Lands*, http://www.religioscope.com/info/doc/jihad/azzam_defence_3_chap1.htm (accessed October 16, 2006).

66. Abou Zahab and Roy, *Islamist Networks*, 18. Massoud was assassinated by al-Qa'ida members posing as journalists immediately before September 11.

67. *Al-Sahab Productions*, interview with Ayman Al-Zawahiri. Posted to jihadist websites on September 11, 2006.

68. "Advice of One Concerned," video by Al-Sahab Media. Posted to jihadist websites on July 5, 2007.

69. Ayman Al-Zawhiri, *Knights under the Prophet's Banner*, quoted in Sageman, *Understanding Terror Networks*, 23.

70. Ayman Al-Zawahiri, *Knights under the Prophet's Banner*, 2001. Originally serialized in *Al-Sharq Al-Awsat* newspaper, 2001. Excerpts found at http://www.fas.org/irp/world/para/ayman_bk.html (accessed May 2005).

71. Ibid.

72. From Ayman Al-Zawahiri, "2005 letter to Al-Zarqawi," released by the Office of the Director of National Intelligence, http://dni.gov/press_releases/20051011_release.htm (accessed August 22, 2006).

73. Al-Iraqi, Abu-Maysarah, "This is Who We Are," AQI *Dhurwat Al-Sanam* online magazine, posted to jihadist websites in March 2005.

74. Usama bin Laden, "To the nation, in general, and the mujahidin in Iraq and Somalia, in particular," audio tape posted to jihadist websites in July 2006.

75. Ayman Al-Zawahiri, "2005 letter to Al-Zarqawi."

76. *Al-Sahab Productions*, interview with Ayman Al-Zawahiri, posted to jihadist websites on September 11, 2006.

77. Harmony document AFGP-2002–600053, quoted in "Harmony and Disharmony: Exploiting Al-Qa'ida's Organizational Vulnerabilities," (West Point, NY: Combating Terrorism Center, U.S. Military Academy, 14 February 2006), www.ctc.usma.edu.

78. Brachman and McCants, "Stealing Al-Qa'ida's Playbook": Lawrence Wright, *The Looming Tower*, 256–61.

79. Gerges, *Journey of the Jihadist*, 54–58, 90–91.

80. Letter found at http://dni.gov/press_releases/20051011_release.htm (accessed August 22, 2006).

81. Abu Muhammad Al-Maqdisi, *Democracy: A Religion*, translated by Abu Muhammad Al-Maleki and Abu Sayf Muwahhid (Al-Tibyan Publications, n.d.), http://www.islamicthinkers.com (accessed August 22, 2006).

82. Statement posted to jihadist websites on January 28, 2005.

83. Quoted in part 7 of the serialized book, "Al-Zarqawi: The Second Generation of Al-Qa'ida," by Fu'ad Husayn, which appeared in *Al-Quds Al-Arabi* newspaper, May 20, 2005. See also interview with *Al-Jazeera* TV, July 5, 2005; and interview in *Al-Ghadd* newspaper, July 5, 2005. Al-Zarqawi later directly responded to al-Maqdisi's criticisms in a written statement that appeared on jihadist websites on July 12, 2005.

84. Part 6 of the serialized book, "Al-Zarqawi: The Second Generation of Al-Qa'ida," by Fu'ad Husayn, which appeared in *Al-Quds Al-Arabi* newpaper, May 19, 2005.

85. Muhammad Saeed Al-Qahtani, "Al Wala' Wal Bara' According to the Aqeedah of the Salaf," translated by Omar Johnstone (n.d.). Posted to www.islamworld.net/wala.html (accessed December 5, 2006).

86. Cook, *Understanding Jihad*, 141.

87. Abu-Muhammad Al-Maqdisi, *Millat Ibrahim*, translated and published by Al-Tibyan Publications (n.d.); posted on jihadist websites.

88. Ibn Abd-al-Aziz, "The Key Guide to Preparations" [Al-Umdah fi 'Idad al-Udah], posted to jihadist websites (accessed August 30, 2007), 181, 199.

89. Abu-Yahya Al-Libi, "The Magi's Hellfire in the Arabian Peninsula," posted to jihadist websites, January 5, 2007.

90. "The Islamic Perspective on Kitman," posted to http://www.islamonline.net/servlet/Satellite?cid = 1123996016204&pagename = Is lamOnline-English-AAbout_Islam/AskAboutIslamE/AskAboutIslamE on November 6, 2003 (accessed January 2, 2007); Shultz and Beitler, "Tactical Deception and Strategic Surprise in Al-Qa'ida's Operations."

91. Kepel, *Muslim Extremism in Egypt*, 117.

92. Qutb, *Milestones*, 12.

93. Abou Zahab and Roy, *Islamist Networks*, 71.

94. Al-Suri, *The Call to Global Islamic Resistance*, 1456.

95. Qur'an, 2:256.

96. Disagreement exists within the jihadist movement as to the legitimacy of actions in which Muslim civilians are killed as collateral damage in attacks against non-Muslims.

97. Bruce Lincoln, "Mr. Atta's Meditations, Sept. 10, 2001: A Close Reading of the Text," *Religion and Culture Web Forum* (Chicago: Martin Marty Center, University of Chicago, December 2002)," http://marty-center.uchicago.edu/webforum/122002/com mentary.shtml (accessed August 2005).

98. Quoted in Gerges, *The Far Enemy*, 257.

99. Gerges, *Journey of the Jihadist*, 2, 209.

100. A comprehensive English-language biography of Abu Mus'ab al-Suri is provided by Brynjar Lia, *Architect of Global Jihad*.

101. Literally translated as meaning "ancestors" in Arabic. The Salaf often refers to Muslims in the time of the Prophet; they were the inspiration for the austere Salafi Islamic perspective to which violent jihadists adhere.

102. Al-Suri, *The Call to Global Islamic Resistance*, 1458.

103. Brian Jenkins, *Unconquerable Nation,* 76.

104. This perspective was expressed by Kamal el-Said Habib, a former Egyptian militant whom Gerges interviewed. Gerges, *Journey of the Jihadist*, 271.

Chapter 2

1. World Islamic Front statement, February 23, 1998, quoted in Lawrence, *Messages to the World*, 61.

2. Scheuer, "Al-Qaeda's Insurgency Doctrine."

3. Ayman al-Zawahiri, *Knights under the Prophet's Banner*, originally serialized in *Al-Sharq Al-Awsat* newspaper (2001). Excerpts found at http://www.fas.org/irp/world/para/ayman_bk.html (accessed May 2005).

4. Ibid.

5. Ibid. This perspective is not limited to militants. For example, as a nonmilitant but certainly radical Islamist group dedicated to establishing an Islamic state in the United Kingdom and elsewhere, the al-Muhajirun movement teaches its students that "success does not matter, since individuals are judged on whether they work to fulfill divine duties such as the establishment of the caliphate. In other words, salvation does not hinge on

whether activists are successful in reaching stated movement goals; they are judged according to whether they worked toward these objectives. The duty is the effort and not the outcome of collective action" (Wiktorowicz, *Radical Islam Rising*, 181).

6. Center for Islamic Studies and Research, "The Operation of 11 Rabi Al-Awwal [12 May]: The East Riyadh Operation and Our War with the United States and Its Agents," posted to jihadist websites August 2003, www.why-war.com/files/alqaida _statements.pdf (accessed May 14, 2006). The Center for Islamic Studies and Research is thought by some terrorism experts to be a media front for al-Qa'ida.

7. Scheuer, "Coalition Warfare."

8. Quoted in Scheuer, "Coalition Warfare."

9. Each of the maps in the figure was produced using ArcGis 9.1, using WGS84 in Geographical Coordinates. The information for the two historical maps is derived from W. C. Brice, *An Historical Atlas of Islam*, http://ccat.sas.upenn.edu/~rs143/map.html (accessed January 16, 2007). The information for the contemporary map is derived from *Populations of Muslims around the World*, http://islamicweb.com (accessed January 16, 2007).

10. The first four caliphs were Muhammad's disciples (*Sahaba*): (1) Abu Bakr, (2) Umar bin al-Khattab, (3) Uthman ibn Affan, and (4) Ali ibn Abi Talib. Although Abu-Bakr is recognized by Sunnis as the first caliph, Shiites consider Ali ibn Abi Talib to have been the first truly legitimate caliph.

11. Gregorian, *Islam*, 2.

12. Gerges, *Journey of the Jihadist*, 177–80.

13. Cullison, "Inside Al-Qaeda's Hard Drive."

14. Ibid.

15. The ability of al-Qa'aida to resolve the financial problems facing al-Zawahiri's EIG group was a major consideration in his decision to join the World Islamic Front and sign bin Laden's fatwa. Gerges, *The Far Enemy*, 162, 170–71.

16. From a 2005 letter to al-Zarqawi, accessible at http://dni.gov/press_releases/ 20051011_release.htm (accessed August 22, 2006).

17. Al-Zawahiri, *Knights under the Prophet's Banner*.

18. Ibid.

19. Al-Zayyat, *The Road to Al-Qaeda*, 64–68. Another description of the process that led al-Zawahiri to shift to the Far Enemy approach is provided in Gerges, *The Far Enemy*, 121–22.

20. The GSPC originally announced its allegiance to al-Qa'ida on September 11, 2003. See Schanzer, *Al-Qaeda's Armies*.

21. *Al-Sahab Productions*, interview with Ayman al-Zawahiri, posted to jihadist websites on September 11, 2006.

22. The statement announcing the name change signaled that bin Laden had blessed the new name. Statement posted to jihadist websites, January 2007. The group claimed responsibility for killing four Mauritanian soldiers in Mauritania in December 2007. Statement posted to jihadist websites on December 26, 2007.

23. Kathryn Haahr suggests the alliance between the two groups could be due to either of two possibilities: first, that al-Qa'ida is strengthening itself by forming partnerships with other jihadist groups; or second, that a weakened al-Qa'ida is actually relying on groups like the GSPC. Haahr, "GSPC Joins Al-Qaeda and France Becomes Top Enemy."

24. Abd-al-Qadir Ibn Abd-al-Aziz, "The Key Guide to Preparations," posted to jihadist websites (accessed August 30, 2007), 90.

25. Gerges, *The Far Enemy*, 51. See also al-Zawhiri, *Knights under the Prophet's Banner*, quoted in Sageman, *Understanding Terror Networks*, 44.

26. See Pavlova, "From Counter-Society to Counter-State"; Abuza, "Jemaah Islamiya Enters Regrouping Phase."

27. Abu-Mus'ab al-Zarqawi, 2004 Letter released by the Coalition Provisional Authority, http://www.state.gov/p/nea/rls/31694.htm.

28. Fishman, "After Zarqawi."

29. Fradkin, "Recent Statements of Islamist Ideology."

30. Statement from Al-Qa'ida website; text available at http://www.mepc.org/journal_vol10/alqaeda.html (accessed November 6, 2006).

31. Abu-Ubayd, al-Qurashi, "The 11 September Raid: The Impossible Becomes Possible," www.why-war.com/files/alqaida_statements.pdf (accessed May 14, 2006).

32. Al-Sahab Media interview with Abu-Yahya al-Libi, posted to jihadist websites, September 10, 2007.

33. AQAP actually had four leaders during the campaign who were killed and replaced. Al-Muqrin, though promoting a local jihad, was a veteran of several jihads around the world: against the Soviets in Afghanistan, against the Serbs in Bosnia, and against Americans in Somalia and Afghanistan. "Al-Qaeda in the Arabian Peninsula: Shooting, Hostage Taking, Kidnapping Wave—May/June 2004," IntelCenter, www.intelcenter.com; Usama bin Abd-al-Aziz al-Khalidi, "What Do the Al-Salul Want?" *Sawt Al-Jihad Magazine*, issue 6 (2003).

34. Quoted in Benjamin and Simon, *The Next Attack*, 100–101.

35. Several articles making this argument appeared in *Sawt Al-Jihad* until mid-2004, when the magazine began to give more favorable coverage to the jihad in Iraq. According to Thomas Hegghammer, the softening of the position on Iraq may have undermined AQAP's recruitment. For examples of anti-Iraqi jihad articles in *Sawt Al-Jihad*, see Anonymous, "Questions Regarding the Jihad against the Crusaders in the Arabian Peninsula," *Sawt Al-Jihad Magazine*, issues 11 and 12 (2004); Muhammad bin Ahmad al-Salim, "Do Not Go to Iraq: Advice for the Mujahidin," *Sawt Al-Jihad Magazine*, issue 7 (2003) and "Woe to You, Iraq," *Sawt Al-Jihad Magazine*, issue 11 (2004), all posted to jihadist websites; Hegghammer, "Global Jihadism after the Iraq War."

36. "Al-Qaeda in the Arabian Peninsula: Shooting, Hostage Taking, Kidnapping Wave – May/June 2004," IntelCenter, www.intelcenter.com.

37. Abu-Mus'ab al-Suri, *The Call to Global Islamic Resistance*, 1114, distributed on jihadist websites.

38. Ibid., 1367.

39. Al-Sahab Media interview, posted to jihadist websites, September 10, 2007.

40. Al-Suri, *The Call to Global Islamic Resistance*, 1380–81.

41. Ibid., 1389–90.

42. Ibid., 1385–87.

43. This does not mean, however, that one should assume that al-Suri's writings were the inspiration for AQAP's campaign.

44. Statement posted to jihadist websites, May 30, 2004.

45. Qutb, *Milestones*, 131.

46. Al-Zawahiri, *Knights Under the Prophet's Banner*.

47. Ibid.

48. Scheuer, *Through Our Enemies Eyes*, 122.

49. Harmony doc AFGP-2002–600053, ctc.usma.edu/aq.asp.

50. Al-Zayyat, *The Road to Al-Qaeda*, 58.

51. Qutb, *Milestones*, 12.

52. Detailed information for the descriptions of all seven stages is found in Fu'ad Husayn, parts 14 and 15 of "Al-Zarqawi . . . The Second Generation of Al-Qa'ida," serialized in *Al-Quds Al-Arabi* newspaper, May 28 and 30, 2005.

53. Qutb, *Milestones*, 131.

54. Al-Zawahiri, *Knights Under the Prophet's Banner*, 161.

55. Abu-Bakr Naji, *The Management of Savagery*, translated by William McCants (Cambridge, MA: Olin Institute, Harvard University), http://www.ctc.usma.edu/naji.asp (accessed September 18, 2006); also, for an excellent review of Naji's—and many other strategists'—works, see Brachman and McCants, "Stealing Al-Qa'ida's Playbook."

56. Al-Zawahiri, *Knights Under the Prophet's Banner*, 162.

57. Naji, *The Management of Savagery*, 9–10.

58. Sayf al-Din al-Ansari, "The Raid on New York and Washington," www.why-war.com/files/alqaida_statements.pdf (accessed December 14, 2006).

59. Al-Zawahiri, *Knights Under the Prophet's Banner*, 19, 44.

60. Naji, *The Management of Savagery*, 25–26.

61. Ibid., 40.

62. As discussed in Brachman and McCants, "Stealing Al-Qa'ida's Playbook"; Naji, *The Management of Savagery*, 34.

63. Naji, *The Management of Savagery*, 46.

64. Jihadist website postings: Al-Shammari interview (October 2006); IAI's *Al-Fursan Magazine* interview (July 2006).

65. The group has also declared that it has a special brigade created to observe Jews and the Mossad, and to defend the al-Aqsa Mosque in Jerusalem. Although it claims to be locally focused, this could signal that the group's ambitions extend beyond Iraq.

66. The Badr Corps is the armed wing of the Supreme Council for the Islamic Revolution in Iraq (SCIRI), a pro-Iranian group. SCIRI is the primary Shi'ite rival of Muqtada al-Sadr's group.

67. Jihadist website postings: Interview with IAI spokesman Dr. Ibrahim Al-Shammari (October 5, 2006); IAI group "Creed and Methodology" (August 25, 2005); IAI's *Al-Fursan Magazine* interview with unidentified group Amir (July 30, 2006).

68. Other similarly oriented insurgent groups in Iraq have claimed the same, including the Al-Rashidin Army. See interview with Al-Rashidin Army Amir, posted to jihadist websites in August 2007.

69. Al-Shammari interview, released on jihadist websites (October 5, 2006); and Al-Shammari interview with *Al-Jazeera* (23 March 2006).

70. Khalil, "Islamic Army in Iraq Pursues Strategy of Negotiation and Violence."

71. The group, however, appears to consider members of the Iraqi Army and police forces as apostates.

72. Al-Rishawi was killed on September 13, 2007, by a bomb planted under his car in Ramadi, ten days after his ninety-minute meeting with President Bush, and two days after the sixth anniversary of the 9/11 attacks.

73. Al-Shammari interview with *Al-Jazeera* (October 19, 2006).

74. The IAI has a history of some cooperation in operations with other jihadist groups in Iraq and says that it does not "in principle" refuse cooperation with fellow mujahidin. More specifically, al-Shammari stated that, although it has not cooperated with the Mujahidin Shura Council or the mujahidin in Afghanistan, the IAI would like to do so.

75. Harmony database document AFGP-2002–600080, http://www.ctc.usma.edu/aq_600080.asp (accessed September 19, 2006).

76. Ibid.

77. Ibid.

78. "Harmony and Disharmony: Exploiting Al-Qa'ida's Organizational Vulnerabilities," (West Point, NY: Combating Terrorism Center, U.S. Military Academy, February 14, 2006), www.ctc.usma.edu.

79. Ibid.

80. Usama bin Laden, quoted in Bonney, *Jihad*, 321–22.

81. Muhammad al-Shafi'i, "Abu-Ubayd al-Qurashi, bin Ladin's Most Prominent Aide: Perpetrators of September Attacks Studied Security Mistakes That Led to Downfall of Ayyash and Ramzi," *Al-Sharq Al-Awsat*, March 23, 2002.

82. Abu-Ubayd Al-Qurashi, quoted in "Bin Laden Lieutenant Admits to September 11 and Explains al-Qaeda's Combat Doctrine," Memri Special Dispatch 344 (February 10, 2002), http://www.memri.org/bin/articles.cgi?Area = sd&ID = SP34402.

83. "The Operation of 11 Rabi Al-Awwal [12 May]: The East Riyadh Operation and Our War with the United States and Its Agents," Center for Islamic Studies and Research, posted to jihadist websites in August 2003. www.why-war.com/files/alqaida_statements .pdf (accessed May 14, 2006).

84. "U.S. Forces Poised In Al-Fallujah As Delegates Continue To Broker Talks," *GlobalSecurity.org*, www.globalsecurity.org/military/library/news/2004/04/mil-040412-rferl02.h tm (accessed February 1, 2008).

85. Al-Ayiri's discussion of urban guerrilla warfare's impact on air operations was in the context of how Iraqi forces could best wage war against the United States after the

invasion, but its lessons are equally applicable for jihadist insurgents. Yusuf al-Ayiri, *The Crusaders' War on Iraq*, posted to jihadist websites.

86. Mao's first phase of protracted war, "strategic defensive," is one in which political strength is built and military action is limited and takes place in the form of mobile warfare, supplemented by guerrilla and positional warfare. In this phase, operations are carried out for their propaganda value. All information on Mao's military doctrine found in Mao Tse-Tung, *On Protracted War*, 35–46, and Thomas X. Hammes, *The Sling and the Stone*, 52.

87. Abd-al-Aziz al-Muqrin, *Al-Battar Camp*, number 2 (January 2004), www.e-prism.org/articlesbyotherscholars.html (accessed September 19, 2006).

88. Mao calls the second phase of protracted warfare "strategic balance"; in it, the enemy is put on the defensive and is met by heavy guerrilla forces that work to wear them down. Insurgents, in this phase, gain strength and consolidate control of base areas, and in some cases actively administer portions of the contested area. The insurgents gather arms.

89. Abd-al-Aziz al-Muqrin, *Al-Battar Camp*, number 3 (February 2004), http://www.e-prism.org/articlesbyotherscholars.html (accessed 19 September 2006).

90. Mao's third phase is that of the insurgents' "strategic counter-offensive," in which they recover lost territories. The third stage is characterized by one in which the insurgency shifts from guerrilla operations to positional warfare, carried out by regular forces in a final offensive against the regime.

91. Mao's insurgent forces became the nucleus of his army; Guevara similarly wrote that the guerrilla force "is an armed nucleus, the fighting vanguard of the people." Guevara, *Guerrilla Warfare*, 10.

92. Abd-Al-Aziz Al-Muqrin, *Al-Battar Camp*, number 3.

93. Ayman Al-Zawahiri, "Letter from Al-Zawahiri to Al-Zarqawi," released on October 11, 2005, by the Office of the Director of National Intelligence, www.dni.gov/release_letter_101105.html (accessed September 19, 2006).

94. Al-Suri, *The Call to Global Islamic Resistance*, 1442.

95. Mao is not the only classic insurgent to have influenced al-Ayiri and al-Qurashi. Their writings resemble—and, in Al-Qurashi's case, cite—the writings of others, including Che Guevara and Carlos Marighella (author of the *Minimanual of the Urban Guerrilla*). In his article, al-Qurashi also includes discussions of various insurgencies, including those in Nicaragua, Vietnam, and Cuba. See Yusuf al-Ayiri, *The Crusaders' War on Iraq*; Abu-Ubayd al-Qurashi, "Revolutionary Wars," posted to jihadist websites; and Abu-Ubayd al-Qurashi ("Fourth Generation Wars," 2002), quoted in "Bin Laden Lieutenant Admits to September 11 and Explains al-Qaeda's Combat Doctrine," Memri Special Dispatch 344 (February 10, 2002), www.memri.org/bin/articles.cgi?Area = sd&ID = SP34402.

96. Ellen Knichmeyer, "Zarqawi Said to Be Behind Iraq Raid," *Washington Post*, April 5, 2005; Al-Zarqawi group statement, posted to jihadist websites (April 3, 2005).

97. David Kilcullen applies this directly to the Iraq insurgency, which he terms a "resistance insurgency," one in which "multiple groups are seeking to paralyze and fragment the state" and provoke the Coalition—rather than a "revolutionary insurgency," one in which the insurgents aim to displace the government and administer the territory themselves. Kilcullen, "Counterinsurgency Redux."

98. The need to gain and sustain popular support may have forced Iraqi insurgents, most notably al-Qa'ida in Iraq, to stop recording and releasing videos of beheading hostages. The number of beheading tapes released to the media or posted on websites diminished noticeably starting in 2005.

Chapter 3

1. See Arquilla and Ronfeldt, *The Advent of Netwar*; Arquilla and Ronfeldt, *Swarming and the Future of Conflict*; Arquilla and Ronfeldt, *Networks and Netwars*.

2. Yusuf al-Ayiri, *The Crusaders' War on Iraq*, posted to jihadist websites.

3. Sageman, *Understanding Terror Networks*, 141.

4. Valdis Krebs, "Uncloaking Terrorist Networks," *First Monday*, vol. 7, no. 4, www.firstmonday.org/issues/issue7_4/krebs/ (accessed November 11, 2006).

5. Lesser et al., *Countering the New Terrorism*, 51.

6. See Abuza, *Militant Islam in Southeast Asia*, 132–40; and Sageman, *Understanding Terrorist Networks*, 137–52.

7. See Johnson, "Analyses of the Groupe Salafiste pour la Prédication et le Combat (GSPC)"; Gunaratna, *Inside Al Qaeda*, 96–97; Sageman, *Understanding Terrorist Networks*, 137–52; Brisard with Martinez, *Zarqawi*, 137.

8. Ayman al-Zawahiri, *Knights under the Prophet's Banner*, 176.

9. The leaderless resistance model was popularized by Louis Beam, an American extremist from the Aryan Nations group.

10. See Al-Suri, *The Call to Global Islamic Resistance*, 51.

11. Brachman and McCants, "Stealing Al-Qa'ida's Playbook."

12. "The Frightening Evolution of Al-Qa'ida," *MSNBC.com*, June 24, 2005, http://msnbc.msn.com/id/8307333/print/1/displaymode/1098/ (accessed August 22, 2006).

13. Al-Suri, *The Call to Global Islamic Resistance*, 665–66, 668, 1408; Lia Brynjar, "Abu-Mus'ab Al-Suri: Profile of a Jihadist Leader," *Joint FFI/King's College Conference—"The Changing Faces of Jihadism"* (April 28, 2006), www.mil.no/felles/ffi/start/English/ (accessed February 6, 2007).

14. Sageman, *Understanding Terror Networks*, 121–24.

15. Al-Suri, *The Call to Global Islamic Resistance*, 54.

16. Pavlova, "From Counter-Society to Counter-State."

17. It should be noted that, although al-Suri came out against the bay'ah, he did pledge to Mullah Omar.

18. Al-Suri, *The Call to Global Islamic Resistance*, 1352–64.

19. Muhammad Khalil al-Hakaymah, "How to Kill Alone" and "Toward a New Strategy," both published on jihadist websites in 2006.

20. Yusuf al-Ayiri, *The Crusaders' War against Iraq*, posted to jihadist websites in 2002.

21. Al-Suri, *The Call to Global Islamic Resistance*, 1396–97.

22. Ibid., 1393.

23. Ibid., 1396.

24. Ibid., 838.

25. See Jaspert, *The Crusades*; Riley-Smith, *The Crusades*. For an Islamic perspective, see Hillenbrand, *The Crusades*.

26. Al-Suri, *The Call to Global Islamic Resistance*, 1446–48.

27. Ibid., 1447–1500.

28. "Declaration of War against the Americans Occupying the Land of the Two Holy Places," www.pbs.org/newshour/terrorism/international/fatwa_1996.html (accessed on August 29, 2006).

29. See al-Qa'ida training manual released by the U.S. Department of Justice, http://www.fas.org/irp/world/para/manualpart1.html (accessed December 29, 2006); Khalid Al-Hammadi, interview with Nasir Al-Bahri, aka Abu-Jandal, *Al-Quds Al-Arabi* newspaper, March 24, 2005; Gerges, *The Far Enemy*, 183; "Atiyah Letter," released by Iraqi National Security Advisor on September 18, 2006, English translation provided by the Combating Terrorism Center at West Point, www.ctc.usma.edu.

30. Quoted in Gerges, *The Far Enemy*, 257.

31. Muhammad al-Shafi'i, *Al-Sharq Al-Awsat* (19 January 2003).

32. Al-Zawahiri, *Knights under the Prophet's Banner*.

33. Quoted in Scheuer, "Al-Zawahiri's September 11 Video."

34. Abu-Mus'ab al-Suri, *The Confrontation between the Sunni Population of Al Sham against Al-Naserieh, Crusaders and Jews*, 2002. Harmony document # AGFP 2002–600966, http://ctc.usma.edu/aq.asp (accessed 29 December 2006).

35. Karen DeYoung, "Letter Gives Glimpse of Al-Qaeda's Leadership," *The Washington Post*, October 2, 2006.

36. Letter released by Iraqi National Security Advisor on September 18, 2006. English translation provided by the Combating Terrorism Center at West Point, www.ctc.usma.edu.

37. Ulph, "Al-Zarqawi's Group under Pressure and Seeking Allies."

38. Message posted on jihadist websites on January 15, 2006. The proper communication of a clear position is a classic al-Zawahiri approach, one that he wrote about in his 2001 autobiography.

39. Quoted in Scheuer, "Al-Qaeda in Iraq." Quotes originally appeared in Arabic publications: *Daily Star* (April 3, 2006) and *al-Bawaba* (April 2, 2006).

40. Quoted in Michael Scheuer, "Al-Qaeda in Iraq." Quotes originally appeared in Arabic publications: *Daily Star* (April 3, 2006) and *al-Bawaba* (April 2, 2006).

41. "Jihadist Websites Community on Formation of Iraqi Islamic State," posted to Centcom's "What Extremists Are Saying" website, http://www.centcom.mil/sites/

uscentcom1/What%20Extremists%20Say/JihadistWebsitesCommunityonFormationof IraqiIslamicState.aspx?PageView = Shared (accessed November 13, 2006).

42. Posted to jihadist websites, January 8, 2007.

43. The following were listed as Abu-Umar al-Baghdadi's ministers: Abu Abd-al-Rahman al-Filahi, Prime Minister; Abu-Hamzah al-Muhajir (aka Abu-Ayyub al-Masri, leader of Al-Qa'ida in Iraq after al-Zarqawi's death), Minister of War; Abu-Uthman al-Tamimi, Minster of the Shari'ah Commission; Abu-Bakr al-Jaburi, Minister of Public Relations; Abu Abd-al-Jabbar al-Janabi, Minister of National Security; Abu-Muhammad al-Mashhadani, Minister of Information; Abu Abd-al-Qadir al-Issi, Minister of Captive and Detainee Affairs; Abu-Ahmad al-Janabi, Minister of Petroleum; Mustafa al-A'raji, Minister of Agriculture; Abu-Abdullah al-Zayyi, Minister of Health. Posted to jihadist websites, April 19, 2007.

44. Letter to Abu-Umar al-Baghdadi, posted to jihadist websites, April 5, 2007.

45. Statement posted to jihadist websites, April 16, 2007.

46. Statements posted to jihadist websites on March 13, 15, 24, and 30, and April 7, 13, and 18, 2007.

47. Letter released by Combating Terrorism Center at West Point.

48. Statements posted to jihadist websites on May 2, and June 20, 2007.

49. Judging by the rhetoric in its statements, the Islamic Army in Iraq was probably the driving force behind the Jihad and Reform Front. Additionally, registration details from the JRF's website obtained by open-source WhoIs searches indicated that the website's main contact was money_detailsiai@yahoo.com, and that the website was registered to the same server as a number of Islamic Army websites.

50. This is probably a reference to al-Qa'ida in Iraq's attacks on Shi'ite civilians.

51. Posted to jihadist websites, June 6, 2007.

52. Statement posted to jihadist websites, January 1, 2008.

53. Statements posted to jihadist websites on March 18, 2007 (initial split of 1920 Revolution Brigades), and March 28 and 29, 2007 (creation of Hamas-Iraq and Islamic Jihad Corp's readoption of 1920 name).

54. Statements posted to jihadist websites on March 28 and April 22, 2007; interview with Hamas-Iraq's Political Office, posted to jihadist websites on July 18, 2007. See also Khalil, "Divisions within the Iraqi Insurgency.".

55. Statements posted to jihadist websites on March 28 and April 22, 2007; interview with Hamas-Iraq's Political Office, posted to jihadist websites on July 18, 2007.

56. Devji, *Landscapes of the Jihad.*

57. In his study of the environmental activist movement, Luther Gerlach describes four factors that contribute to the segmentation and division of social movements. First, personal power and individualism taking the initiative in "achieving those movement goals the person or group considers important"; personal emphasis helps to exacerbate differences over the perceived importance of certain points of the ideology. Second, preexisting cleavages—such as socioeconomic differences, factionalism, and personal conflicts—all contribute to segmentation and division. The third factor is competition among members.

The fourth is ideological difference. Segmentation and division results in a variety of groups and subgroups working to achieve the movement's goals; a variety of groups makes it easier for a social movement to do different things and reach out to different populations. See Arquilla and Ronfeldt, *Networks and Netwars*, 291–92.

58. O'Neill, *Insurgency and Terrorism*, 128–31.

59. The group includes the 1920 Revolution Brigades, al-Rashidin Army, Army of the Muslims, Islamic Movement of Iraq's Mujahidin, Jund al-Rahman Brigade, Call and Encampment Brigades, al-Tamkin Brigades, and the Muhammad al-Fatih Brigades. Statement posted to jihadist websites, September 6, 2007.

60. Statement posted to jihadist websites, May 1, 2007.

Chapter 4

1. For example, al-Suri's decentralization theory depends on successful, wide-scale radicalization of individuals and small groups.

2. Sageman, *Leaderless Jihad*.

3. Wiktorowicz, *Radical Islam Rising*, 34.

4. People and groups who desire to become trusted authorities must invest significant attention in how others perceive their public and private reputations. Wiktorowicz points out that individuals and groups must "establish the movement's reputation and sacred authority so that religious seekers are more likely to . . . be exposed to the process of movement socialization." Similarly, given the decentralized nature of sacred authority in Islam, a movement must convince adherents that its scholarly interpretation is not only legitimate but also more authentic than alternatives. In essence, an adherent must trust the spiritual guide's credibility in order to be receptive to the religious education offered by the movement. See Wiktorowicz, *Radical Islam Rising*, 6, 27, 137.

5. Ibid., 5, 97, 167.

6. For examples of the risks posed to terrorist groups, see Pipes, *The Degaev Affair*, and Giorgio, *Memoirs of an Italian Terrorist*

7. One jihadist group, Asbat al-Ansar, thought to have around 300 members, found safe haven and was headquartered in the 44,000- to 75,000-person Ayn al-Hilwah camp, which erupted into a full-blown battle between an Asbat al-Ansar splinter group and Fatah. Asbat al-Ansar's target set has proven to be quite wide, with the group having targeted Hamas, Fatah, an American missionary, and the Russian embassy in Beirut, in addition to a disrupted plot to target Jordanian, U.S., and British embassies in Lebanon. Schanzer, *Al-Qaeda's Armies*, 47–61.

8. *Violent Jihad in the Netherlands*. See also Robert S. Leiken, "Europe's Angry Muslims," *Foreign Affairs* 84 (2005), www.foreignaffairs.org/20050701faessay84409/robert-s-leiken/europe-s-angry-mus lims.html (accessed January 18, 2008); Lt. Col. Scott Morrison, "What if there is no terrorist network?" *Armed Forces Journal,* www.armed forcesjournal.com/2007/08/2872696 (accessed January 18, 2008).

9. "Al-Qa'ida Foreign Fighters in Iraq: A First Look at the Sinjar Records" (West Point, NY: Combating Terrorism Center, U.S. Military Academy, 2007), www.ctc.usma.edu.

10. For an extensive summary of various theories that have been proposed to explain terrorism, see Victoroff, "The Mind of the Terrorist."

11. Wiktorowicz, *Radical Islam Rising*, 12.

12. Neuroscientists have examined anger and violence and discovered genetic variations, expressed as concentrations of a molecule in the brain, which are both congenital and predispose an individual to a violent temper.

13. For an empirically based critique of psychological theories of the underlying motivations for acts of terrorism, see Horgan, *The Psychology of Terrorism.*

14. Intelligence and Security Committee, *Report into the London Terrorist Attacks on 7 July 2005.*

15. Hegghammer, "Terrorist Recruitment and Radicalization in Saudi Arabia."

16. Al-Suri, *The Call to Global Islamic Resistance*, 1458

17. This is a common feature of religious fundamentalist groups that engage in violent action. For example, the violent elements of the anti-abortion movement in the United States have engaged in domestic terrorism.

18. For a description of the Pew Global Attitudes Project and copies of the reports it has produced, which provide the data analyzed in this section, see http://pewglobal.org/ (accessed November 7, 2006).

19. These results are based on surveys conducted in Indonesia, Jordan, Lebanon, Morocco, Pakistan, and Turkey.

20. "Muslim Alienation Risk in Europe," *BBC News*, http://news.bbc.co.uk/2/hi/europe/6189675.stm (accessed February 1, 2008).

21. Historically, volunteering for military service goes up in the initial stages of conflicts. Recruiting individuals to a cause is not difficult when people agree there is a threat that must be met. This pattern occurred during the initial months of World War I for both the Allies and Central Powers. Similarly, it has happened in the United States during the early stages of various military engagements, including the Civil War, both World Wars, and after the September 11 terrorist attacks. While we do not imply comparability between September 11 and the U.S.-led coalition invasion of Iraq to overthrow Saddam Hussein, it is readily apparent that the insurgency in Iraq has successfully used the image of an occupying power attacking a Muslim country for recruitment purposes both inside and outside Iraq.

22. Grossman, *On Killing.*

23. For a discussion of isolation and its effects on ideological and motivational reinforcement, see Ferracuti, "Ideology and Repentance," 61. For more on group pressures and underground groups, see Post, "Terrorist Psycho-logic," 33.

24. Grossman, *On Killing,* 150–51; and Bandura, "Mechanisms of Moral Disengagement," 176.

25. Grossman, *On Killing,* 187–89.

26. Bandura, "Mechanisms of Moral Disengagement," 164–72; and Post, "Terrorist Psycho-logic," 35.

27. Sageman, *Understanding Terror Networks*, 184.

28. See "Testimony of Robert S. Mueller, III, Director Federal Bureau of Investigation, before the Senate Committee on Intelligence of the United States Senate, February 16, 2005," www.fbi.gov/congress/congress05/mueller021605.htm; and "A Review of the Bureau of Prisons' Selection of Muslim Religious Services Providers," U.S. Department of Justice, http://www.usdoj.gov/oig/special/0404/; Kepel, *Muslim Extremism in Egypt*; Siegel, "Radical Islam and the French Muslim Prison Population"; and Vindino, *Al Qaeda in Europe: The New Battleground of International Jihad.*

29. Owen Bowcott, "Torture Trail to September 11," *The Guardian*, January 24, 2003, www.guardian.co.uk/alqaida/story/0,,881096,00.html; and al-Zayyat, *The Road to Al-Qaeda.*

30. Gerges, *Journey of the Jihadist*, 38, 58–59; and Zambelis, "Egyptian Gama'a Al-Islamiyya's Public Relations Campaign." Some believe that prisons can also act as moderating forces, deradicalizing ideology; Chris Zambelis explains, "According to some observers, as documented in a November 2003 report from the al-Ahram Center for Political and Strategic Studies, lengthy prison stints for ideologues such as Ibrahim and his colleagues encouraged a closer study of religious texts, which in and of itself may have contributed to a revision of the group's radical doctrine."

31. Jihadist websites (further identification withheld).

32. Al-Suri, *The Call to Global Islamic Resistance*, 1423, discusses the foundations of their training.

33. Ibid., 1425.

34. Stern, *Terror in the Name of God*, 243

35. Ibid., 237–80, provides a more in-depth treatment of Islamic terrorist networks, franchises, and freelancers.

36. Al-Suri, *The Call to Global Islamic Resistance*, 1414–19.

37. Al-Suri recommends that explosive training in private homes be limited to theoretical explanations so as to avoid accidents that might lead to discovery. Al-Suri, *The Call to Global Islamic Resistance*, 1425

38. Intelligence and Security Committee, *Report into the London Terrorist Attacks on 7 July 2005.*

39. The Global Islamic Media Front, a jihadist Internet group, has distributed on jihadist websites technical training on a variety of topics, including encryption and secure electronic communications.

40. See www.defenselink.mil/Releases/Release.aspx?ReleaseID = 7530 (accessed December 15, 2006).

41. Two of the detainees—one Saudi and one Yemeni—committed suicide on June 10, 2006, while in U.S. custody.

42. The Guantánamo list includes information about the citizenship of each detainee: Afghanistan (n = 217; 28.6%); Azerbaijan (n = 1; 0.1%); Bangladesh (n = 1; 0.1%); Kazakhstan (n = 3; 0.4%); Pakistan (n = 66; 8.7%); Pakistan/Afghanistan (n = 1; 0.1%); Pakistan/Bangladesh (n = 1; 0.1%); Tajikistan (n = 12; 1.6%); Turkmenistan (n = 1; 0.1%);

and Uzbekistan (n = 8; 1.1%). Percentages are computed based on the total number of detainees (n = 759).

43. In addition to the Pakistani nationals, detainees in the "locals" classification have been released from Tajikistan (n = 6), Turkmenistan (n = 1), and Uzbekistan (n = 1).

44. Ideology as a motivator is not unique to the jihadis. For example, the American volunteers commonly referred to as the Abraham Lincoln Brigade fought on the side of the antifascist Spanish Republican forces in the Spanish Civil War (against the Nationalists under Franco) as part of the International Brigade that was loosely organized by the Comintern and made up of volunteers from nations around the globe. See Carroll, *The Odyssey of the Abraham Lincoln Brigade.*

45. The following countries are defined as core Arab: Bahrain (n = 6, 0.8%); Egypt (n = 6, 0.8%); Iraq (n = 8, 1.1%); Jordan (n = 8, 1.1%); Kuwait (n = 12, 1.6%); Lebanon (n = 1, 0.1%); Palestine (n = 3, 0.4%); Qatar (n = 1, 0.1%); Saudi Arabia (n = 138; 18.2%); Syria (n = 10, 1.3%); United Arab Emirates (n = 2, 0.3%); and Yemen (n = 108, 14.2%). Percentages are computed based on the total number of detainees (n = 759).

46. The Maghreb is the region of Africa that encompasses Algeria (n = 25, 3.3%); Libya (n = 11, 1.4%); Mauritania (n = 3, 0.4%); Morocco (n = 15, 2.0%); and Tunisia (n = 12, 1.6%). Percentages are computed based on the total number of detainees (n = 759).

47. We include detainees from the following countries in the "Other" category for region: Australia (0.3%, n = 2); Azerbaijan (0.1%, n = 1); Canada (0.3%, n = 2); China (2.9%, n = 22); Iran (0.4%, n = 3); and Turkey (0.7%, n = 5). Percentages are computed based on the total number of detainees (n = 759).

48. The "Travelers" category includes detainees from the following regions: Core Arabs, Maghreb Arabs, Europe, Sub-Saharan Africa, and Other. The "Afghans and Locals" category includes the following regions: Afghanistan and Locals.

49. A West Point study of an over-600-person list of AQI foreign fighters conducted by the Combatting Terrorism Center at West Point found that "Saudis made up the largest contingent of foreign fighters entering Iraq. Libyans were second (first if measured in per capita terms) and Syrians a distant third." The West Point study also noted that Saudis "contributed the most overall suicide bombers, but the percentage of Suadi fighters listed as suicide bombers was actually lower than non-Saudis." "Al-Qa'ida's Foreign Fighters in Iraq: A First Look at the Sinjar Records" (West Point, NY: Combatting Terrorism Center, U.S. Military Academy, 2007), www.ctc.usma.edu.

50. The "Other" category consists of the following: French (0.8%, n = 3); Sudanese (0.8%, n = 3); and Turkish (0.3%, n = 1). Percentages are computed based on the total number of martyrs (n = 395).

51. The nationalities of 24 of the 27 individuals on the AQI/MSC Martyrs list were as follows: Algeria (3.7 %, n = 1); Egypt (7.4%, n = 2); Iraq (14.8%, n = 4); Libya (3.7 %, n = 1); Morocco (3.7 %, n = 1); Palestine (11.1%, n = 3); Saudi Arabia (11.1%, n = 3); Syria (11.1%, n = 3); Tunisia 3.7 %, n = 1); Turkey (3.7 %, n = 1); United Arab Emirates (3.7 %, n = 1); Yemen (3.7 %, n = 1); and unknown (18.5%, n = 5). Percentages are computed based on the total number of martyrs (n = 27).

Chapter 5

1. Lal and Jackson, "Change and Continuity in Terrorism Revisited: Terrorist Tactics, 1980–2005."

2. C. M. J. Drake, "The Role of Ideology in Terrorists' Target Selection."

3. Quoted in "Al-Qaeda Tactic/Target Brief–v1.5," IntelCenter (June 14, 2004), www.intelcenter.com.

4. According to a U.S. Army War College study, "what Al-Qaeda and its franchises fear most are Islamic laws, histories, and principles that do not conform to their militant ideologies." Youssef Aboul-Enein and Sherifa Zuhur, "Islamic Rulings on Warfare," *Strategic Studies Institute*, October 2004, www.strategicstudiesinstitute.army.mil.

5. Grossman, *On Killing*, 172.

6. Abd-al-Aziz al-Muqrin, "The Targets inside Cities—Al Qaeda Targeting Guidance," trans. IntelCenter–Al Qaeda Targeting Guidance, v1.0, www.intelcenter.com/Qaeda-Targeting-Guidance-v1–0.pdf (accessed September 15, 2006).

7. Yusuf al-Ayiri, "Operation Moscow Theatre: What Did the Mujahidin Gain from It and What Did They Lose?" Summarized in William McCants, ed., *Militant Ideology Atlas*, http://ctc.usma.edu/atlas/Atlas-ResearchCompendium.pdf (accessed December 29, 2006).

8. Al-Muqrin, "The Targets inside Cities."

9. Ibid.

10. Ibid.

11. Ibid.

12. Quoted in Bergen, *The Osama Bin Laden I Know*, 244–46.

13. Al-Suri, *The Call to Global Islamic Resistance*, 1388–89; Letter to al-Zarqawi, released by the Office of the Director of National Intelligence, http://dni.gov/press_releases/letter_in_english.pdf (accessed December 29, 2006).

14. Usama bin Laden, February 11, 2003; quoted in Lawrence, *Messages to the World*, 183.

15. Regimes in Iraq, Saudi Arabia, Jordan, and Egypt are all targeted by al-Zawahiri in this statement. Video statement posted to jihadist websites, April 29, 2006.

16. See al-Zawahiri statements: *Al-Jazeera*, September 28, 2003; *Al-Jazeera*, March 25, 2004; and others posted to jihadist websites, February 20, 2006 and April 29, 2006.

17. Muni Ahmad, "Fugitive Named in 2 Pakistan Plots," *Associated Press—CBS News Online*, May 28. 2004. www.cbsnews.com/stories/2004/05/26/world/main619660.shtml (accessed September 11, 2006).

18. Usama bin Laden, December 16, 2004; quoted in Lawrence, *Messages to the World*, 272.

19. Ulph, "Al-Zawahiri Encourages Targeting of Gulf Oil."

20. The Egyptian Islamist movements were split about methods also, with some believing that revolution could only be achieved through a military coup, and others believing that, upon the assassination of major leaders, the Egyptian masses would rise up.

21. Ulph, "Schism and Collapse of Morale."

22. Usama Bin Laden, 1977, *CNN* interview with Peter Arnett; quoted in Lawrence, *Messages to the World*, 47.

23. World Islamic Front statement, February 23, 1998; quoted in Lawrence, *Messages to the World*, 61.

24. From video by al-Qa'ida's media group, *Al-Sahab*, "Knowledge for Acting Upon: The Manhattan Raid," released on September 11, 2006.

25. This letter is a perfect example of how al-Qa'ida "shops" for like-minded clerics to provide legitimacy to their actions. Cullison, "Inside Al-Qaeda's Hard Drive."

26. Ibid.

27. Wiktorowicz, "A Genealogy of Radical Islam."

28. According to Brian Fishman, al-Zarqawi had four major ideological influences in his life: (1) Abu-Muhammad al-Maqdisi; (2) Abu-Abdullah al-Muhajir; (3) Abu-Anas al-Shami; and (4) Abu-Hamzah al-Baghdadi. Al-Maqdisi's influence on al-Zarqawi's takfiri targeting is immense, but al-Muhajir has been credited by al-Zarqawi as the person who changed his mind about the legality of martyrdom operations as a legitimate form of resistance. After studying with al-Muhajir, al-Zarqawi, who had no previous involvement in suicide terrorism, began to rely on the tactic heavily in his campaign in Iraq. Al-Shami, as al-Zarqawi's primary legal advisor in Iraq, set up the theological basis for al-Zarqawi's war against the Shi'ites. Even though al-Zarqawi probably was anti-Shi'ite before contact with al-Shami, al-Shami's justifications were perceived by the Legal Council as sufficient to begin and escalate a campaign against the sect. Brian Fishman, "Zarqawi's Jihad: Inside the Mind of Iraq's Most Notorious Man," Working Paper (West Point, NY: Combating Terrorism Center, U.S. Military Academy, April 26, 2006). See also Jackson et al., *Aptitude for Destruction*, 45–46.

29. Quoted in Fishman, "Zarqawi's Jihad"; Abu-Anas al-Shami, audio sermon posted to alsaha.fares.net on July 28, 2004; and Abu-Mus'ab al-Zarqawi, audio sermon posted to jihadist websites on May 18, 2005.

30. "Harmony and Disharmony: Exploiting Al-Qa'ida's Organizational Vulnerabilities" (West Point, NY: Combating Terrorism Center, U.S. Military Academy, February 14, 2006).

31. Cruickshank and Ali, "Abu Musab Al Suri," 7.

32. Al-Suri, *The Call to Global Islamic Resistance*, 1389.

33. "The Key Guide to Preparations," posted to jihadist websites, 191 (accessed August 30, 2007).

34. "Instructions to Abu-Usamah," document number IZ-060316–02, April 20, 2006, www.ctc.usma.edu/harmony_docs.asp.

35. Letter released by Iraqi National Security Advisor, September 18, 2006. English translation provided by the Combating Terrorism Center at West Point, www.ctc .usma.edu.

36. Letter released by Iraqi National Security Advisor, September 18, 2006.

37. Ibid.

38. Muqaddam, "Algeria: Acute Crisis inside the Leadership of Al-Qa'ida."

39. Sensual descriptions of the Islamic paradise and its rewards can be found in the Qur'an and the Hadiths, giving rise to the popular notion that martyrs will receive 72 virgins. For instance, in sura 55, verses 72–74, N. J. Dawood translates the Arabic word *hur* as virgins, and the context makes clear that virgin is the appropriate translation: "Dark-eyed virgins sheltered in their tents (which of your Lord's blessings would you deny?) whom neither man nor jinnee will have touched before." *The Koran*, 7th edition, translated by N. J. Dawood (New York: Penguin, 2000). It is important to note, however, that there is no mention anywhere in the Qur'an of the actual number of virgins available in paradise for all Muslims, not just martyrs. Some maintain the Hadiths specify 72 virgins in heaven. For example, Ibn Kathir (1301–1373 CE), in his commentary (*Tafsir*), refers to Hadith 2687 in discussing sura 55: "It was mentioned by Daraj Ibn Abi Hatim, that Abu Al-Haytham 'Adullah Ibn Wahb narrated from Abu Sa'id Al-Khudhri, who heard the Prophet Muhammad (Allah's blessings and peace be upon him) saying, 'The smallest reward for the people of Heaven is an abode where there are 80,000 servants and 72 wives, over which stands a dome decorated with pearls, aquamarine and ruby, as wide as the distance from Al-Jabiyyah to San'a.'" This assertion, however, does not appear in other compilations, such as the Sahih Muslim.

40. For a list of the benefits of martyrdom, see al-Suri, *The Call to Global Islamic Resistance*, 1475–78. Jihadists frequently say that they "consider" a particular person to be a martyr, but that only God can decide for sure.

41. Gerges, *The Far Enemy*, 142.

42. Abu-Muhammad al-Maqdisi, "Regarding the Fatwa of the Saudi Mufti on 'Acts of Martyrdom,'" summarized in William McCants, ed., *Militant Ideology Atlas* (West Point, NY: Combating Terrorism Center, U.S. Military Academy), http://ctc.usma.edu/atlas/Atlas-ResearchCompendium.pdf (accessed December 29, 2006).

43. The Arabic word for martyr is *shahid*.

44. Muhammad's sayings and deeds are called Sunnah and are transmitted through Hadith. The Sahih Muslim, one of the six major Sunni Hadith collections, was compiled by Imam Muslim (Abul Husain Muslim bin al-Hajjaj al-Nisapuri, 824–883 CE). Imam Muslim never claimed to collect all authentic traditions, but only to assemble traditions that all Muslims should agree were based on accurate reports. Imam Muslim checked each report he included for compatibility with the Qur'an and for the veracity of the chain of reporters. The Salih Muslim is the second most famous Hadith collection, although it is dismissed as inauthentic by Shi'ites. Sahih Muslim, chapter 782, *"The Merit of Martyrdom,"* translation by Abdul Hamid Siddiqui (accessed November 8, 2006), www.usc.edu/dept/MSA/fundamentals/hadithsunnah/muslim.

45. Based on his interviews with former jihadists, Fawaz Gerges argues the tactic was pioneered and justified by al-Zawahiri during his years as an Egyptian militant. Gerges, *The Far Enemy*, 142.

46. Paz, "Global Jihad and WMD."

47. Pape, *Dying to Win*, 28–29, 38.

48. Usama bin Laden, audio message posted to jihadist websites on December 28, 2004.

49. Abu-Ubayd al-Qurashi, "The 11 September Raid: The Impossible Becomes Possible," www.why-war.com/files/alqaida_statements.pdf (accessed May 14, 2006).

50. In the Amman attacks, only one of the multiple bombers was female. This woman's bomb apparently failed to explode, and she left the hotel as her husband exploded his device. The woman lived and soon after appeared on Jordanian television, confessing her role. Ali, "Ready to Detonate."

51. Al-Faqih points out that, although jihad is generally carried out by men, there are no Islamic injunctions against women fighting. Abedin, "New Security Realities and Al-Qaeda's Changing Tactics."

52. *Al-Khansaa Magazine* (a jihadist women's magazine published by al-Qa'ida in the Arabian Peninsula), posted to jihadist websites in September 2004.

53. "Umm Usama," 2003 interview with *Al-Sharq Al-Awsat*, quoted in Ali, "Ready to Detonate."

54. Al-Suri, *The Call to Global Islamic Resistance*, 1390.

55. Al-Zawhiri, *Knights under the Prophet's Banner*, quoted in Sageman, *Understanding Terror Networks*, 23.

56. Al-Suri, *The Call to Global Islamic Resistance*, 1381.

57. Quoted in Benjamin and Simon, *The Next Attack*, 69.

58. Quoted in Benjamin and Simon, *The Next Attack*, 69. See also Bergen, *The Osama Bin Laden I Know*, 337–49.

59. Cullison, "Inside Al-Qaeda's Hard Drive."

60. Statement posted to jihadist websites on September 28, 2006.

61. Quoted in Cruickshank and Ali, "Abu Musab Al Suri," 7. As discussed earlier, although al-Suri promotes a general decentralization of the jihad, he believes that such decentralization should take place mostly at the "everyday foot-soldier" level; in his book, al-Suri explains that the Global Islamic Resistance will be composed of several kinds of brigades, one of which is a "strategic operations brigade" with a number of responsibilities, including knowledge of and capabilities in obtaining and using weapons of mass destruction against the United States. Al-Suri, *The Call to Global Islamic Resistance*, 1400.

62. Al-Suri, letter released to jihadist websites in January 2005.

63. Quoted in Bergen, *The Osama Bin Laden I Know*, 337.

64. Al-Fahd, *A Treatise on the Legal Status of Using Weapons of Mass Destruction against Infidels*, posted to jihadist websites in 2003; Scheuer, *Imperial Hubris*, 154–56. Although it is not an official fatwa, al-Fahd's treatise is to date the most extensive jurisprudential justification for WMD use.

65. Both Abu Ghaith's 4 million and al-Fahd's 10 million figures are based on their calculations of the number of Muslim deaths for which the United States is responsible, both directly and indirectly. Al-Fahd, *A Treatise on the Legal Status of Using Weapons of Mass Destruction Against Infidels*, posted to jihadist websites in 2003.

66. U.S. Department of State, *Patterns of Global Terrorism, 2000—Appendix B: Background Information on Terrorist Groups* (Washington, DC: U.S. Department of State, April 30, 2000), www.state.gov/s/ct/rls/pgtrpt/2000/2450.htm

67. "GIA Threatens "Dissuasive" Measures Against Students, Teachers," *Agence France Presse*, August 6, 1994.

68. U.S. Department of State, *Patterns of Global Terrorism, 2003—Appendix B: Background Information on Designated Foreign Terrorist Organizations* (Washington, DC: U.S. Department of State, April 2004), www.state.gov/s/c/rls/crt/2003/c12153.htm.

69. "Europeans in Algeria Released for Ransom, Not by Army Assault: Report," *Agence France Presse*, May 16, 2003. See also U.S. Department of State, *Patterns of Global Terrorism, 2003—Appendix A: Chronology of Significant International Terrorist Incidents, 2003* (Washington, DC: U.S. Department of State, April 2004), www.state.gov/s/ct/rls/pgtrpt/2003/33773.htm.

70. U.S. Department of State, *Patterns of Global Terrorism, 2003—Appendix A: Chronology of Significant International Terrorist Incidents, 2003*.

71. "Yemeni Kidnapper Admits Planning "Liquidation" of US Nationals," *Agence France Presse*, February 18, 1999.

72. This number goes up as time progresses. See statements in Lawrence, *Messages to the World*. References to alleged effects of sanctions on Iraq appeared in bin Laden's statements no fewer than eleven times between 1996 and 2004.

73. MIPT, "Group Profile: Harakat-ul-Mujahidin (HUM)," *MIPT Terrorism Knowledge Base* (Oklahoma City, OK: National Memorial Institute for the Prevention of Terrorism), www.tkb.org/Group.jsp?groupID = 50.

74. In Pakistan, many of the more radical elements within the population tend to believe that a reporter is the same as an intelligence agent.

75. Douglas Jehl, "Suspect Says Reporter Was Slain in January as Part of Wider Plot," *The New York Times*, February 23, 2002.

76. "Al-Qaeda Ups Ante by Threatening to Kill US Hostage," *ONASA News Agency*, June 16, 2004. See also MIPT, "Incident Profile: Al-Qaeda Attacked Government Target (May 30, 2004, Saudi Arabia)," *MIPT Terrorism Knowledge Base*, www.tkb.org/Incident.jsp?incID = 18746. For more information on Western targeting, see Abd-al-Aziz al-Muqrin, "Al-Qaeda Targeting Guidance," translated and edited by IntelCenter, www.intelcenter.com/reports-charts.html. In this series of articles, which appeared in AQAP's *Al-Battar Camp* magazine in 2004, al-Muqrin created a target guidance system focusing on "Faith Targets," "Economic Targets," and "Human Targets," in addition to listing targets in descending importance in relation to occupation and nationality.

77. For the low estimate, see *Iraq Body Count*, www.iraqbodycount.net (accessed October 16, 2006). For the highest estimate, see Gilbert Burnham, Riyadh Lafta, Shannon Doocy, and Les Roberts, "Mortality after the 2003 Invasion of Iraq," *The Lancet*, October 11, 2006, www.thelancet.com (accessed October 13, 2006).

78. For examples of the wide variation in methodology, time periods, and estimates of violent deaths, see U.S. Department of Defense, *Measuring Stability and Security in*

Iraq; Hannah Fischer, "Iraqi Civilian, Police, and Security Forces Casualty Estimates," *CRS Report for Congress* RS22441 (Washington, DC: Congressional Research Service, 2006); *Iraq Body Count*, www.iraqbodycount.net (accessed October 16, 2006); United Nations Assistance Mission for Iraq, *Human Rights Report*, http://tinyurl .com/ml6c8 (accessed October 17, 2006); Les Roberts, Riyadh Lafta, Richard Garfield, Jamal Khudairi, and Gilbert Burnham, "Mortality before and after the 2003 Invasion of Iraq," *The Lancet* 364 (2004), 1857–64; Gilbert Burnham, Riyadh Lafta, Shannon Doocy, and Les Roberts, "Mortality after the 2003 Invasion of Iraq," *The Lancet*, October 11, 2006, www.thelancet.com (accessed October 13, 2006); and http://news.bbc.co.uk/2/hi/middle_east/6135526.stm (accessed November 10, 2006).

79. For details on the UNAMI report, see www.uniraq.org (accessed January 17, 2006).

80. "Humanitarian Crisis in Iraq Facts and Figures," www.uniraq.org (accessed February 1, 2008).

81. Iraq Body Count, "The Baghdad 'Surge' and Civilian Casualties," www.iraqbody count.org/analysis/numbers/baghdad-surge (accessed January 20, 2008); Iraq Body Count, "Database," www.iraqbodycount.org/database/ (accessed January 20, 2008).

82. Jill Carroll, "Iraq's Rising Industry: Domestic Kidnapping," *The Christian Science Monitor*, April 22, 2005. See also Ellen Knickmeyer and Jonathan Finer, "In Iraq, 425 Foreigners Estimated Kidnapped since 2003," *The Washington Post*, December 25, 2005; Brian Jenkins, Meg Williams, and Ed Williams, "Kidnappings in Iraq Strategically Effective," *The Chicago Tribune*, April 29, 2005, www.rand.org/commentary/042905CT.html.

83. Knickmeyer and Finer, "In Iraq, 425 Foreigners Estimated Kidnapped since 2003."

84. Brisard with Martinez, *Zarqawi: The New Face of Al Qaeda*.

85. Group statement, September 3, 2004, www.albasrah.net. This group likely has a more Ba'athist orientation than Islamist—their website choice is one that is popular among Ba'athist and Sadaamist groups.

86. The overall fatality rate for kidnappings in Iraq is twice that seen in Colombia and other countries where kidnapping is endemic, but economic in nature. See Jenkins, Williams, and Williams, "Kidnappings in Iraq Strategically Effective." Responsibility for Iraqi kidnapping cases is rarely claimed publicly by insurgent groups; the incentive is monetary, with the average ransom for Iraqi hostages being around $30,000. See Knickmeyer and Finer, "In Iraq, 425 Foreigners Estimated Kidnapped since 2003."

87. Group statement, November 1, 2005. Posted to jihadist websites.

88. Group statement, July 7, 2005. Posted to jihadist websites.

89. Group statement, November 4, 2005. Posted to jihadist websites.

90. Group statement, December 29, 2005. Posted to jihadist websites.

91. Group statement, January 17, 2006. Posted to jihadist websites.

92. Group statement (GSPC), July 26, 2005. Group Statements (al-Zarqawi group), July 23, 2005; July 27, 2005; July 28, 2005; July 30, 2005. Posted to jihadist websites.

93. International Crisis Group, *In Their Own Words: Reading the Iraqi Insurgency* (Brussels, Belgium: International Crisis Group, 15 February 2006).

94. Benjamin and Simon, *The Next Attack*, 63.

95. Upon its public release, some expressed doubts as to the authenticity of this letter. However, the language of the letter and many of its concerns match perfectly with previous al-Zawahiri statements. We consider the letter to be authentic and think it offers an important glimpse into al-Zawahiri's greater strategy for al-Qa'ida. In this letter, al-Zawahiri focused on four issues that needed improvement: (1) decreasing the targeting of Iraq's Shi'ite population; (2) decreasing the use of beheading of hostages and releasing video of the executions; (3) unification of the various jihadist groups in Iraq and putting them under Iraqi leadership, as foreign leadership of the groups has worked against Iraqi sensitivities; and (4) al-Zawahiri instructed al-Zarqawi to do the political fieldwork necessary in preparation to protect against secular-nationalists and "traitors" who might try to come to power after the United States exits Iraq. Ayman al-Zawahiri, "Letter from Al-Zawahiri to Al-Zarqawi," released on October 11, 2005, by the Office of the Director of National Intelligence, www.dni.gov/release_letter_101105.html.

96. International Crisis Group, *In Their Own Words*.

97. "Al Qa'ida in Iraq Situation Report," document number IZ-06–316–01, released on April 20, 2006, www.ctc.usma.edu/harmony_docs.asp.

98. For example, in post-9/11 statements, bin Laden has claimed that the United States sustained at least $1 trillion in losses. See bin Laden interview with *Al-Jazeera* television on October 21, 2001, quoted in Lawrence, *Messages to the World*, 111–12.

99. Cullison, "Inside Al-Qaeda's Hard Drive."

100. Usama bin Laden, Autumn 2004, quoted in Lawrence, *Messages to the World*, 241.

101. Abd-al-Aziz Bin Rashid al-Anzi, "The Religious Rule on Targeting Oil Interests," posted to jihadist websites on February 26, 2006.

102. Abu-Mus'ab al-Najdi, "Al-Qa'ida's Battle is Economic, Not Military," found in a compilation of al-Najdi's articles, posted to jihadist websites, April 7, 2006. This is a core argument of al-Qa'ida activists in Saudi Arabia. As discussed earlier, Abu-Hajir Abd-al-Aziz al-Muqrin, the deceased leader of al-Qa'ida in the Arabian Peninsula, strongly encouraged attacks on economic targets as a way to force the withdrawal of foreign investments. Abd-al-Aziz al-Muqrin, "The Targets inside Cities," translated by Intel-Center—Al Qaeda Targeting Guidance, v1.0, www.intelcenter.com/Qaeda-Targeting-Guidance-v1–0.pdf (accessed September 15, 2006).

103. Anonymous, "Jihad in Iraq: Hopes and Dangers," www.e-prism.org/images/book_-_Iraq_Al-Jihad.doc (accessed September 14, 2006); and Abu-Bakr al-Naji, *The Management of Savagery*, translated by William McCants (West Point, NY: Combating Terrorism Center, U.S. Military Academy, 2006), www.ctc.usma.edu.

104. Al-Suri, *The Call to Global Islamic Resistance*, 1384.

105. Ulph, "Al-Zawahiri Encourages Targeting of Gulf Oil."

106. "Yemen Foils Two Suicide Attacks," CNN.com, September 15, 2006, http://edition.cnn.com/2006/WORLD/meast/09/15/yemen.attacksfoiled/index.html. For an overview of Yemen's vulnerability, see Solomon and Regens, "Expansion of Yemen's Refining Capacity Raises Terrorism Concerns."

107. Anonymous, "Jihad in Iraq: Hopes and Dangers," www.e-prism.org/images/book_-_Iraq_Al-Jihad.doc (accessed September 14, 2006).

108. Quoted in Brynjar Lia and Thomas Hegghammer, "FFI Explains Al-Qaida Document," Forsvarets Forskningsinstitutt, March 19, 2004, www.mil.no/felles/ffi/start/article
.jhtml?articleID = 71589; Lia and Hegghammer, "Jihadi Strategic Studies."

109. In April 2006, Spanish authorities released an indictment of the surviving members of the Madrid cell, stating that two of the plot's key planners had extensively visited a jihadist website on which the document was hosted. Thomas Hegghammer, "Strategic Studies in Jihadist Literature," Address to the Middle East Institute, Washington, DC (Oslo: Norwegian Defence Research Establishment, May 17, 2006), www.mil.no/felles/ffi/start/English (accessed February 6, 2007).

110. Roland Jacqard and Uthman Tzagarit, "Al-Hayat publishes a letter signed by Usama bin Laden defining to the Algerian Salafi Group targets that must be hit in the southern and eastern parts of France; Al-Qa'ida plans to repeat the Spanish scenario during the French presidential elections," *Al-Hayat*, February 9, 2007.

111. Al-Suri cites the Madrid attack as a successful deterrent operation. Al-Suri, *The Call to Global Islamic Resistance*, 1391–93.

112. Chalk, "Maritime Terrorism in the Contemporary Era."

113. Quoted in Sageman, *Understanding Terror Networks*, 21.

114. Sunni versus Shi'ite sectarian violence is most likely to play out in countries with significant Shi'ite populations that have been ruled by Sunnis. The following countries traditionally ruled by Sunnis have large Shi'ite populations: Azerbaijan (15%); Bahrain (75%); Iraq (65%); Lebanon (45%); Pakistan (20%); Qatar (16%); Saudi Arabia (10%); and the United Arab Emirates (15%). See Nasr, *The Shia Revival*.

Chapter 6

1. Gunaratna, *Inside Al Qaeda*, 58.

2. Qutb, *Milestones*, 21.

3. Wiktorowicz, *Radical Islam Rising*, 181.

4. This is not to say that simply denying jihadists the opportunity to exploit the Internet is the key. Such a strategy, while tempting, would likely be an impossible endeavor due to the large number of jihadist websites. These websites are constantly evolving and often disappear for days at a time or longer. Those sites that do reappear—and most active sites do—often do so at a different web address or server location. When a site disappears altogether, its community simply shifts to the next site. To target sites across the board with the objective of destroying every jihadist website would resemble a continuous game of "whack-a-mole," expending vast resources for a disappointing impact.

5. The April 2004 statement is found in Lawrence, *Messages to the World*, 233–36; the January 2006 statement is quoted in "Bin Laden Offers Americans Truce," *Al-Jazeera .net*, English edition, January 19, 2006, http://english.aljazeera.net/NR/exeres/593298 A0-3C1A-4EB4-B29D-EA1A9678D922.htm (accessed August 29, 2006); Hadiths

from al-Bukhari: Abdullah bin Abbas, vol. 4, book 52, #253, and Sahl bin Sad vol. 5, book 59, #521, www.usc.edu/dept/MSA/fundamentals/hadithsunnah/bukhari (accessed September 4, 2006); al-Zawahiri statement posted to jihadist websites, February 21, 2006.

6. While al-Qa'ida has historically required its allies to submit to its Far Enemy targeting doctrine, the merger with al-Zarqawi's group shows al-Qa'ida's willingness to compromise this agenda if beneficial to the overall movement.

7. The "Atiyah" letter to al-Zarqawi demonstrates the cautious strategic nature of al-Qa'ida's senior leaders: Atiyah warns al-Zarqawi to focus on operations in Iraq and not to spread out into neighboring countries like Jordan because of the alienation of Sunnis that results from such attacks. Keeping jihadist battles inside a single nation may prove difficult. The start-up of a jihadist group in one country, as al-Suri advises in his critique of the Syrian campaign, often leads to operations in neighboring countries—even before there is victory in the main arena. In an effort to distract the intelligence and law enforcement authorities of the nearby countries, and to prevent cooperation between the host country and its regional allies, expansion of the battle into nearby regions is often necessary. Likewise, the use of neighboring territory as a safe haven or a staging area often leads to conflict spilling over the borders.

8. Center for Islamic Studies and Research, "The Operation of 11 Rabi Al-Awwal: The East Riyadh Operation and Our War with the United States and Its Agents," www.why-war.com/files/qaeda_east_riyadh_operation.txt.

9. "Al-Qa'ida's (Mis)Adventures in the Horn of Africa" (West Point, NY: Combating Terrorism Center, U.S. Military Academy, May 2007), www.ctc.usma.edu.

10. Because both of these attacks took place in Jordan, firmly within the regional operational reach of the AQI network and the Iraq War theater, they are not considered true external attacks.

11. Al-Sahab Institute for Media Production interview with al-Zawahiri, posted to jihadist websites, May 5, 2007.

12. John Arquilla and David Ronfeldt, who have done some of the most interesting and well-known research on organizational structures and networks, have also done a great deal of research on a battle strategy known as "swarming." Described as a sustainable pulsing of violence in which groups quickly strike and disperse, swarming offers nonstate actors, such as those in the jihadist movement, the ability to "blanket the battlespace" and to "mitigate the risk imposed by enemy countermeasures." Although many of these characteristics are explained in military terms, they can be adapted to explain al-Suri's ideal mode of conflict. Arquilla and Ronfeldt offer two simple requirements for swarming: (1) the ability to strike from multiple directions, and (2) forces must provide the intelligence necessary to create and maintain an overall view of the battle. See Arquilla and Ronfeldt, *Swarming and the Future of Conflict*, 21–23, 48.

13. Perhaps the most explicit radical discussion of carrying out the administrative duties of a state comes from exiled al-Muhajiroun leader Sheikh Omar Bakri Muhammad in his pamphlet, "The First 24 Hours after the Establishment of the Islamic State." In this pamphlet, Sheikh Bakri gives a brief outline of the composition and duties of the

various departments and ministries in the caliphate, including the departments of agriculture, war, health, education and culture, energy, and customs and foreign trade. Pamphlet acquired from jihadist website, March 2007.

14. Benjamin and Simon, *The Next Attack*, 130.

15. Although the United States does import natural gas, net imports historically are below 20% of U.S. consumption; thus, the interruption of natural gas imports is not a primary vulnerability of U.S. energy supplies. The majority of natural gas imports are from Canada (95%) through pipelines. Liquefied natural gas (LNG)—natural gas is liquefied by refrigeration to -260 F ($\sim$ -163 C) to reduce its volume > 600%, making it easier to transport—is imported from Algeria, Trinidad & Tobago, Qatar, Malaysia, Australia, and the United Arab Emirates. See Energy Information Agency, Office of Oil and Gas, *U.S. Natural Gas Imports and Exports: Issues and Trends 2005* (Washington, DC: U.S. Department of Energy, February 2007).

16. The al-Suri model closely resembles what Shaul Mishal and Maoz Rosenthal have termed "dune organization." In a dune organization, the organization (or overall movement) is based more on "movement and constant flow and entrepreneurship rather than determining a structural mode of action." This organizational model allows for continued fighting even with the loss (or absence) of leadership, since the organization and affiliated or inspired group all carry out attacks. This entrepreneurship can encourage new tactics and targeting doctrines that may not seem to make any strategic sense. To truly utilize the dune organization model, an overarching ideology must be present, such as that of al-Qa'ida. Jihadists around the world have been inspired by this ideology and have carried out attacks even without operation-specific guidance or support.

17. The names under which countries are known internationally are often seen as products of colonialism and are therefore not recognized by al-Qa'ida subgroups. Subgroups often base their names, therefore, not on the countries in which they are operating but instead on traditional regional names. The GSPC's name change to the al-Qa'ida Organization in the Lands of the Islamic Maghreb refers to North Africa, and not to Algeria specifically. Al-Zarqawi's branch, known before the creation of the Mujahidin Shura Council as the al-Qa'ida of Jihad Organization in the Land of the Two Rivers (Mesopotamia), refrained from using "Iraq" in its name, even though Iraq was its zone of primary operation. Similarly, al-Qa'ida in the Arabian Peninsula refrained from using the name Saudi Arabia, and al-Qa'ida in the Land of al-Kinanah—the group headed by Muhammad Khalil al-Hakaymah—refrained from using Egypt in its name.

18. The merger was announced by al-Zawahiri and Abu-Layth al-Libi, thought to be a dual member of al-Qa'ida and LIFG, in an al-Sahab video on November 3, 2007, posted to jihadist websites. Other shared members include Atiyah Abd-al-Rahman and Abu-Yahya al-Libi. Craig Whitlock and Munir Ladaa, "Abu Laith al-Libi, Field Commander and Spokesman" and "Abu Yahya al-Libi, Religious Scholar," *The Washington Post*, www.washingtonpost.com/wp-srv/world/specials/terror/binladen.html (accessed January 4, 2008). See also Gambill, "The Libyan Islamic Fighting Group (LIFG)"; U.S. House of Representatives, *Al-Qaeda: The Many Faces of an Islamic Extremist Threat, Report*

of the House Permanent Select Committee on Intelligence (Washington, DC: U.S. House of Representatives, Permanent Select Committee on Intelligence, June 2006), www.fas.org/irp/congress/2006_rpt/hpsci0606.pdf (accessed January 4, 2007).

19. Harmony document #AFGP-2002–600048, provided by the Combating Terrorism Center at West Point, www.ctc.usma.edu.

20. "Declassified Key Judgments of the National Intelligence Estimate 'Trends in Global Terrorism: Implications for the United States, dated April 2006," released at www.dni.gov on September 26, 2006.

21. Jackson et al., *Aptitude for Destruction*, 38.

22. Ulph, "Al-Zawahiri Encourages Targeting of Gulf Oil"; Daly, "Saudi Oil Facilities: Al-Qadea's Next Target?" Shaykh Abd-al-Aziz bin Rashid al-Anzi, *The Religious Rule on Targeting Oil Interests*, posted to the Islamic Renewal Organization's Internet forum, http://tajdeed.co.uk, on February 26, 2006; Abd al-Aziz al-Muqrin, "Al-Qaeda Targeting Guidance," translated and edited by IntelCenter, www.intelcenter.com/reports-charts.html.

23. Nasiri, *Inside the Jihad*.

24. The problem with fundamentalism per se is not its requirement to return to the basis of the religious belief but a concurrent tendency of such groups to be extremely hostile towards those who are not members. While fundamentalists may see the nonmember as a possible recruit and target for evangelical activity, those who reject the call are easily cast into an enemy camp. Logical discussion is difficult with group members. Having identified and accepted the "one true religion," members of fundamentalist sects tend to be at best dismissive of alternative views and quickly show extreme irritation with interlocutors who do not get the point. Members of competing faiths are often demonized and tagged with unflattering names. Muslim extremists often talk of Christians as "Crusaders," while some Christian fundamentalists have used terms like "Islamo-fascist." When a given conflict is between opposing fundamentalist camps, it seems a daunting task to find any common ground on which to build a consensus that might lead to resolution. Any attack from one group on another prompts a counterattack of equal or greater proportion. Fundamentalists who are attacked by nonbelievers are not dissuaded but instead see the attack as part of an apocalyptic struggle between good and evil.

25. The fanaticism that is apparent when we look at a young person trained in a jihadist paramilitary camp who returns to his home and yet is immediately ready to reenter the jihad when called to service years later is an example of this dedication. Members who leave the movement usually do so because of disenchantment with the ways in which fundamentalism is carried out or when they are confronted with leadership figures whose dedication turns out to be flawed.

Chapter 7

1. Keefe, *Chatter*.

2. National Commission on Terrorist Attacks upon the United States, *The 9/11 Commission Report*, 127.

3. *Inside the Jihad* is one example, written by a man who claims to have worked for the French and German intelligence agencies and to have taken both basic and advanced training in the Afghanistan camps. See Nasiri, *Inside the Jihad.*

4. While intelligence collection was always less successful than desired, the use of Afghanistan and tribal areas in neighboring Pakistan by al-Qa'ida as an operational base and sanctuary from which its leadership could openly operate offered some clear advantages for intelligence collection about the organization.

Conclusion

1. Doran, "The Pragmatic Fanaticism of al Qaeda," 178.

2. As reported in the Hadith, the Prophet Muhammad said, "And he who accuses a believer of kufr (disbelief) then it is like killing him." Quoted in Wiktorowicz, *Radical Islam Rising*, 175.

3. For example, according to Sunni legend, Ibn-al-Alqami was a Shi'ite minister who opened the gates of Baghdad to the invading Mongols who sacked the city in 1258 C.E. References to al-Alqami's purported historical act of treason are used in modern jihadists' websites and writings to refer to the current Shi'ite-dominated government of Iraq as being similarly traitorous to Islam.

4. The rift between al-Qa'ida's central leadership and al-Zarqawi over the mass targeting of Shi'ites and nonjihadist civilians—as seen through al-Zawahiri's and Atiyah Abd-al-Rahman's letters to al-Zarqawi—is drawn mostly on strategic lines instead of theological ones: Al-Qa'ida leaders like al-Zawahiri and bin Laden have remained noticeably quiet over the targeting of Shi'ites, but their silence should not be mistaken as disagreements with al-Zarqawi over whether Shi'ites are apostate. This is a widely accepted position in the jihadist community.

5. Quintan Wiktorowicz, "The New Global Threat: Transnational Salafis and Jihad," http://groups.colgate.edu/aarislam/wiktorow.htm.

6. Letter published by the Combating Terrorism Center at West Point, http://ctc .usma.edu (accessed February 25, 2007).

7. Interview posted to jihadist websites on September 10, 2007.

8. Dr. Fadl also is known as Sayyid Imam and Abd-al-Qadir Ibn Abd-al-Aziz.

9. OPEC adopted an unadjusted-for-inflation (i.e., nominal) price band of $22–28 per barrel for its market basket of crude on March 28, 2000. The world average price was $32.32 (September 8, 2001) the OPEC average price was $25.02 (September 7, 2001), and the U.S. average price was $23.89 (September 7, 2001) for the week immediately prior to September 11. Nominal prices per barrel of crude oil remained low even after the tragic events of September 11, as reflected in prices the week immediately following September 11: world average price $30.63 (September 15, 2001); OPEC average price $25.02 (September 14, 2001); and U.S. average price $23.89 (September 14, 2001). It was not until 2005, with limited spare production capacity, that OPEC finally abandoned its price band and was powerless to stem a surge in oil prices that was reminiscent of the late

1970s. For example, the average prices per barrel for the week of January 11, 2008, were as follows: world average price $92.82; OPEC average price $92.69; and U.S. average price $89.60. The OPEC averages are based on affiliations for the stated period of time, which may differ from current affiliations. See http://tonto.eia.doe.gov/dnav/pet/pet_pri_wco_k_w.htm (accessed January 23, 2008).

10. For a detailed discussion of how the United States can better deploy its assets to counter the global jihad, see Byman, *The Five Front War.*

GLOSSARY

Al-Farag, Abd-al-Salam: Egyptian jihadist leader; author of the influential book *The Neglected Duty*.

Al-Libi, Abu-Layth: A Libyan Islamic Fighting Group member and senior al-Qa'ida leader who was field commander in Afghanistan; U.S. military blamed him for a suicide bombing that killed twenty-three people outside Bagram Air Base in Afghanistan during a February 2007 visit by Vice President Cheney; killed in January 2008 in Pakistan's North Waziristan tribal area by a missile launched in a U.S. unmanned Predator air strike.

Al-Libi, Abu-Yahya: Abu-Yahya al-Libi frequently appears in official al-Qa'ida/al-Sahab releases and has become one of the most visible figures in al-Qa'ida, after al-Zawahiri; escaped from Bagram Prison in Afghanistan on July 11, 2005.

Al-Maqdisi, Abu-Muhammad: Jordanian jihadist cleric; mentor to al-Zarqawi; author of *Democracy Is a Religion*, among other influential books and articles.

Al-Suri, Abu-Mus'ab: Al-Qa'ida trainer and strategist; author of numerous texts, including *The Call to Global Islamic Resistance*.

Al-wala' wa al-bara': Literally "allegiance and disavowal," a term used to order Muslims to remain loyal to other Muslims and to show open hatred for infidels.

Al-Zarqawi, Abu-Mus'ab (AMZ): Jordanian-born leader of al-Qa'ida in Iraq; swore allegiance to bin Laden in 2004; killed by U.S. forces in June 2006.

Al-Zawahiri, Ayman: Ayman Muhammad Rabaie al-Zawahiri, commonly referred to as al-Zawahiri, is the second-in-command of al-Qa'ida and bin Laden's principal deputy. Born in 1951; one of his uncles, who was a follower of Sayyid Qutb, influenced al-Zawahiri's political views. Al-Zawahiri reportedly joined the Muslim Brotherhood as a 14-year-old boy. After attending Cairo University, he served as a surgeon in the Egyptian Army. As a member of the Egyptian Islamic Jihad, he was arrested and imprisoned after Anwar Sadat's 1981 assignation. Al-Zawahiri was released in 1984. He succeeded 'Abbud al-Zummar as the leader of Egyptian Islamic Jihad when al-Zummar was sentenced to life imprisonment. By 1987, al-Zawahiri was in Pakistan, where he joined other militants—including Usama bin Laden—supporting the fight against the Soviet forces in Afghanistan. Starting in the early 1990s, EIJ became increasingly more violent under al-Zawahiri's leadership and launched numerous terrorist attacks aimed at undermining Hosni Mubarak's regime. Al-Zawahiri was sentenced to death *in absentia* by a military tribunal in 1999. Like bin Laden, he was expelled from Sudan in 1996 and ultimately made his way to Afghanistan, where the two were reunited. In 1998 he formally merged Egyptian Islamic Jihad into al-Qa'ida; he has emerged as the primary al-Qa'ida spokesman since September 11 and is presumed to be operating from the Waziristan region of Pakistan.

Amir: Literally prince, commander; title given to leader of jihadist groups.

Atiyah: Libyan believed to be senior al-Qa'ida figure Atiyah Abd-al-Rahman; wrote a letter to al-Zarqawi in which he chastised the AQI leader for his attacks on civilians and Shi'ites, and for being too exclusionary.

Azzam, Abdullah: Palestinian cleric who led the mujahidin in Afghanistan against Soviet forces in the 1980s; mentor to bin Laden, with whom he ran the Maktab al-Khidmat (MAK), or Services Bureau, a foreign fighter facilitation organization.

Bin Laden, Usama (UBL): Usama bin Muhammad bin 'Awad bin Laden, commonly referred to as Usama bin Laden, is the Saudi-born founder of al-Qa'ida. UBL was born in 1957; his father was a wealthy Yemeni businessman with close ties to the Saudi royal family. Bin Laden left Saudi Arabia in 1979 to fight against the Soviet invasion of Afghanistan. He was instrumental, along with Adbullah Azzam, in organizing the MAK. After the Soviet withdrawal from Afghanistan, UBL returned to Saudi Arabia shortly before Saddam Hussein invaded Kuwait; when the Saudi monarchy rejected his call to use only Muslim forces to defend the Kingdom, UBL denounced the decision to use U.S. and other Western troops. He moved to Sudan in 1992 and subsequently returned to Afghanistan in 1996 after Saudi, Egyptian, and U.S. pressure on the Sudanese government forced UBL to leave. UBL spent the 1990s building the al-Qa'ida network, planning and executing terrorist attacks against the United States and friendly governments, and issuing fatwas—one in 1996, and another in 1998—declaring that Muslims should kill civilians and military personnel from the United States and allied countries until they withdraw military forces from Islamic countries and withdraw support for Israel. Following the overthrow of the Taliban regime as part of the U.S. response to September 11, UBL and Ayman al-Zawahiri, along with the rest of the al-Qa'ida senior leadership, are presumed to be operating from the Waziristan region of Pakistan.

Caliph: Arabic for successor to the Prophet Muhammad, with temporal authority as leader of the faithful, but not with the authority to establish religious doctrine.

Caliphate: The term "caliphate," *al-Khilafah* in Arabic, refers to a unified system of temporal authority exercised by a successor to the Prophet Muhammad over the community of believers.

Far Enemy: The Western governments, such as the United States and the United Kingdom, that support local regimes opposed by the jihadists.

Ibn-Taymiyyah: Thirteenth-century Islamic cleric; frequently cited by jihadists.

Jahiliyah: Literally "ignorance"; the term generally is used to describe pre-Islamic times, characterized as pagan and chaotic. Also applied to modern times, as popularized by Sayyid Qutb.

Jihad: Means "to strive" or "to struggle" in Arabic; the term has a religious connotation, involving an outwardly directed struggle against oppression and tyranny, as well as an inwardly directed personal struggle for holiness. The spiritual jihad in quest of holiness, or *jihad bil-nafs*, is seen by most Muslims as the "greater jihad." The concept of *jihad bil-sayf*, literally "jihad by the sword," or violent jihad, traditionally is viewed as the "lesser jihad."

Kafir: Infidel (plural is *kuffar*).

Naji, Abu-Bakr: Author of *The Management of Savagery*.

Near Enemy: Secular "apostate" regimes in Muslim countries, such as Egypt or Syria, that the jihadists oppose.

Qutb, Sayyid: Egyptian writer executed by the Egyptian State in 1966; wrote a number of commentaries on the Qur'an and the revolutionary text *Milestones*, widely regarded as one of the biggest influences on the modern jihadist movement.

Salafi: Means "following the forefathers of Islam."

Salafi Islam: Fundamentalist school of Islamic thought followed by Sunnis; principal tenet of Salafism is that Islam was perfect and complete during the days of Muhammad and his companions, but that undesirable innovations have been added over the later centuries due to materialist and cultural influences; followers of this form of Islam call themselves *Muwahhidun* ("Unitarians", or "unifiers of Islamic practice"); term is often used interchangeably with Wahhabism, but these terms are not necessarily synonymous.

Shura: Arabic for "consultation."

Takfir: To declare a Muslim to be a kafir, or infidel.

Ulema: Islamic scholars.

Ummah: Community or nation of believers (Muslims).

Wahhabi Islam: Particular orientation within the Salafi school of Islamic thought followed by Sunnis; based on the teachings of Abd al-Wahhab; sometimes the term Wahhabi is used to refer to Salafi Islam because most jihadists are Salafis who adhere to the Wahhabi variant.

BIBLIOGRAPHY

Abedin, Mahan. "New Security Realities and Al-Qaeda's Changing Tactics: An Interview with Saad Al-Faqih." *Jamestown Foundation Terrorism Focus* 3 (December 15, 2005).

Abou Zahab, Mariam, and Olivier Roy. *Islamist Networks: The Afghan-Pakistan Connection*. New York: Columbia University Press, 2004.

Abuza, Zachary. *Militant Islam in Southeast Asia: Crucible of Terror*. Boulder, CO: Lynne Rienner, 2003.

———. "Jemaah Islamiya Enters Regrouping Phase." *Jamestown Foundation Terrorism Focus* 3 (November 21, 2006).

Ahmed, Akbar. *Islam under Siege: Living Dangerously in a Post-Honor World*. Cambridge: Polity, 2003.

Ajami, Fouad. *The Dream Palace of the Arabs: A Generation's Odyssey*. New York: Pantheon, 1998.

Alexander, Yonah. *Combating Terrorism: Strategies of Ten Countries*. Ann Arbor: University of Michigan Press, 2002.

Ali, Farhana. "Ready to Detonate: The Diverse Profiles of Female Bombers." *MIPT Terrorism Annual*, 43–52. Oklahoma City: National Memorial Institute for the Prevention of Terrorism, 2006.

Ali, Tariq. *The Clash of Fundamentalisms: Crusades, Jihads and Modernity*. New York: Verso, 2002.

Allison, Graham T. *Nuclear Terrorism: The Ultimate Preventable Catastrophe*. New York: Holt, 2004.

Allison, Graham T., P. X. Kelley, and Richard L. Garwin. *Nonlethal Weapons and Capabilities: Report of an Independent Task Force Sponsored by the Council on Foreign Relations*. Washington, DC: Council on Foreign Relations Press, 2004.

Al-Hafani, Abd-al-Mun'im. *Musu'ah Al-Farq wa Al-Jama'at wa Al-Madhahib wa Al-Ahzab wa Al-Harakat Al-Islamiyah* [Encyclopedia of Companies, Groups, Schools, Parties, and Islamic Movements]. Cairo: Maktab Madbuli, 2005.

Al-Muqaddam, Muhammad. *Al-Afghan Al-Jaza'iriyun: Min Al-Jama'ah ila Al-Qa'ida* [The Afghan Algerians: From Al-Jama'ah to Al-Qa'ida]. Algeria: Al-Mu'asasah Al-Wataniyah Lil-Itisal wa Al-Nashar wa Al-Ishhar, 2002.

Al-Musali, Ahmad. *Musu'ah Al-Hakarakt Al-Islamiyah fil-Watan Al-Arabi wa Iran wa Turkiyah* [Encyclopedia of Islamic Movements in the Arab Nation, Iran, and Turkey]. Beirut: Center for the Studies of Arab Unity, 2004.

Al-Zayyat, Montasser. *The Road to Al-Qaeda: The Story of Bin Laden's Right-Hand Man*. London: Pluto Press, 2004.

Antokol, Norman, and Mayer Nudell. *No One a Neutral: Political Hostage-Taking in the Modern World*. Medina, OH: Alpha, 1990.

Arberry, Arthur J. *The Koran Interpreted: A Translation*. New York: Touchstone, 1996.

Armstrong, Karen. *Muhammad: A Biography of the Prophet*. New York: Harper-Collins, 1992.

Arquilla, John, and David Ronfeldt. *The Advent of Netwar*. Santa Monica, CA: RAND, 1996.

———. *Swarming and the Future of Conflict*. Santa Monica, CA: RAND, 2000.

———, eds. *Networks and Netwars: The Future of Terror, Crime, and Militancy*. Santa Monica, CA: RAND, 2001.

Aslan, Reza. *No god but God: The Origins, Evolution, and Future of Islam*. New York: Random House, 2006.

Aussaresses, Paul. *The Battle of the Casbah: Terrorism and Counter-Terrorism in Algeria, 1955–1957*. Translated by Robert L. Miller. New York: Enigma, 2002.

Azzam, Abdullah. *Join the Caravan*. London: Azzam Publications, 2001.

Baer, Robert. *See No Evil: The True Story of a Ground Soldier in the CIA's War on Terrorism*. New York: Three Rivers Press, 2002.

———. *Sleeping with the Devil: How Washington Sold Our Soul for Saudi Crude*. New York: Crown, 2003.

Bandura, Albert. "Mechanisms of Moral Disengagement." In *Origins of Terrorism: Psychologies, Ideologies, Theologies, States of Mind*, edited by Walter Reich, 161–91. Washington: Woodrow Wilson Center Press, 1998.

Barber, Benjamin R. *Fear's Empire: War, Terrorism, and Democracy*. New York: Norton, 2003.

———. *Jihad vs. McWorld*. New York: Ballantine, 1996.

Baudrillard, Jean. *The Spirit of Terrorism; And Other Essays*. London: Verso, 2003.

Benjamin, Daniel, and Steven Simon. *The Age of Sacred Terror: Radical Islam's War against America*. New York: Random House, 2003.

———. *The Next Attack: The Failure of the War on Terror and a Strategy for Getting It Right*. New York: Times Books, 2005.

Bergen, Peter. *The Osama Bin Laden I Know: An Oral History of Al Qaeda's Leader*. New York: Free Press, 2006.

Berman, Paul. *Terror and Liberalism*. New York: Norton, 2003.

Berntsen, Gary, and Ralph Pezzullo. *Jawbreaker: The Attack on Bin Laden and Al Qaeda: A Personal Account by the CIA's Key Field Commander*. New York: Crown, 2005.

Bin Laden, Usama. *Messages to the World: The Statements of Osama Bin Laden.* Edited by Bruce Lawrence. Translated by James Howarth. London: Verso 2005.

Bloom, Mia. *Dying to Kill: The Allure of Suicide Terror.* New York: Columbia University Press, 2005.

Bonney, Richard. *Jihad: From Qur'an to bin Laden.* New York: Palgrave Macmillan, 2004.

Brachman, Janet, and William McCants. "Stealing Al-Qa'ida's Playbook." West Point, NY: Combating Terrorism Center, U.S. Military Academy, Feburary 2006.

Braffman, Ori, and Rod A. Beckstrom. *The Starfish and the Spider: The Unstoppable Power of Leaderless Organizations.* New York: Portfolio, 2006.

Brisard, Jean-Charles, and Damien Martinez. *Zarqawi: The New Face of Al-Qaeda.* New York: Other Press, 2005.

Byman, Daniel. *The Five Front War: The Better Way to Fight Global Jihad.* New York: Wiley, 2007.

Carroll, Peter N. *The Odyssey of the Abraham Lincoln Brigade: Americans in the Spanish Civil War.* Palo Alto, CA: Stanford University Press, 1994.

Chalk, Peter. "Maritime Terrorism in the Contemporary Era: Threat and Potential Future Contingencies." *MIPT Terrorism Annual,* 19–42. Oklahoma City: National Memorial Institute for the Prevention of Terrorism, 2006.

Chalk, Peter, and William Rosenau. *Confronting "the Enemy Within": Security Intelligence, the Police, and Counterterrorism in Four Democracies.* Santa Monica, CA: RAND, 2004.

Clarke, Richard A. *Against All Enemies: Inside America's War on Terror.* New York: Free Press, 2004.

Clarke, Richard A., and Glenn P. Aga. *Defeating the Jihadists: A Blueprint for Action: The Report of a Task Force.* New York: Century Foundation Press, 2004.

Clausewitz, Carl von. *On War.* New York: Penguin, 1982.

Coll, Steve. *Ghost Wars: The Secret History of the CIA, Afghanistan, and Bin Laden, from the Soviet Invasion to September 10, 2001.* New York: Penguin, 2004.

Conroy, John. *Unspeakable Acts, Ordinary People: The Dynamics of Torture.* Berkeley: University of California Press, 2000.

Cook, David. *Understanding Jihad.* Berkeley: University of California Press, 2005.

———. *Paradigmatic Jihadi Movements.* West Point, NY: Combating Terrorism Center, U.S. Military Academy, 2006.

Cragin, Kim, and Sara A. Daly. *The Dynamic Terrorist Threat: An Assessment of Group Motivations and Capabilities in a Changing World.* Santa Monica, CA: RAND, 2004.

Cragin, Kim, and Scott Gerwehr. *Dissuading Terror: Strategic Influence and the Struggle against Terrorism*. Santa Monica, CA: RAND, 2004.

Crenshaw, Martha. *Terrorism in Context*. University Park: Pennsylvania State University Press, 1995.

Crile, George. *Charlie Wilson's War: The Extraordinary Story of the Largest Covert Operation in History*. New York: Atlantic Monthly Press, 2003.

Cronin, Isaac. *Confronting Fear: A History of Terrorism*. New York: Thunder's Mouth Press, 2002.

Cruickshank, Paul, and Mohannad Hage Ali. "Abu Musab Al Suri: Architect of the New Al Qaeda." *Studies in Conflict and Terrorism* 30 (2007): 1–14.

Cullison, Alan. "Inside Al-Qaeda's Hard Drive." *The Atlantic*, September 2004.

Daly, John C. K. "Saudi Oil Facilities: Al-Qadea's Next Target?" *Jamestown Foundation Terrorism Monitor* 4 (February 24, 2006).

DeLong-Bas, Natana J. *Wahabi Islam: From Revival and Reform to Global Jihad*. New York: Oxford University Press, 2004.

Devji, Faisal. *Landscapes of the Jihad: Militancy, Morality, Modernity*. Ithaca, NY: Cornell University Press, 2005.

Doran, Michael. "The Pragmatic Fanaticism of al Qaeda: An Anatomy of Extremism in Middle Eastern Politics." *Political Science Quarterly* 117 (2002): 177–90.

Drake, C. M. J. "The Role of Ideology in Terrorists' Target Selection." *Terrorism and Political Violence* 10 (1998): 53–85.

Ekman, Paul. *Emotions Revealed: Recognizing Faces and Feelings to Improve Communication and Emotional Life*. New York: Times Books, 2003.

Enders, Walter, and Todd Sandler. *The Political Economy of Terrorism*. New York: Cambridge University Press, 2006.

Esposito, John L. *The Islamic Threat: Myth or Reality?* New York: Oxford, 1999.

———. *Unholy War: Terror in the Name of Islam*. New York: Oxford University Press, 2002.

Farah, Douglas. *Blood from Stones: The Secret Financial Network of Terror*. New York: Broadway Books, 2004.

Faraj, Muhammad 'Abdus Salam. *Jihad—The Absent Obligation*. Birmingham, UK: Maktabah Al Ansar Publications, 2000.

———. *The Neglected Duty*. Birmingham, UK: Maktabah Al Ansar, 2000.

Feldman, Noah. *After Jihad: America and the Struggle for Islamic Democracy*. New York: Farrar, Straus and Giroux, 2003.

Ferguson, Charles D., William C. Potter, and Amy Sands. *The Four Faces of Nuclear Terrorism*. New York: Routledge, 2005.

Ferracuti, Franco. "Ideology and Repentance." In *Origins of Terrorism: Psychologies, Ideologies, Theologies, States of Mind*, edited by Walter Reich, 59–64. Washington, DC: Woodrow Wilson Center Press, 1998.

Fishman, Brian. "After Zarqawi." *Washington Quarterly* 29 (2006): 19–32.

Flynn, Stephen E. *America the Vulnerable: How Our Government Is Failing to Protect Us from Terrorism.* New York: HarperCollins, 2004.

Forest, James J. F. *The Making of a Terrorist: Recruitment, Training, and Root Causes.* Westport, CT: Praeger Security International, 2006.

Forestier, Patrick, and Ahmed Salam. *Confession D'Un Emir Du GIA.* Paris: Bernard Grasset, 1999.

Fouda, Yosri, and Nick Fielding. *Masterminds of Terror: The Truth behind the Most Devastating Terrorist Attack the World Has Ever Seen.* New York: Arcade Publishing, 2003.

Fox, Jonathan. "Do Religious Institutions Support Violence or the Status Quo?" *Studies in Conflict and Terrorism* 22 (1999): 119–35.

Fradkin, Hillel. "Recent Statements of Islamist Ideology: Bin Ladin and Zarqawi Speak." *Current Trends in Islamist Ideology.* Vol. 1, 5–11. Washington, DC: Hudson Institute, 2005.

Freeman, Charles W., Jr. *Arts of Power: Statecraft and Diplomacy.* Washington, DC: U.S. Institute of Peace, 1997.

Friedman, George. *America's Secret War: Inside the Hidden Worldwide Struggle between America and Its Enemies.* New York: Doubleday, 2004.

Friedman, Norman. *Terrorism, Afghanistan, and America's New Way of War.* Annapolis, MD: Naval Institute Press, 2003.

Friedman, Thomas L. *From Beirut to Jerusalem.* New York: Anchor, 1990.

Fromkin, David. *A Peace to End All Peace: Creating the Modern Middle East, 1914–1922.* New York: Holt, 2001.

Fuller, Graham E. *A Sense of Siege: The Geopolitics of Islam and the West.* Santa Monica, CA: RAND, 1995.

———. *The Future of Political Islam.* New York: Palgrave, 2003.

Füredi, Frank. *Politics of Fear.* New York: Continuum, 2005.

Gaddis, John Lewis. *Surprise, Security, and the American Experience.* Cambridge, MA: Harvard University Press, 2004.

Gambill, Gary. "The Libyan Islamic Fighting Group (LIFG)." *Jamestown Foundation Terrorism Monitor* 3 (March 24, 2006).

Gerges, Fawaz A. *The Far Enemy: Why Jihad Went Global.* New York: Cambridge University Press, 2005.

———. *Journey of the Jihadist: Inside Muslim Militancy.* Orlando, FL: Harcourt, 2006.

Giorgio. *Memoirs of an Italian Terrorist.* Translated by Anthony Shugaar. New York: Carroll & Graf, 2003.

Gompert, David C., Hans Pung, Kevin A. O'Brien, and Jefferey Petterson. *Stretching the Network: Using Transformed Forces in Demanding Contingencies Other than War.* Santa Monica, CA: RAND, April 2004.

Gordon, Avishag. "The Effect of Database and Website Inconstancy on the Terrorism Field's Delineation." *Studies in Conflict and Terrorism* 27 (2004): 79–88.

Gray, John. *Al Qaeda and What It Means to Be Modern.* New York: New Press, 2003.

Gregorian, Vartan. *Islam: A Mosaic, Not a Monolith.* Washington, DC: Brookings, 2003.

Grossman, Dave. *On Killing: The Psychological Cost of Learning to Kill in War and Society.* New York: Back Bay Books, 1996.

Guevara, Ché. *Guerrilla Warfare.* Lincoln: University of Nebraska Press, 1998.

Gunaratna, Rohan. *Inside Al Qaeda: Global Network of Terror.* New York: Columbia University Press, 2002.

Gurr, Nadine, and Benjamin Cole. *The New Face of Terrorism: Threats from Weapons of Mass Destruction.* New York: I. B. Tauris 2000.

Haahr, Kathryn. "GSPC Joins Al-Qaeda and France Becomes Top Enemy." *Jamestown Foundation Terrorism Focus* 3 (September 26, 2006).

Habeck, Mary R. *Knowing the Enemy: Jihadist Ideology and the War on Terror.* New Haven, CT: Yale University Press, 2006.

Hammes, Thomas X. *The Sling and the Stone: On War in the 21st Century.* St. Paul, MN: Zenith Press, 2004.

Hedges, Chris. *War Is a Force that Gives Us Meaning.* New York: Anchor Books, 2003.

Hegghammer, Thomas. "Global Jihadism after the Iraq War." *Middle East Journal* 60 (2006): 11–32.

———. "Terrorist Recruitment and Radicalization in Saudi Arabia." *Middle East Policy* 14 (2006): 39–60.

Heymann, Philip B. *Terrorism, Freedom, and Security: Winning without War.* Cambridge, MA: MIT Press, 2003.

Hillenbrand, Carole. *The Crusades: Islamic Perspectives.* New York: Routledge, 2000.

Hoffman, Bruce. *Al Qaeda, Trends in Terrorism, and Future Potentialities: An Assessment.* Santa Monica, CA: RAND, 2003.

———. *Inside Terrorism.* New York: Columbia University Press, 1998.

Hoge, James F., Jr., and Gideon Rose, eds. *How Did This Happen?* NY: Council on Foreign Relations, 2001.

Hopkirk, Peter. *The Great Game: The Struggle for Empire in Central Asia.* New York: Kodansha International, 1994.

Horgan, John. *The Psychology of Terrorism.* New York: Routledge, 2005.

Howard, Russell D., and Reid L. Sawyer. *Terrorism and Counterterrorism: Understanding the New Security Environment: Readings & Interpretations.* 2nd ed. Dubuque, IA: McGraw Hill, 2006.

Hroub, Khaled. *HAMAS: Political Thought and Practice.* Washington, DC: Institute for Palestine Studies, 2000.

Huntington, Samuel P. *The Clash of Civilizations and the Remaking of World Order.* New York: Simon & Schuster, 1996.

Intelligence and Security Committee. *Report into the London Terrorist Attacks on 7 July 2005.* London: Intelligence and Security Committee, May 2006.

Jackson, Brian A., John C. Baker, Peter Chalk, Kim Cragin, John V. Parachini, and Horacio R. Trujillo. *Aptitude for Destruction: Organizational Learning in Terrorist Groups and Its Implications for Combating Terrorism.* Santa Monica, CA: RAND, 2005.

Jalali, Ali Ahmad, and Lester W. Grau. *Afghan Guerrilla Warfare: In the Words of the Mujahideen Fighters.* London: Compendium Publishing, 2001.

Jaspert, Nikolas. *The Crusades.* Translated by Phyllis G. Jestice. Oxford: Routledge, 2006.

Jenkins, Brian. *Unconquerable Nation: Knowing Our Enemy, Strengthening Ourselves.* Santa Moncia, CA: RAND, 2006.

Jenkins, Philip. *Images of Terror: What We Can and Can't Know about Terrorism.* Hawthorne, NY: Aldine de Gruyter, 2003.

Johnson, Thomas. "Analyses of the Groupe Salafiste pour la Prédication et le Combat (GSPC)." *Strategic Insights* 5 (November 2006). www.ccc.nps.navy.mil/si.

Juergensmeyer, Mark. *Terror in the Mind of God: The Global Rise of Religious Violence.* 3rd ed. Berkeley: University of California Press, 2003.

Kaplan, Robert D. *Soldiers of God: With Islamic Warriors in Afghanistan and Pakistan.* New York: Vintage, 2001.

Keefe, Patrick Radden. *Chatter: Dispatches from the Secret World of Global Eavesdropping.* New York: Random House, 2006.

Kennedy, Hugh. *The Prophet and the Age of the Caliphates: The Islamic Near East from the 6th to the 11th century.* 2nd ed. New York: Longman: 2004.

Kepel, Gilles. *Muslim Extremism in Egypt: The Prophet and Pharaoh.* Translated by John Rothschild. Berkeley: University of California Press, 1985.

————. *Jihad: The Trail of Political Islam*. Translated by Anthony F. Roberts. Cambridge, MA: Harvard University Press, 2003.

————. *The War for Muslim Minds: Islam and the West*. Translated by Pascale Ghazaleh. Cambridge, MA: Belknap Press of Harvard University Press, 2004.

Khalidi, Rashid. *Resurrecting Empire: Western Footprints and America's Perilous Path in the Middle East*. Boston: Beacon, 2004.

Khalil, Lydia. "Divisions within the Iraqi Insurgency." *Jamestown Foundation Terrorism Monitor* 5 (April 12, 2007).

————. "Islamic Army in Iraq Pursues Strategy of Negotiation and Violence." *The Jamestown Foundation Terrorism Focus* 3 (October 24, 2006).

Kilcullen, David. "Counterinsurgency Redux." *Survival* 28 (December 2006): 111–13.

Kleveman, Lutz. *The New Great Game: Blood and Oil in Central Asia*. New York: Atlantic Monthly Press, 2003.

Lal, Rollie, and Brian A. Jackson. "Change and Continuity in Terrorism Revisited: Terrorist Tactics, 1980–2005." *MIPT Terrorism Annual*, 3–18. Oklahoma City: National Memorial Institute for the Prevention of Terrorism, 2006.

Laqueur, Walter. *The New Terrorism: Fanaticism and the Arms of Mass Destruction*. New York: Oxford, 2000.

————. *Voices of Terror: Manifestos, Writings, and Manuals of Al Qaeda, Hamas, and Other Terrorists from around the World and throughout the Ages*. New York: Reed Press, 2004.

Lawrence, Bruce, ed. *Messages to the World: The Statements of Osama bin Laden*. Translated by James Howarth. New York: Verso, 2005.

Leshan, Lawrence. *The Psychology of War: Comprehending Its Mystique and Its Madness*. New York: Helios Press, 2002.

Lesser, Ian O., Bruce Hoffman, John Arquilla, David F. Ronfeldt, Michele Zanini, and Brian M. Jenkins. *Countering the New Terrorism*. Santa Monica, CA: RAND, 1999.

Levitt, Matthew. *Targeting Terror: U.S. Policy toward Middle Eastern State Sponsors and Terrorist Organizations, Post–September 11*. Washington, DC: Washington Institute for Near East Policy, 2002.

————. *HAMAS: Politics, Charity, and Terrorism in the Service of Jihad*. New Haven, CT: Yale University Press, 2006.

Lewis, Bernard. *The Crisis of Islam: Holy War and Unholy Terror*. New York: Modern Library, 2003.

————. *From Babel to Dragomans: Interpreting the Middle East*. New York: Oxford University Press, 2004.

————. *The Middle East*. New York: Touchstone, 1997.

————. *The Muslim Discovery of Europe*. New York: Norton, 1982.

————. *What Went Wrong?: Western Impact and Middle Eastern Response*. New York: Perennial, 2003.

Lia, Brynjar. *Architect of Global Jihad: The Life of Al-Qaida Strategist Abu Mus'ab Al-Suri*. New York: Columbia University Press, 2008.

Lia, Brynjar, and Thomas Hegghammer. "Jihadi Strategic Studies: The Alleged Al Qaida Policy Study Preceding the Madrid Bombings." *Studies in Conflict and Terrorism* 27 (2004): 355–75.

Mandaville, Peter. *Global Political Islam*. New York: Routledge, 2007.

Maududi, Abu-al-A'la. *Toward Understanding Islam*. Translated by Ahmad Khushid. Lahore, Pakistan: Idara Tarjuman-ul-Quran, 2000.

Mayer, Jean Francois. "Cults, Violence and Religious Terrorism." *Studies in Conflict and Terrorism* 24 (2001): 361–76.

McCants, William, ed. *Militant Ideology Atlas: Research Compendium*. West Point, NY: U.S. Military Academy, Combating Terrorism Center, 2006.

McCrisken, Trevor B. *American Exceptionalism and the Legacy of Vietnam: U.S. Foreign Policy Since 1974*. New York: Palgrave Macmillan, 2003.

McDermott, Terry. *Perfect Soldiers: The Hijackers: Who They Were, Why They Did It*. New York: Harper Collins, 2005.

Mickolus, Edward F., and Susan L. Simmons. *Terrorism, 1996–2001: A Chronology*. Vols. I and II. Westport, CT: Greenwood, 2002.

Mishal, Shaul, and Avraham Sela. *The Palestinian HAMAS: Vision, Violence, and Coexistence*. New York: Columbia University Press, 2000.

Moore, Robin. *The Hunt for Bin Laden: Task Force Dagger*. New York: Random House, 2003.

Mueller, John E. *Overblown: How Politicians and the Terrorism Industry Inflate National Security Threats, and Why We Believe Them*. New York: Free Press, 2006.

Muqaddam, Muhammad. "Algeria: Acute Crisis inside the Leadership of Al-Qa'ida, Points of Reference inside the Organization Oppose the Trend of the Amir." *Al-Hayat* 8 (May 2007).

Murray, Williamson, and Robert H. Scales. *The Iraq War: A Military History*. Cambridge, MA: Belknap Press of Harvard University Press, 2003.

Naftali, Timothy J. *Blind Spot: The Secret History of American Counterterrorism*. New York: Basic Books, 2005.

Nasiri, Omar. *Inside the Jihad: My Life with Al Qaeda, A Spy's Story*. New York: Perseus, 2006.

Nasr, Seyyed Vali Reza. *The Shia Revival: How Conflicts within Islam Will Shape the Future*. New York: Norton, 2006.

National Commission on Terrorist Attacks upon the United States. *The 9/11 Commission Report: Final Report of the National Commission on Terrorist Attacks upon the United States*. New York: Norton, 2004.

O'Hanlon, Michael E. *Protecting the American Homeland: A Preliminary Analysis*. Washington: Brookings, 2002.

O'Neill, Bard. *Insurgency and Terrorism: From Revolution to Apocalypse*. Washington, DC: Brassey's, 2005.

Oliver, Anne Marie, and Paul Steinberg. *The Road to Martyrs' Square: A Journey into the World of the Suicide Bomber*. New York: Oxford University Press, 2005.

Oren, Michael B. *Power, Faith, and Fantasy: America in the Middle East, 1776 to the Present*. New York: Norton, 2007.

Pape, Robert Anthony. *Dying to Win: The Strategic Logic of Suicide Terrorism*. New York: Random House, 2005.

Pavlova, Elena. "From Counter-Society to Counter-State: Jemaah Islamiyah According to PUPJI." Singapore: Institute of Defence and Strategic Studies, Nanyang Technological University, 2006. www.idss.edu.sg/publications/workingpapers/wp117.pdf.

Paz, Reuven. "Global Jihad and WMD: Between Martyrdom and Mass Destruction." In *Current Trends in Islamist Ideology*, vol. 2, edited by Hillel Fradkin, Husain Haggani, and Eric Brown, 74–86. Washington, DC: Hudson Institute, 2005.

Peters, Ralph. *Beyond Baghdad: Postmodern War and Peace*. Mechanicsburg, PA: Stackpole, 2003.

———. *Beyond Terror: Strategy in a Changing World*. Mechanicsburg, PA: Stackpole, 2002.

Pillar, Paul R. *Terrorism and US Foreign Policy*. Washington, DC: Brookings, 2001.

Pipes, Richard. *The Degaev Affair: Terror and Treason in Tsarist Russia*. New Haven, CT: Yale University Press, 2003.

Post, Jerrold. "Terrorist Psycho-logic." In *Origins of Terrorism: Psychologies, Ideologies, Theologies, States of Mind*, edited by Walter Reich, 25–40. Washington, DC: Woodrow Wilson Center Press, 1998.

Qutb, Sayyid. *Milestones*. New Delhi, India: Islamic Book Service, 2002.

Rabasa, Angel. *The Muslim World after 9/11*. Santa Monica, CA: RAND, 2004.

Rabasa, Angel, Peter Chalk, Kim Cragin, Sara A. Daly, Heather S. Gregg, Theodore W. Karasik, Kevin A. O'Brien, and William Rosenau. *Beyond al-Qaeda*. Parts 1 and 2. Santa Monica, CA: RAND, 2006.

Rashid, Ahmed. *Jihad: The Rise of Militant Islam in Central Asia*. New York: Penguin, 2003.

———. *Taliban: Militant Islam, Oil, and Fundamentalism in Central Asia*. New Haven, CT: Yale Nota Bene, 2001.

Reich, Walter, ed. *Origins of Terrorism: Psychologies, Ideologies, Theologies, States of Mind*. Washington, DC: Woodrow Wilson Center Press, 1998.

Riley-Smith, Jonathan. *The Crusades: A History*. 2nd ed. New Haven, CT: Yale University Press, 2005.

Robins, Robert S., and Jerrold M. Post. *Political Paranoia: The Psychopolitics of Hatred*. New Haven, CT: Yale University Press, 1997.

Rosen, Lawrence. *Bargaining for Reality: The Construction of Social Relations in a Muslim Community*. Chicago: University of Chicago Press, 1984.

Roy, Olivier. *The Failure of Political Islam*. Cambridge, MA: Harvard University Press, 1994.

———. *Globalized Islam: The Search for a New Ummah*. New York: Columbia University Press, 2004.

Rubin, Barry M., and Judith Colp Rubin. *Anti-American Terrorism and the Middle East: A Documentary Reader*. New York: Oxford University Press, 2002.

Ruthven, Malise. *A Fury for God: The Islamist Attack on America*. New York: Granta, 2002.

Sageman, Marc. *Leaderless Jihad: Terror Networks in the Twenty-First Century*. Philadelphia: University of Pennsylvania Press, 2007.

———. *Understanding Terror Networks*. Philadelphia: University of Pennsylvania Press, 2004.

Schanzer, Johnathan. *Al-Qaeda's Armies: Middle East Affiliate Groups & the Next Generation of Terror*. New York: Specialist Press International, 2005.

Scheuer, Michael. "Al-Qaeda in Iraq: Has Al-Zawahiri Reined in Al-Zarqawi?" *Jamestown Foundation* 3 (April 11, 2006).

———. "Al-Qaeda's Insurgency Doctrine: Aiming for a 'Long War.'" *Jamestown Foundation Terrorism Focus* 3 (February 28, 2006).

———. "Al-Zawahiri's September 11 Video Hits Main Themes of Al-Qaeda Doctrine." *Jamestown Foundation Terrorism Focus* 3 (September 19, 2006).

———. "Coalition Warfare: How Al-Qaeda Uses the World Islamic Front Against Crusaders and Jews, Part I," *Jamestown Foundation Terrorism Focus* 2 (March 31, 2005).

———. *Imperial Hubris: Why the West Is Losing the War on Terror*. Washington, DC: Brassey's, 2004.

———. *Through Our Enemies' Eyes: Osama bin Laden, Radical Islam, and the Future of America*. 2nd ed. Washington, DC: Potomac, 2006.

Schmid, Alex Peter, and A. J. Jongman. *Political Terrorism: A New Guide to Actors, Authors, Concepts, Data Bases, Theories, & Literature*. New Brunswick, NJ: Transaction, 2005.

Schroen, Gary C. *First In: An Insider's Account of How the CIA Spearheaded the War on Terror in Afghanistan.* New York: Presidio, 2005.

Selengut, Charles. *Sacred Fury: Understanding Religious Violence.* Walnut Creek, CA: Alta Mira Press, 2003.

Shadid, Anthony. *Legacy of the Prophet: Despots, Democrats, and the New Politics of Islam.* Boulder, CO: Westview, 2002.

Shay, Shaul. *The Shahids: Islam and Suicide Attacks.* New Brunswick, NJ: Transaction, 2004.

Shultz, Richard H., Jr., and Andrea J. Dew. *Insurgents, Terrorists, and Militias: The Warriors of Contemporary Combat.* New York: Columbia University Press, 2006.

Shultz, Richard H., Jr., and Ruth Marolies Beitler. "Tactical Deception and Strategic Surprise in Al-Qa'ida's Operations." *Middle East Review of International Affairs* 8 (June 2004): 56–79.

Siegel, Pascale Combelles. "Radical Islam and the French Muslim Prison Population." *Jamestown Foundation Terrorism Monitor* 4 (July 27, 2006).

Smelser, Neil J. and Faith Mitchell. *Terrorism: Perspectives from the Behavioral and Social Sciences.* Washington, DC: National Academy Press, 2002.

Solomon, John, and Kent Regens. "Expansion of Yemen's Refining Capacity Raises Terrorism Concerns." *Jamestown Foundation Terrorism Focus* 4 (May 29, 2007).

Stern, Jessica. *Terror in the Name of God: Why Religious Militants Kill.* New York: Ecco, 2003.

———. *The Ultimate Terrorists.* Cambridge, MA: Harvard University Press, 2003.

Sun Tzu. *The Art of War: Leadership and Strategy from the Chinese Military Classics.* Translated by Ralph D. Sawyer. Boulder, CO: Westview, 1994.

Suskind, Ron. *The One Percent Doctrine: Deep Inside America's Pursuit of its Enemies since 9/11.* New York: Simon & Schuster, 2006.

Teitelbaum, Joshua. *Holier Than Thou: Saudi Arabia's Islamic Opposition.* Washington, DC: Washington Institute for Near East Policy, 2000.

Tilly, Charles. *Social Movements, 1768–2004.* Boulder, CO: Paradigm, 2004.

Timmerman, Kenneth R. *Preachers of Hate: Islam and the War on America.* New York: Crown Forum, 2003.

Tse-Tung, Mao. *On Guerrilla Warfare.* Translated by Samuel B. Griffith II. Urbana: University of Illinois Press, 2000.

———. *On Protracted War.* Honolulu, HI: University Press of the Pacific, 2001.

Ullman, Harlan. *Finishing Business: Ten Steps to Defeat Global Terror.* Annapolis, MD: Naval Institute Press, 2004.

Ulph, Stephen. "Al-Zarqawi's Group under Pressure and Seeking Allies." *Jamestown Foundation Terrorism Focus* 3 (January 18, 2006).

———. "Al-Zawahiri Encourages Targeting of Gulf Oil." *Jamestown Foundation Terrorism Focus* 2 (December 13, 2005).

———. "Schism and Collapse of Morale in Algeria's GSPC." *Jamestown Foundation Terrorism Focus* 2 (March 31, 2005).

U.S. Department of Defense. *Measuring Stability and Security in Iraq.* Washington, DC: U.S. Department of Defense, 2006.

Victoroff, Jeff. "The Mind of the Terrorist." *Journal of Conflict Resolution* 49 (2005): 3–42.

Vindino, Lorenzo. *Al Qaeda in Europe: The New Battleground of International Jihad.* New York: Prometheus, 2005.

Violent Jihad in the Netherlands. The Hague, Netherlands: General Intelligence and Security Service, Ministry of the Interior and Kingdom Affairs, 2006.

Wardlaw, Grant. *Political Terrorism: Theory, Tactics, and Counter-Measures.* New York: Cambridge University Press, 1989.

Weaver, Mary Anne. *Pakistan: In the Shadow of Jiihad and Afghanistan.* New York: Farrar, Straus and Giroux, 2002.

Webel, Charles. *Terror, Terrorism, and the Human Condition.* New York: Palgrave Macmillan, 2004.

White, Jeffrey. *An Adaptive Insurgency.* Policy Focus #58. Washington, DC: Washington Institute for Near East Policy, 2006.

Wiktorowicz, Quintan. "A Genealogy of Radical Islam." *Studies in Conflict and Terrorism* 28 (2005): 75–97.

———. *Radical Islam Rising: Muslim Extremism in the West.* Lanham, MD: Rowman & Littlefield, 2005.

Wright, Lawrence. *The Looming Tower: Al-Qaeda and the Road to 9/11.* New York: Knopf, 2006.

Zambelis, Chris. "Egyptian Gama'a Al-Islamiyya's Public Relations Campaign." *Jamestown Foundation Terrorism Focus* 3 (September 12, 2006).

Zeidan, David. "The Islamic Fundamentalist View of Life as a Perennial Battle." *Middle East Review of International Affairs* 5 (2001): 26–53.

THE AUTHORS

Devin R. Springer is a research associate in the Center for Biosecurity Research at the University of Oklahoma Health Sciences Center. Mr. Springer is an Arabic linguist and he has extensive experience monitoring jihadist media and the use of the Internet by the jihadist movement. His research focuses on jihadist ideology and strategic thought. Mr. Springer is a graduate of the University of Oklahoma in international relations.

James L. Regens is Presidential Professor of Occupational and Environmental Health and adjunct professor of psychiatry and behavioral sciences at the University of Oklahoma Health Sciences Center. Dr. Regens serves as associate dean for research in the College of Public Health and is founding director of the Center for Biosecurity Research. His research focuses on chemical, biological, radiological, and nuclear countermeasures; the transmission dynamics of infectious diseases; and nonproliferation. Dr. Regens has held positions at research universities, in government, and in national laboratories. He has been a consultant to and on review panels for numerous organizations, including the International Atomic Energy Agency, National Institutes of Health, Defense Threat Reduction Agency, National Academy of Engineering, Organization for Economic Cooperation and Development, Department of Homeland Security, and the Department of Energy. He is the author of over two hundred publications, including eight books, and is a member of the Council on Foreign Relations.

David N. Edger is a professor at the University of Oklahoma Health Sciences Center; he is also a faculty member in the political science department on the Norman campus. Prior to coming to the University of Oklahoma, Mr. Edger spent thirty-five years in the Central Intelligence Agency. At CIA, Mr. Edger worked around the world in all aspects of the work of the National Clandestine Service (formerly called the Directorate of Operations). Mr. Edger's most senior position was as head of operations of the Clandestine Service. Mr. Edger's awards from CIA include the Distinguished Intelligence Medal, the Distinguished

Career Intelligence Medal, the Intelligence Medal of Merit, and the Donovan Medal. He has received numerous awards from other government agencies and from several nations. Since retiring from CIA, Mr. Edger has been a consultant for businesses and governments, primarily in the field of counterterrorism.

INDEX